KING'S RANSOM

WRITER	**NICK SPENCER**

AMAZING SPIDER-MAN #61-62

ARTIST	**PATRICK GLEASON**
COLOR ARTIST	**EDGAR DELGADO**
COVER ART	PATRICK GLEASON & EDGAR DELGADO

AMAZING SPIDER-MAN #63-65

ARTISTS	**FEDERICO VICENTINI** WITH **FEDERICO SABBATINI** (#65)
COLOR ARTIST	**ALEX SINCLAIR**
COVER ART	MARK BAGLEY & JOHN DELL WITH EDGAR DELGADO (#63-64) & BRIAN REBER (#65)

GIANT-SIZE AMAZING SPIDER-MAN: KING'S RANSOM

ARTISTS	**ROGÊ ANTÔNIO** WITH **CARLOS GÓMEZ** & **ZÉ CARLOS**
COLOR ARTIST	**ALEX SINCLAIR**
COVER ART	MARK BAGLEY, JOHN DELL & BRIAN REBER

"SINISTER WAR PRELUDE"

PENCILER	**MARK BAGLEY**
INKER	**ANDREW HENNESSY**
COLOR ARTIST	**BRIAN REBER**

LETTERER	**VC's JOE CARAMAGNA**

ASSISTANT EDITOR	**LINDSEY COHICK**
EDITOR	**NICK LOWE**

61

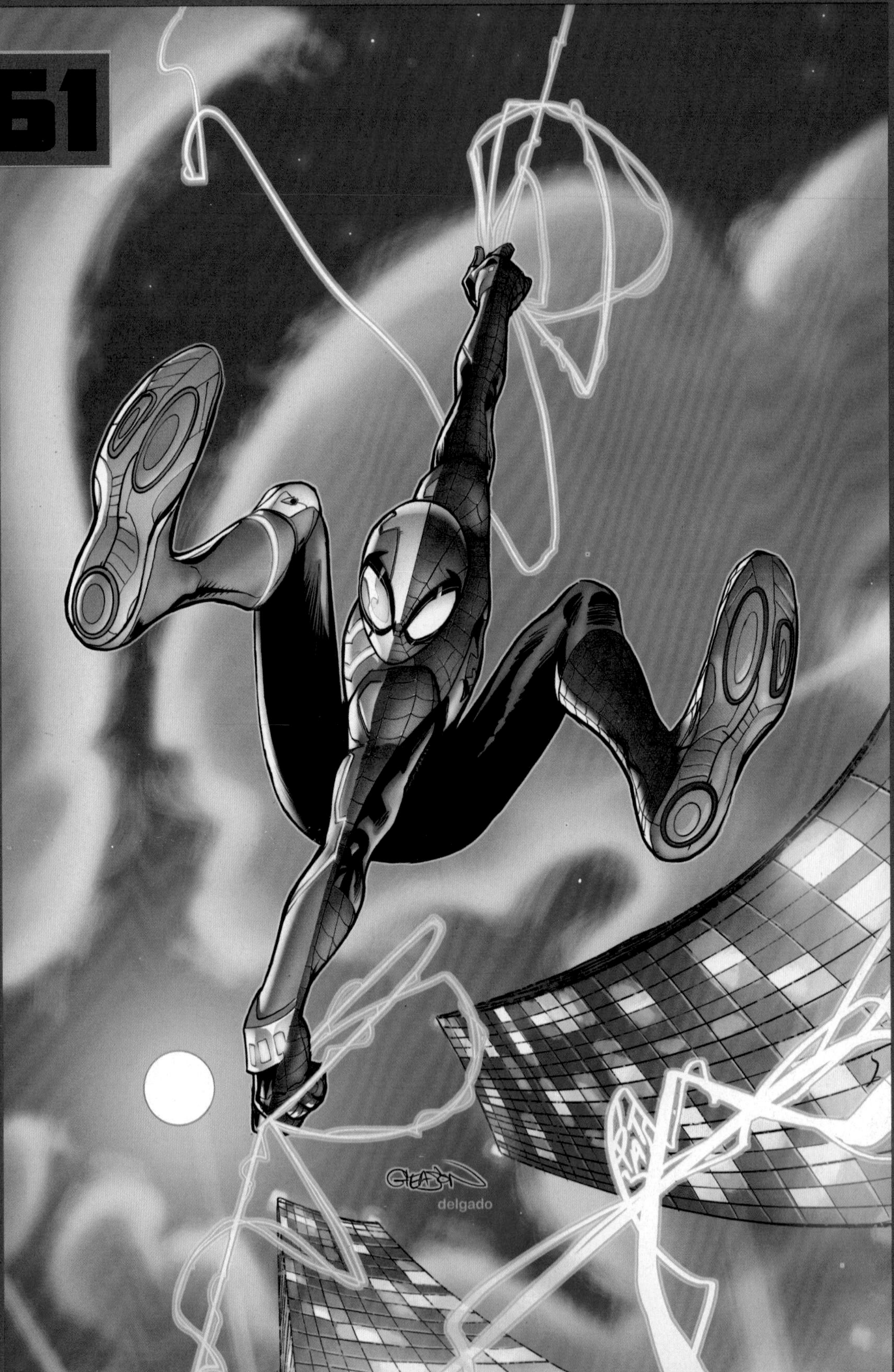
delgado

LET'S TRY SOMETHING NEW!

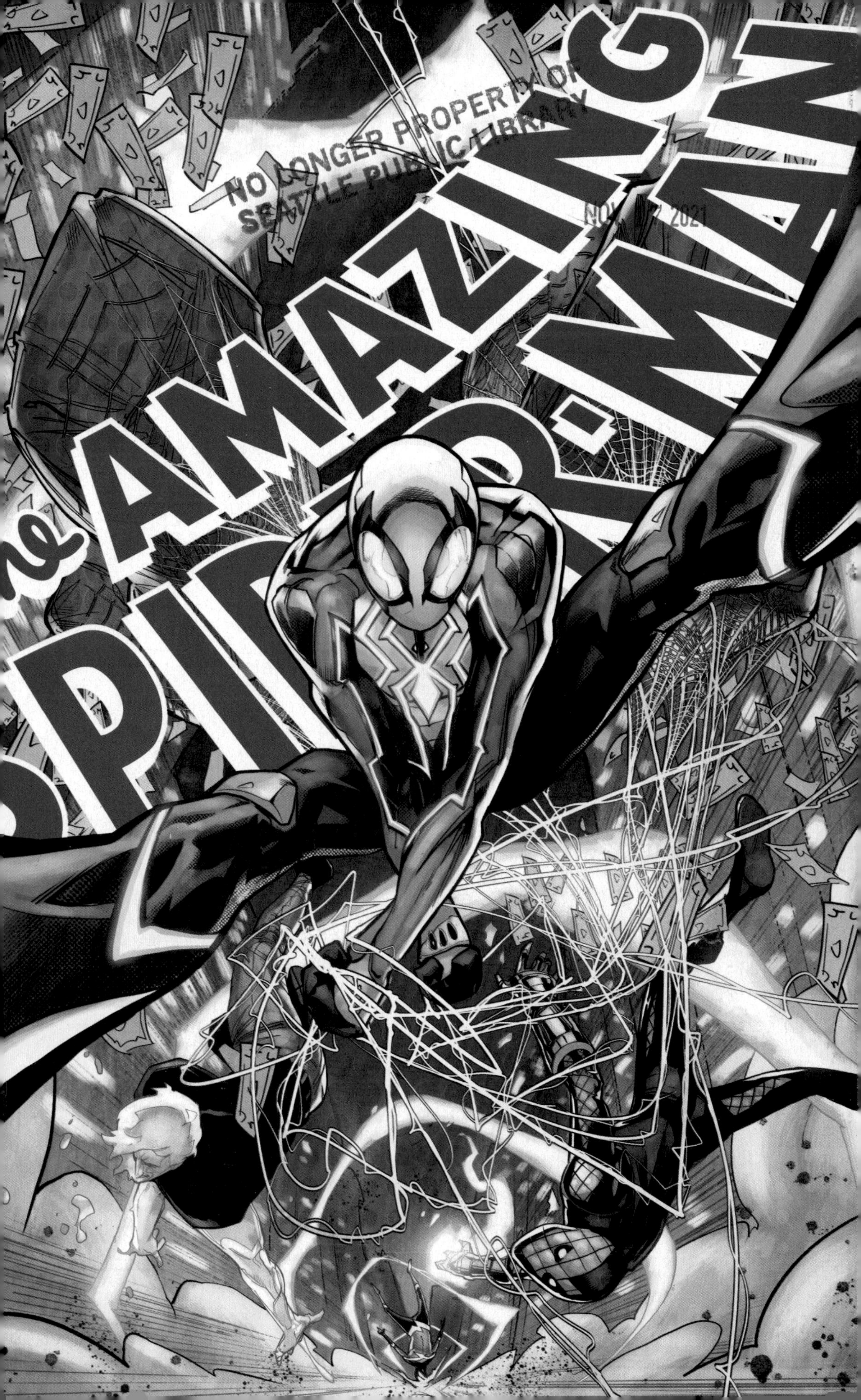
AMAZING

Kindred turned Peter's world upside down. Norman Osborn, the Green Goblin, having been "cleansed" of his sins by the Sin-Eater, revealed that Kindred is actually his son, Harry Osborn. Harry's reign of terror over Peter Parker ended when Norman and Mayor Wilson Fisk, A.K.A. the Kingpin, trapped Kindred in a Darkforce cage. With Kindred put away, Peter was finally ready to put the Osborn family drama behind him and return to his normal life.

Peter now shares an apartment with "reformed villain" Fred Myers, A.K.A Boomerang, Randy Robertson and their pet alien, Gog. Gog used to guard the pieces of the powerful Lifeline Tablet, which Boomerang and Spider-Man are endeavoring to keep out of Kingpin's hands. But Kingpin has plans of his own...

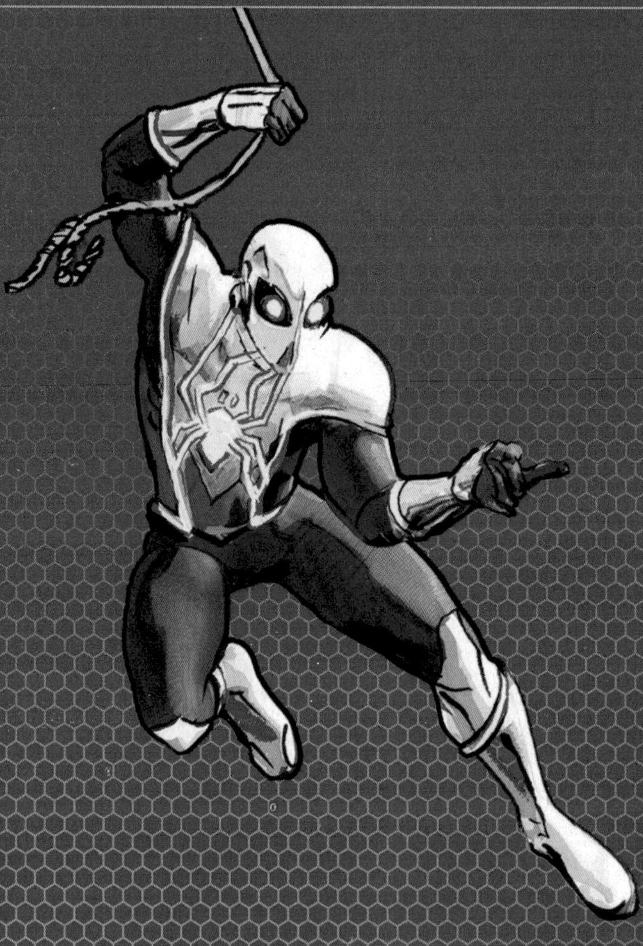

SPIDER-MAN CREATED BY STAN LEE & STEVE DITKO

COLLECTION EDITOR JENNIFER GRÜNWALD
ASSISTANT EDITOR DANIEL KIRCHHOFFER ✱ ASSISTANT MANAGING EDITOR MAIA LOY
ASSISTANT MANAGING EDITOR LISA MONTALBANO ✱ VP PRODUCTION & SPECIAL PROJECTS JEFF YOUNGQUIST
BOOK DESIGNERS ADAM DEL RE WITH JAY BOWEN
SVP PRINT, SALES & MARKETING DAVID GABRIEL ✱ EDITOR IN CHIEF C.B. CEBULSKI

AMAZING SPIDER-MAN BY NICK SPENCER VOL. 13: KING'S RANSOM. Contains material originally published in magazine form as AMAZING SPIDER-MAN (2018) #61-65 and GIANT-SIZE AMAZING SPIDER-MAN: KING'S RANSOM (2021) #1. First printing 2021. ISBN 978-1-302-92606-9. Published by MARVEL WORLDWIDE, INC., a subsidiary of MARVEL ENTERTAINMENT, LLC. OFFICE OF PUBLICATION: 1290 Avenue of the Americas, New York, NY 10104. **Printed in Canada.** KEVIN FEIGE, Chief Creative Officer; DAN BUCKLEY, President, Marvel Entertainment; JOE QUESADA, EVP & Creative Director; DAVID BOGART, Associate Publisher & SVP of Talent Affairs; TOM BREVOORT, VP, Executive Editor; NICK LOWE, Executive Editor, VP of Content, Digital Publishing; DAVID GABRIEL, VP of Print & Digital Publishing; JEFF YOUNGQUIST, VP of Production & Special Projects; ALEX MORALES, Director of Publishing Operations; DAN EDINGTON, Managing Editor; RICKEY PURDIN, Director of Talent Relations; JENNIFER GRÜNWALD, Senior Editor, Special Projects; SUSAN CRESPI, Production Manager; STAN LEE, Chairman Emeritus. For information regarding advertising in Marvel Comics or on Marvel.com, please contact Vit DeBellis, Custom Solutions & Integrated Advertising Manager, at vdebellis@marvel.com. For Marvel subscription inquiries, please call 888-511-5480. **Manufactured between 6/18/2021 and 7/20/2021 by SOLISCO PRINTERS, SCOTT, QC, CANADA.**

10 9 8 7 6 5 4 3 2 1

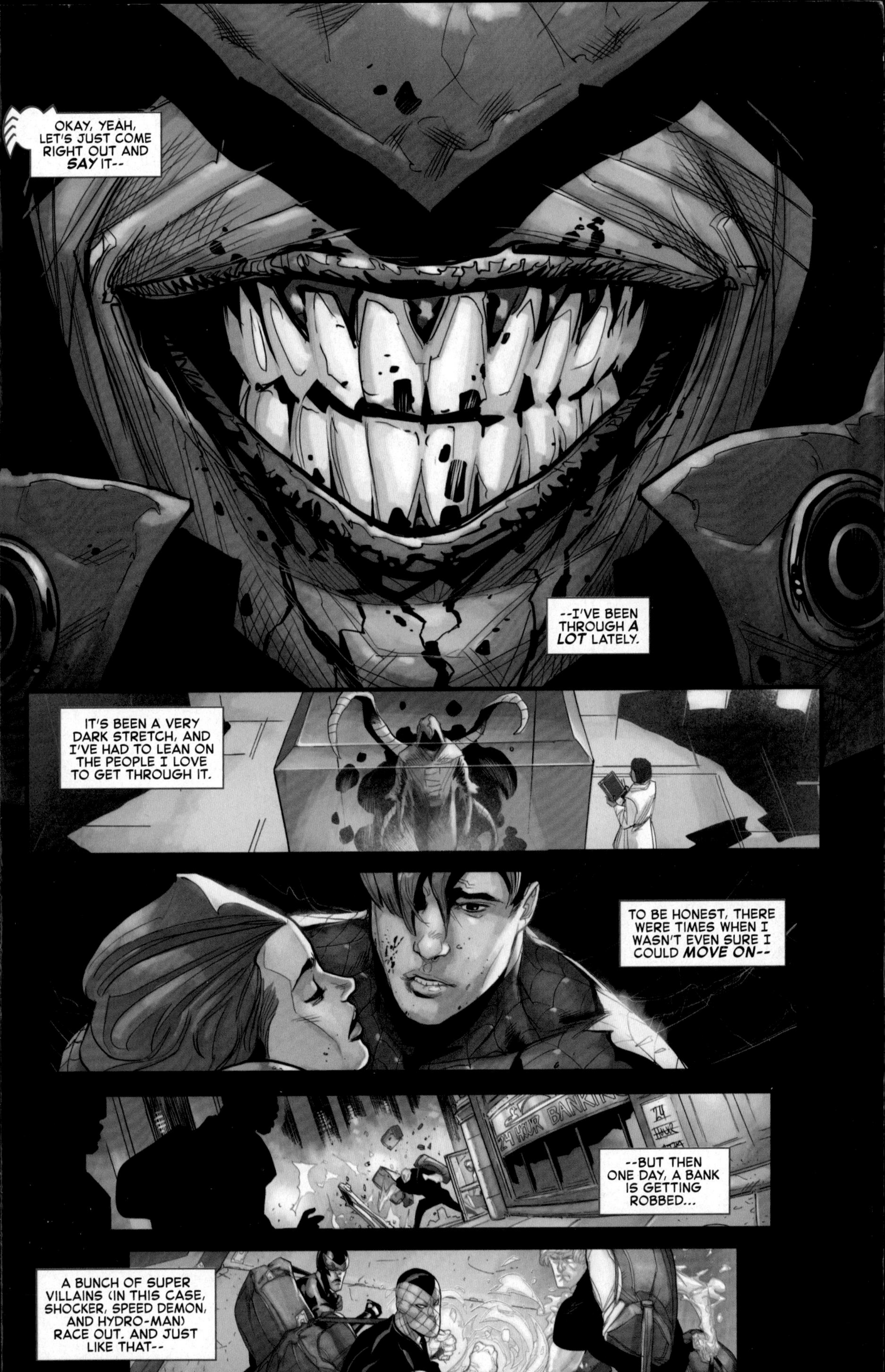
OKAY, YEAH, LET'S JUST COME RIGHT OUT AND SAY IT--
--I'VE BEEN THROUGH A LOT LATELY.
IT'S BEEN A VERY DARK STRETCH, AND I'VE HAD TO LEAN ON THE PEOPLE I LOVE TO GET THROUGH IT.
TO BE HONEST, THERE WERE TIMES WHEN I WASN'T EVEN SURE I COULD MOVE ON--
24 HOUR BANKING
--BUT THEN ONE DAY, A BANK IS GETTING ROBBED...
A BUNCH OF SUPER VILLAINS (IN THIS CASE, SHOCKER, SPEED DEMON, AND HYDRO-MAN) RACE OUT. AND JUST LIKE THAT--

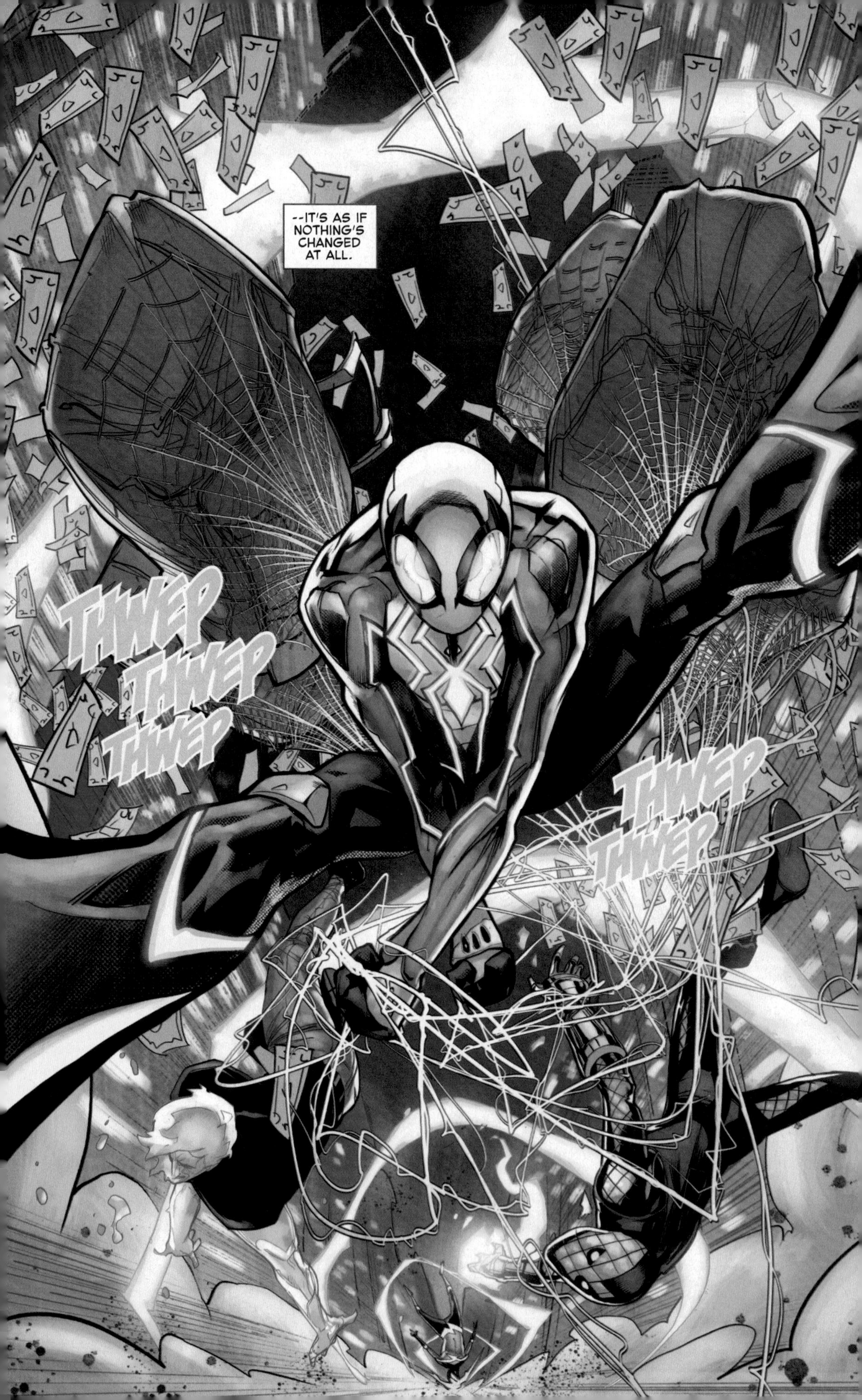
--IT'S AS IF NOTHING'S CHANGED AT ALL.
THWEP THWEP THWEP
THWEP THWEP

I WANT TO THANK ALL OF YOU FOR YOUR TIME AND FOR YOUR WILLINGNESS TO MEET WITH ME.

I UNDERSTAND HOW *BUSY* YOU ALL ARE. AFTER ALL--

--BUSINESS HAS BEEN *BOOMING*, HASN'T IT?

YOU'LL GET NO COMPLAINTS OUT OF ME, FISK. LAST QUARTER WAS THE *MAGGIA'S* BEST YET.

HH. YES, OF COURSE, *HAMMERHEAD*, YOU WOULDN'T COMPLAIN-- YOU'VE BEEN EXPANDING SO RAPIDLY INTO *MY* TERRITORY.

YOU GOT SOMETHING TO *SAY*, OWL? 'CAUSE I DON'T SEE YOUR NAME ON ANYTHING IN RED HOOK.

WELL, PERHAPS YOU SHOULD VISIT AGAIN, JUST THE *TWO* OF US. I'LL BE HAPPY TO SHOW YOU--

GENTLEMEN, PLEASE-- *ENOUGH!*

THERE'S NO NEED FOR THESE KINDS OF PETTY SQUABBLES ANYMORE.

NOT ONLY IS THERE MORE THAN ENOUGH TO GO AROUND, BUT THESE SORTS OF DISPUTES CAN BE ADJUDICATED AND ARBITRATED BY MY ADMINISTRATION IF NEEDED.

UH, NAH, KINGPIN, THAT WON'T BE NECESSARY--

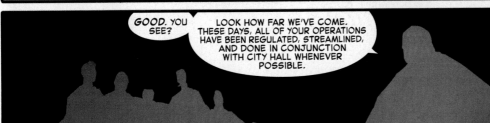

GOOD. YOU SEE?

LOOK HOW FAR WE'VE COME. THESE DAYS, ALL OF YOUR OPERATIONS HAVE BEEN REGULATED, STREAMLINED, AND DONE IN CONJUNCTION WITH CITY HALL WHENEVER POSSIBLE.

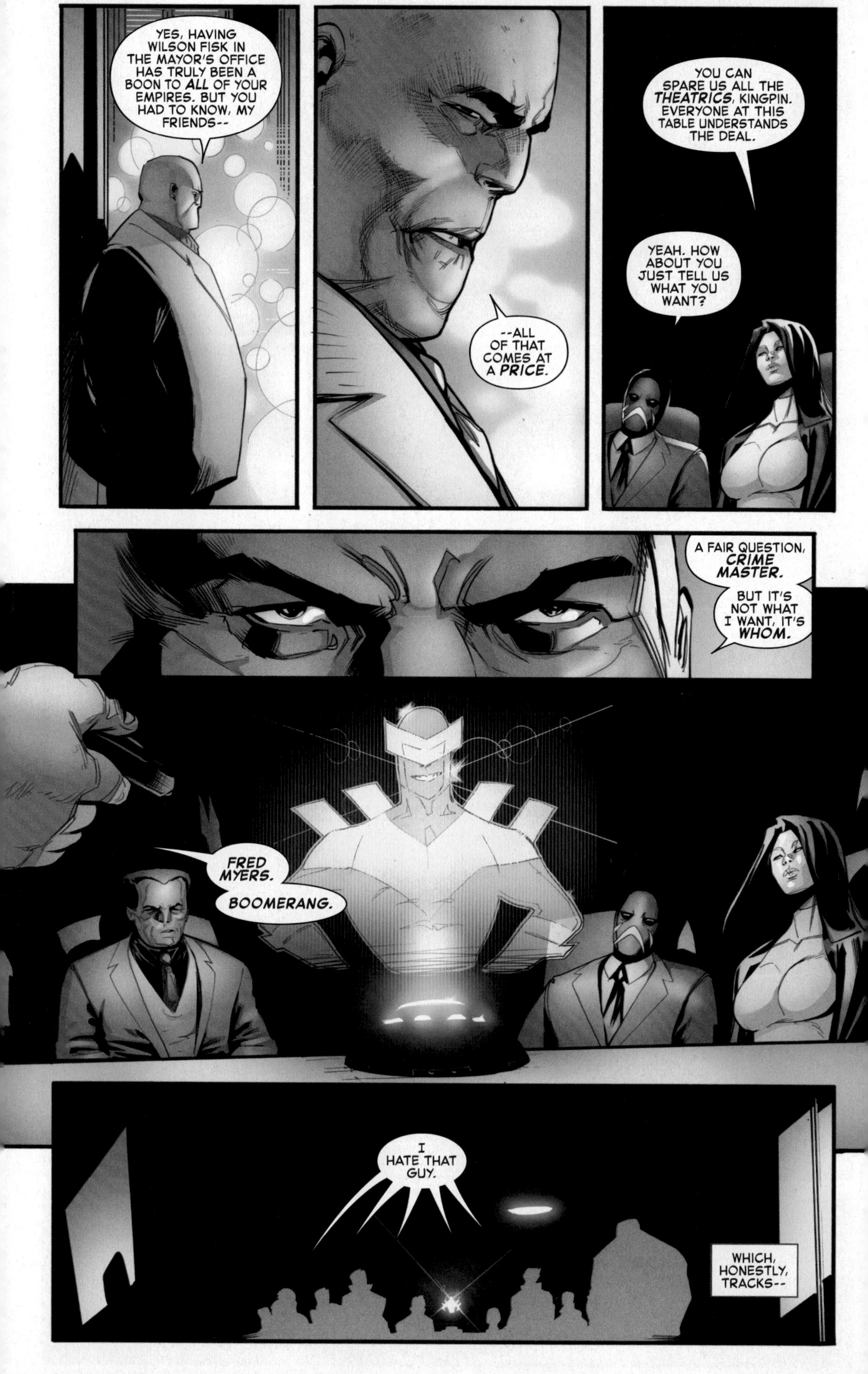
YES, HAVING WILSON FISK IN THE MAYOR'S OFFICE HAS TRULY BEEN A BOON TO ALL OF YOUR EMPIRES. BUT YOU HAD TO KNOW, MY FRIENDS--
--ALL OF THAT COMES AT A PRICE.
YOU CAN SPARE US ALL THE THEATRICS, KINGPIN. EVERYONE AT THIS TABLE UNDERSTANDS THE DEAL.
YEAH. HOW ABOUT YOU JUST TELL US WHAT YOU WANT?
A FAIR QUESTION, CRIME MASTER.
BUT IT'S NOT WHAT I WANT, IT'S WHOM.
FRED MYERS.
BOOMERANG.
I HATE THAT GUY.
WHICH, HONESTLY, TRACKS--

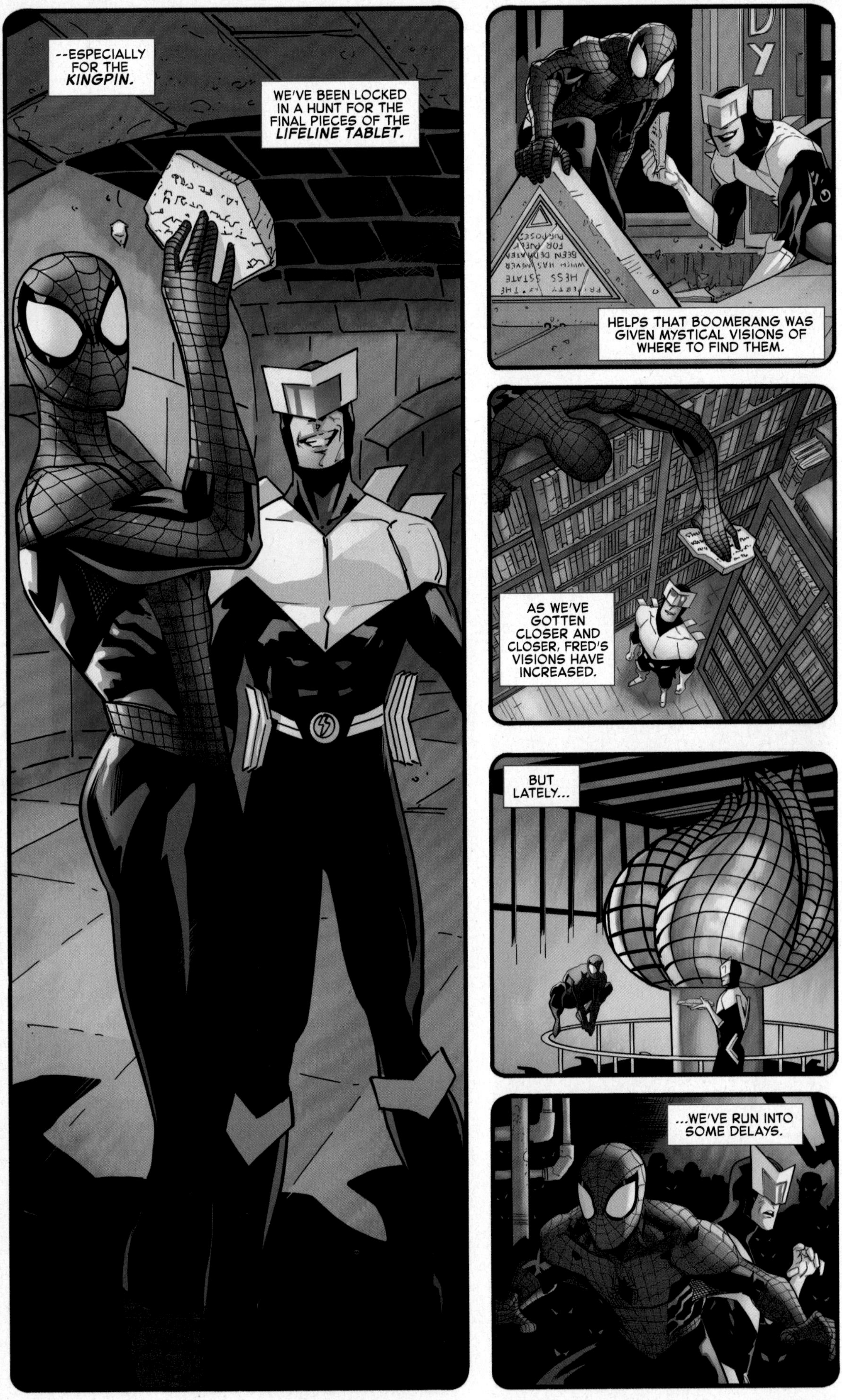
--ESPECIALLY FOR THE *KINGPIN.*
WE'VE BEEN LOCKED IN A HUNT FOR THE FINAL PIECES OF THE *LIFELINE TABLET.*
HELPS THAT BOOMERANG WAS GIVEN MYSTICAL VISIONS OF WHERE TO FIND THEM.
AS WE'VE GOTTEN CLOSER AND CLOSER, FRED'S VISIONS HAVE INCREASED.
BUT LATELY...
...WE'VE RUN INTO SOME DELAYS.

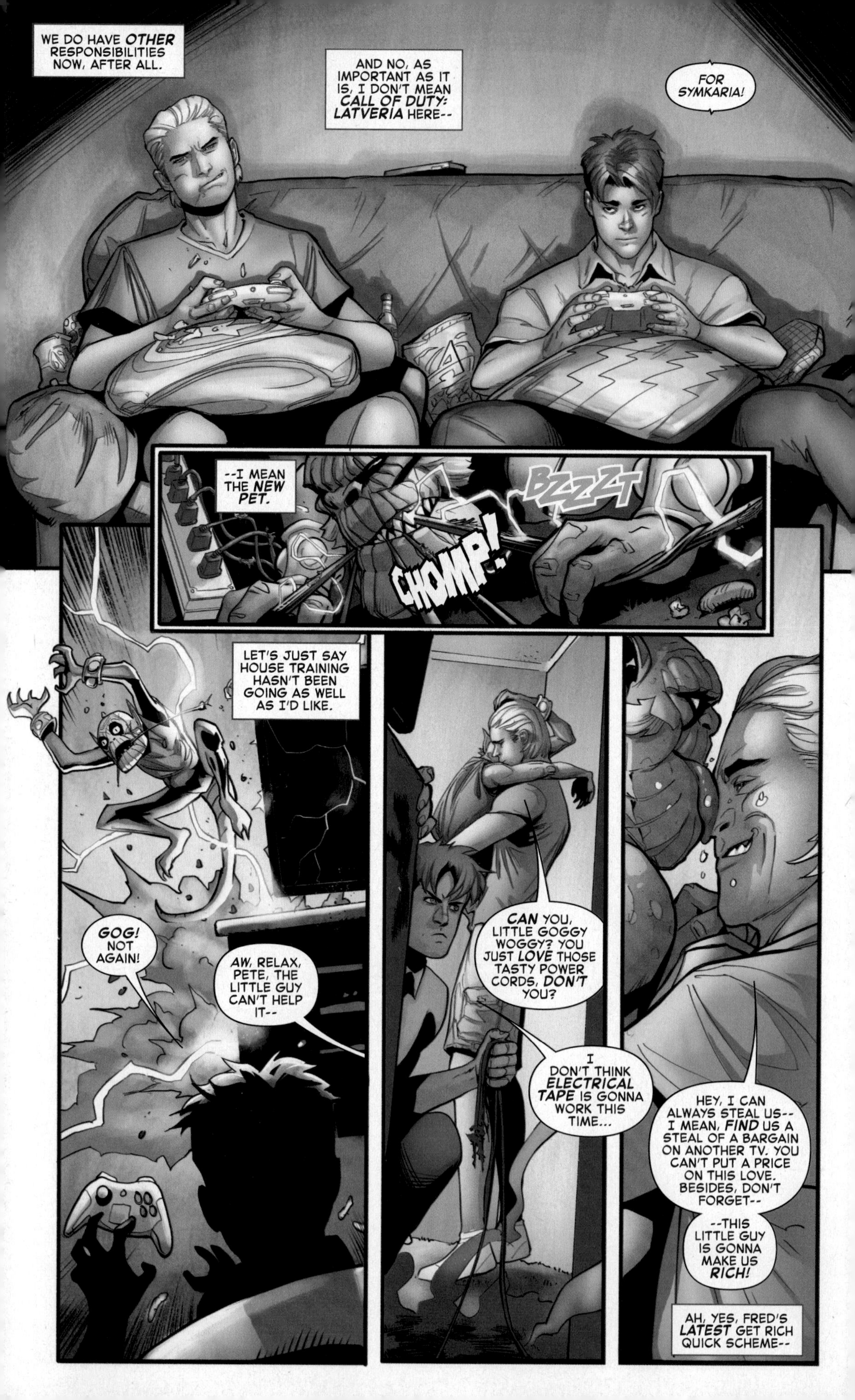
WE DO HAVE OTHER RESPONSIBILITIES NOW, AFTER ALL.
AND NO, AS IMPORTANT AS IT IS, I DON'T MEAN CALL OF DUTY: LATVERIA HERE--
FOR SYMKARIA!
--I MEAN THE NEW PET.
BZZZT
CHOMP!
LET'S JUST SAY HOUSE TRAINING HASN'T BEEN GOING AS WELL AS I'D LIKE.
GOG! NOT AGAIN!
AW, RELAX, PETE, THE LITTLE GUY CAN'T HELP IT--
CAN YOU, LITTLE GOGGY WOGGY? YOU JUST LOVE THOSE TASTY POWER CORDS, DON'T YOU?
I DON'T THINK ELECTRICAL TAPE IS GONNA WORK THIS TIME...
HEY, I CAN ALWAYS STEAL US-- I MEAN, FIND US A STEAL OF A BARGAIN ON ANOTHER TV. YOU CAN'T PUT A PRICE ON THIS LOVE. BESIDES, DON'T FORGET--
--THIS LITTLE GUY IS GONNA MAKE US RICH!
AH, YES, FRED'S LATEST GET RICH QUICK SCHEME--

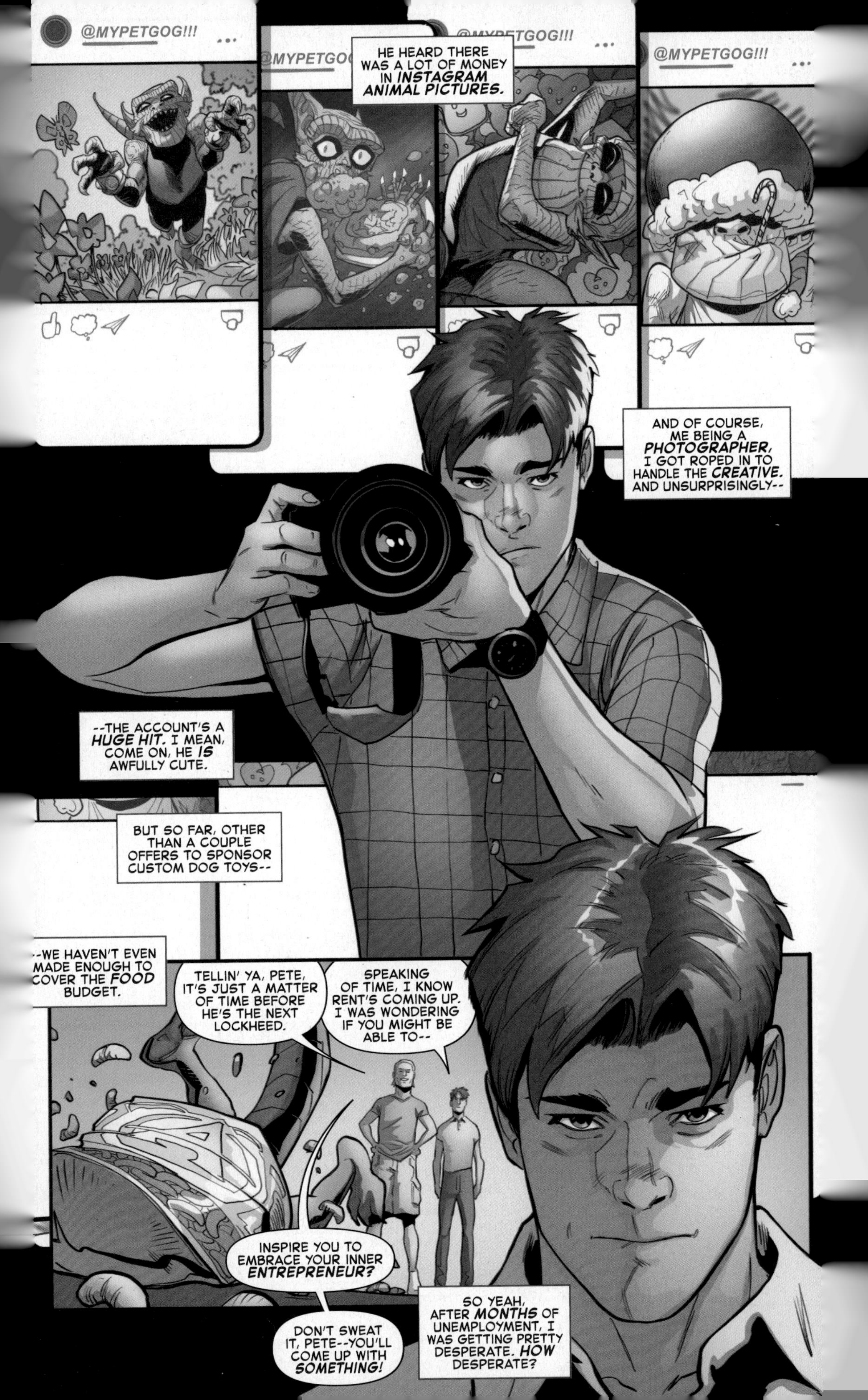
@MYPETGOG!!!
@MYPETGOG
HE HEARD THERE WAS A LOT OF MONEY IN INSTAGRAM ANIMAL PICTURES.
@MYPETGOG!!!
@MYPETGOG!!!
AND OF COURSE, ME BEING A PHOTOGRAPHER, I GOT ROPED IN TO HANDLE THE CREATIVE. AND UNSURPRISINGLY--
--THE ACCOUNT'S A HUGE HIT. I MEAN, COME ON, HE IS AWFULLY CUTE.
BUT SO FAR, OTHER THAN A COUPLE OFFERS TO SPONSOR CUSTOM DOG TOYS--
--WE HAVEN'T EVEN MADE ENOUGH TO COVER THE FOOD BUDGET.
TELLIN' YA, PETE, IT'S JUST A MATTER OF TIME BEFORE HE'S THE NEXT LOCKHEED.
SPEAKING OF TIME, I KNOW RENT'S COMING UP. I WAS WONDERING IF YOU MIGHT BE ABLE TO--
INSPIRE YOU TO EMBRACE YOUR INNER ENTREPRENEUR?
DON'T SWEAT IT, PETE--YOU'LL COME UP WITH SOMETHING!
SO YEAH, AFTER MONTHS OF UNEMPLOYMENT, I WAS GETTING PRETTY DESPERATE. HOW DESPERATE?

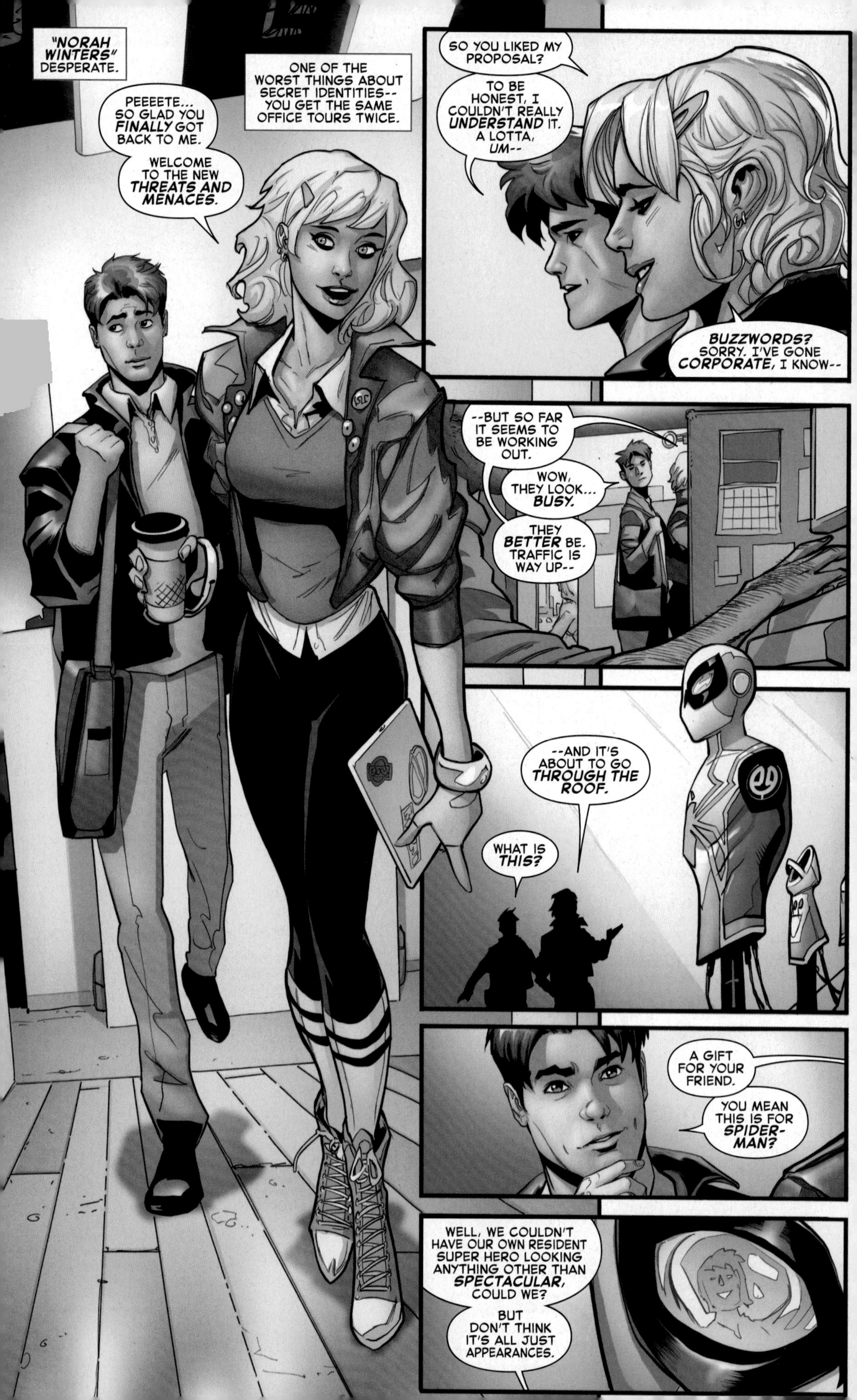
"NORAH WINTERS" DESPERATE.
PEEEETE... SO GLAD YOU FINALLY GOT BACK TO ME.
WELCOME TO THE NEW THREATS AND MENACES.
ONE OF THE WORST THINGS ABOUT SECRET IDENTITIES-- YOU GET THE SAME OFFICE TOURS TWICE.
SO YOU LIKED MY PROPOSAL?
TO BE HONEST, I COULDN'T REALLY UNDERSTAND IT. A LOTTA, UM--
BUZZWORDS? SORRY. I'VE GONE CORPORATE, I KNOW--
--BUT SO FAR IT SEEMS TO BE WORKING OUT.
WOW, THEY LOOK... BUSY.
THEY BETTER BE. TRAFFIC IS WAY UP--
--AND IT'S ABOUT TO GO THROUGH THE ROOF.
WHAT IS THIS?
A GIFT FOR YOUR FRIEND.
YOU MEAN THIS IS FOR SPIDER-MAN?
WELL, WE COULDN'T HAVE OUR OWN RESIDENT SUPER HERO LOOKING ANYTHING OTHER THAN SPECTACULAR, COULD WE?
BUT DON'T THINK IT'S ALL JUST APPEARANCES.

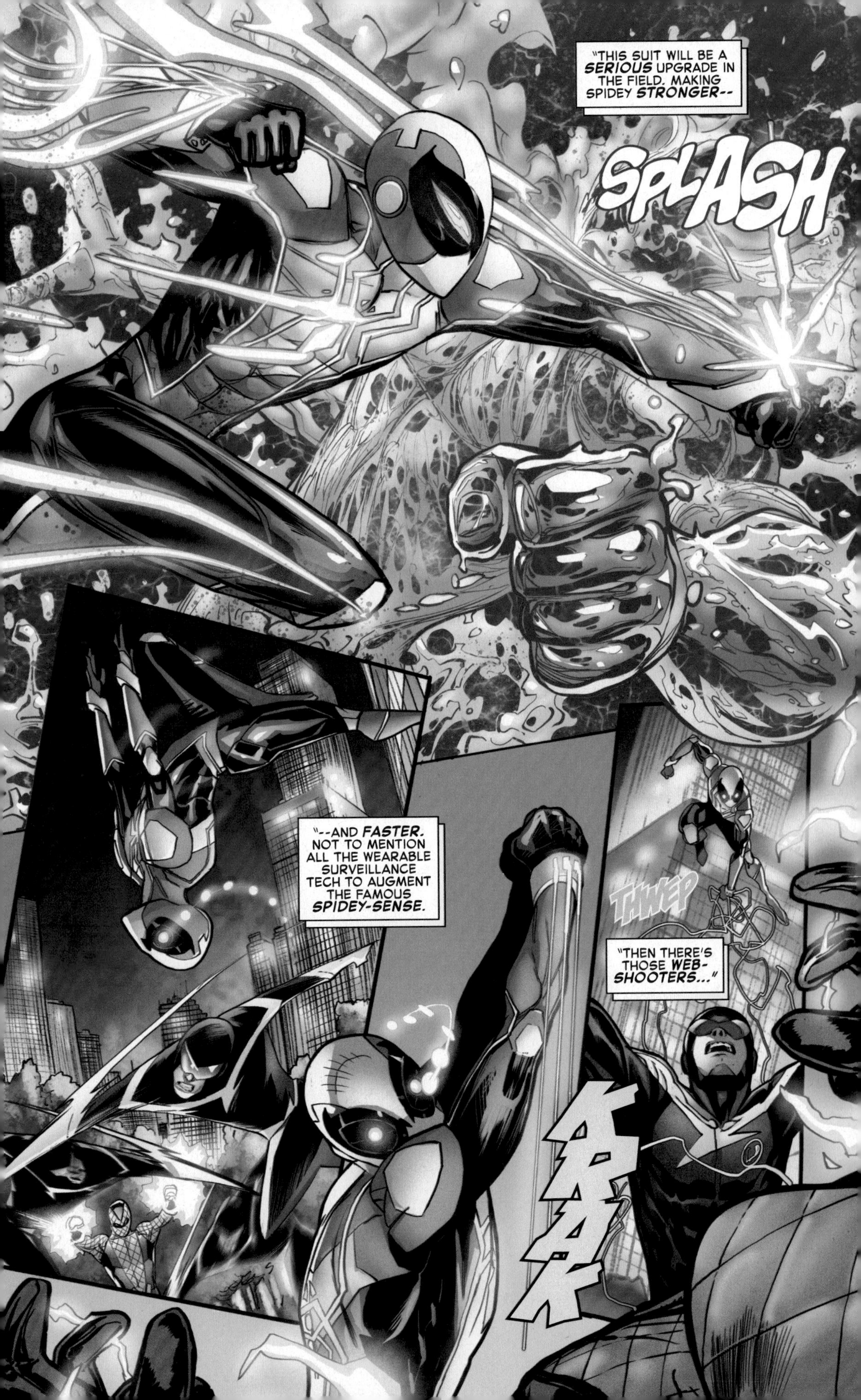
"THIS SUIT WILL BE A SERIOUS UPGRADE IN THE FIELD. MAKING SPIDEY STRONGER--
SPLASH
"--AND FASTER. NOT TO MENTION ALL THE WEARABLE SURVEILLANCE TECH TO AUGMENT THE FAMOUS SPIDEY-SENSE.
THWEP
"THEN THERE'S THOSE WEB-SHOOTERS..."
KRAK

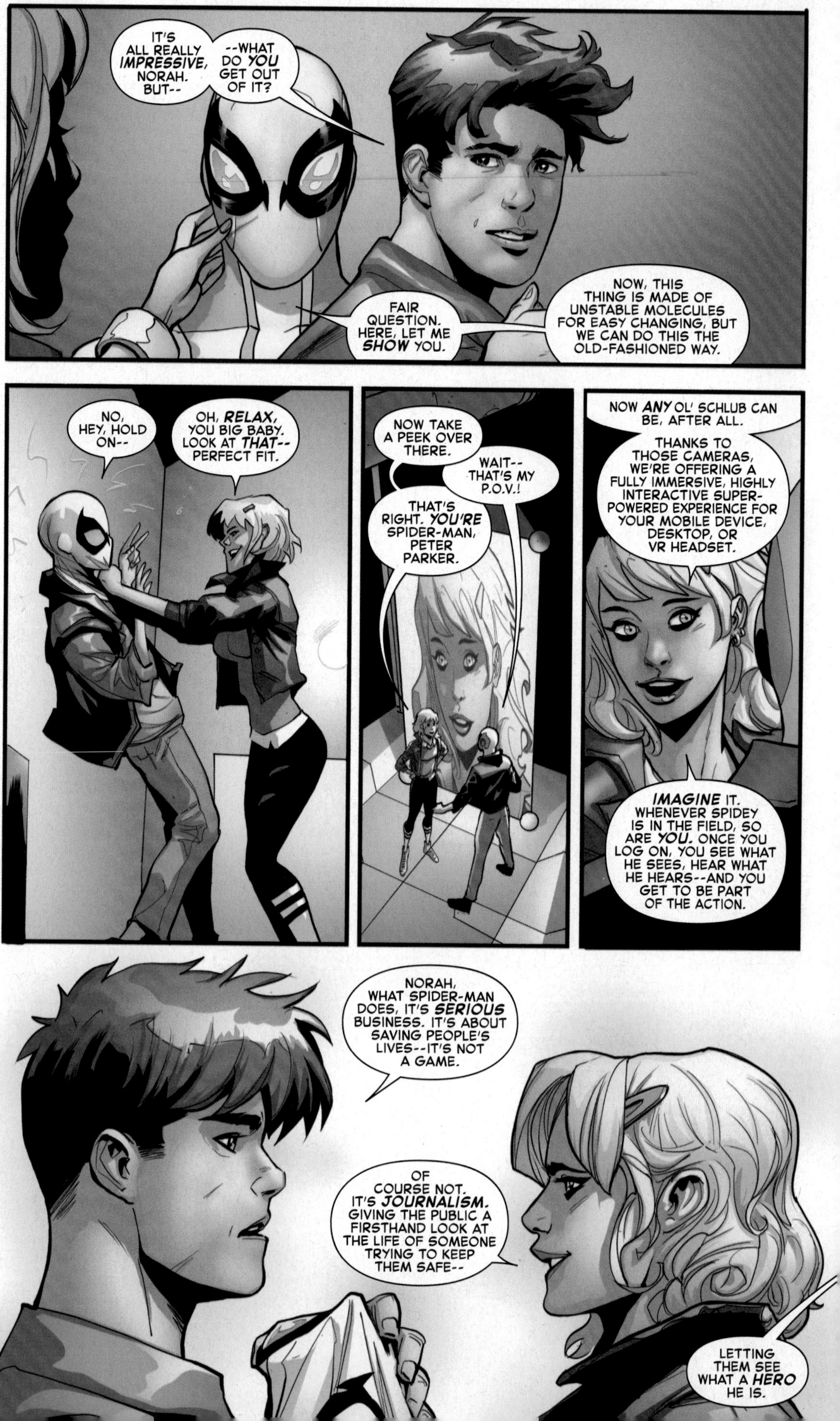
IT'S ALL REALLY *IMPRESSIVE*, NORAH. BUT--
--WHAT DO *YOU* GET OUT OF IT?
FAIR QUESTION. HERE, LET ME *SHOW* YOU.
NOW, THIS THING IS MADE OF UNSTABLE MOLECULES FOR EASY CHANGING, BUT WE CAN DO THIS THE OLD-FASHIONED WAY.
NO, HEY, HOLD ON--
OH, *RELAX*, YOU BIG BABY. LOOK AT *THAT*-- PERFECT FIT.
NOW TAKE A PEEK OVER THERE.
WAIT-- THAT'S MY P.O.V.!
THAT'S RIGHT. *YOU'RE* SPIDER-MAN, PETER PARKER.
NOW *ANY* OL' SCHLUB CAN BE, AFTER ALL.
THANKS TO THOSE CAMERAS, WE'RE OFFERING A FULLY IMMERSIVE, HIGHLY INTERACTIVE SUPER-POWERED EXPERIENCE FOR YOUR MOBILE DEVICE, DESKTOP, OR VR HEADSET.
IMAGINE IT. WHENEVER SPIDEY IS IN THE FIELD, SO ARE *YOU*. ONCE YOU LOG ON, YOU SEE WHAT HE SEES, HEAR WHAT HE HEARS--AND YOU GET TO BE PART OF THE ACTION.
NORAH, WHAT SPIDER-MAN DOES, IT'S *SERIOUS* BUSINESS. IT'S ABOUT SAVING PEOPLE'S LIVES--IT'S NOT A GAME.
OF COURSE NOT. IT'S *JOURNALISM*. GIVING THE PUBLIC A FIRSTHAND LOOK AT THE LIFE OF SOMEONE TRYING TO KEEP THEM SAFE--
LETTING THEM SEE WHAT A *HERO* HE IS.

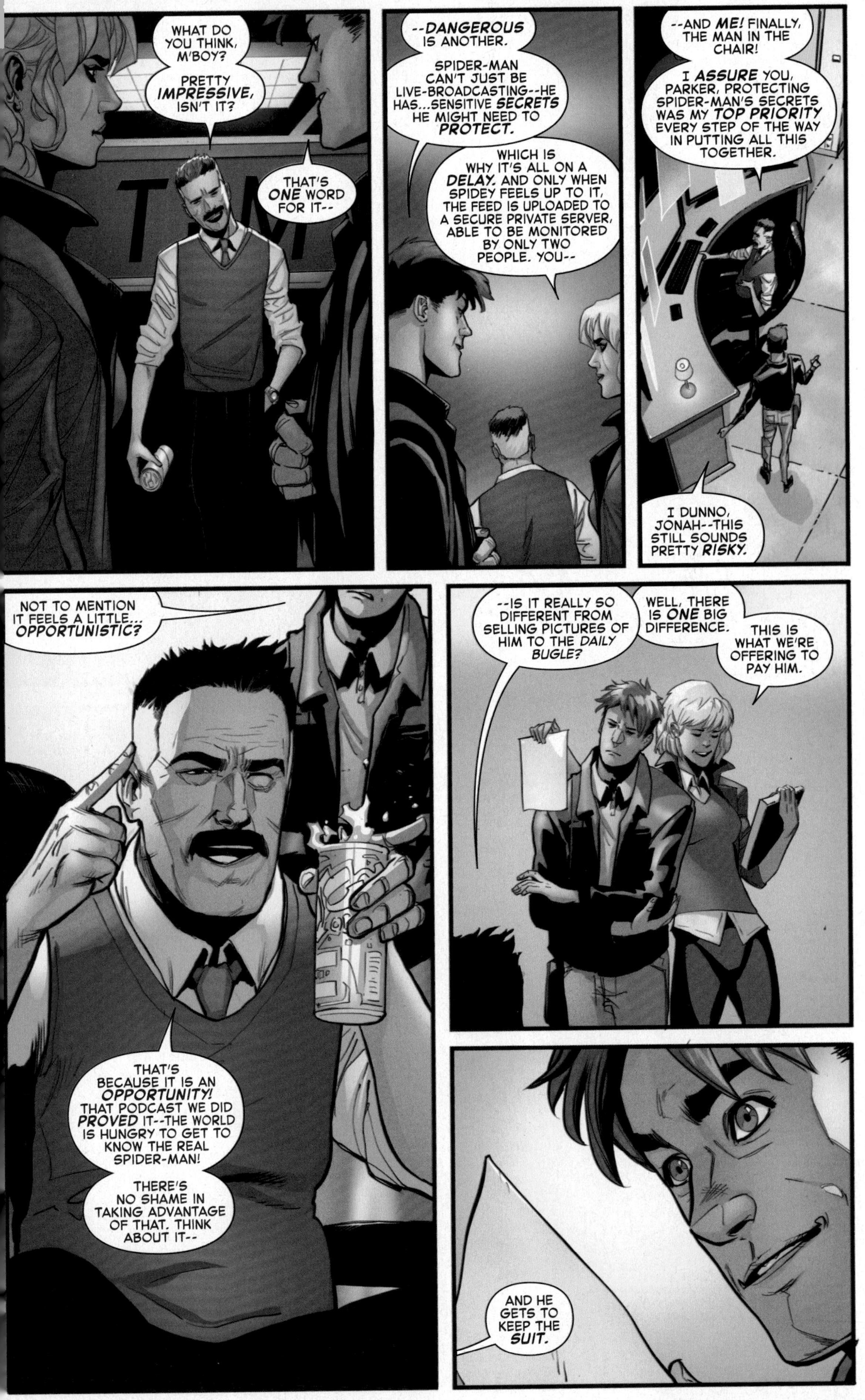
WHAT DO YOU THINK, M'BOY?
PRETTY IMPRESSIVE, ISN'T IT?
THAT'S ONE WORD FOR IT--
--DANGEROUS IS ANOTHER.
SPIDER-MAN CAN'T JUST BE LIVE-BROADCASTING--HE HAS...SENSITIVE SECRETS HE MIGHT NEED TO PROTECT.
WHICH IS WHY IT'S ALL ON A DELAY. AND ONLY WHEN SPIDEY FEELS UP TO IT, THE FEED IS UPLOADED TO A SECURE PRIVATE SERVER, ABLE TO BE MONITORED BY ONLY TWO PEOPLE. YOU--
--AND ME! FINALLY, THE MAN IN THE CHAIR!
I ASSURE YOU, PARKER, PROTECTING SPIDER-MAN'S SECRETS WAS MY TOP PRIORITY EVERY STEP OF THE WAY IN PUTTING ALL THIS TOGETHER.
I DUNNO, JONAH--THIS STILL SOUNDS PRETTY RISKY.
NOT TO MENTION IT FEELS A LITTLE... OPPORTUNISTIC?
THAT'S BECAUSE IT IS AN OPPORTUNITY! THAT PODCAST WE DID PROVED IT--THE WORLD IS HUNGRY TO GET TO KNOW THE REAL SPIDER-MAN!
THERE'S NO SHAME IN TAKING ADVANTAGE OF THAT. THINK ABOUT IT--
--IS IT REALLY SO DIFFERENT FROM SELLING PICTURES OF HIM TO THE DAILY BUGLE?
WELL, THERE IS ONE BIG DIFFERENCE.
THIS IS WHAT WE'RE OFFERING TO PAY HIM.
AND HE GETS TO KEEP THE SUIT.

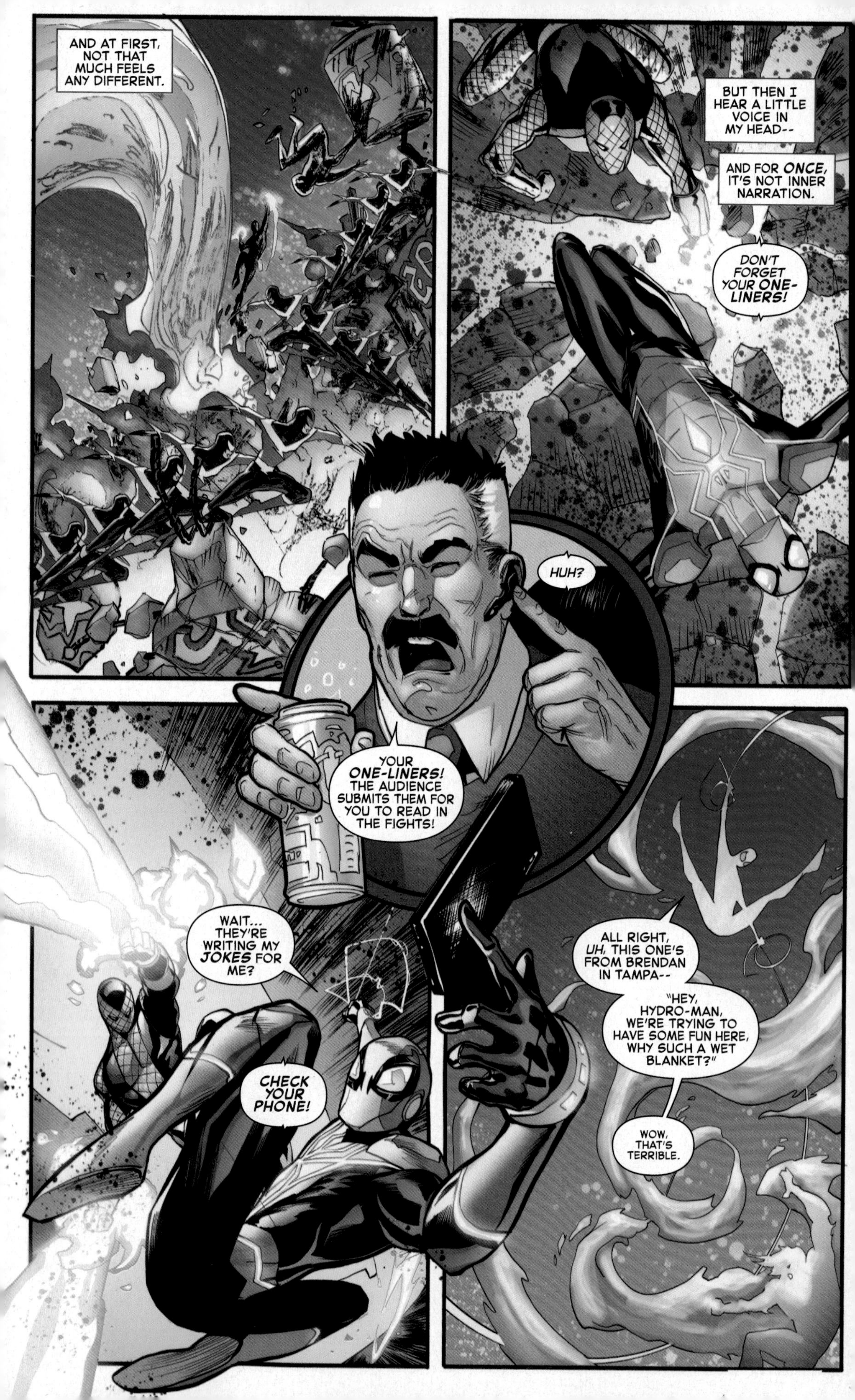
AND AT FIRST, NOT THAT MUCH FEELS ANY DIFFERENT.
BUT THEN I HEAR A LITTLE VOICE IN MY HEAD--
AND FOR ONCE, IT'S NOT INNER NARRATION.
DON'T FORGET YOUR ONE-LINERS!
HUH?
YOUR ONE-LINERS! THE AUDIENCE SUBMITS THEM FOR YOU TO READ IN THE FIGHTS!
WAIT... THEY'RE WRITING MY JOKES FOR ME?
CHECK YOUR PHONE!
ALL RIGHT, UH, THIS ONE'S FROM BRENDAN IN TAMPA--
"HEY, HYDRO-MAN, WE'RE TRYING TO HAVE SOME FUN HERE, WHY SUCH A WET BLANKET?"
WOW, THAT'S TERRIBLE.

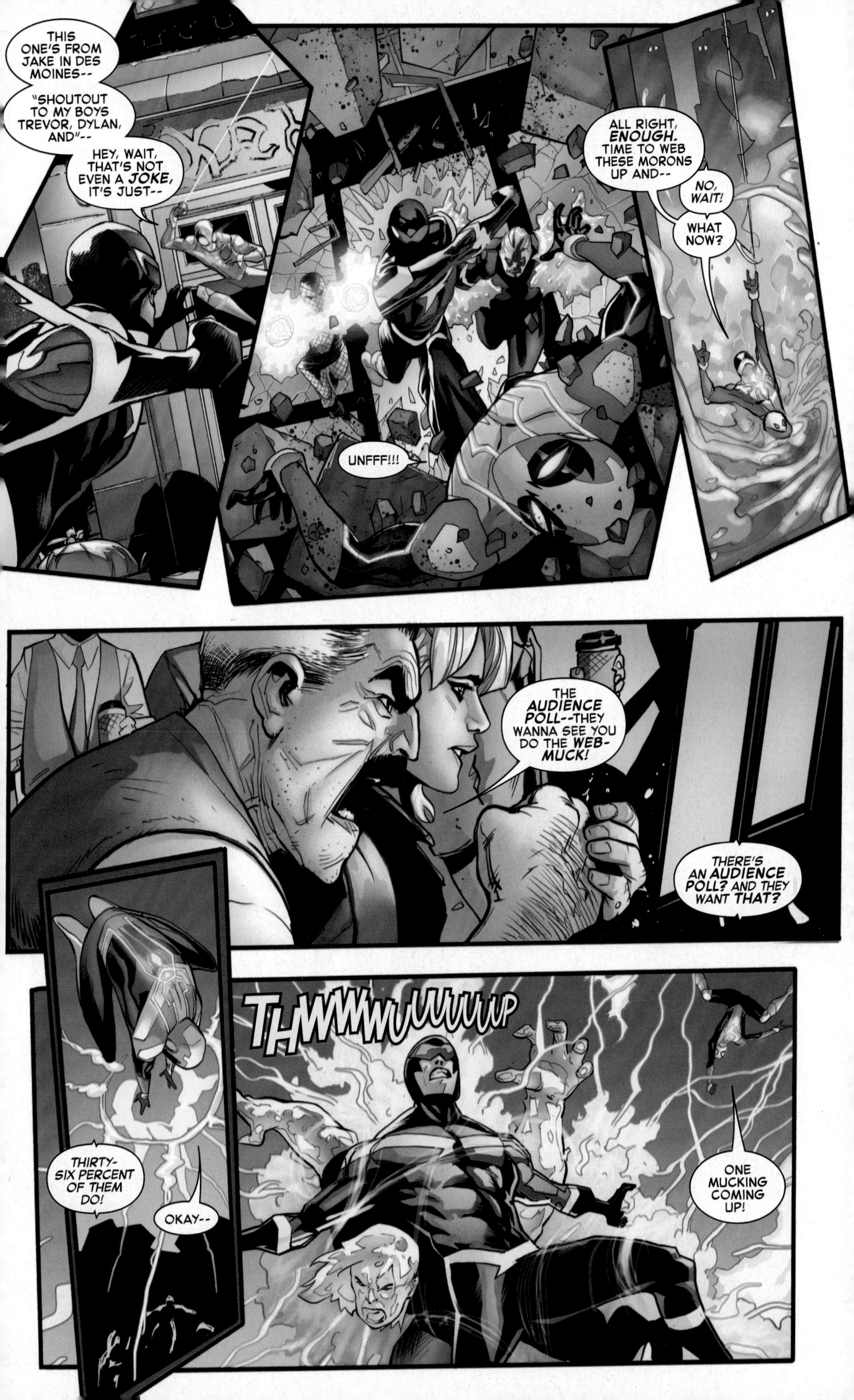
THIS ONE'S FROM JAKE IN DES MOINES--
"SHOUTOUT TO MY BOYS TREVOR, DYLAN, AND"--
HEY, WAIT, THAT'S NOT EVEN A JOKE, IT'S JUST--
UNFFF!!!
ALL RIGHT, ENOUGH. TIME TO WEB THESE MORONS UP AND--
NO, WAIT!
WHAT NOW?
THE AUDIENCE POLL--THEY WANNA SEE YOU DO THE WEB-MUCK!
THERE'S AN AUDIENCE POLL? AND THEY WANT THAT?
THIRTY-SIX PERCENT OF THEM DO!
OKAY--
THWWWUUUUUP
ONE MUCKING COMING UP!

HAPPY NOW?

OVER THE MOON! NOW, JUST SAY, "THIS CRIMINAL APPREHENSION IS BROUGHT TO YOU BY YOU-UNDIES"--

JONAH, THERE IS *NO WAY* I AM GONNA SAY--

You-UNDIES

KAPOW

KAPOW

PHOOM

BUT CIVILIZATION FELT DIFFERENT, I GUESS--

SIGH. YOU KNOW, I HAD A SUPER VILLAIN WHO DID THIS STUFF ONCE.* I THOUGHT IT WAS THE END OF CIVILIZATION.

You UNDIES

*SPIDEY'S REFERRING TO SCREWBALL, OF COURSE, FROM WAY BACK IN ASM #559! --NL

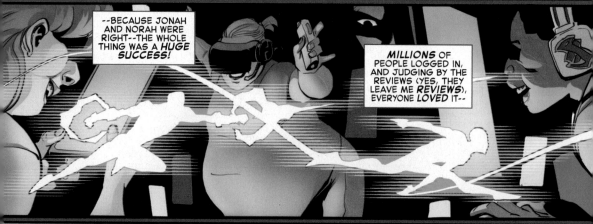

--BECAUSE JONAH AND NORAH WERE RIGHT--THE WHOLE THING WAS A *HUGE* SUCCESS!

MILLIONS OF PEOPLE LOGGED IN, AND JUDGING BY THE REVIEWS (YES, THEY LEAVE ME *REVIEWS*), EVERYONE *LOVED* IT--

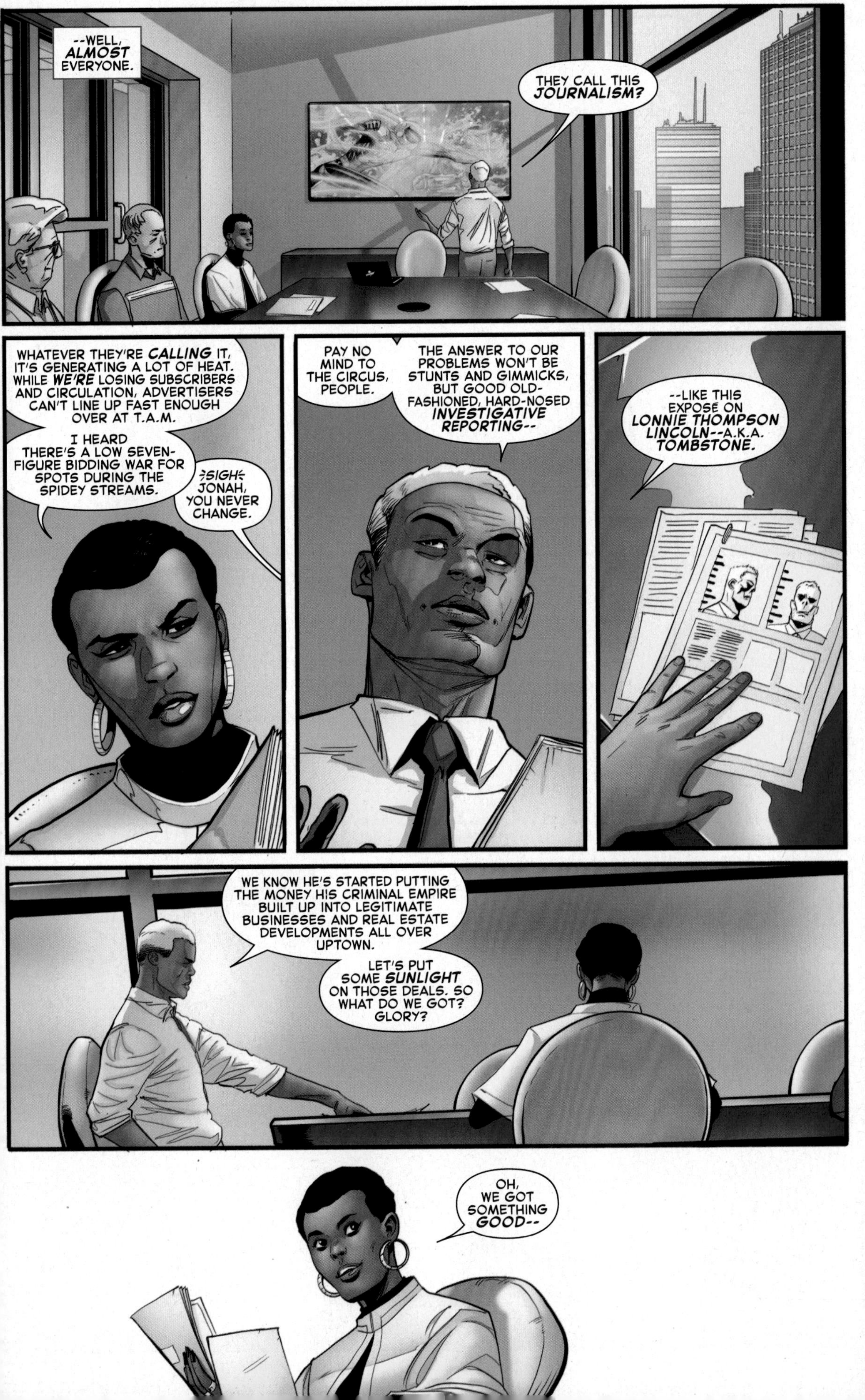
--WELL, ALMOST EVERYONE.
THEY CALL THIS JOURNALISM?
WHATEVER THEY'RE CALLING IT, IT'S GENERATING A LOT OF HEAT. WHILE WE'RE LOSING SUBSCRIBERS AND CIRCULATION, ADVERTISERS CAN'T LINE UP FAST ENOUGH OVER AT T.A.M.
I HEARD THERE'S A LOW SEVEN-FIGURE BIDDING WAR FOR SPOTS DURING THE SPIDEY STREAMS.
SIGH JONAH, YOU NEVER CHANGE.
PAY NO MIND TO THE CIRCUS, PEOPLE.
THE ANSWER TO OUR PROBLEMS WON'T BE STUNTS AND GIMMICKS, BUT GOOD OLD-FASHIONED, HARD-NOSED INVESTIGATIVE REPORTING--
--LIKE THIS EXPOSÉ ON LONNIE THOMPSON LINCOLN--A.K.A. TOMBSTONE.
WE KNOW HE'S STARTED PUTTING THE MONEY HIS CRIMINAL EMPIRE BUILT UP INTO LEGITIMATE BUSINESSES AND REAL ESTATE DEVELOPMENTS ALL OVER UPTOWN.
LET'S PUT SOME SUNLIGHT ON THOSE DEALS. SO WHAT DO WE GOT? GLORY?
OH, WE GOT SOMETHING GOOD--

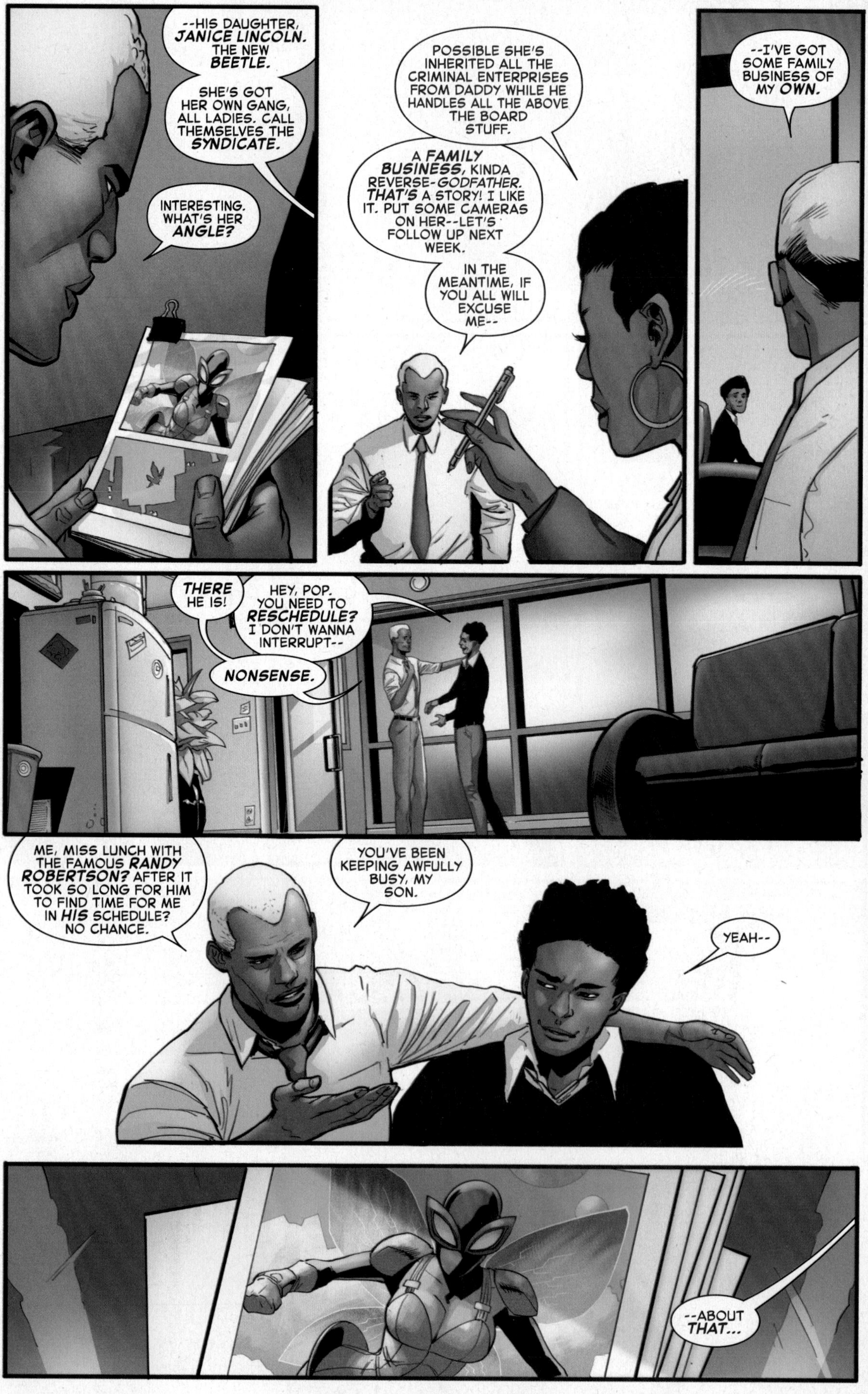
--HIS DAUGHTER, JANICE LINCOLN. THE NEW BEETLE.
SHE'S GOT HER OWN GANG, ALL LADIES. CALL THEMSELVES THE SYNDICATE.
INTERESTING. WHAT'S HER ANGLE?
POSSIBLE SHE'S INHERITED ALL THE CRIMINAL ENTERPRISES FROM DADDY WHILE HE HANDLES ALL THE ABOVE THE BOARD STUFF.
A FAMILY BUSINESS, KINDA REVERSE-GODFATHER. THAT'S A STORY! I LIKE IT. PUT SOME CAMERAS ON HER--LET'S FOLLOW UP NEXT WEEK.
IN THE MEANTIME, IF YOU ALL WILL EXCUSE ME--
--I'VE GOT SOME FAMILY BUSINESS OF MY OWN.
THERE HE IS!
HEY, POP. YOU NEED TO RESCHEDULE? I DON'T WANNA INTERRUPT--
NONSENSE.
ME, MISS LUNCH WITH THE FAMOUS RANDY ROBERTSON? AFTER IT TOOK SO LONG FOR HIM TO FIND TIME FOR ME IN HIS SCHEDULE? NO CHANCE.
YOU'VE BEEN KEEPING AWFULLY BUSY, MY SON.
YEAH--
--ABOUT THAT...

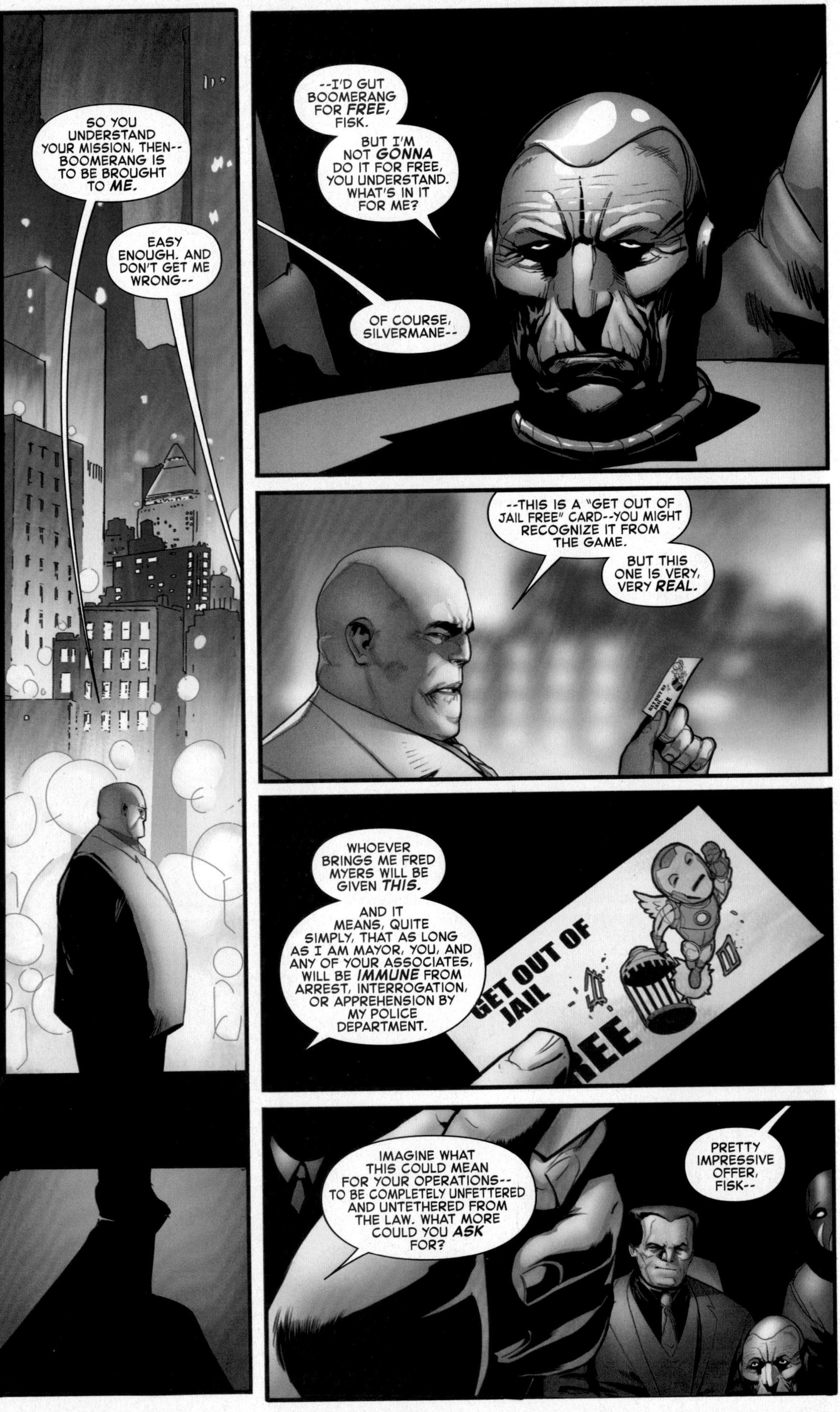

SO YOU UNDERSTAND YOUR MISSION, THEN--BOOMERANG IS TO BE BROUGHT TO ME.
EASY ENOUGH. AND DON'T GET ME WRONG--
--I'D GUT BOOMERANG FOR FREE, FISK.
BUT I'M NOT GONNA DO IT FOR FREE, YOU UNDERSTAND. WHAT'S IN IT FOR ME?
OF COURSE, SILVERMANE--
--THIS IS A "GET OUT OF JAIL FREE" CARD--YOU MIGHT RECOGNIZE IT FROM THE GAME.
BUT THIS ONE IS VERY, VERY REAL.
WHOEVER BRINGS ME FRED MYERS WILL BE GIVEN THIS.
AND IT MEANS, QUITE SIMPLY, THAT AS LONG AS I AM MAYOR, YOU, AND ANY OF YOUR ASSOCIATES, WILL BE IMMUNE FROM ARREST, INTERROGATION, OR APPREHENSION BY MY POLICE DEPARTMENT.
GET OUT OF JAIL
REE
IMAGINE WHAT THIS COULD MEAN FOR YOUR OPERATIONS--TO BE COMPLETELY UNFETTERED AND UNTETHERED FROM THE LAW. WHAT MORE COULD YOU ASK FOR?
PRETTY IMPRESSIVE OFFER, FISK--

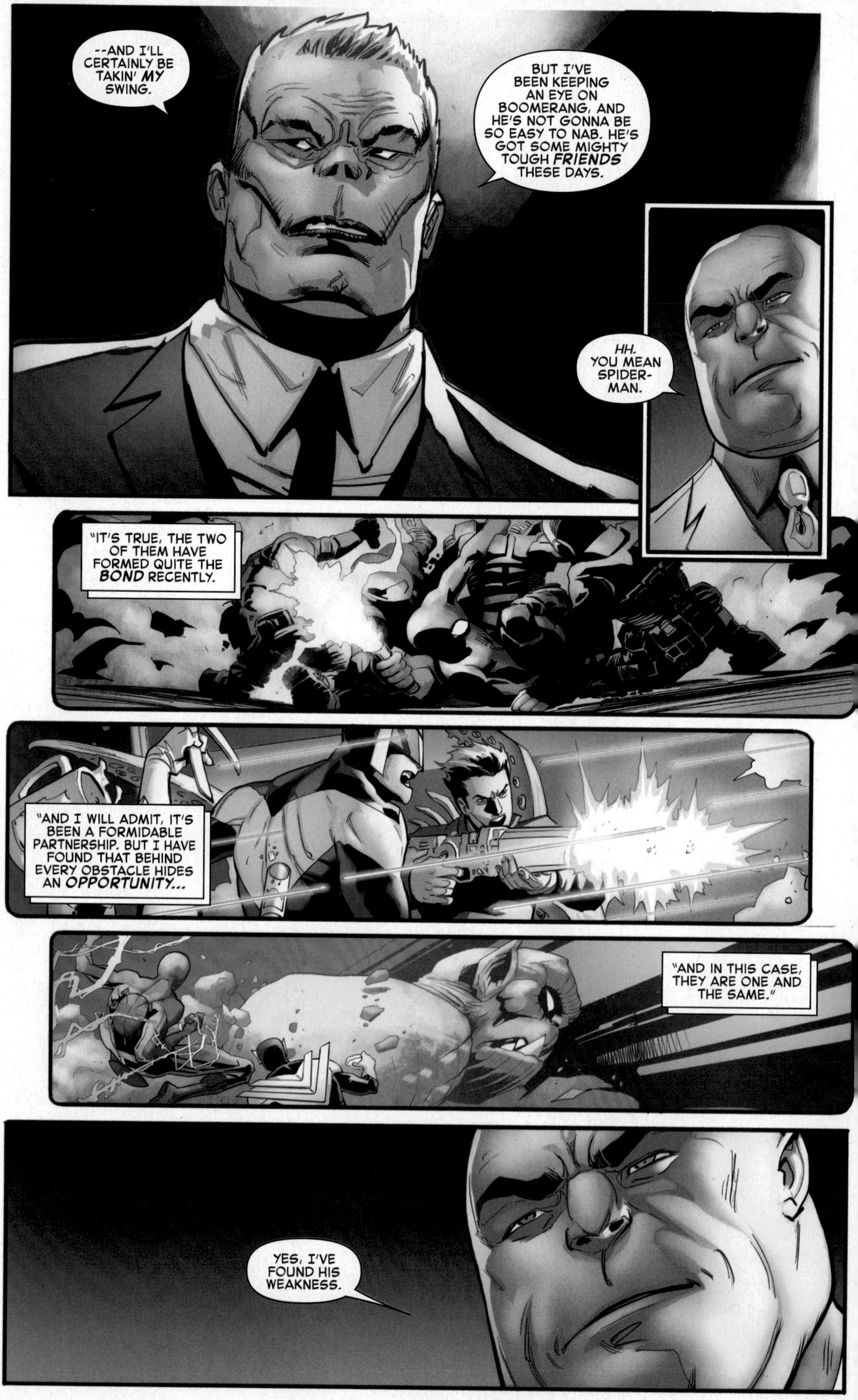
--AND I'LL CERTAINLY BE TAKIN' MY SWING.
BUT I'VE BEEN KEEPING AN EYE ON BOOMERANG, AND HE'S NOT GONNA BE SO EASY TO NAB. HE'S GOT SOME MIGHTY TOUGH FRIENDS THESE DAYS.
HH. YOU MEAN SPIDER-MAN.
"IT'S TRUE, THE TWO OF THEM HAVE FORMED QUITE THE BOND RECENTLY.
"AND I WILL ADMIT, IT'S BEEN A FORMIDABLE PARTNERSHIP. BUT I HAVE FOUND THAT BEHIND EVERY OBSTACLE HIDES AN OPPORTUNITY...
"AND IN THIS CASE, THEY ARE ONE AND THE SAME."
YES, I'VE FOUND HIS WEAKNESS.

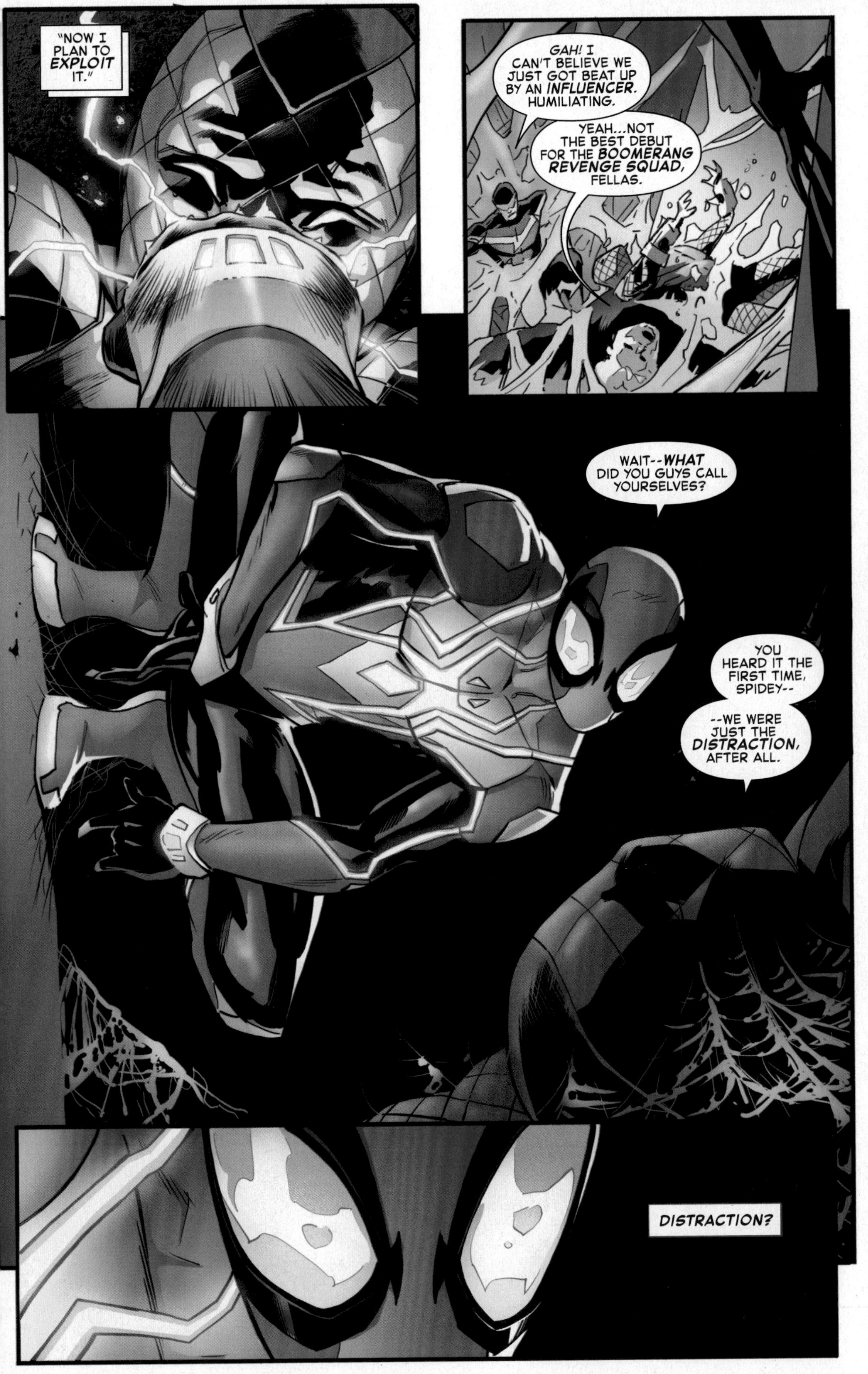
"NOW I PLAN TO EXPLOIT IT."
GAH! I CAN'T BELIEVE WE JUST GOT BEAT UP BY AN INFLUENCER. HUMILIATING.
YEAH...NOT THE BEST DEBUT FOR THE BOOMERANG REVENGE SQUAD, FELLAS.
WAIT--WHAT DID YOU GUYS CALL YOURSELVES?
YOU HEARD IT THE FIRST TIME, SPIDEY--
--WE WERE JUST THE DISTRACTION, AFTER ALL.
DISTRACTION?

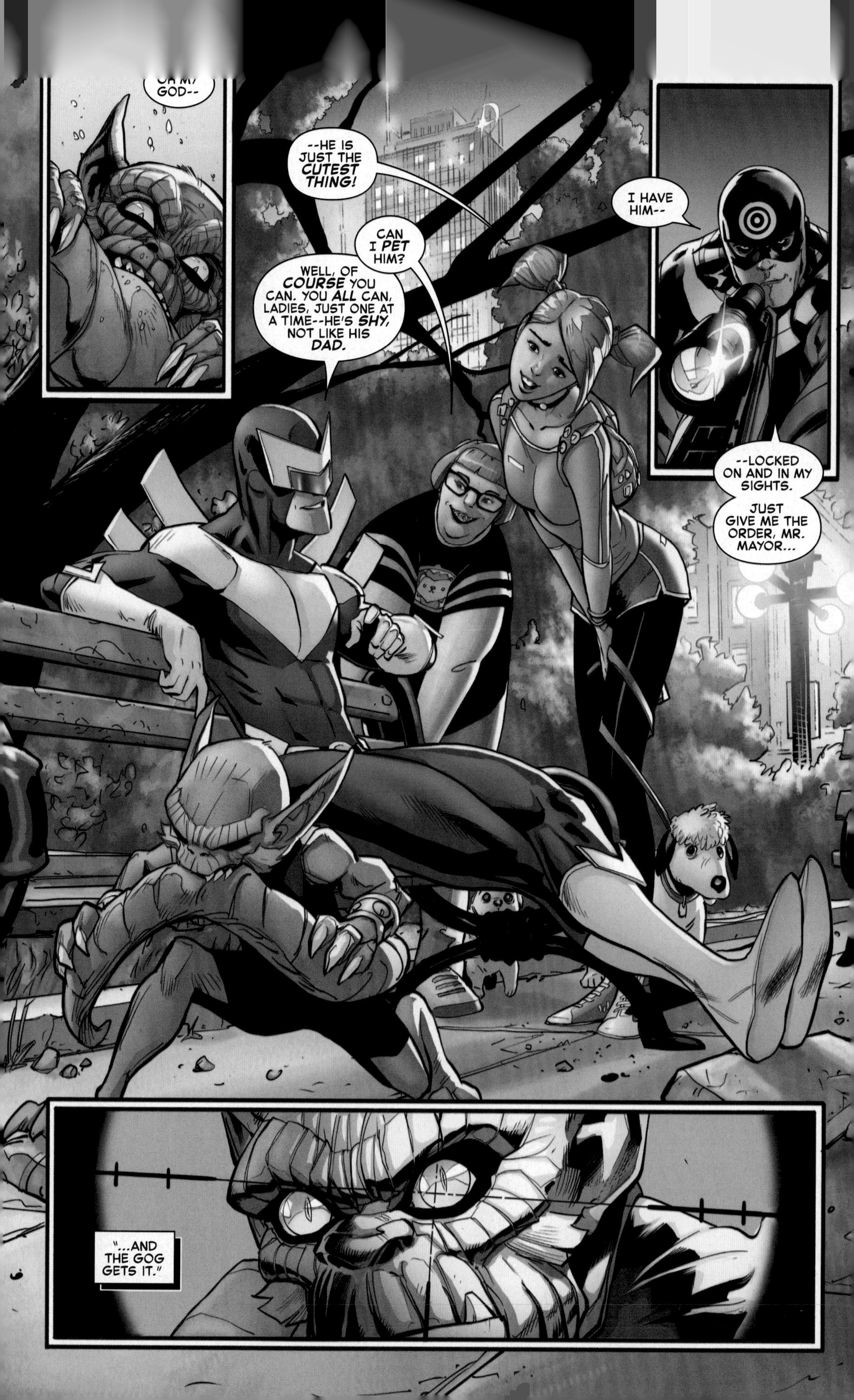
GOD--
--HE IS JUST THE CUTEST THING!
CAN I PET HIM?
WELL, OF COURSE YOU CAN. YOU ALL CAN, LADIES, JUST ONE AT A TIME--HE'S SHY, NOT LIKE HIS DAD.
I HAVE HIM--
--LOCKED ON AND IN MY SIGHTS.
JUST GIVE ME THE ORDER, MR. MAYOR...
"...AND THE GOG GETS IT."

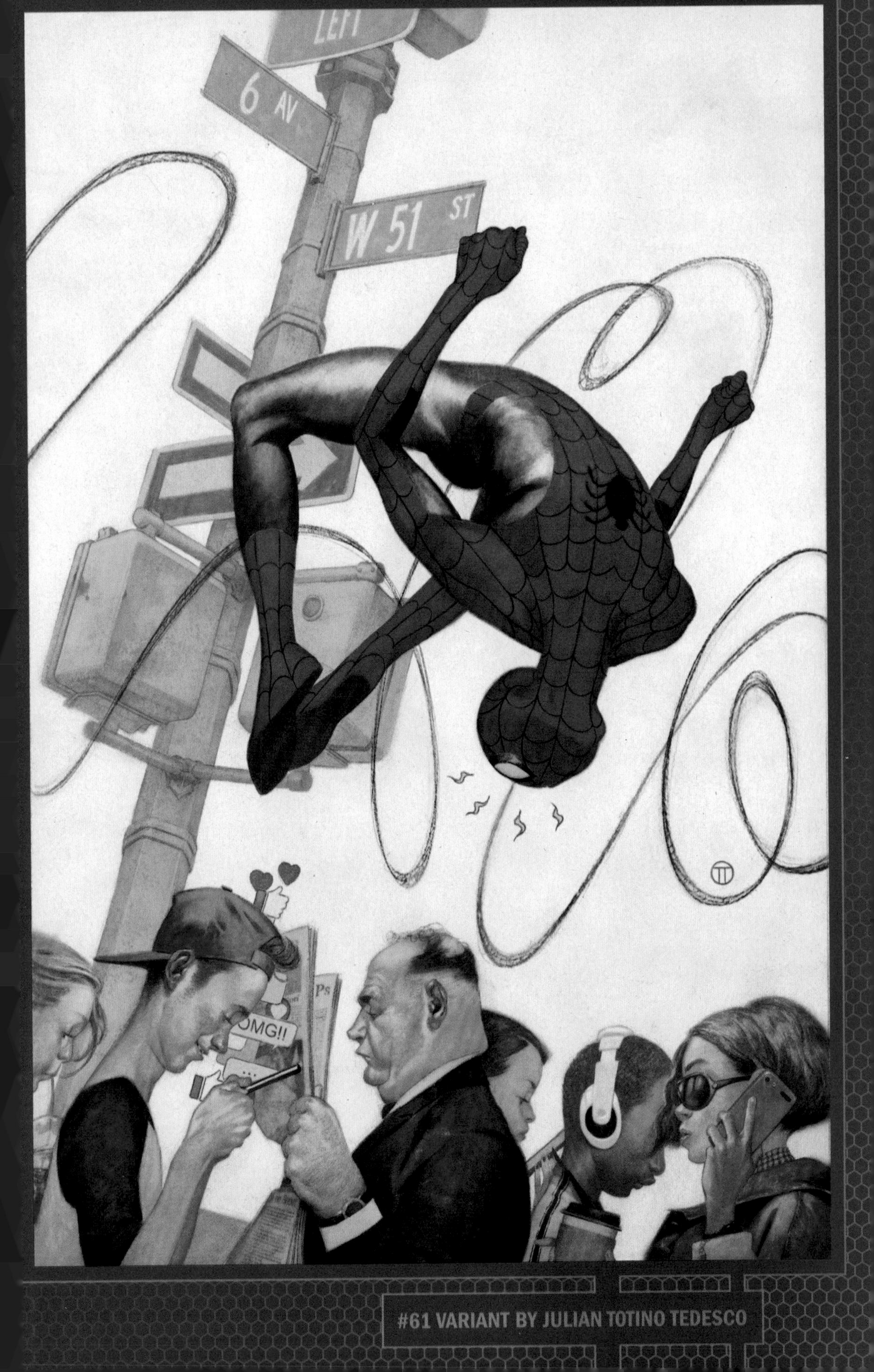
LEFT
6 AV
W 51 ST
OMG!!

#61 VARIANT BY JULIAN TOTINO TEDESCO

62

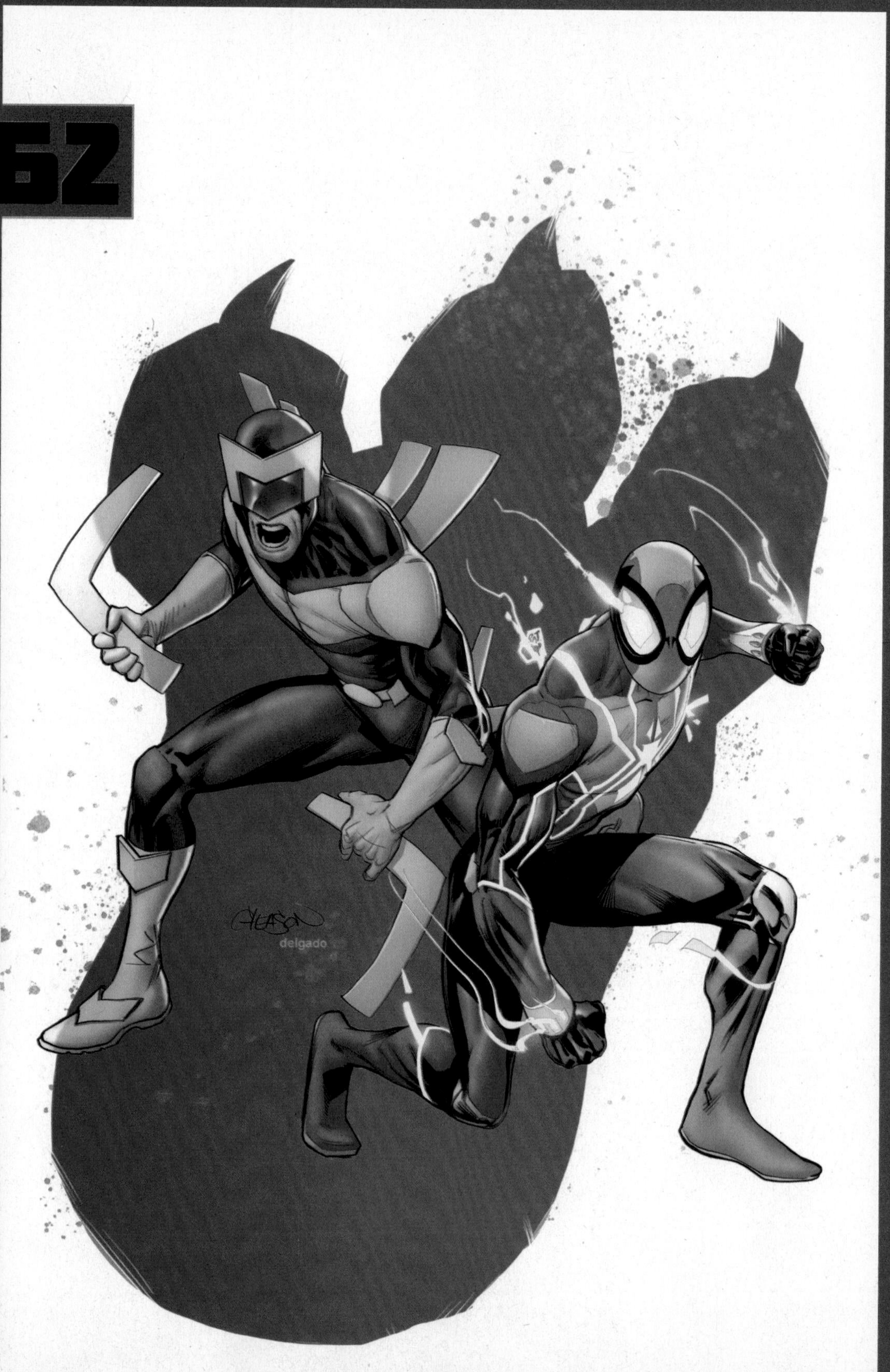

WAG THE GOG

HE'S DONE SO WELL ELUDING ME. ANNOYING ME. INTERFERING WITH MY PLANS.
A ROGUE LIKE BOOMERANG IS MORE DANGEROUS THAN HE MAY SEEM--
THWEP
FASTER!
--ALL CUNNING AND GUILE. BUT I'VE FOUND HIS WEAKNESS.
COME ON! FASTER!
THWEP
HE'S BECOME JUST LIKE THE HERO HE USED TO DESPISE.
IF YOU CAN'T HURT HIM--

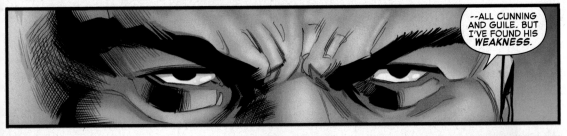

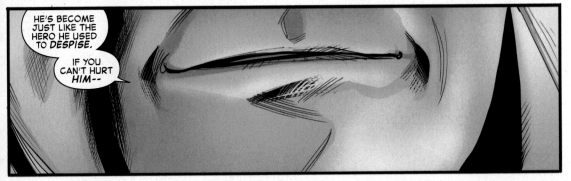

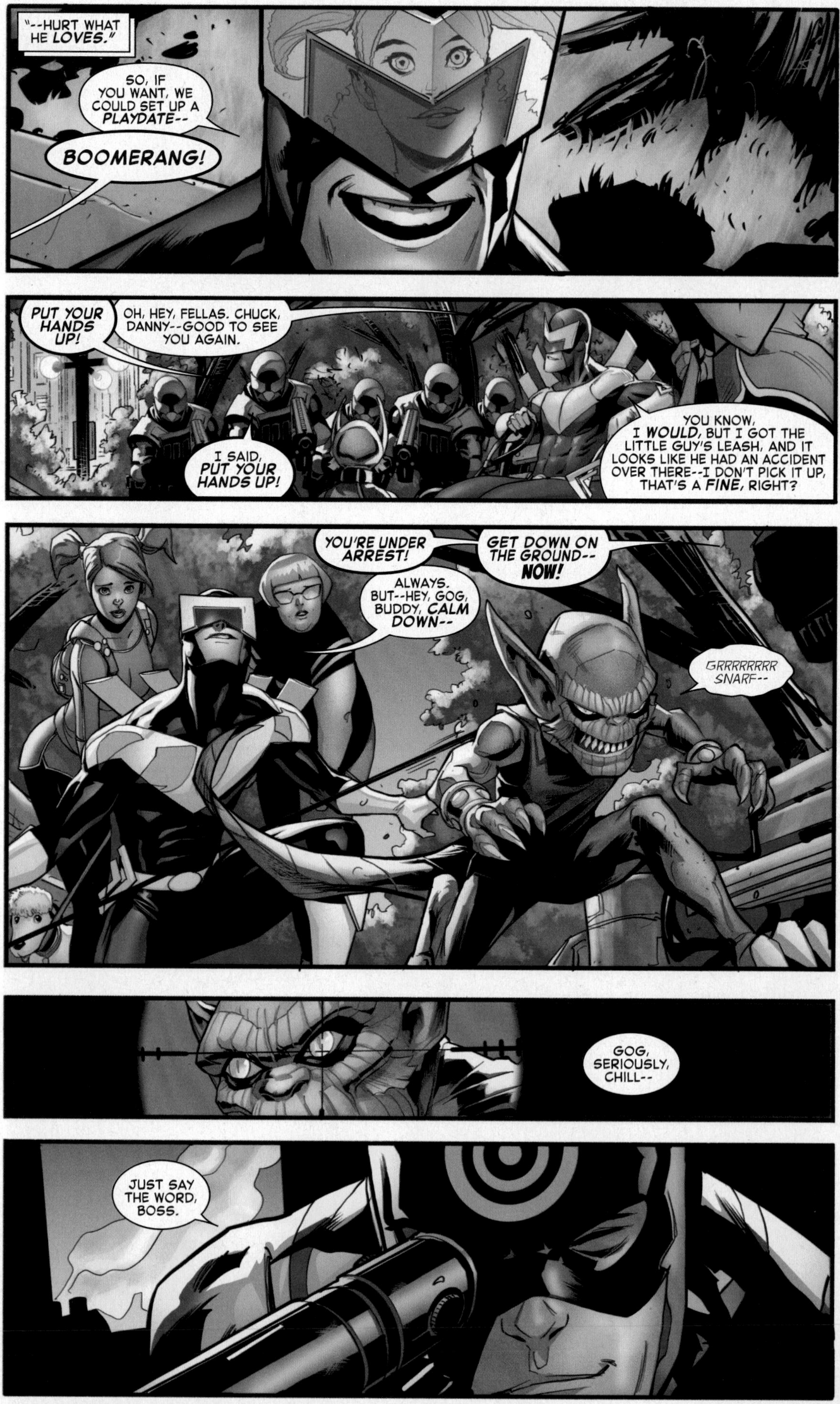
"--HURT WHAT HE LOVES."
SO, IF YOU WANT, WE COULD SET UP A PLAYDATE--
BOOMERANG!
PUT YOUR HANDS UP!
OH, HEY, FELLAS. CHUCK, DANNY--GOOD TO SEE YOU AGAIN.
I SAID, PUT YOUR HANDS UP!
YOU KNOW, I WOULD, BUT I GOT THE LITTLE GUY'S LEASH, AND IT LOOKS LIKE HE HAD AN ACCIDENT OVER THERE--I DON'T PICK IT UP, THAT'S A FINE, RIGHT?
YOU'RE UNDER ARREST!
GET DOWN ON THE GROUND-- NOW!
ALWAYS. BUT--HEY, GOG, BUDDY, CALM DOWN--
GRRRRRRRR SNARF--
GOG, SERIOUSLY, CHILL--
JUST SAY THE WORD, BOSS.

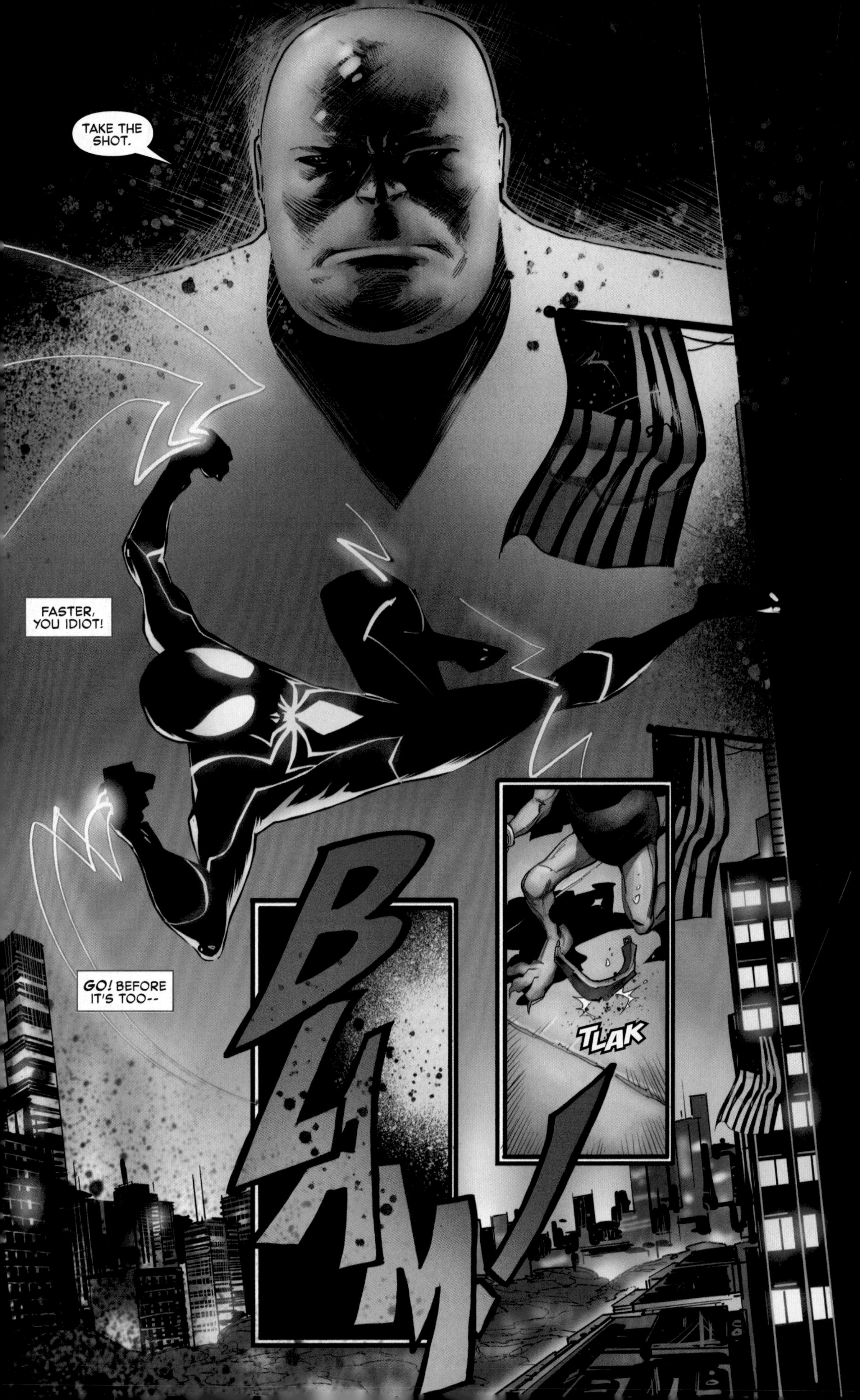
TAKE THE SHOT.
FASTER, YOU IDIOT!
GO! BEFORE IT'S TOO--
BLAM!
TLAK

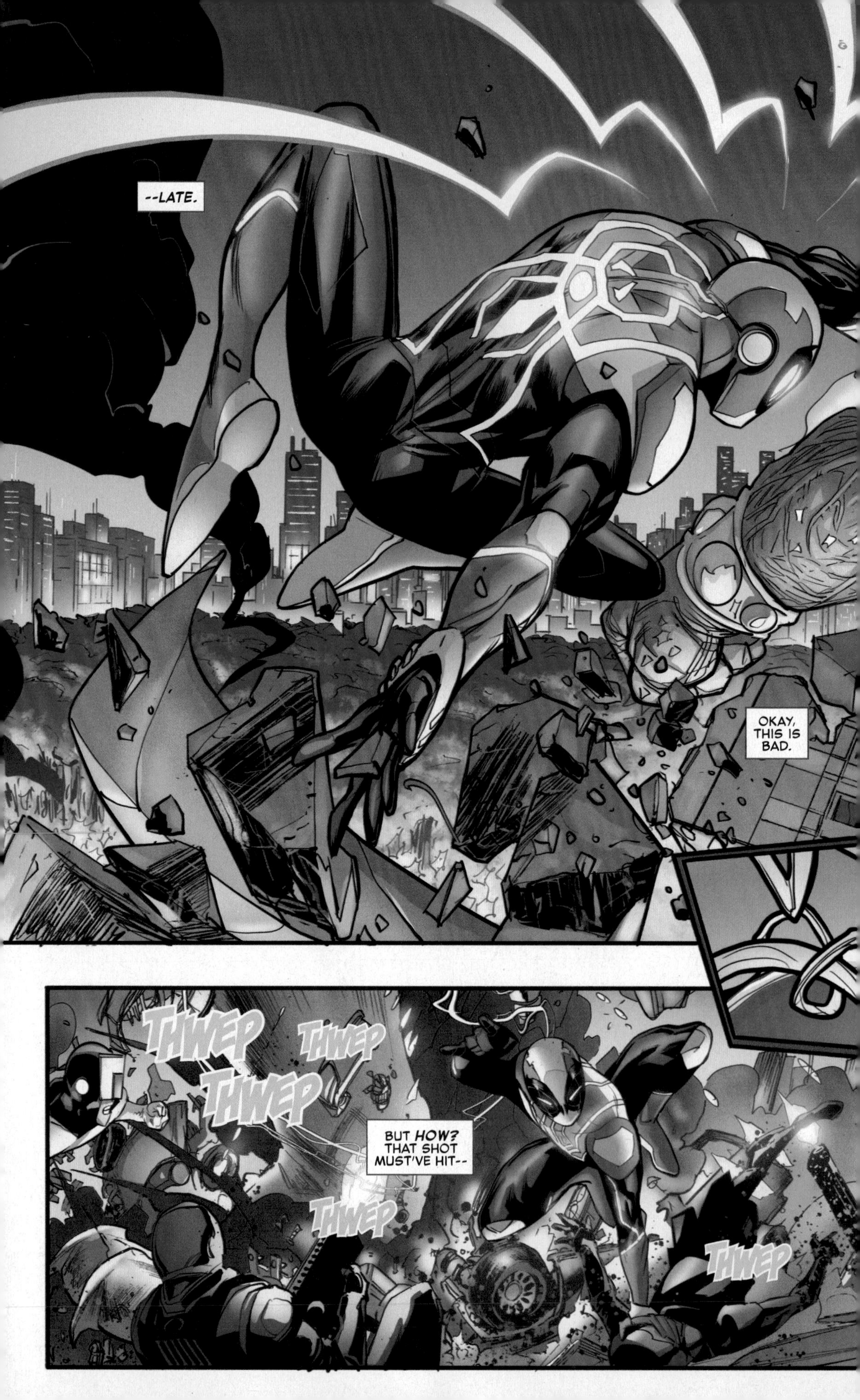
--LATE.
OKAY, THIS IS BAD.
THWEP
THWEP
THWEP
BUT HOW? THAT SHOT MUST'VE HIT--
THWEP
THWEP

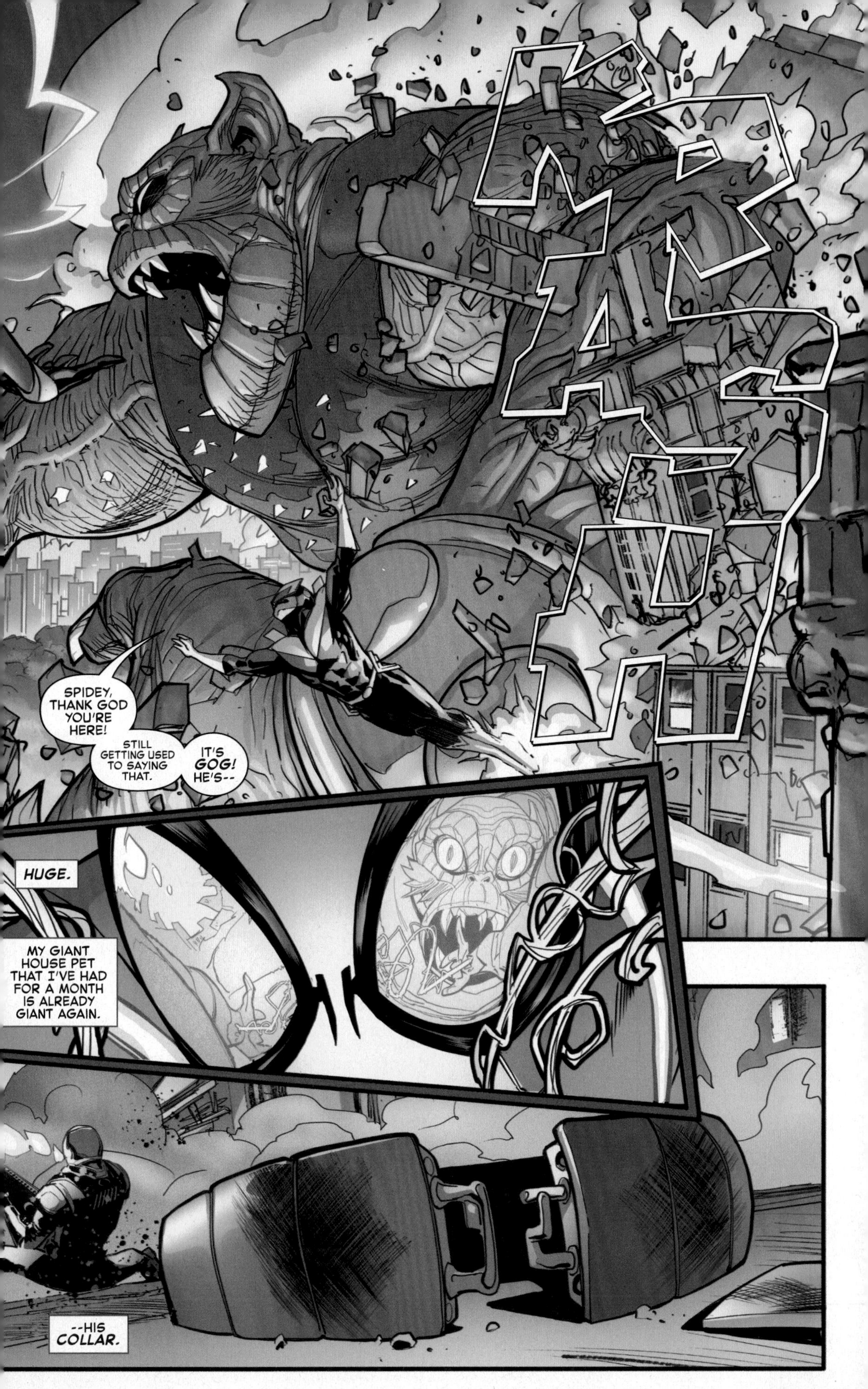

SPIDEY, THANK GOD YOU'RE HERE!
STILL GETTING USED TO SAYING THAT.
IT'S GOG! HE'S--
HUGE.
MY GIANT HOUSE PET THAT I'VE HAD FOR A MONTH IS ALREADY GIANT AGAIN.
--HIS COLLAR.

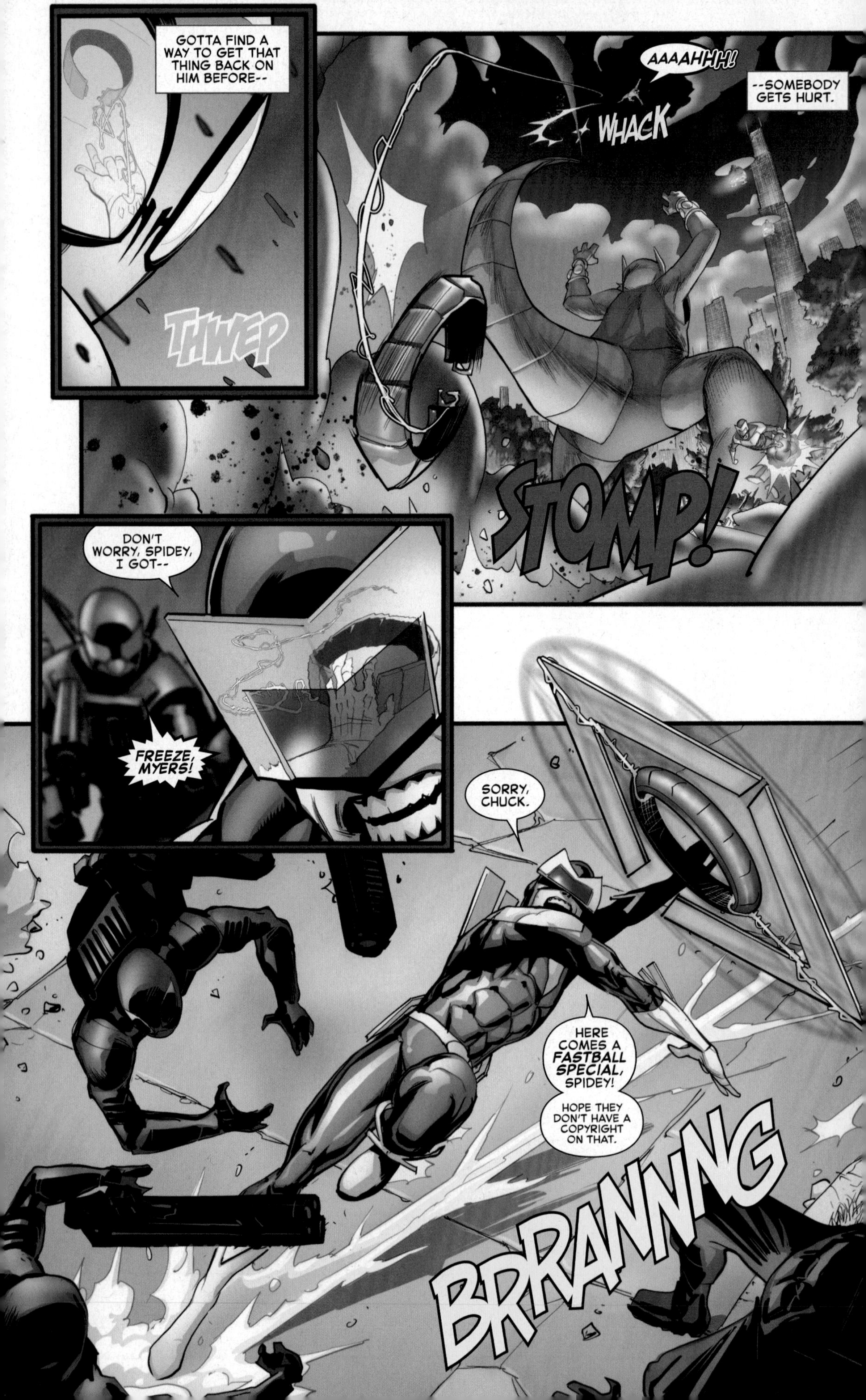
GOTTA FIND A WAY TO GET THAT THING BACK ON HIM BEFORE--
THWEP
AAAAHHH!
--SOMEBODY GETS HURT.
WHACK
STOMP!
DON'T WORRY, SPIDEY, I GOT--
FREEZE, MYERS!
SORRY, CHUCK.
HERE COMES A FASTBALL SPECIAL, SPIDEY!
HOPE THEY DON'T HAVE A COPYRIGHT ON THAT.
BRRANNNG

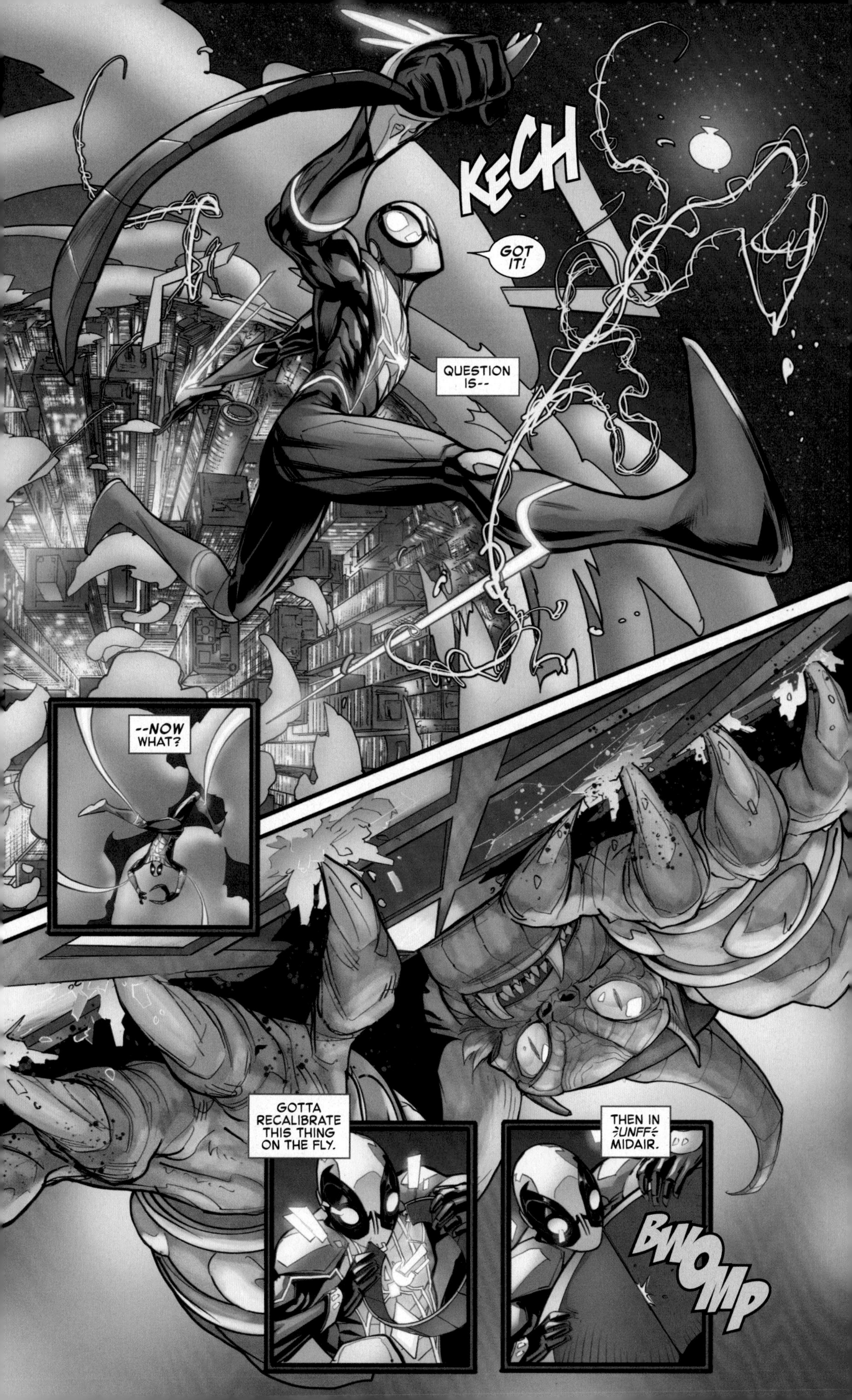
KECH
GOT IT!
QUESTION IS--
--NOW WHAT?
GOTTA RECALIBRATE THIS THING ON THE FLY.
THEN IN ≠UNFF≠ MIDAIR.
BWOMP

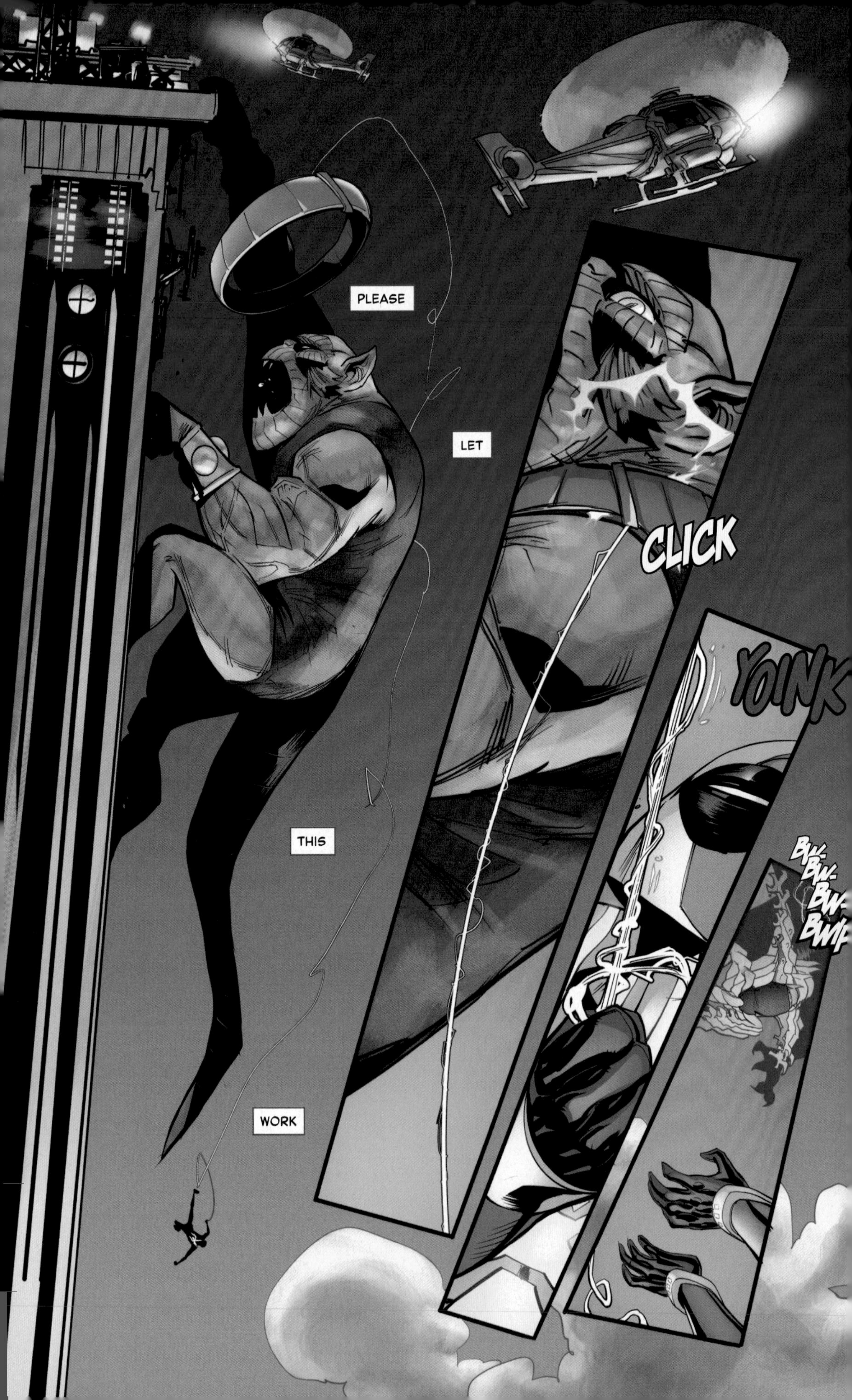
PLEASE
LET
THIS
WORK
CLICK
YOINK
BW-BW-BW-BWIP

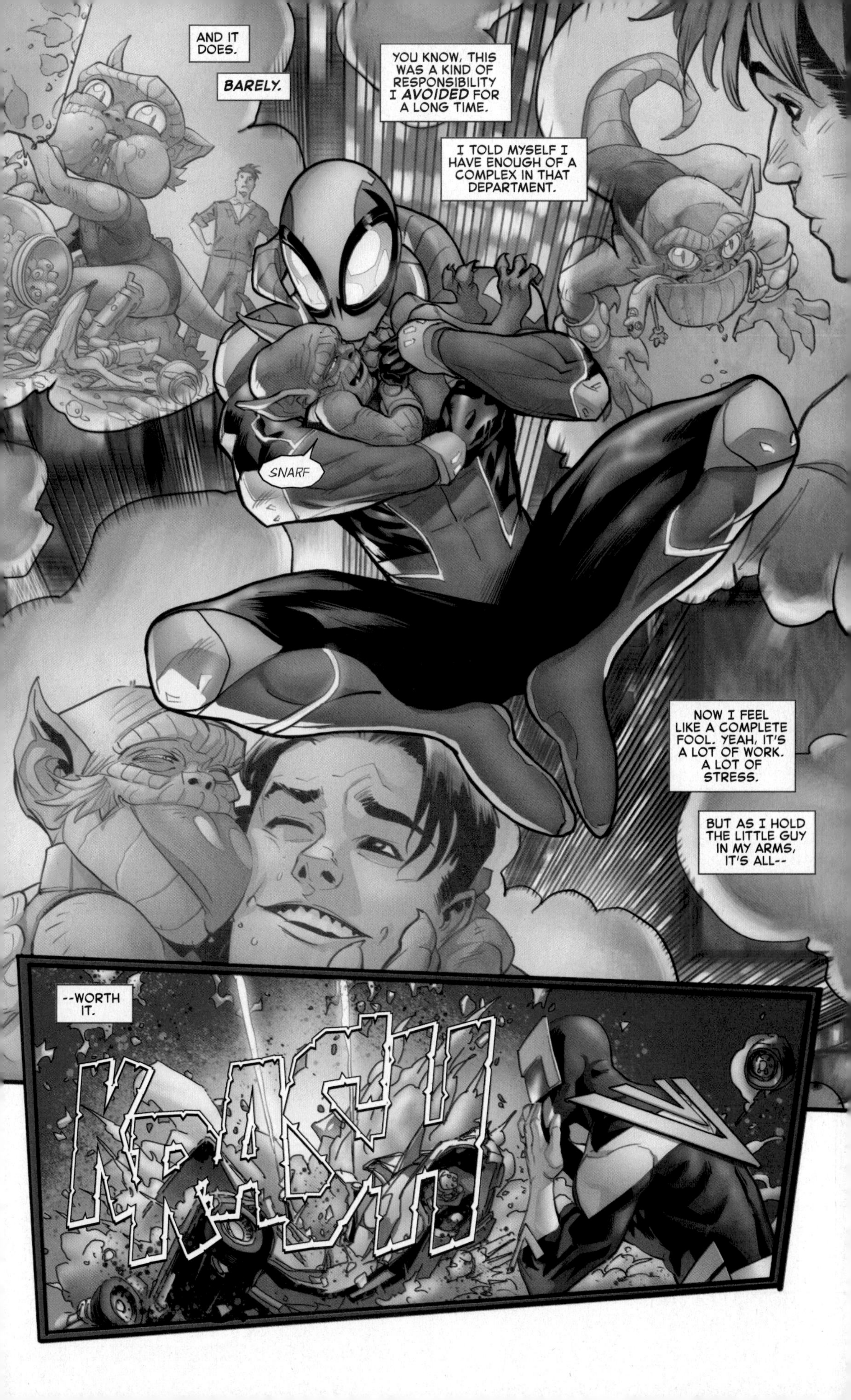
AND IT DOES.
BARELY.
YOU KNOW, THIS WAS A KIND OF RESPONSIBILITY I AVOIDED FOR A LONG TIME.
I TOLD MYSELF I HAVE ENOUGH OF A COMPLEX IN THAT DEPARTMENT.
SNARF
NOW I FEEL LIKE A COMPLETE FOOL. YEAH, IT'S A LOT OF WORK. A LOT OF STRESS.
BUT AS I HOLD THE LITTLE GUY IN MY ARMS, IT'S ALL--
--WORTH IT.
KRASH

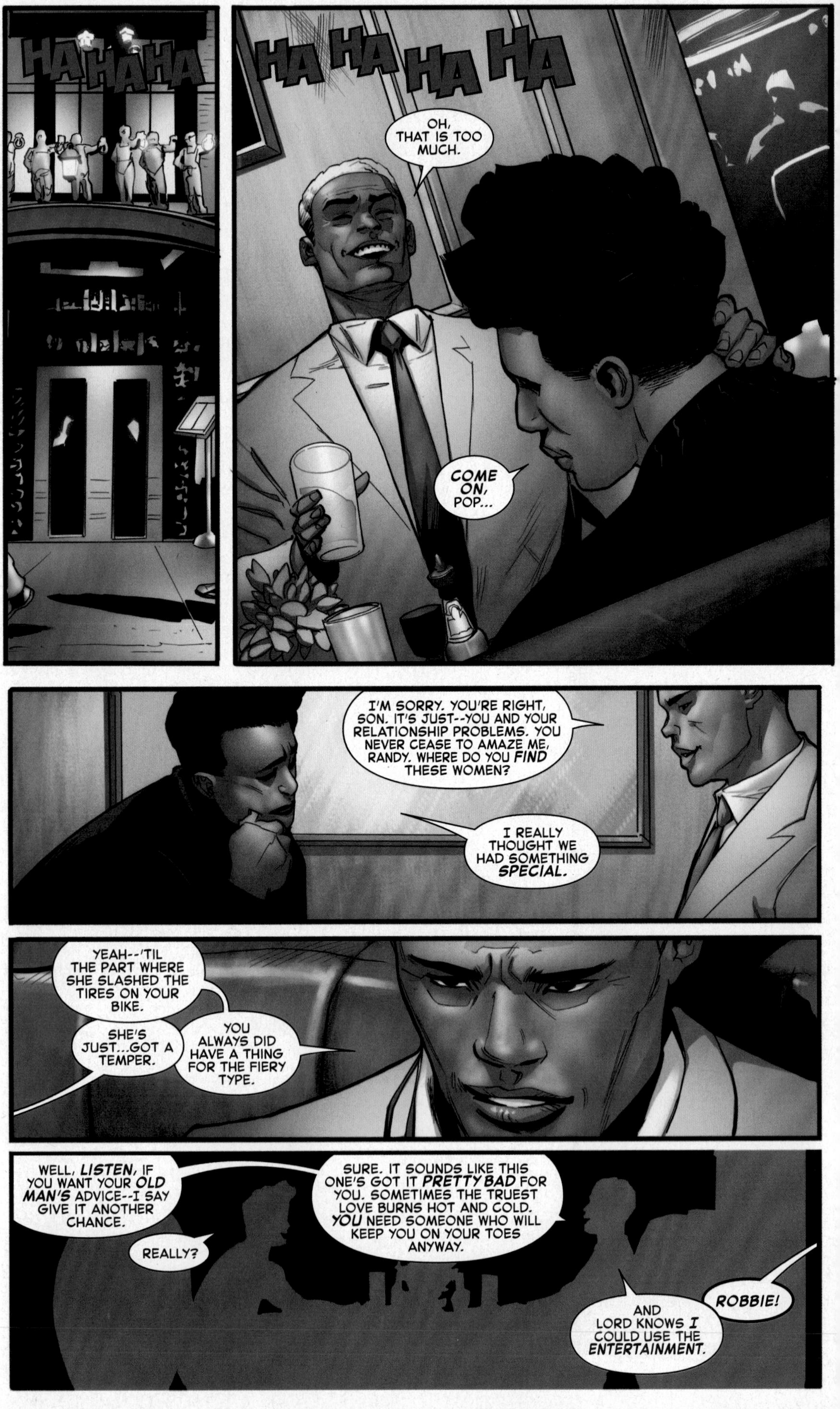

HA HA HA
HA HA HA HA HA
OH, THAT IS TOO MUCH.
COME ON, POP...
I'M SORRY. YOU'RE RIGHT, SON. IT'S JUST--YOU AND YOUR RELATIONSHIP PROBLEMS. YOU NEVER CEASE TO AMAZE ME, RANDY. WHERE DO YOU FIND THESE WOMEN?
I REALLY THOUGHT WE HAD SOMETHING SPECIAL.
YEAH--'TIL THE PART WHERE SHE SLASHED THE TIRES ON YOUR BIKE.
SHE'S JUST...GOT A TEMPER.
YOU ALWAYS DID HAVE A THING FOR THE FIERY TYPE.
WELL, LISTEN, IF YOU WANT YOUR OLD MAN'S ADVICE--I SAY GIVE IT ANOTHER CHANCE.
REALLY?
SURE. IT SOUNDS LIKE THIS ONE'S GOT IT PRETTY BAD FOR YOU. SOMETIMES THE TRUEST LOVE BURNS HOT AND COLD. YOU NEED SOMEONE WHO WILL KEEP YOU ON YOUR TOES ANYWAY.
AND LORD KNOWS I COULD USE THE ENTERTAINMENT.
ROBBIE!

ROBBIE ROBERTSON! THERE YOU ARE!

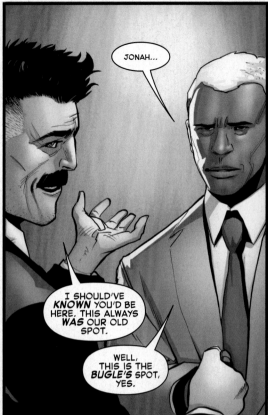

JONAH...

I SHOULD'VE KNOWN YOU'D BE HERE. THIS ALWAYS WAS OUR OLD SPOT.

WELL, THIS IS THE BUGLE'S SPOT, YES.

SAY, I'M LUCKY TO HAVE RUN INTO YOU--I'VE BEEN WANTING TO CATCH UP, SHARE ALL THE BIG NEWS. YOU SAW THE SPIDER-MAN STUFF, RIGHT?

YEAH... I SAW IT...

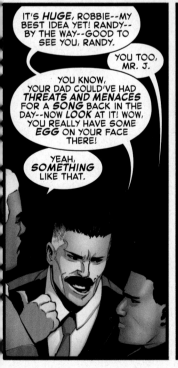

IT'S HUGE, ROBBIE--MY BEST IDEA YET! RANDY--BY THE WAY--GOOD TO SEE YOU, RANDY.

YOU TOO, MR. J.

YOU KNOW, YOUR DAD COULD'VE HAD THREATS AND MENACES FOR A SONG BACK IN THE DAY--NOW LOOK AT IT! WOW, YOU REALLY HAVE SOME EGG ON YOUR FACE THERE!

YEAH, SOMETHING LIKE THAT.

BUT LISTEN, I DON'T WANNA GLOAT. TOO MUCH. I'D LOVE TO TALK TO YOU ABOUT A PARTNERSHIP. WE'VE GOT SO MANY YOUNG PEOPLE VISITING OUR SITE--THEY DON'T EVEN KNOW WHAT A NEWSPAPER IS.

SO I WAS THINKING WE COULD ADD THESE LITTLE POP-UPS, TEXT PIECES FROM BUGLE ARTICLES.

WHAT DO YOU SAY?

YOUR POPS KNOWS WHAT POP-UPS ARE, RIGHT, RANDY?

YEAH... JONAH...

...I DON'T THINK THAT'S A GOOD IDEA.

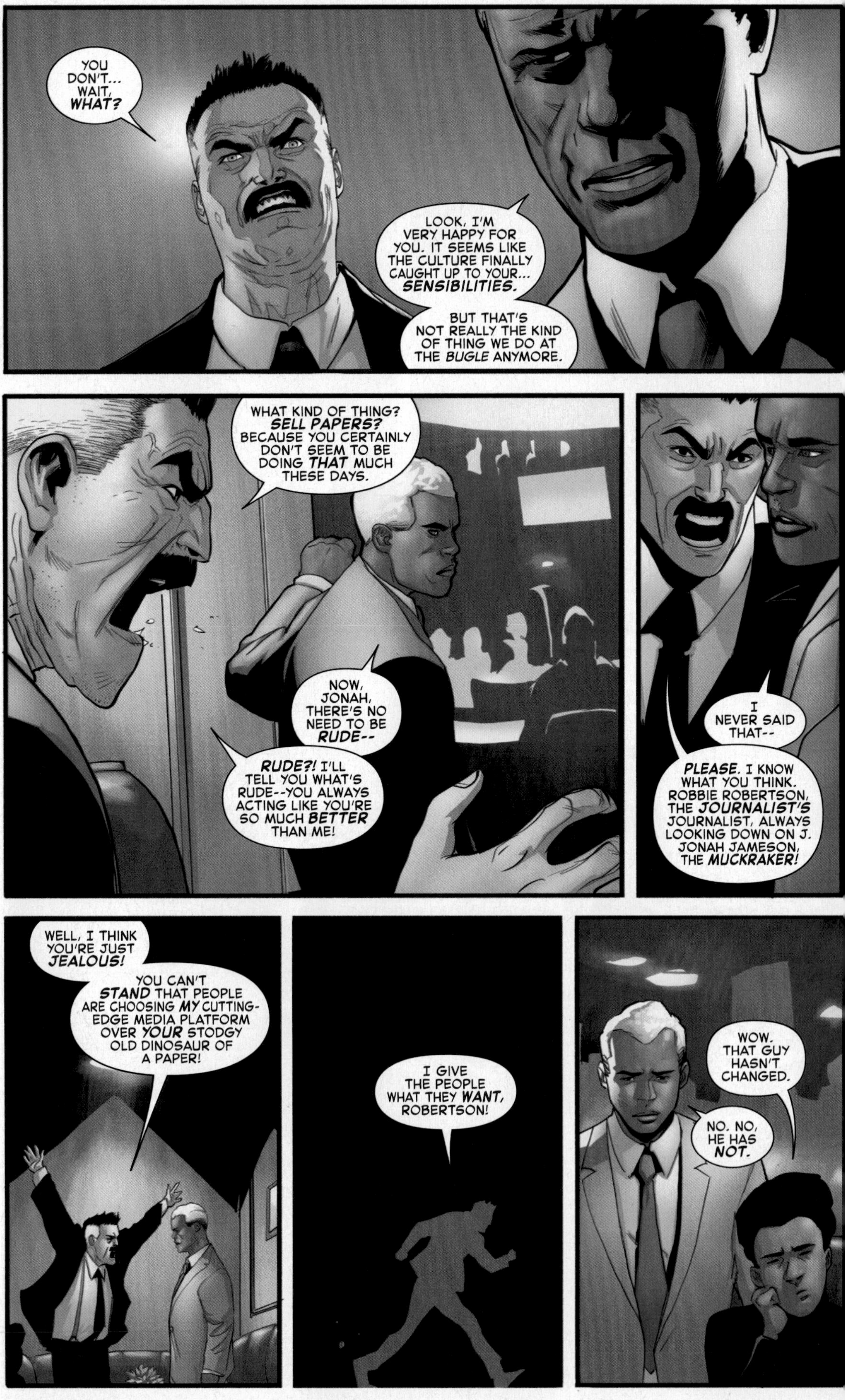
YOU DON'T... WAIT, WHAT?
LOOK, I'M VERY HAPPY FOR YOU. IT SEEMS LIKE THE CULTURE FINALLY CAUGHT UP TO YOUR... SENSIBILITIES.
BUT THAT'S NOT REALLY THE KIND OF THING WE DO AT THE BUGLE ANYMORE.
WHAT KIND OF THING? SELL PAPERS? BECAUSE YOU CERTAINLY DON'T SEEM TO BE DOING THAT MUCH THESE DAYS.
NOW, JONAH, THERE'S NO NEED TO BE RUDE--
RUDE?! I'LL TELL YOU WHAT'S RUDE--YOU ALWAYS ACTING LIKE YOU'RE SO MUCH BETTER THAN ME!
I NEVER SAID THAT--
PLEASE. I KNOW WHAT YOU THINK. ROBBIE ROBERTSON, THE JOURNALIST'S JOURNALIST, ALWAYS LOOKING DOWN ON J. JONAH JAMESON, THE MUCKRAKER!
WELL, I THINK YOU'RE JUST JEALOUS!
YOU CAN'T STAND THAT PEOPLE ARE CHOOSING MY CUTTING-EDGE MEDIA PLATFORM OVER YOUR STODGY OLD DINOSAUR OF A PAPER!
I GIVE THE PEOPLE WHAT THEY WANT, ROBERTSON!
WOW. THAT GUY HASN'T CHANGED.
NO. NO, HE HAS NOT.

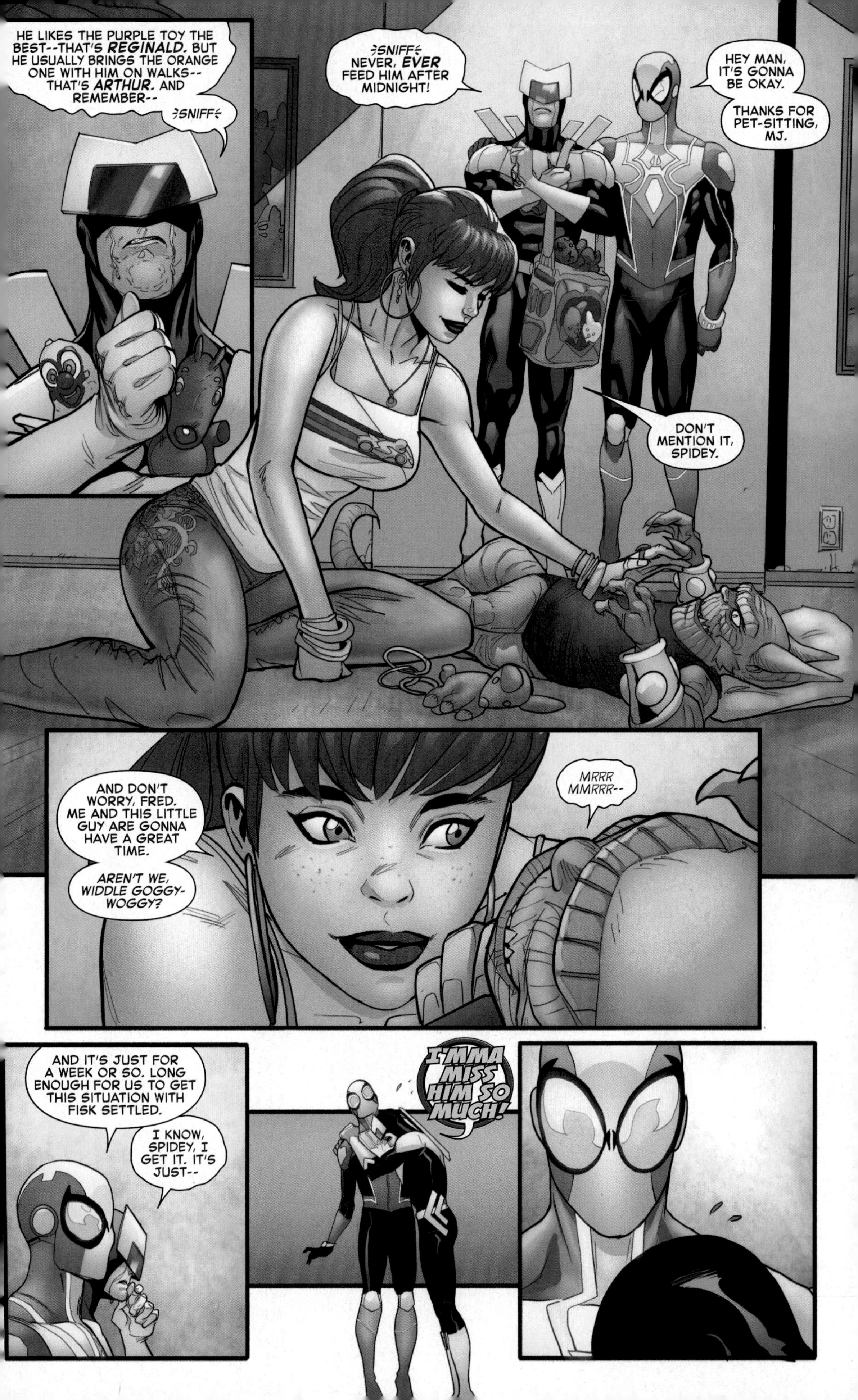
HE LIKES THE PURPLE TOY THE BEST--THAT'S REGINALD. BUT HE USUALLY BRINGS THE ORANGE ONE WITH HIM ON WALKS--THAT'S ARTHUR. AND REMEMBER--
SNIFF
SNIFF
NEVER, EVER FEED HIM AFTER MIDNIGHT!
HEY MAN, IT'S GONNA BE OKAY.
THANKS FOR PET-SITTING, MJ.
DON'T MENTION IT, SPIDEY.
AND DON'T WORRY, FRED. ME AND THIS LITTLE GUY ARE GONNA HAVE A GREAT TIME.
ARE'NT WE, WIDDLE GOGGY-WOGGY?
MRRR MMRRR--
AND IT'S JUST FOR A WEEK OR SO. LONG ENOUGH FOR US TO GET THIS SITUATION WITH FISK SETTLED.
I KNOW, SPIDEY, I GET IT. IT'S JUST--
I'MMA MISS HIM SO MUCH!

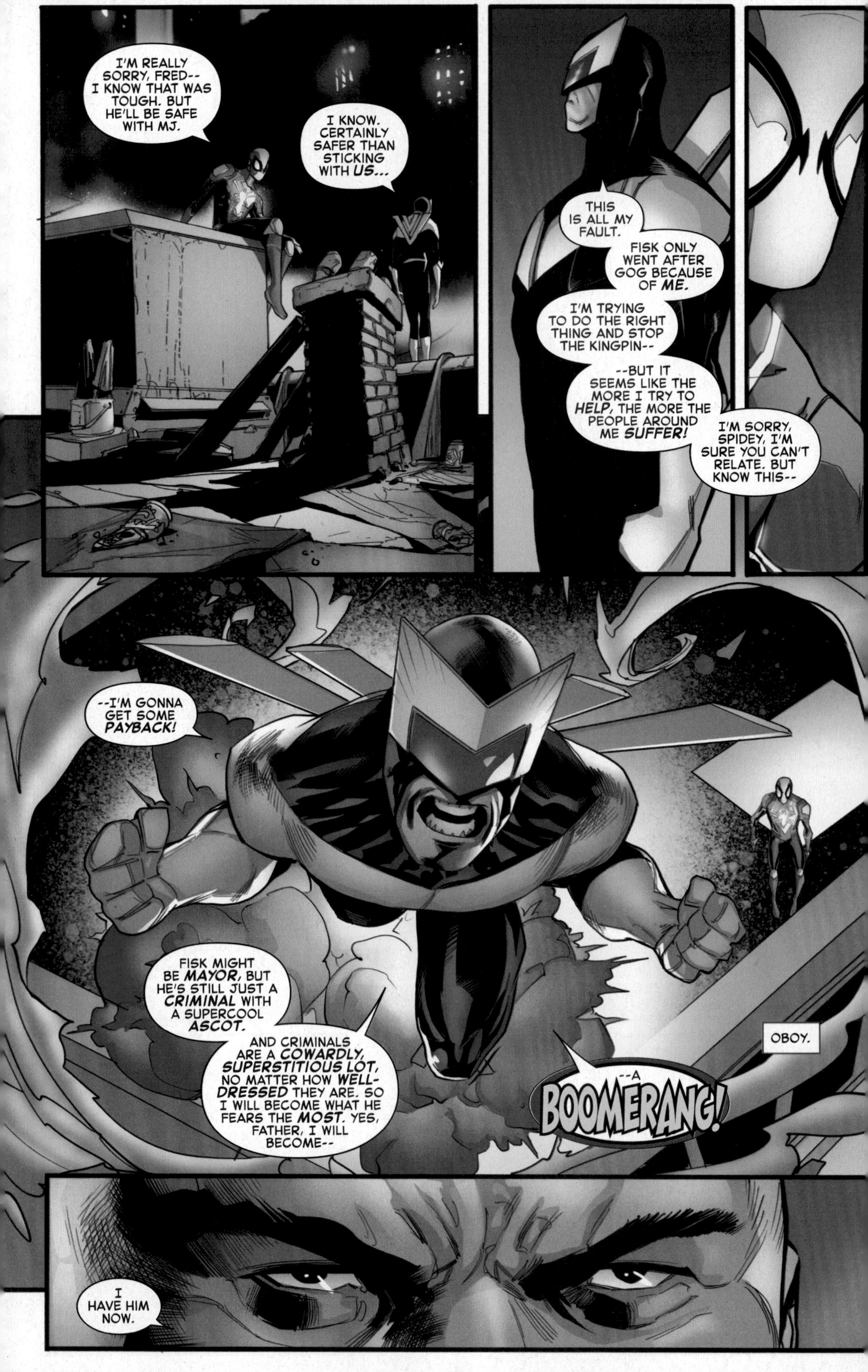

I'M REALLY SORRY, FRED-- I KNOW THAT WAS TOUGH. BUT HE'LL BE SAFE WITH MJ.
I KNOW. CERTAINLY SAFER THAN STICKING WITH US...
THIS IS ALL MY FAULT.
FISK ONLY WENT AFTER GOG BECAUSE OF ME.
I'M TRYING TO DO THE RIGHT THING AND STOP THE KINGPIN--
--BUT IT SEEMS LIKE THE MORE I TRY TO HELP, THE MORE THE PEOPLE AROUND ME SUFFER!
I'M SORRY, SPIDEY, I'M SURE YOU CAN'T RELATE. BUT KNOW THIS--
--I'M GONNA GET SOME PAYBACK!
FISK MIGHT BE MAYOR, BUT HE'S STILL JUST A CRIMINAL WITH A SUPERCOOL ASCOT.
AND CRIMINALS ARE A COWARDLY, SUPERSTITIOUS LOT, NO MATTER HOW WELL-DRESSED THEY ARE. SO I WILL BECOME WHAT HE FEARS THE MOST. YES, FATHER, I WILL BECOME--
--A BOOMERANG!
OBOY.
I HAVE HIM NOW.

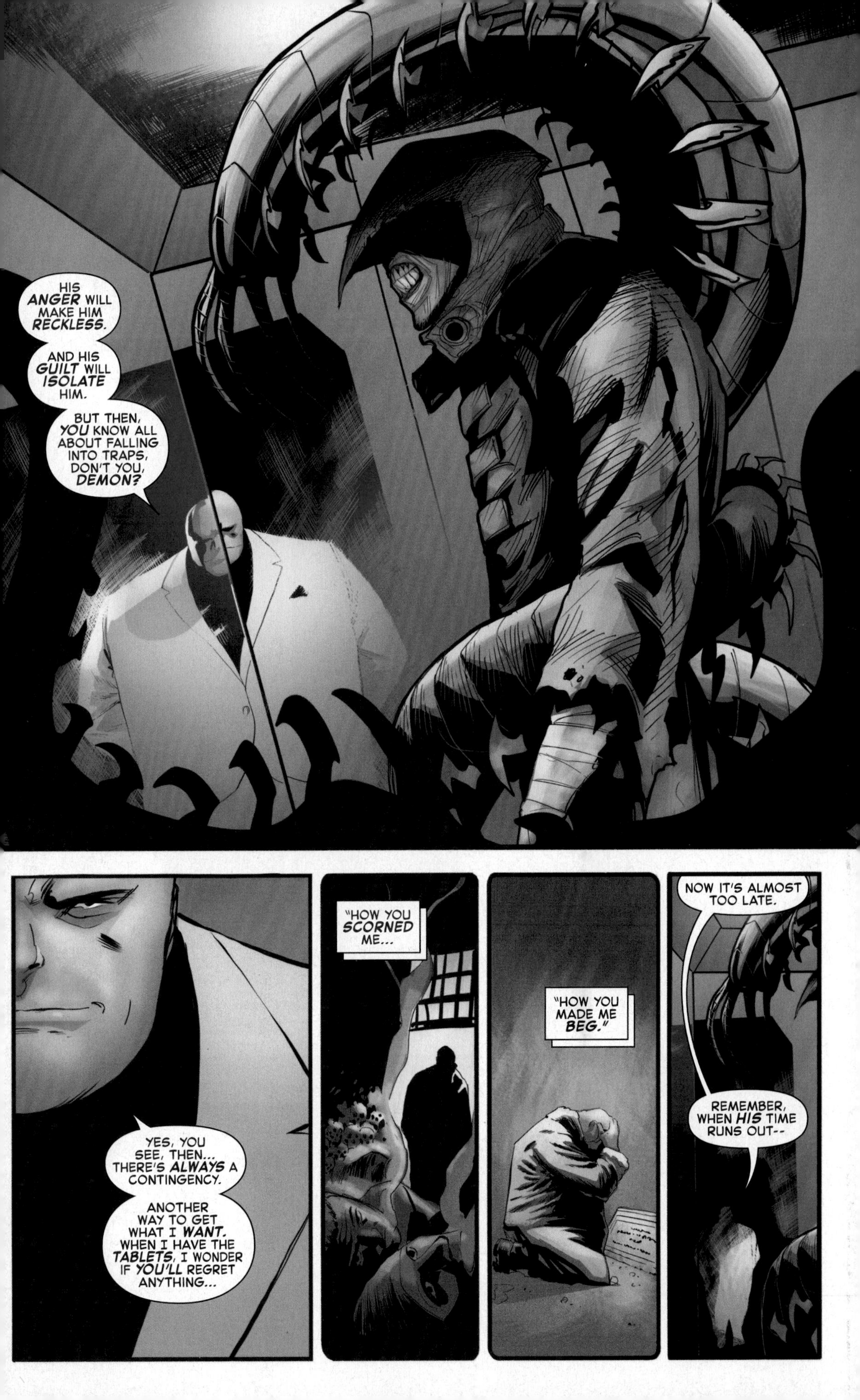
HIS ANGER WILL MAKE HIM RECKLESS.
AND HIS GUILT WILL ISOLATE HIM.
BUT THEN, YOU KNOW ALL ABOUT FALLING INTO TRAPS, DON'T YOU, DEMON?
YES, YOU SEE, THEN... THERE'S ALWAYS A CONTINGENCY.
ANOTHER WAY TO GET WHAT I WANT. WHEN I HAVE THE TABLETS, I WONDER IF YOU'LL REGRET ANYTHING...
"HOW YOU SCORNED ME...
"HOW YOU MADE ME BEG."
NOW IT'S ALMOST TOO LATE.
REMEMBER, WHEN HIS TIME RUNS OUT--

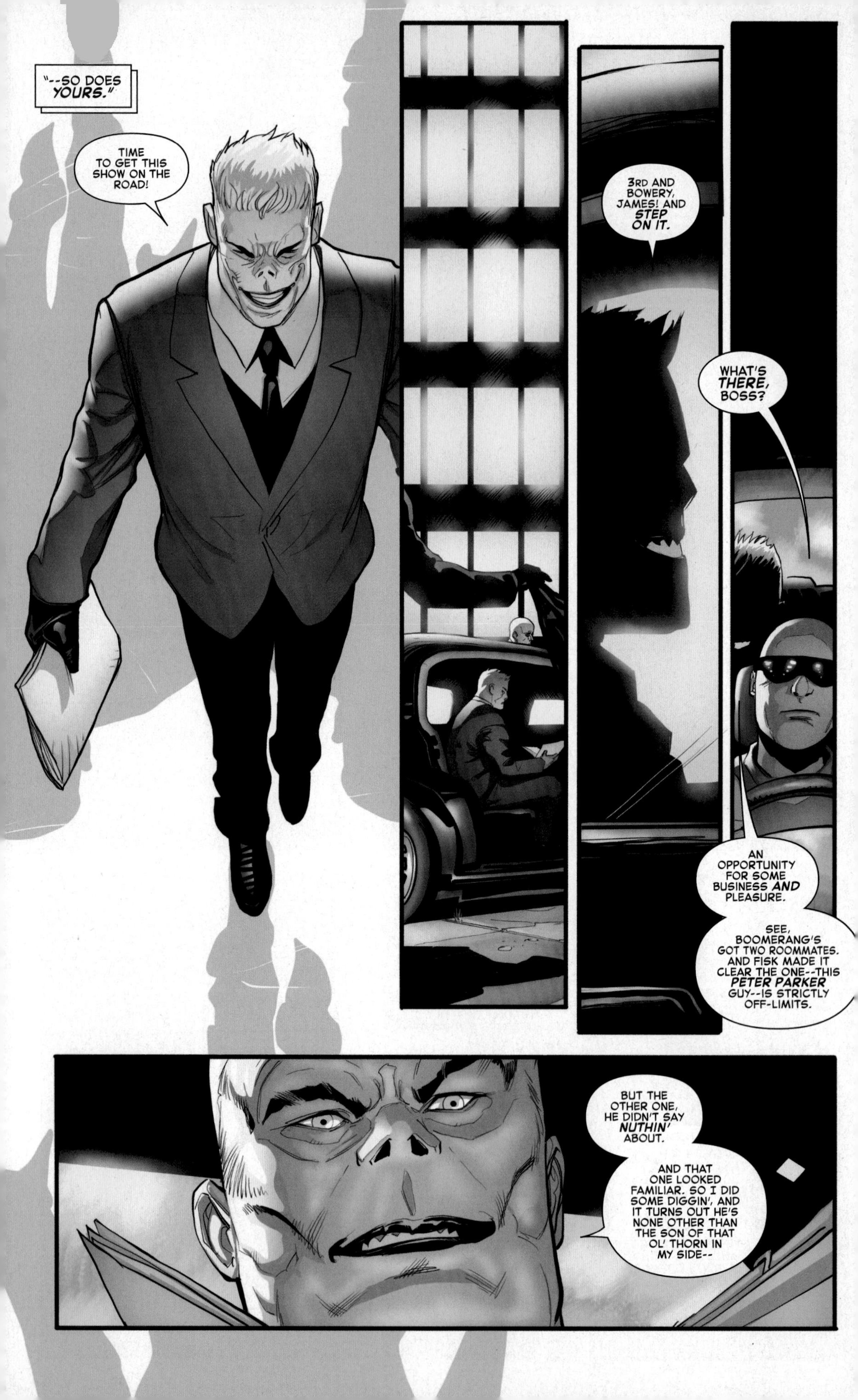
"--SO DOES YOURS."
TIME TO GET THIS SHOW ON THE ROAD!
3RD AND BOWERY, JAMES! AND STEP ON IT.
WHAT'S THERE, BOSS?
AN OPPORTUNITY FOR SOME BUSINESS AND PLEASURE.
SEE, BOOMERANG'S GOT TWO ROOMMATES. AND FISK MADE IT CLEAR THE ONE--THIS PETER PARKER GUY--IS STRICTLY OFF-LIMITS.
BUT THE OTHER ONE, HE DIDN'T SAY NUTHIN' ABOUT.
AND THAT ONE LOOKED FAMILIAR. SO I DID SOME DIGGIN', AND IT TURNS OUT HE'S NONE OTHER THAN THE SON OF THAT OL' THORN IN MY SIDE--

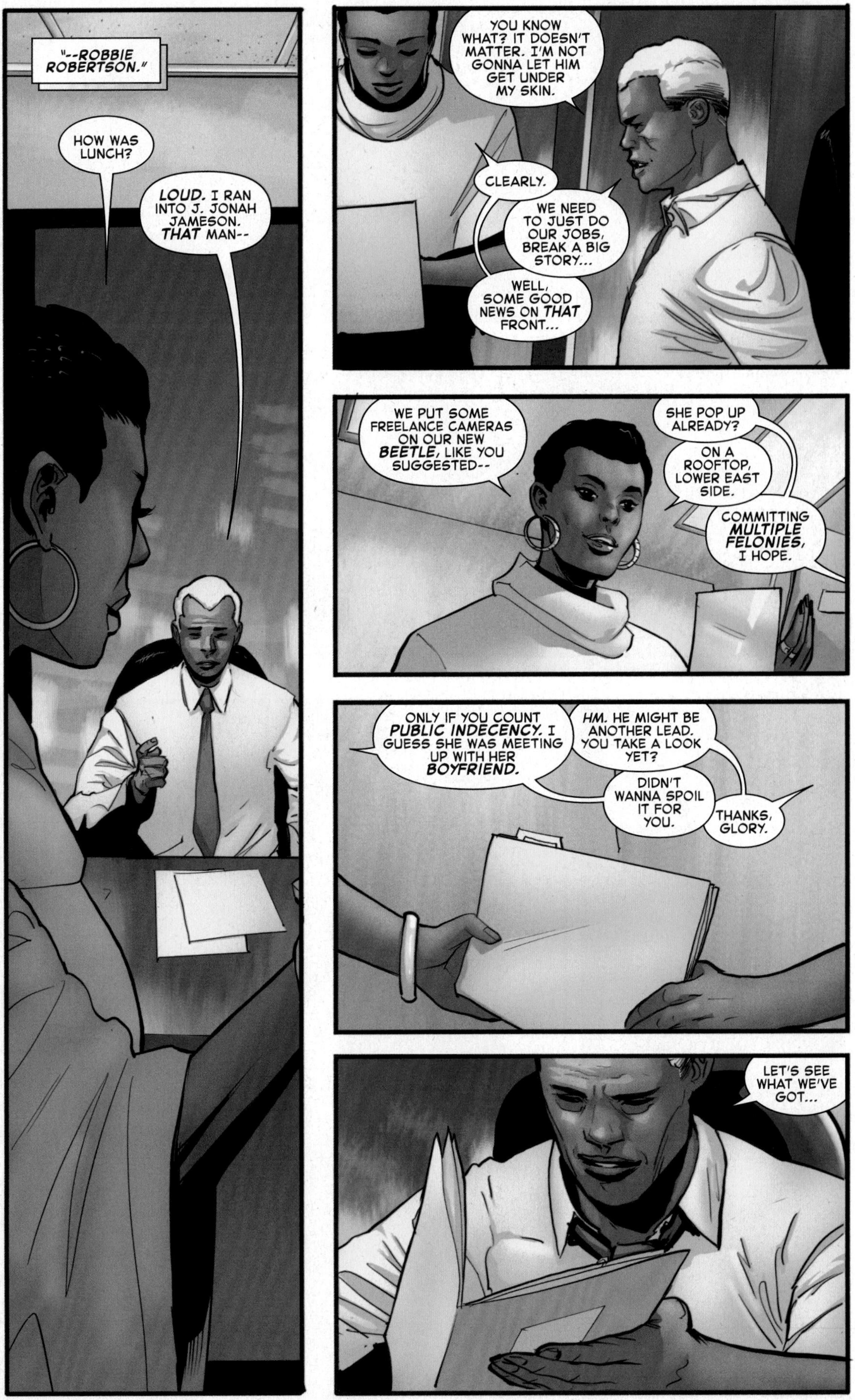
"--ROBBIE ROBERTSON."
HOW WAS LUNCH?
LOUD. I RAN INTO J. JONAH JAMESON. THAT MAN--
YOU KNOW WHAT? IT DOESN'T MATTER. I'M NOT GONNA LET HIM GET UNDER MY SKIN.
CLEARLY.
WE NEED TO JUST DO OUR JOBS, BREAK A BIG STORY...
WELL, SOME GOOD NEWS ON THAT FRONT...
WE PUT SOME FREELANCE CAMERAS ON OUR NEW BEETLE, LIKE YOU SUGGESTED--
SHE POP UP ALREADY?
ON A ROOFTOP, LOWER EAST SIDE.
COMMITTING MULTIPLE FELONIES, I HOPE.
ONLY IF YOU COUNT PUBLIC INDECENCY. I GUESS SHE WAS MEETING UP WITH HER BOYFRIEND.
HM. HE MIGHT BE ANOTHER LEAD. YOU TAKE A LOOK YET?
DIDN'T WANNA SPOIL IT FOR YOU.
THANKS, GLORY.
LET'S SEE WHAT WE'VE GOT...

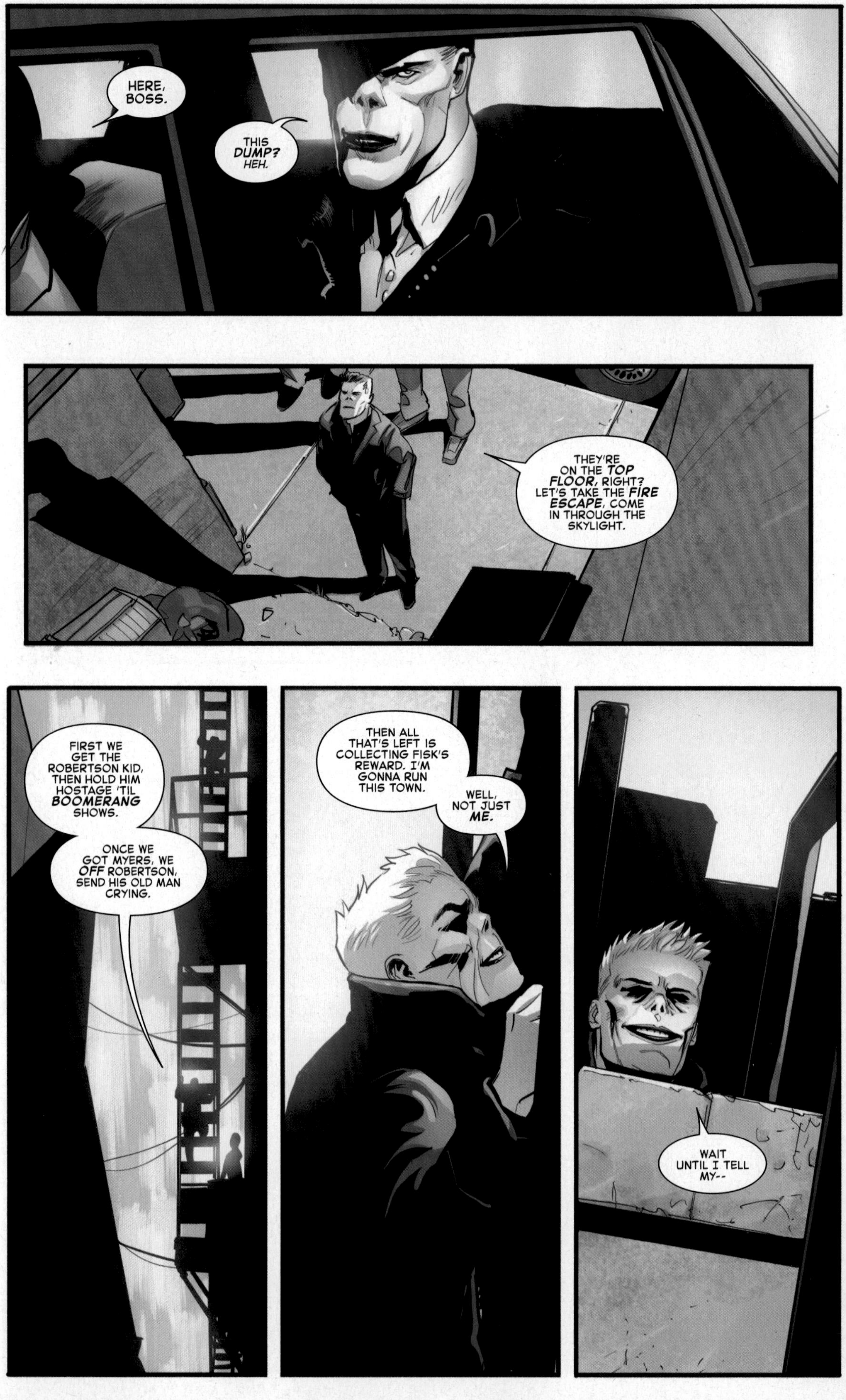
HERE, BOSS.
THIS DUMP? HEH.
THEY'RE ON THE TOP FLOOR, RIGHT? LET'S TAKE THE FIRE ESCAPE, COME IN THROUGH THE SKYLIGHT.
FIRST WE GET THE ROBERTSON KID, THEN HOLD HIM HOSTAGE 'TIL BOOMERANG SHOWS.
ONCE WE GOT MYERS, WE OFF ROBERTSON, SEND HIS OLD MAN CRYING.
THEN ALL THAT'S LEFT IS COLLECTING FISK'S REWARD. I'M GONNA RUN THIS TOWN.
WELL, NOT JUST ME.
WAIT UNTIL I TELL MY--

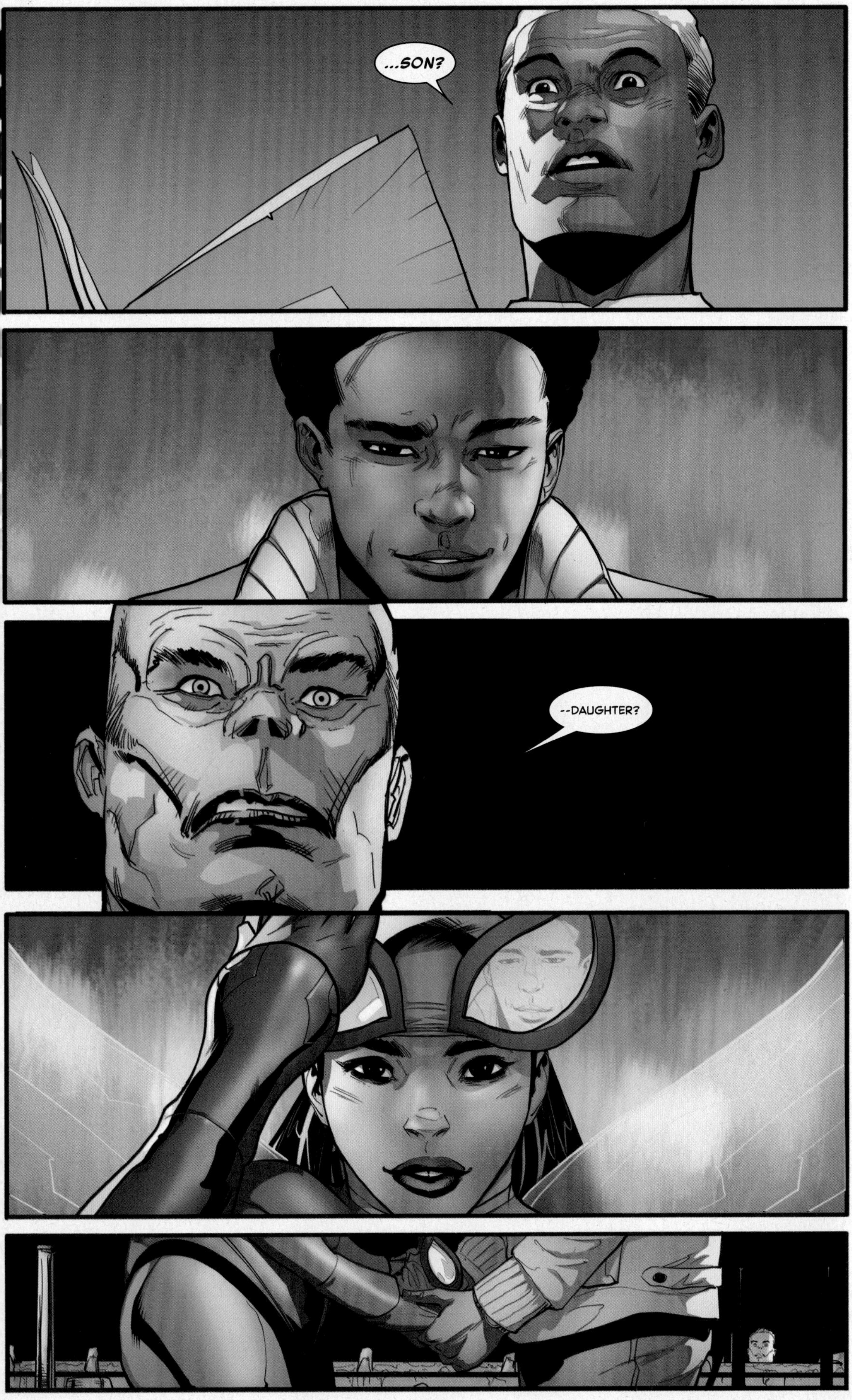
...SON?
--DAUGHTER?

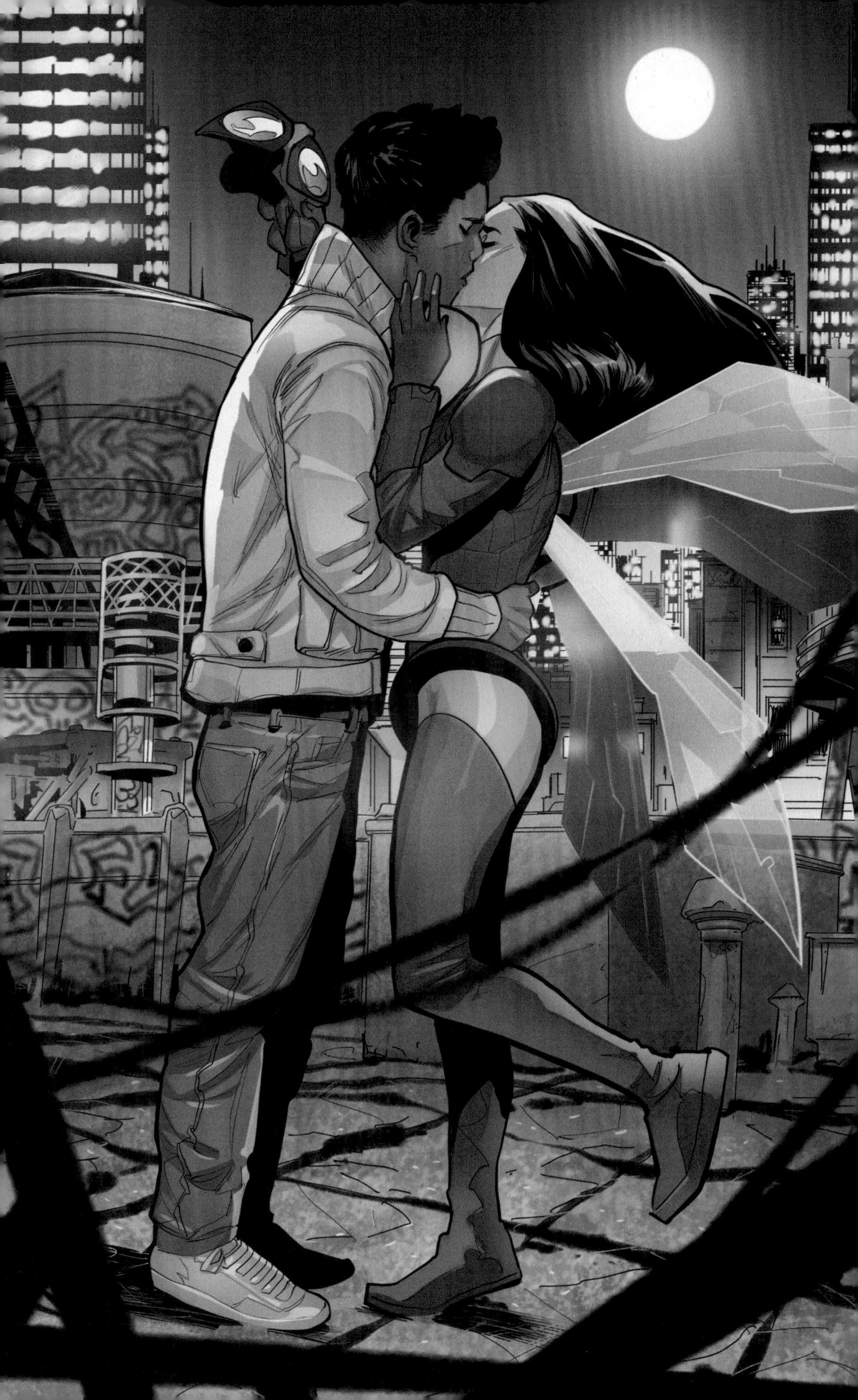

63

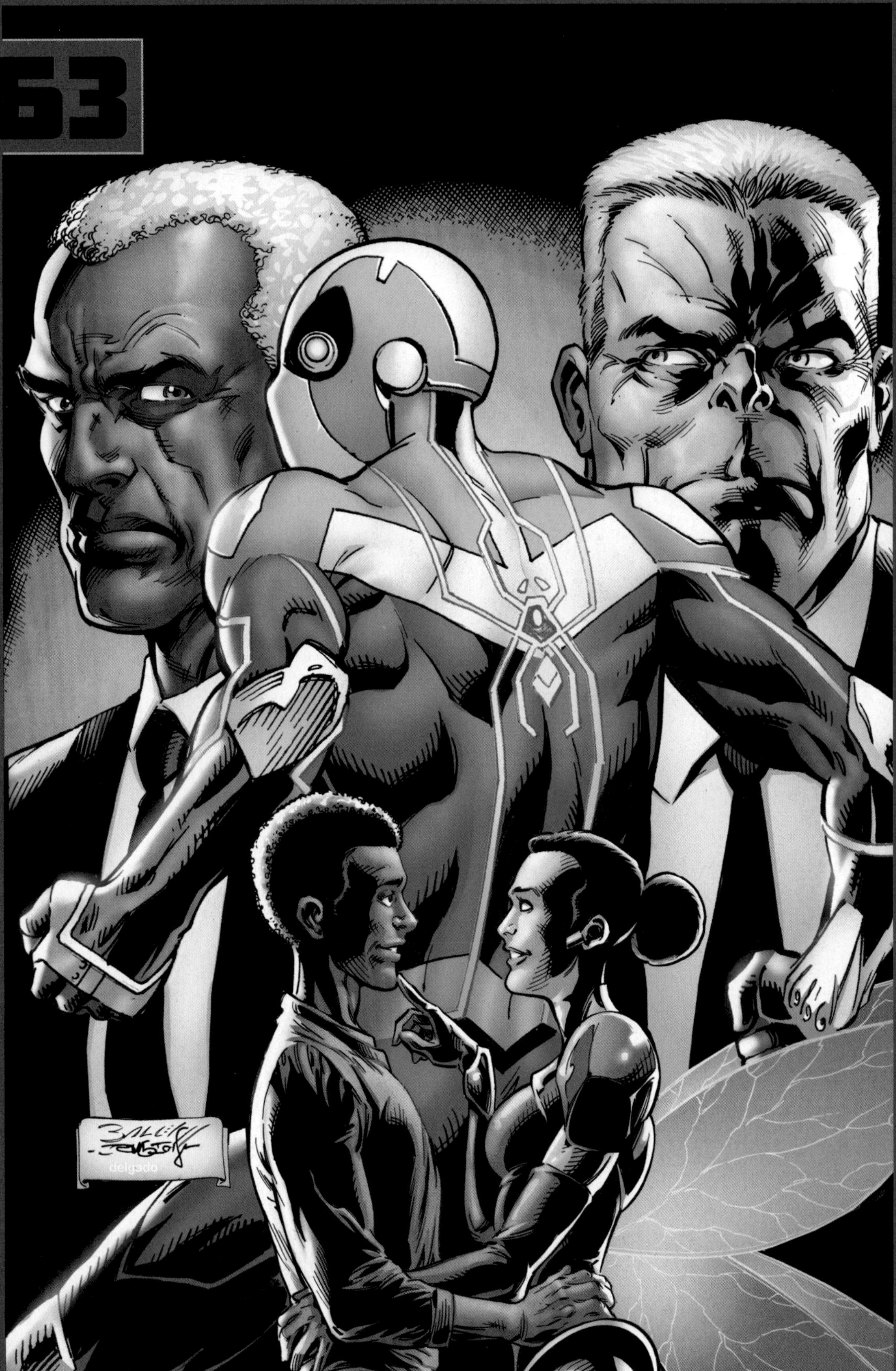

KING'S RANSOM PART 1

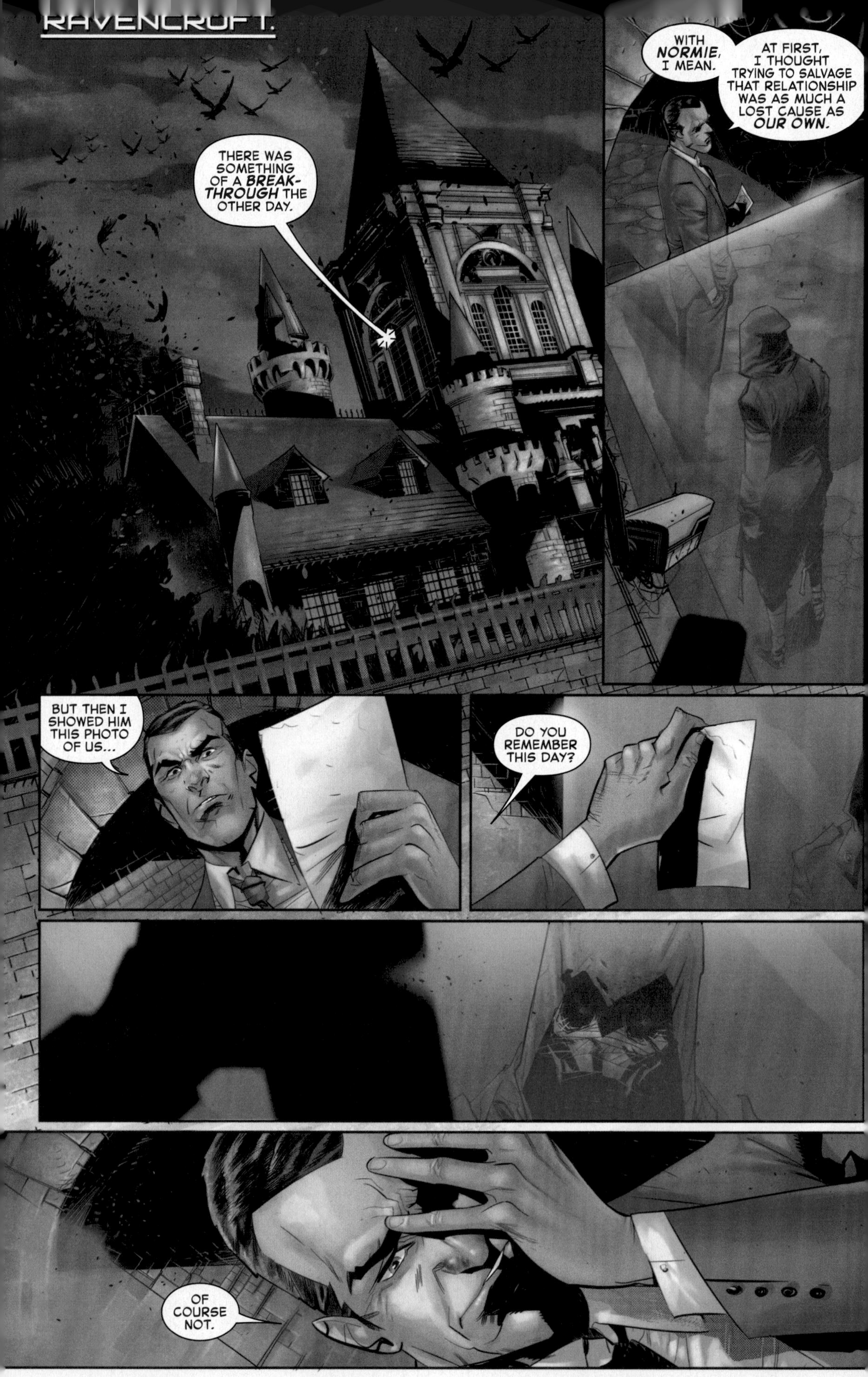
RAVENCROFT.
THERE WAS SOMETHING OF A BREAK-THROUGH THE OTHER DAY.
WITH NORMIE, I MEAN.
AT FIRST, I THOUGHT TRYING TO SALVAGE THAT RELATIONSHIP WAS AS MUCH A LOST CAUSE AS OUR OWN.
BUT THEN I SHOWED HIM THIS PHOTO OF US...
DO YOU REMEMBER THIS DAY?
OF COURSE NOT.

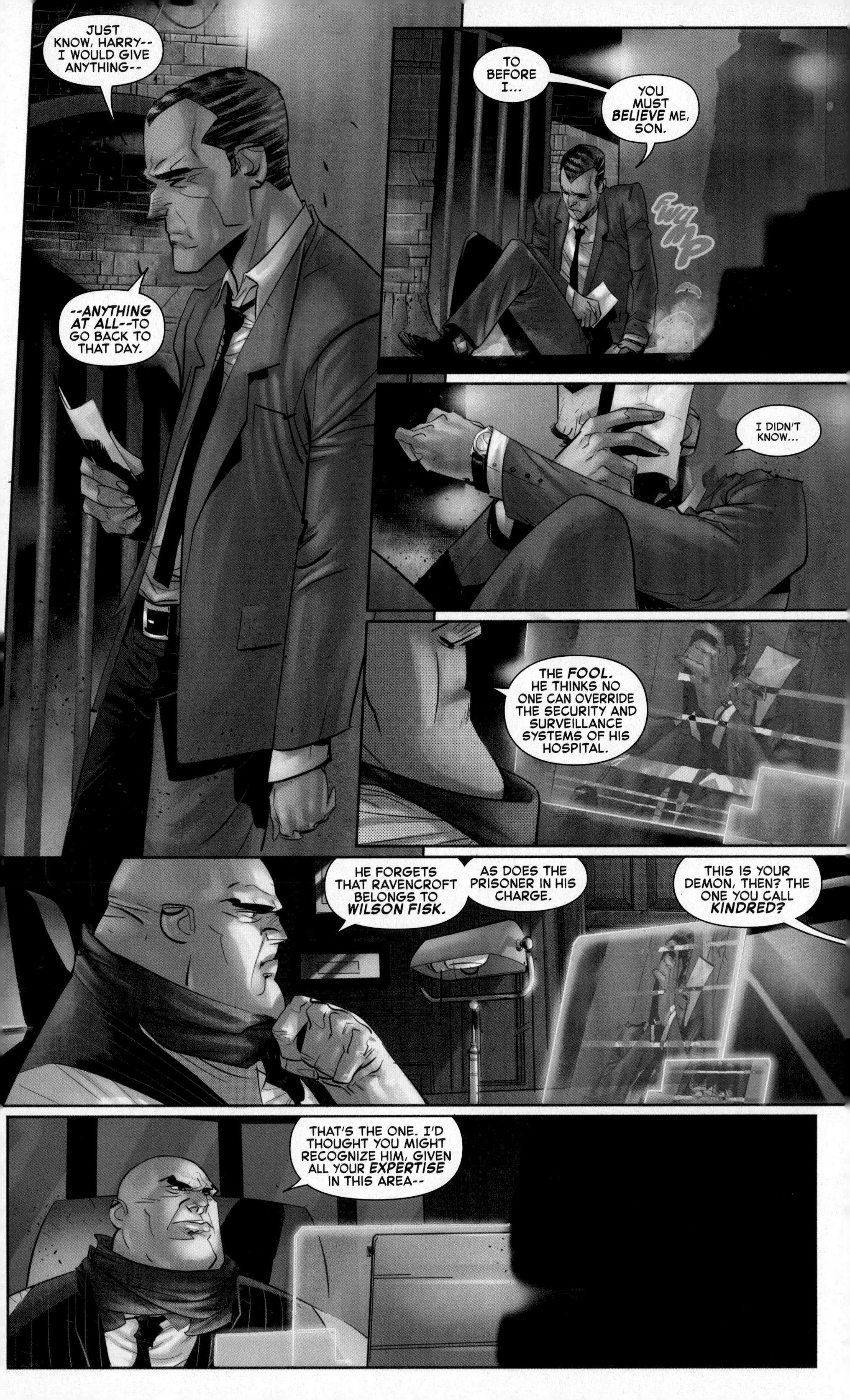
JUST KNOW, HARRY-- I WOULD GIVE ANYTHING--
--ANYTHING AT ALL--TO GO BACK TO THAT DAY.
TO BEFORE I...
YOU MUST BELIEVE ME, SON.
FWUMP
I DIDN'T KNOW...
THE FOOL. HE THINKS NO ONE CAN OVERRIDE THE SECURITY AND SURVEILLANCE SYSTEMS OF HIS HOSPITAL.
HE FORGETS THAT RAVENCROFT BELONGS TO WILSON FISK.
AS DOES THE PRISONER IN HIS CHARGE.
THIS IS YOUR DEMON, THEN? THE ONE YOU CALL KINDRED?
THAT'S THE ONE. I'D THOUGHT YOU MIGHT RECOGNIZE HIM, GIVEN ALL YOUR EXPERTISE IN THIS AREA--

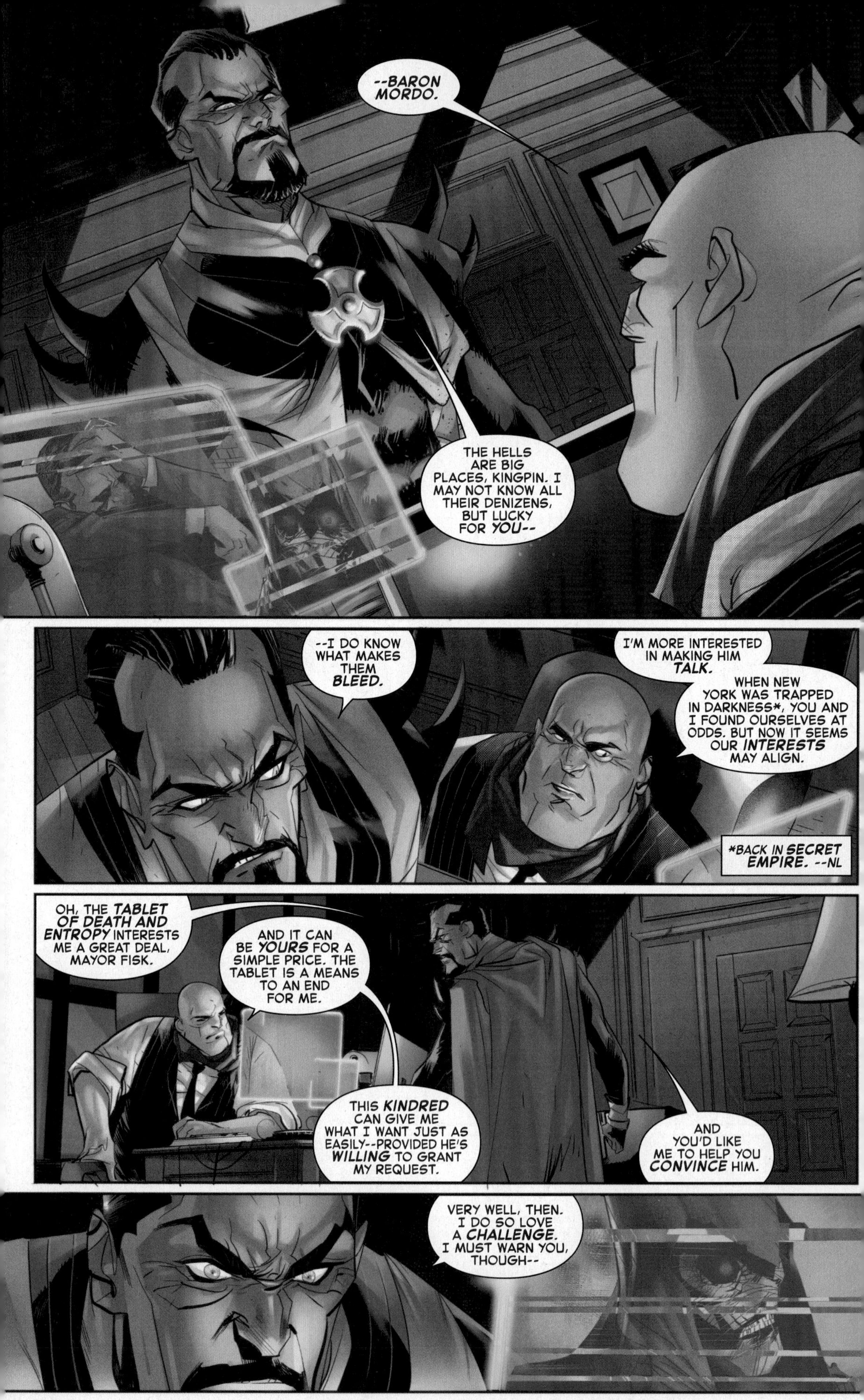
--BARON MORDO.
THE HELLS ARE BIG PLACES, KINGPIN. I MAY NOT KNOW ALL THEIR DENIZENS, BUT LUCKY FOR YOU--
--I DO KNOW WHAT MAKES THEM BLEED.
I'M MORE INTERESTED IN MAKING HIM TALK.
WHEN NEW YORK WAS TRAPPED IN DARKNESS*, YOU AND I FOUND OURSELVES AT ODDS. BUT NOW IT SEEMS OUR INTERESTS MAY ALIGN.
*BACK IN SECRET EMPIRE. --NL
OH, THE TABLET OF DEATH AND ENTROPY INTERESTS ME A GREAT DEAL, MAYOR FISK.
AND IT CAN BE YOURS FOR A SIMPLE PRICE. THE TABLET IS A MEANS TO AN END FOR ME.
THIS KINDRED CAN GIVE ME WHAT I WANT JUST AS EASILY--PROVIDED HE'S WILLING TO GRANT MY REQUEST.
AND YOU'D LIKE ME TO HELP YOU CONVINCE HIM.
VERY WELL, THEN. I DO SO LOVE A CHALLENGE. I MUST WARN YOU, THOUGH--

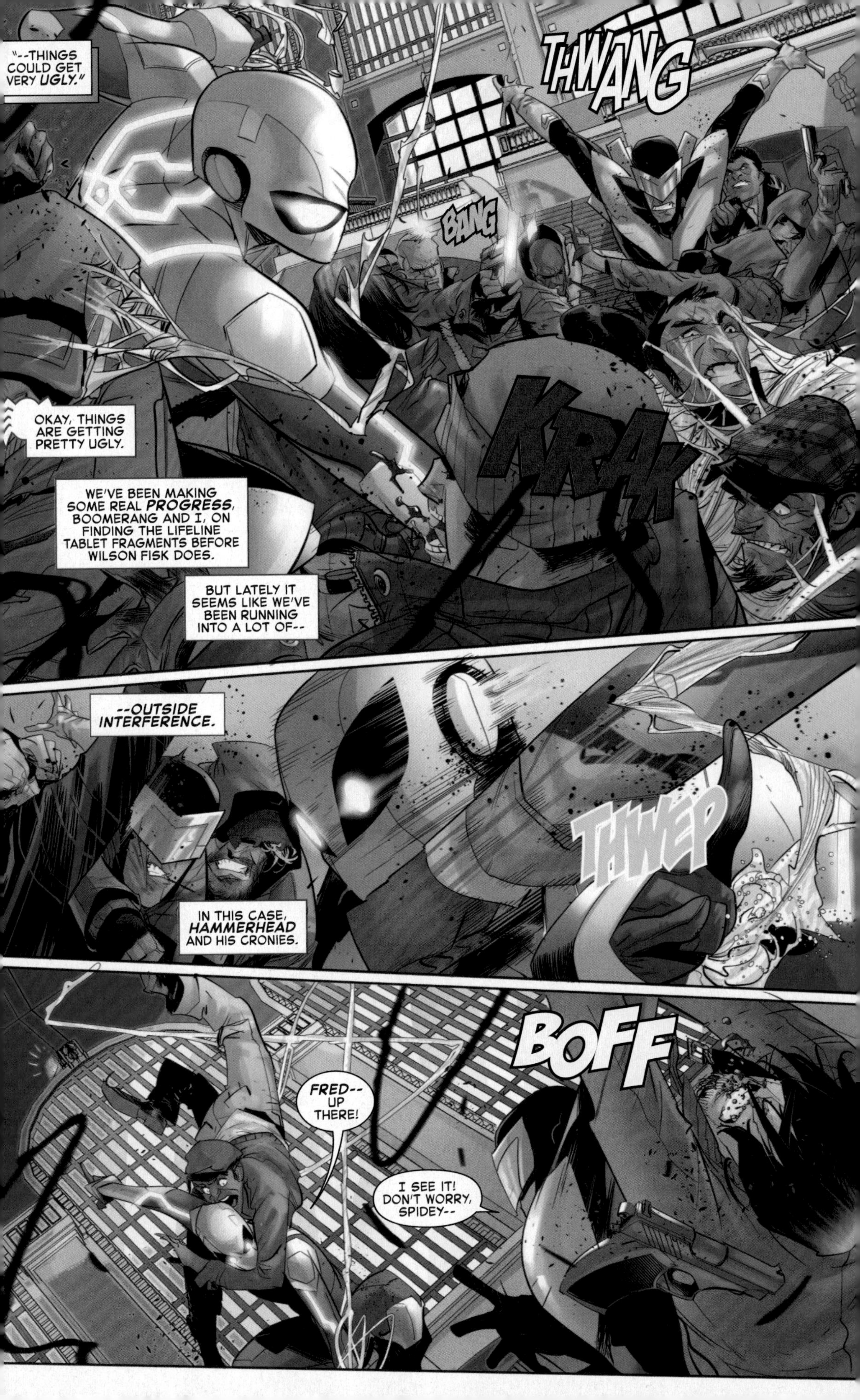
"--THINGS COULD GET VERY *UGLY*."
THWANG
BANG
OKAY, THINGS ARE GETTING PRETTY UGLY.
KRAK
WE'VE BEEN MAKING SOME REAL *PROGRESS*, BOOMERANG AND I, ON FINDING THE LIFELINE TABLET FRAGMENTS BEFORE WILSON FISK DOES.
BUT LATELY IT SEEMS LIKE WE'VE BEEN RUNNING INTO A LOT OF--
--OUTSIDE *INTERFERENCE*.
THWEP
IN THIS CASE, *HAMMERHEAD* AND HIS CRONIES.
BOFF
FRED-- UP THERE!
I SEE IT! DON'T WORRY, SPIDEY--

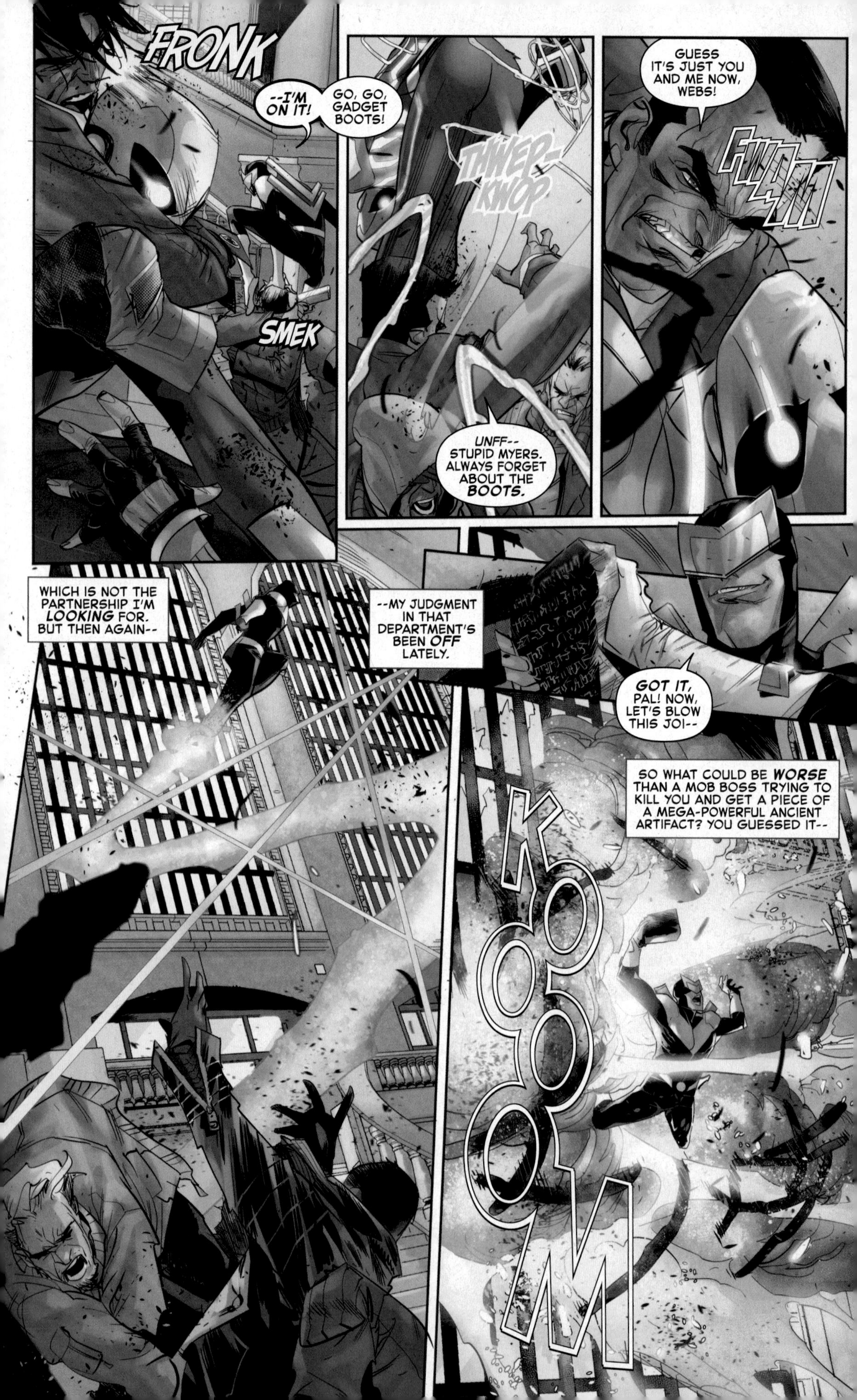
FRONK
--I'M ON IT!
GO, GO, GADGET BOOTS!
SMEK
THWEP-KWOP
UNFF-- STUPID MYERS. ALWAYS FORGET ABOUT THE BOOTS.
GUESS IT'S JUST YOU AND ME NOW, WEBS!
FWOOM
WHICH IS NOT THE PARTNERSHIP I'M LOOKING FOR. BUT THEN AGAIN--
--MY JUDGMENT IN THAT DEPARTMENT'S BEEN OFF LATELY.
GOT IT, PAL! NOW, LET'S BLOW THIS JOI--
SO WHAT COULD BE WORSE THAN A MOB BOSS TRYING TO KILL YOU AND GET A PIECE OF A MEGA-POWERFUL ANCIENT ARTIFACT? YOU GUESSED IT--
KOOOOOM

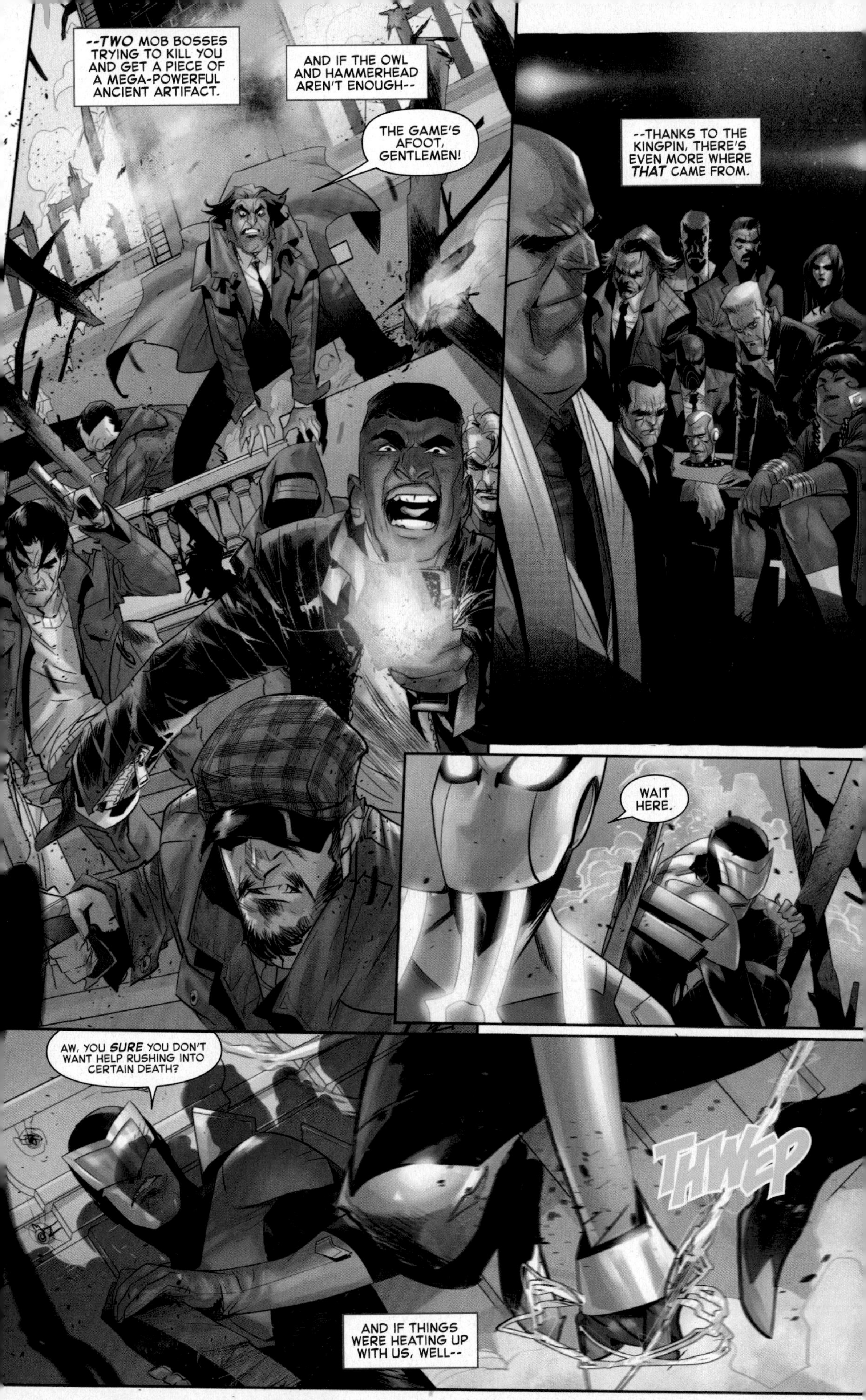
--TWO MOB BOSSES TRYING TO KILL YOU AND GET A PIECE OF A MEGA-POWERFUL ANCIENT ARTIFACT.
AND IF THE OWL AND HAMMERHEAD AREN'T ENOUGH--
THE GAME'S AFOOT, GENTLEMEN!
--THANKS TO THE KINGPIN, THERE'S EVEN MORE WHERE THAT CAME FROM.
WAIT HERE.
AW, YOU SURE YOU DON'T WANT HELP RUSHING INTO CERTAIN DEATH?
THWEP
AND IF THINGS WERE HEATING UP WITH US, WELL--

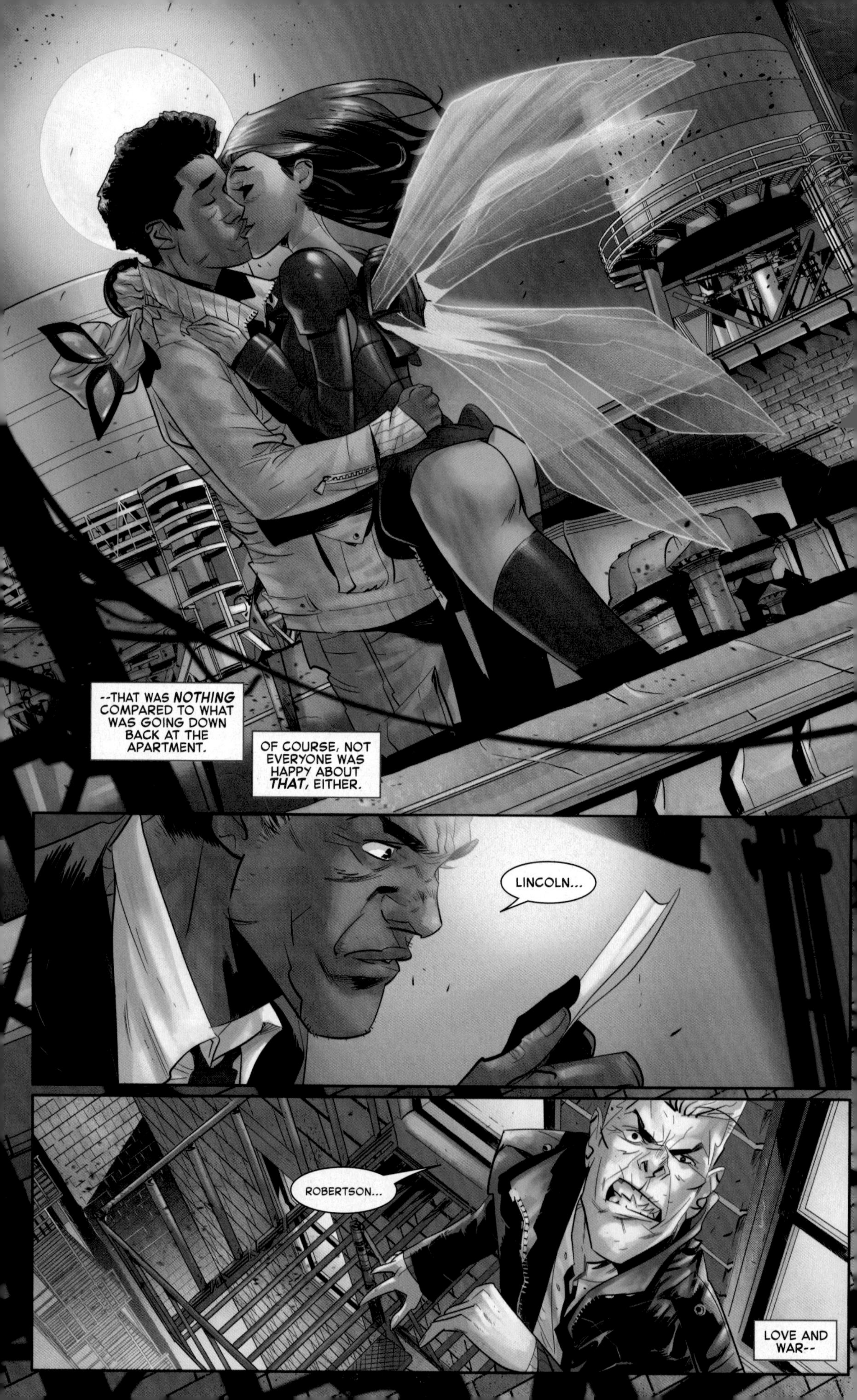
--THAT WAS *NOTHING* COMPARED TO WHAT WAS GOING DOWN BACK AT THE APARTMENT.
OF COURSE, NOT EVERYONE WAS HAPPY ABOUT *THAT,* EITHER.
LINCOLN...
ROBERTSON...
LOVE AND WAR--

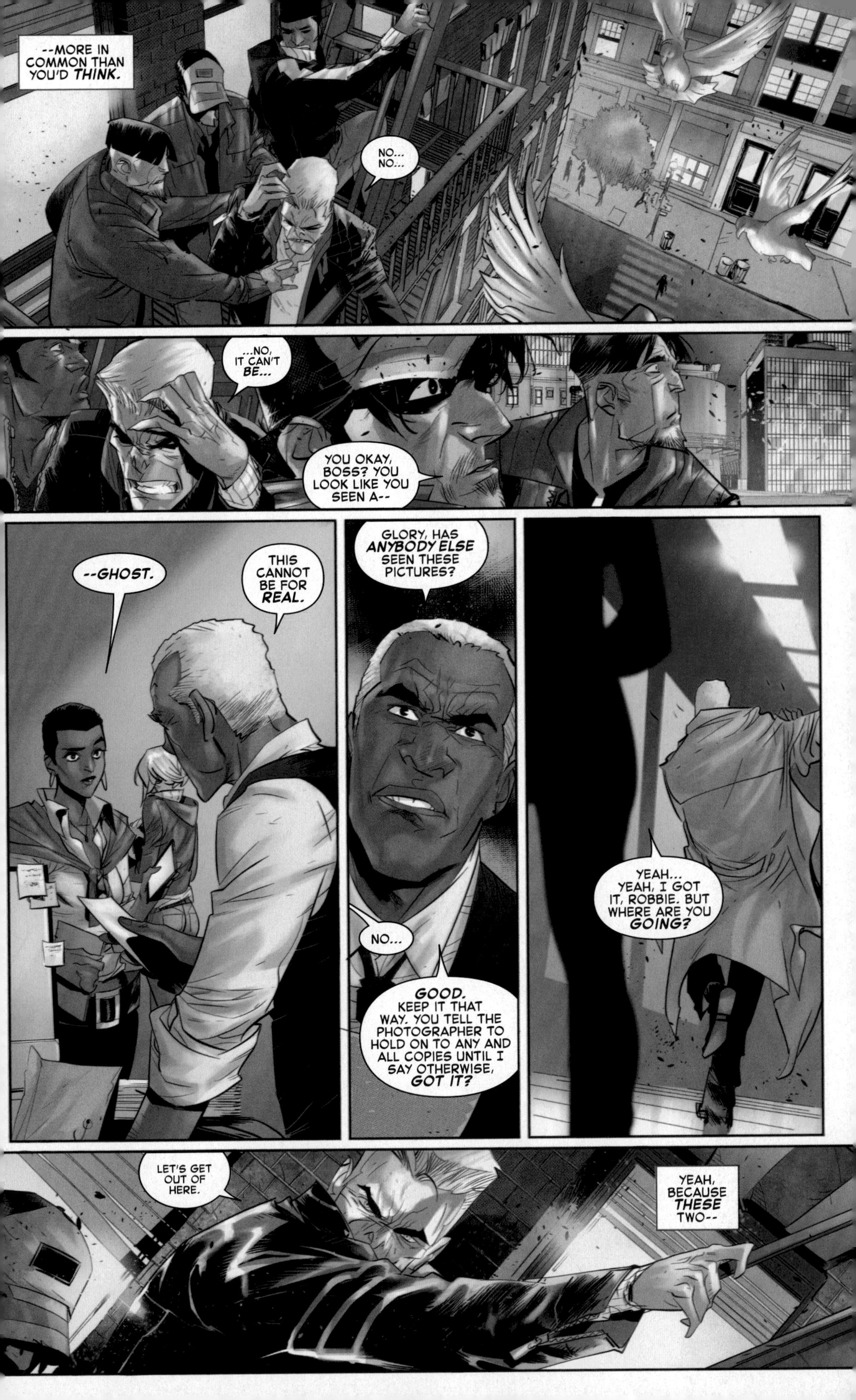
--MORE IN COMMON THAN YOU'D THINK.
NO... NO...
...NO, IT CAN'T BE...
YOU OKAY, BOSS? YOU LOOK LIKE YOU SEEN A--
--GHOST.
THIS CANNOT BE FOR REAL.
GLORY, HAS ANYBODY ELSE SEEN THESE PICTURES?
NO...
GOOD. KEEP IT THAT WAY. YOU TELL THE PHOTOGRAPHER TO HOLD ON TO ANY AND ALL COPIES UNTIL I SAY OTHERWISE, GOT IT?
YEAH... YEAH, I GOT IT, ROBBIE. BUT WHERE ARE YOU GOING?
LET'S GET OUT OF HERE.
YEAH, BECAUSE THESE TWO--

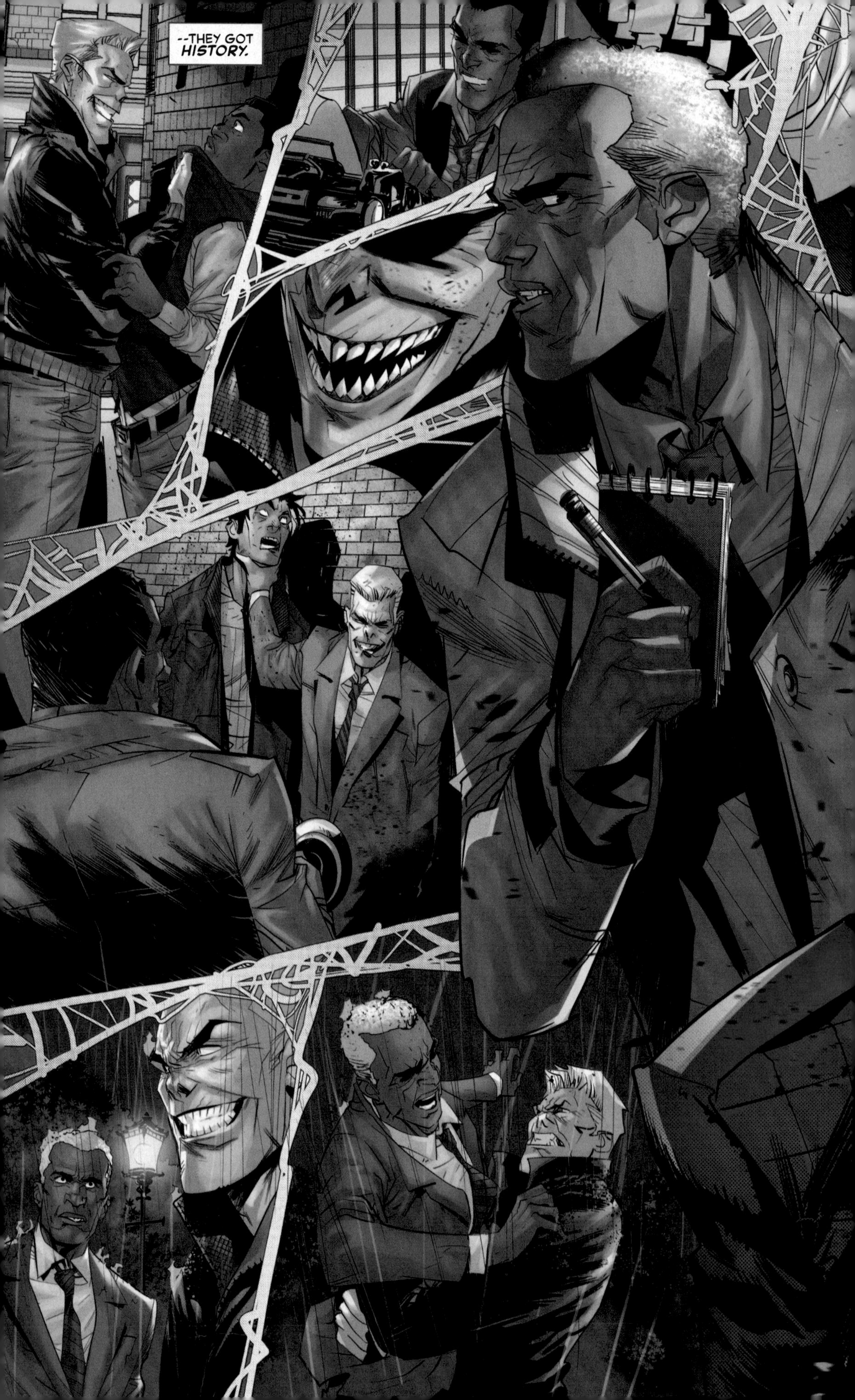
--THEY GOT
HISTORY.

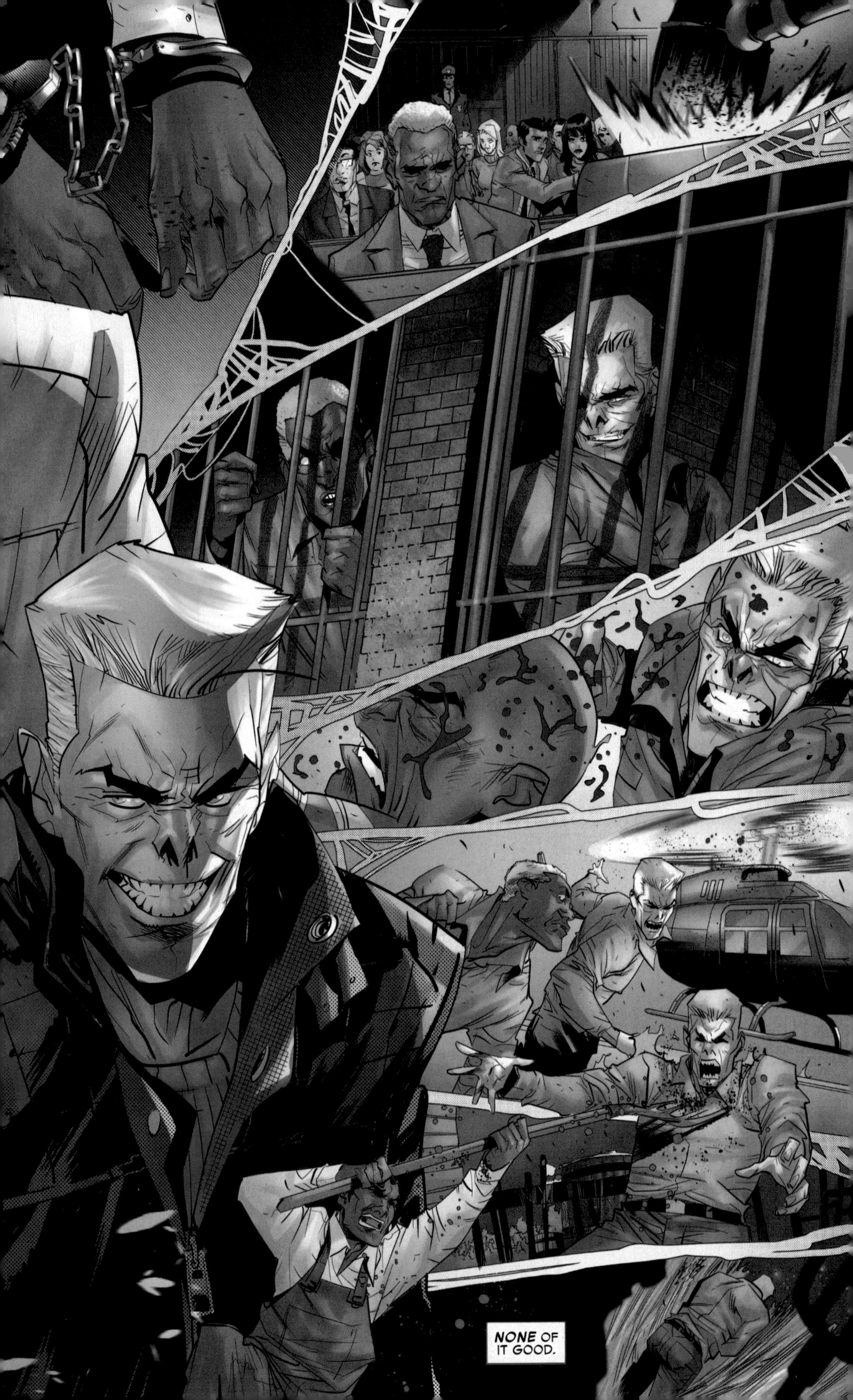
NONE OF IT GOOD.

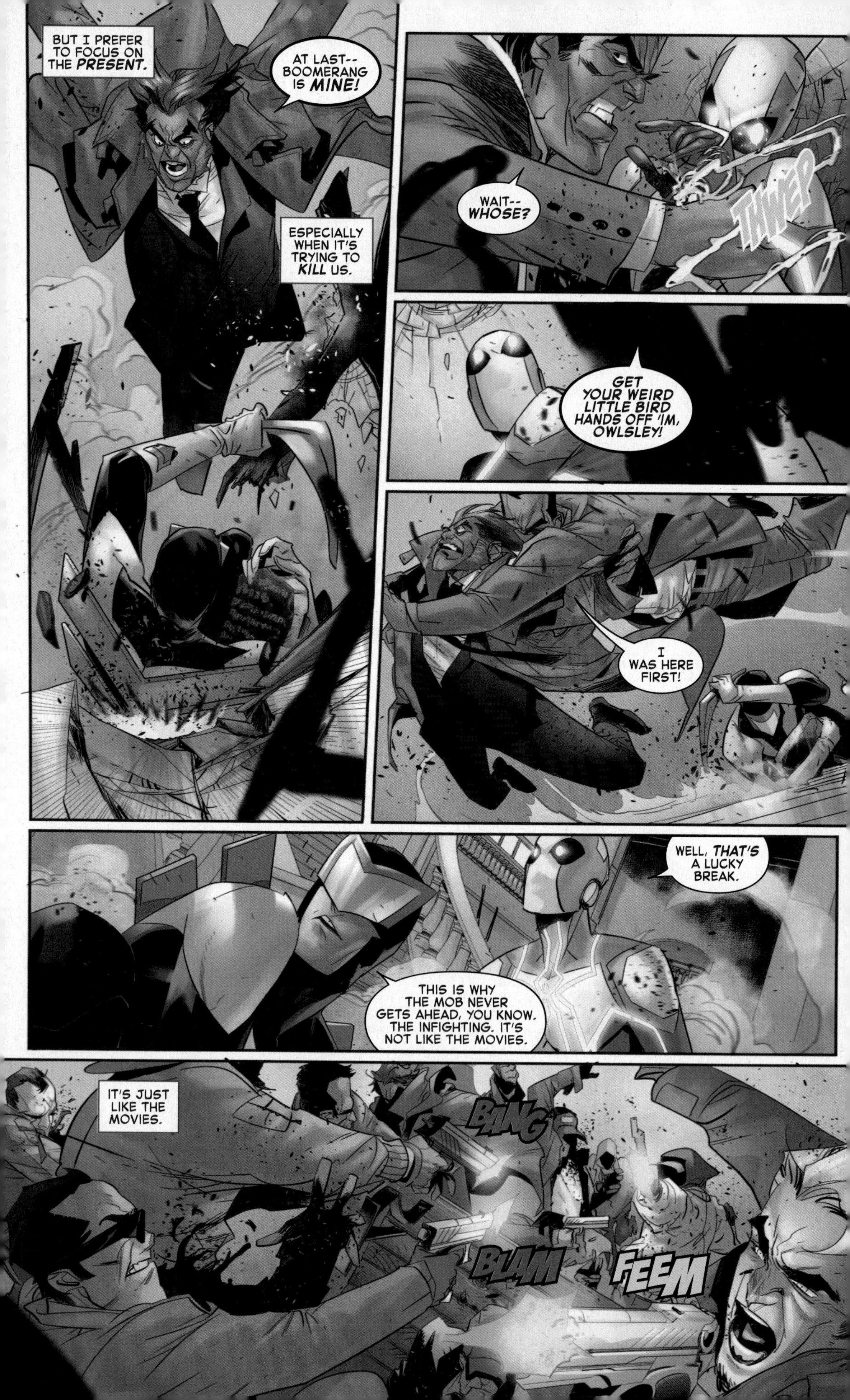

BUT I PREFER TO FOCUS ON THE PRESENT.
AT LAST-- BOOMERANG IS MINE!
ESPECIALLY WHEN IT'S TRYING TO KILL US.
WAIT-- WHOSE?
THWEP
GET YOUR WEIRD LITTLE BIRD HANDS OFF 'IM, OWLSLEY!
I WAS HERE FIRST!
WELL, THAT'S A LUCKY BREAK.
THIS IS WHY THE MOB NEVER GETS AHEAD, YOU KNOW. THE INFIGHTING. IT'S NOT LIKE THE MOVIES.
IT'S JUST LIKE THE MOVIES.
BANG
BLAM
FEEM

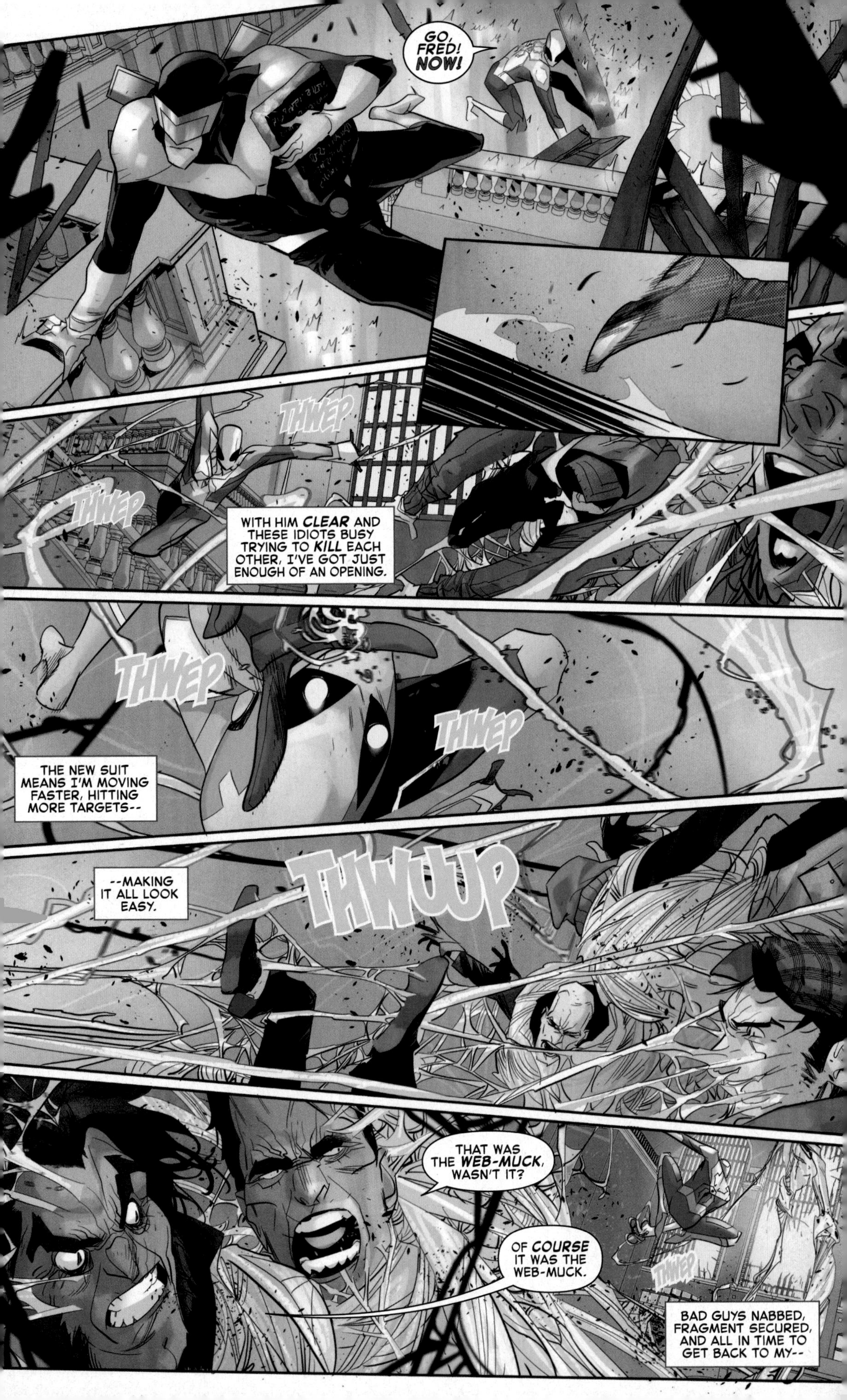
GO, FRED! NOW!
THWEP
THWEP
WITH HIM CLEAR AND THESE IDIOTS BUSY TRYING TO KILL EACH OTHER, I'VE GOT JUST ENOUGH OF AN OPENING.
THWEP
THWEP
THE NEW SUIT MEANS I'M MOVING FASTER, HITTING MORE TARGETS--
--MAKING IT ALL LOOK EASY.
THWUUP
THAT WAS THE WEB-MUCK, WASN'T IT?
OF COURSE IT WAS THE WEB-MUCK.
THWEP
BAD GUYS NABBED, FRAGMENT SECURED, AND ALL IN TIME TO GET BACK TO MY--

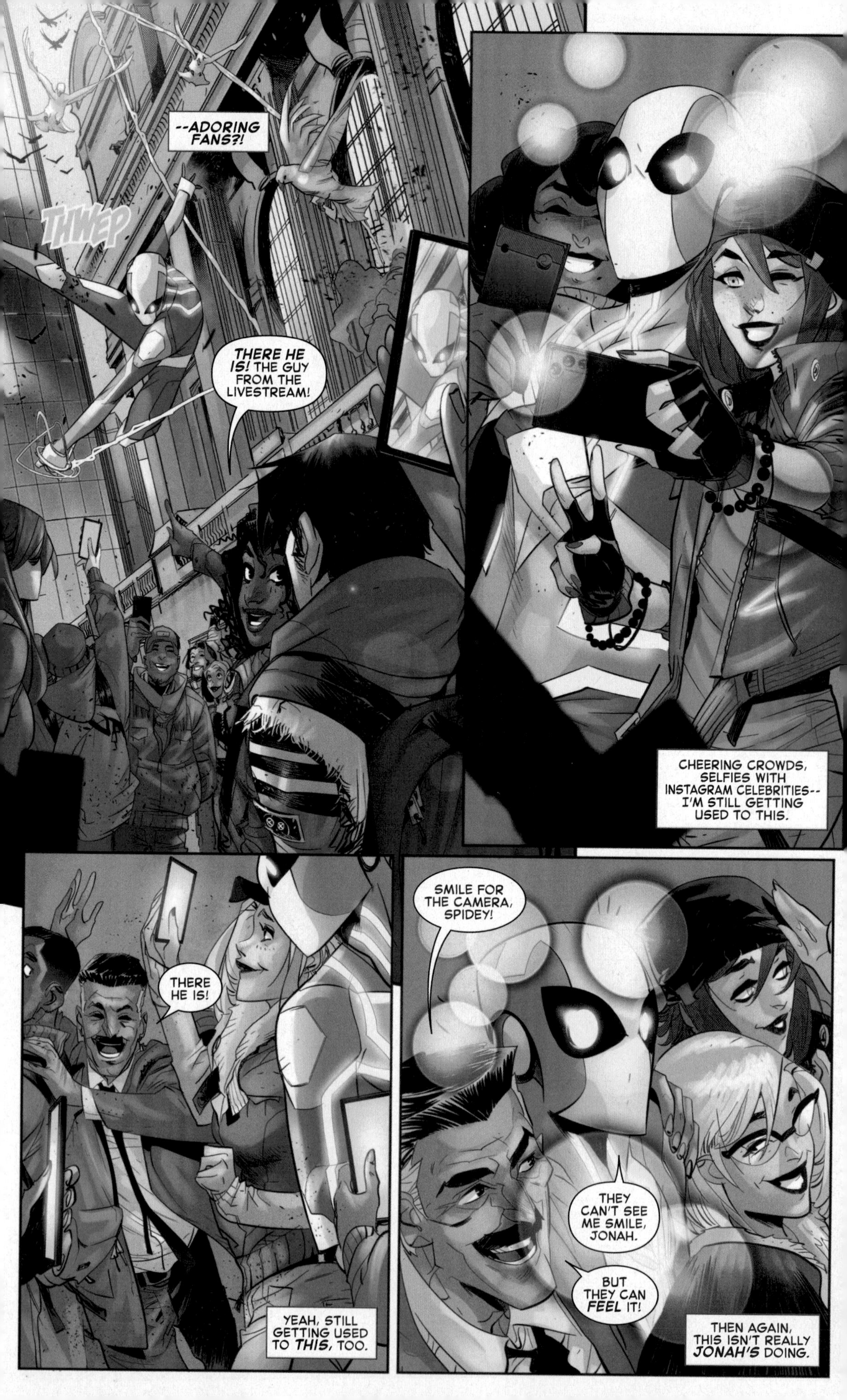
--ADORING FANS?!
THWEP
THERE HE IS! THE GUY FROM THE LIVESTREAM!
CHEERING CROWDS, SELFIES WITH INSTAGRAM CELEBRITIES-- I'M STILL GETTING USED TO THIS.
THERE HE IS!
YEAH, STILL GETTING USED TO THIS, TOO.
SMILE FOR THE CAMERA, SPIDEY!
THEY CAN'T SEE ME SMILE, JONAH.
BUT THEY CAN FEEL IT!
THEN AGAIN, THIS ISN'T REALLY JONAH'S DOING.

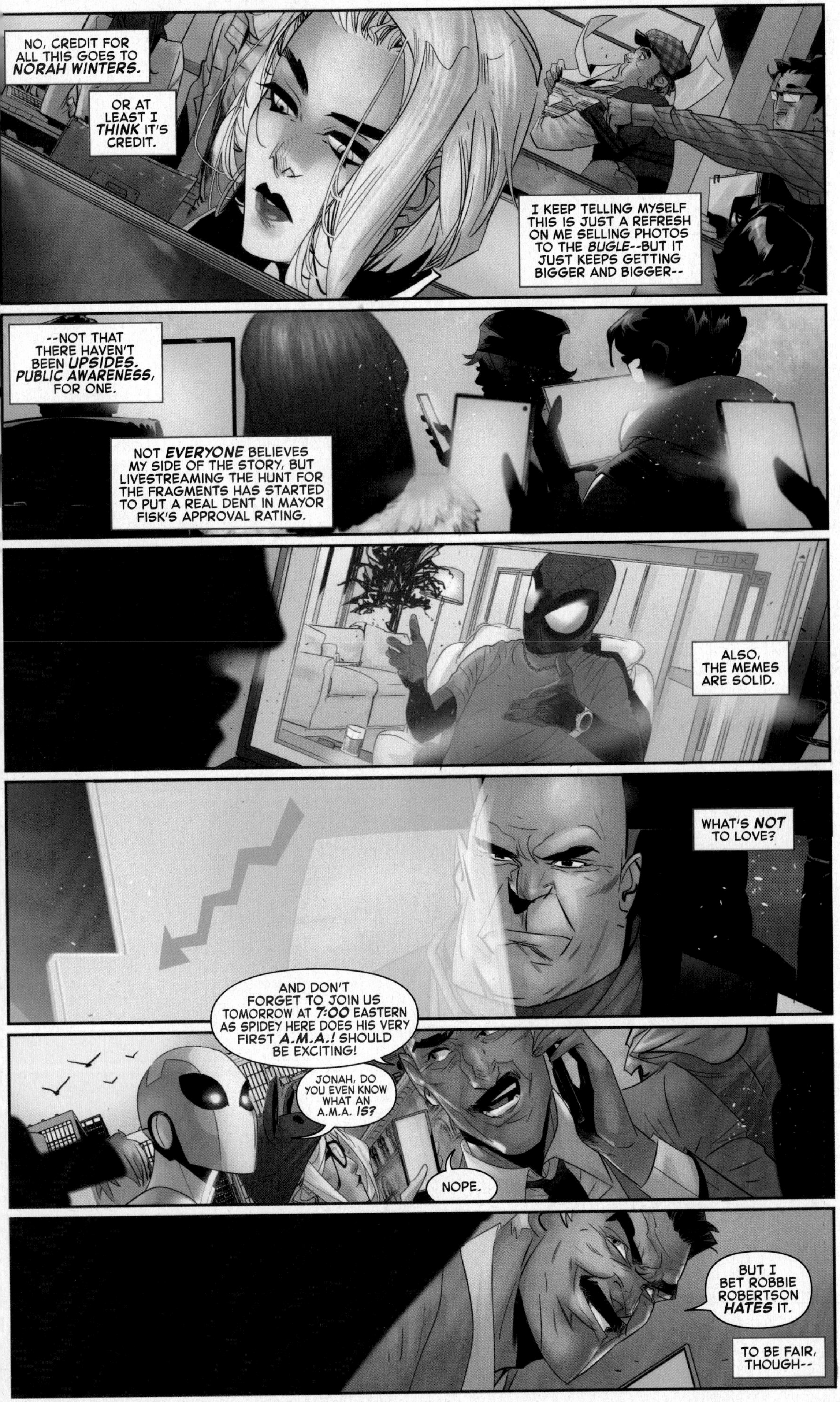
NO, CREDIT FOR ALL THIS GOES TO NORAH WINTERS.
OR AT LEAST I THINK IT'S CREDIT.
I KEEP TELLING MYSELF THIS IS JUST A REFRESH ON ME SELLING PHOTOS TO THE BUGLE--BUT IT JUST KEEPS GETTING BIGGER AND BIGGER--
--NOT THAT THERE HAVEN'T BEEN UPSIDES. PUBLIC AWARENESS, FOR ONE.
NOT EVERYONE BELIEVES MY SIDE OF THE STORY, BUT LIVESTREAMING THE HUNT FOR THE FRAGMENTS HAS STARTED TO PUT A REAL DENT IN MAYOR FISK'S APPROVAL RATING.
ALSO, THE MEMES ARE SOLID.
WHAT'S NOT TO LOVE?
AND DON'T FORGET TO JOIN US TOMORROW AT 7:00 EASTERN AS SPIDEY HERE DOES HIS VERY FIRST A.M.A.! SHOULD BE EXCITING!
JONAH, DO YOU EVEN KNOW WHAT AN A.M.A. IS?
NOPE.
BUT I BET ROBBIE ROBERTSON HATES IT.
TO BE FAIR, THOUGH--

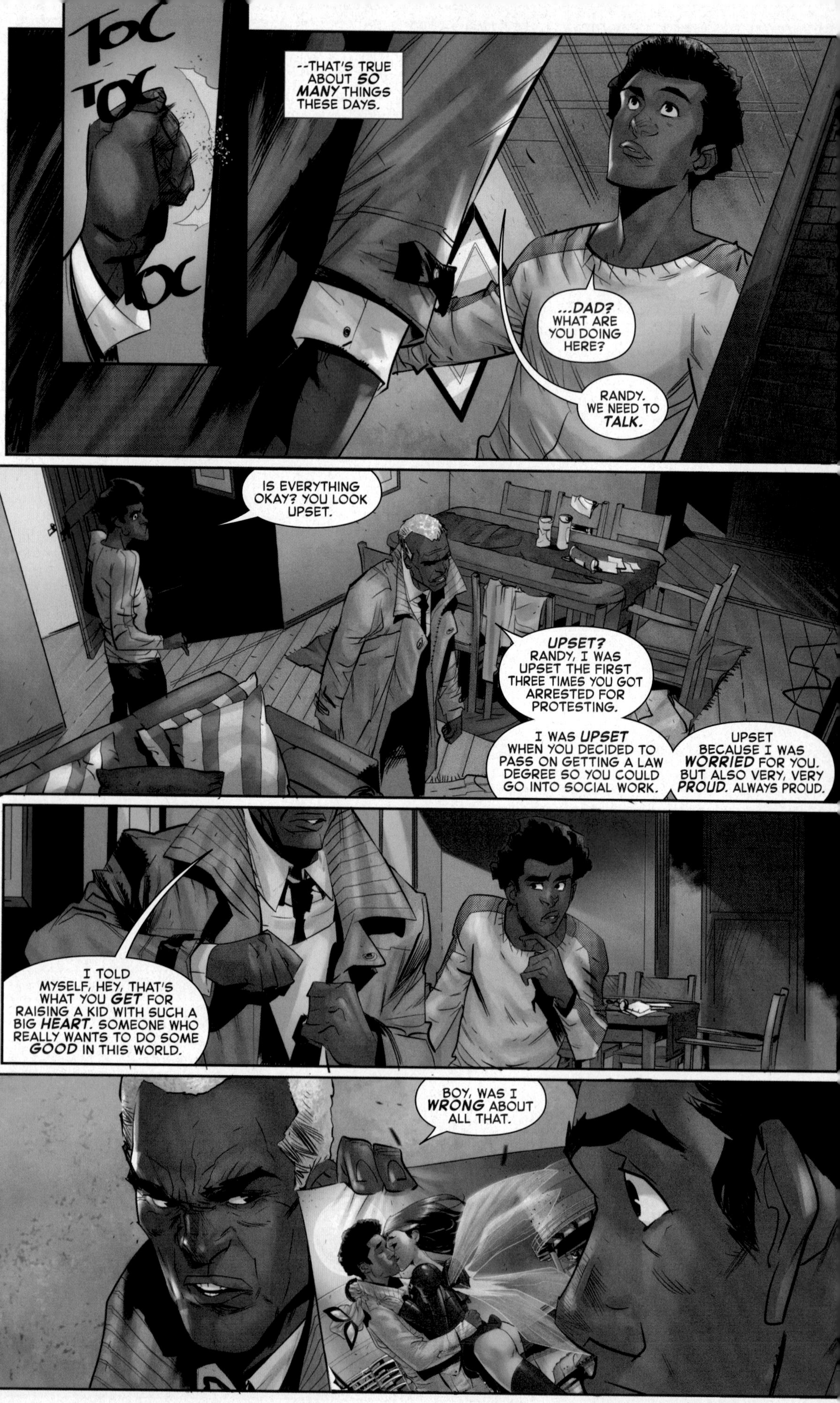
TOC
TOC
TOC
--THAT'S TRUE ABOUT SO MANY THINGS THESE DAYS.
...DAD? WHAT ARE YOU DOING HERE?
RANDY. WE NEED TO TALK.
IS EVERYTHING OKAY? YOU LOOK UPSET.
UPSET? RANDY, I WAS UPSET THE FIRST THREE TIMES YOU GOT ARRESTED FOR PROTESTING.
I WAS UPSET WHEN YOU DECIDED TO PASS ON GETTING A LAW DEGREE SO YOU COULD GO INTO SOCIAL WORK.
UPSET BECAUSE I WAS WORRIED FOR YOU. BUT ALSO VERY, VERY PROUD. ALWAYS PROUD.
I TOLD MYSELF, HEY, THAT'S WHAT YOU GET FOR RAISING A KID WITH SUCH A BIG HEART. SOMEONE WHO REALLY WANTS TO DO SOME GOOD IN THIS WORLD.
BOY, WAS I WRONG ABOUT ALL THAT.

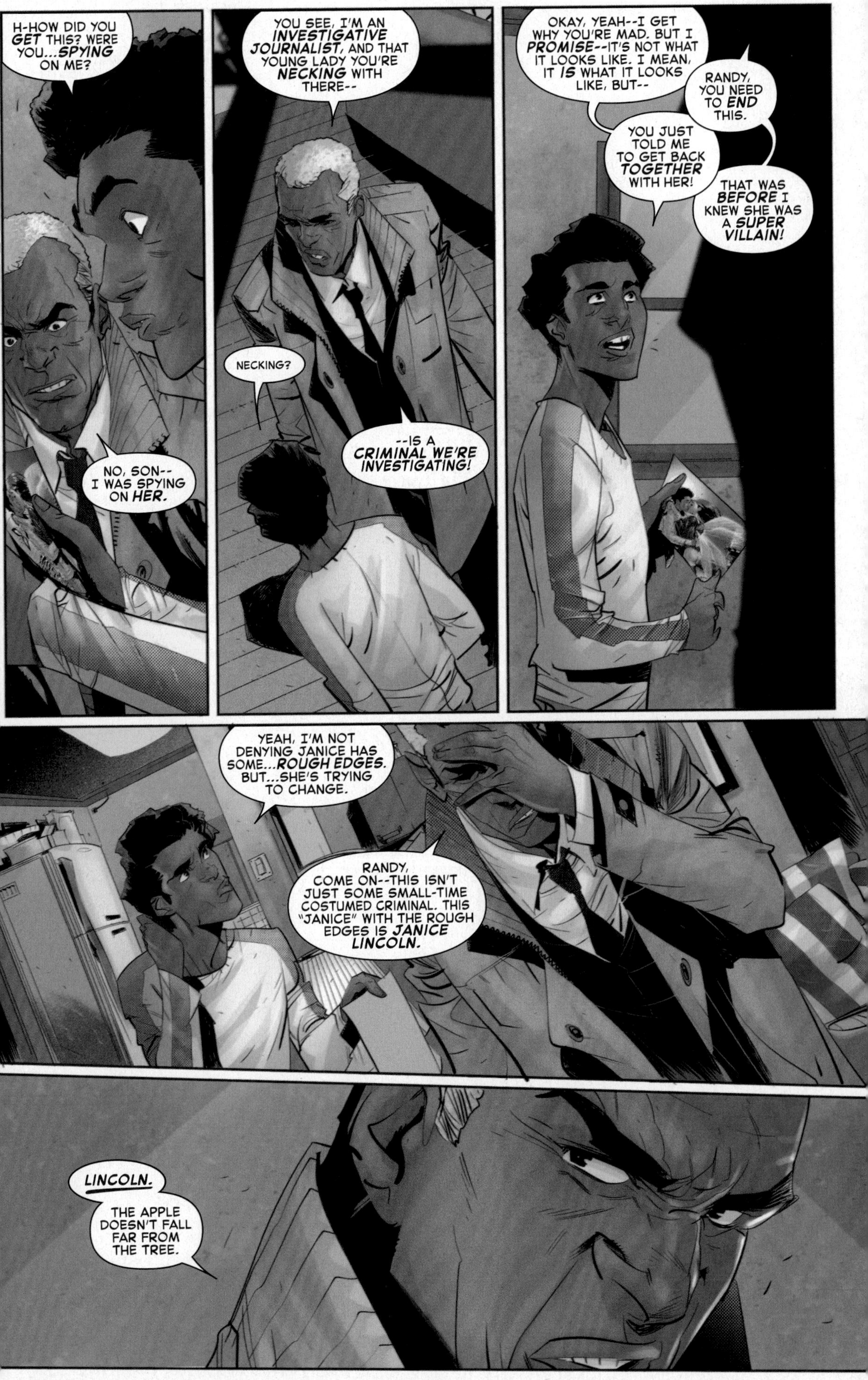
H-HOW DID YOU GET THIS? WERE YOU...SPYING ON ME?
NO, SON--
I WAS SPYING ON HER.
YOU SEE, I'M AN INVESTIGATIVE JOURNALIST, AND THAT YOUNG LADY YOU'RE NECKING WITH THERE--
NECKING?
--IS A CRIMINAL WE'RE INVESTIGATING!
OKAY, YEAH--I GET WHY YOU'RE MAD. BUT I PROMISE--IT'S NOT WHAT IT LOOKS LIKE. I MEAN, IT IS WHAT IT LOOKS LIKE, BUT--
RANDY, YOU NEED TO END THIS.
YOU JUST TOLD ME TO GET BACK TOGETHER WITH HER!
THAT WAS BEFORE I KNEW SHE WAS A SUPER VILLAIN!
YEAH, I'M NOT DENYING JANICE HAS SOME...ROUGH EDGES. BUT...SHE'S TRYING TO CHANGE.
RANDY, COME ON--THIS ISN'T JUST SOME SMALL-TIME COSTUMED CRIMINAL. THIS "JANICE" WITH THE ROUGH EDGES IS JANICE LINCOLN.
LINCOLN.
THE APPLE DOESN'T FALL FAR FROM THE TREE.

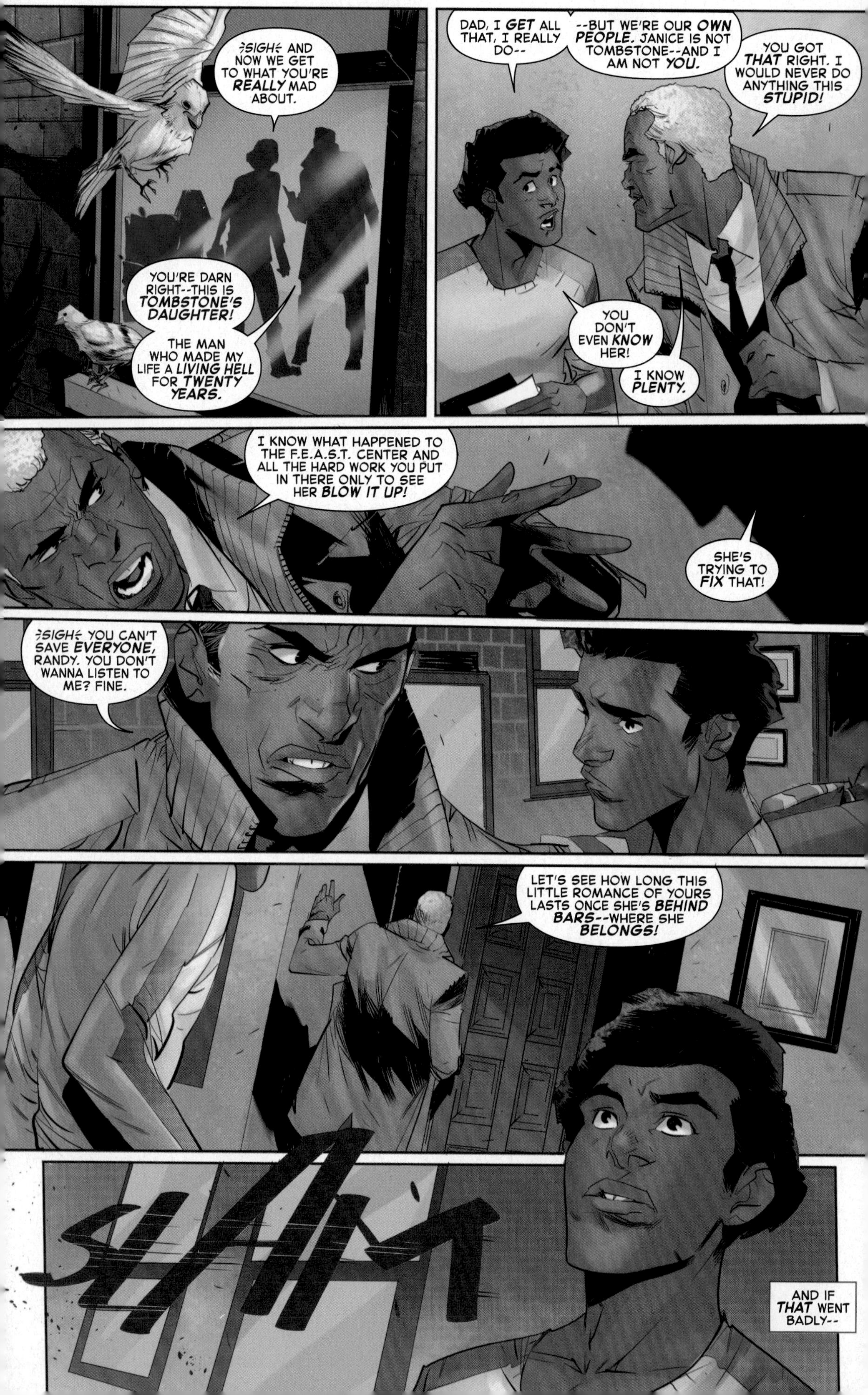

⇒SIGH⇐ AND NOW WE GET TO WHAT YOU'RE REALLY MAD ABOUT.
YOU'RE DARN RIGHT--THIS IS TOMBSTONE'S DAUGHTER!
THE MAN WHO MADE MY LIFE A LIVING HELL FOR TWENTY YEARS.
DAD, I GET ALL THAT, I REALLY DO--
--BUT WE'RE OUR OWN PEOPLE. JANICE IS NOT TOMBSTONE--AND I AM NOT YOU.
YOU GOT THAT RIGHT. I WOULD NEVER DO ANYTHING THIS STUPID!
YOU DON'T EVEN KNOW HER!
I KNOW PLENTY.
I KNOW WHAT HAPPENED TO THE F.E.A.S.T. CENTER AND ALL THE HARD WORK YOU PUT IN THERE ONLY TO SEE HER BLOW IT UP!
SHE'S TRYING TO FIX THAT!
⇒SIGH⇐ YOU CAN'T SAVE EVERYONE, RANDY. YOU DON'T WANNA LISTEN TO ME? FINE.
LET'S SEE HOW LONG THIS LITTLE ROMANCE OF YOURS LASTS ONCE SHE'S BEHIND BARS--WHERE SHE BELONGS!
SLAM
AND IF THAT WENT BADLY--

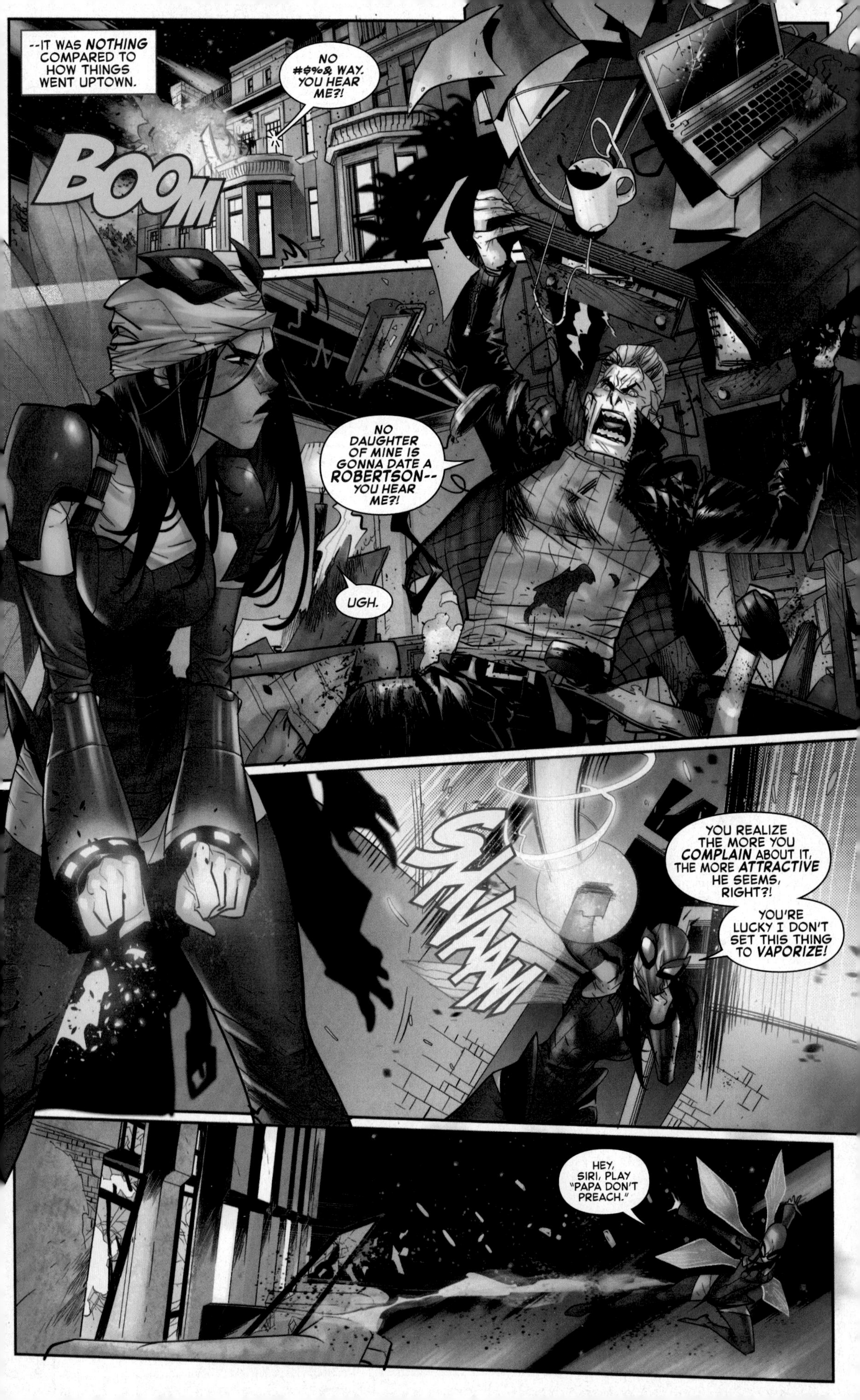
--IT WAS NOTHING COMPARED TO HOW THINGS WENT UPTOWN.
BOOM
NO #$%& WAY. YOU HEAR ME?!
NO DAUGHTER OF MINE IS GONNA DATE A ROBERTSON-- YOU HEAR ME?!
UGH.
SHVAAM
YOU REALIZE THE MORE YOU COMPLAIN ABOUT IT, THE MORE ATTRACTIVE HE SEEMS, RIGHT?!
YOU'RE LUCKY I DON'T SET THIS THING TO VAPORIZE!
HEY, SIRI, PLAY "PAPA DON'T PREACH."

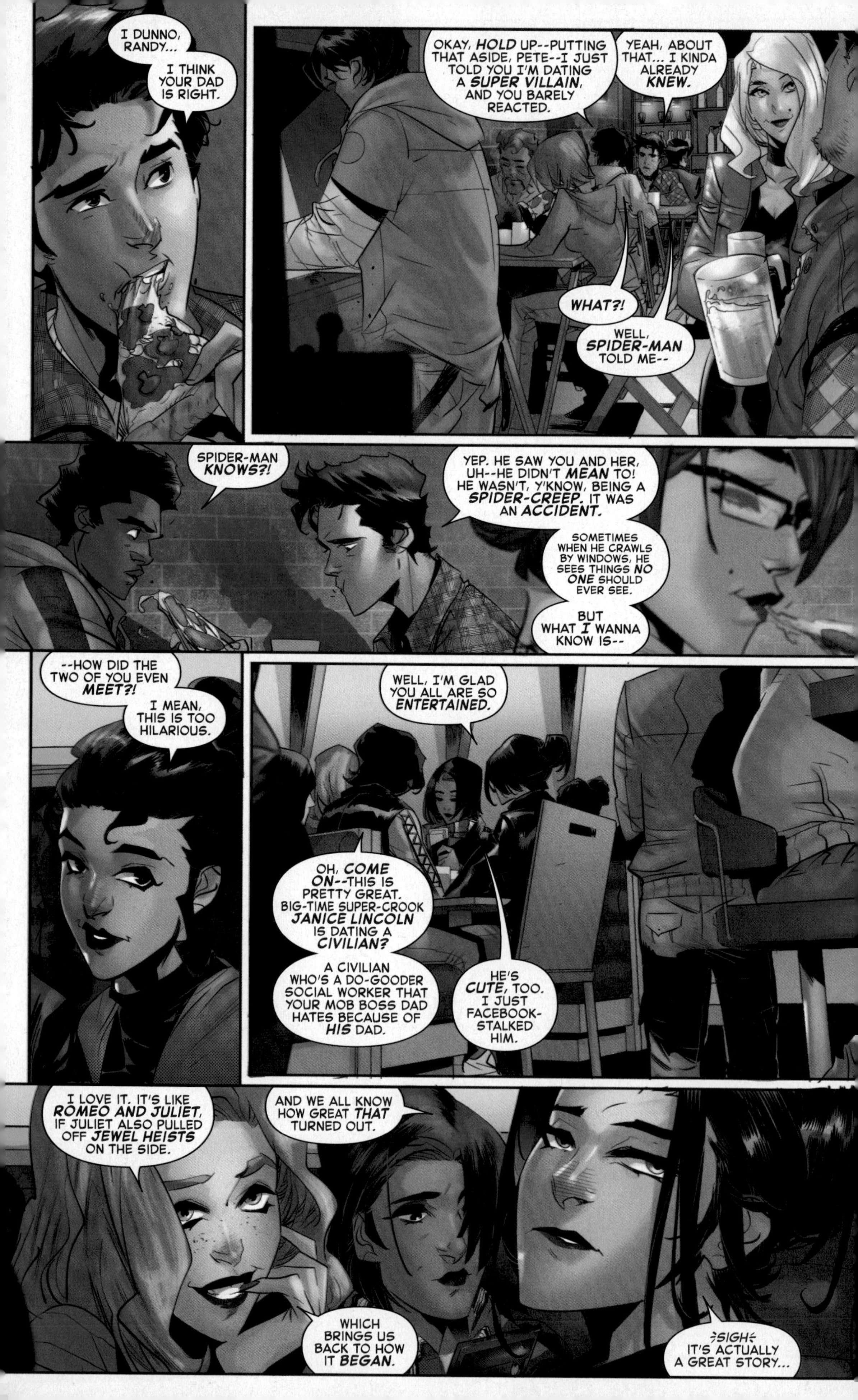
I DUNNO, RANDY...
I THINK YOUR DAD IS RIGHT.
OKAY, HOLD UP--PUTTING THAT ASIDE, PETE--I JUST TOLD YOU I'M DATING A SUPER VILLAIN, AND YOU BARELY REACTED.
YEAH, ABOUT THAT... I KINDA ALREADY KNEW.
WHAT?!
WELL, SPIDER-MAN TOLD ME--
SPIDER-MAN KNOWS?!
YEP. HE SAW YOU AND HER, UH--HE DIDN'T MEAN TO! HE WASN'T, Y'KNOW, BEING A SPIDER-CREEP. IT WAS AN ACCIDENT.
SOMETIMES WHEN HE CRAWLS BY WINDOWS, HE SEES THINGS NO ONE SHOULD EVER SEE.
BUT WHAT I WANNA KNOW IS--
--HOW DID THE TWO OF YOU EVEN MEET?!
I MEAN, THIS IS TOO HILARIOUS.
WELL, I'M GLAD YOU ALL ARE SO ENTERTAINED.
OH, COME ON--THIS IS PRETTY GREAT. BIG-TIME SUPER-CROOK JANICE LINCOLN IS DATING A CIVILIAN?
A CIVILIAN WHO'S A DO-GOODER SOCIAL WORKER THAT YOUR MOB BOSS DAD HATES BECAUSE OF HIS DAD.
HE'S CUTE, TOO. I JUST FACEBOOK-STALKED HIM.
I LOVE IT. IT'S LIKE ROMEO AND JULIET, IF JULIET ALSO PULLED OFF JEWEL HEISTS ON THE SIDE.
AND WE ALL KNOW HOW GREAT THAT TURNED OUT.
WHICH BRINGS US BACK TO HOW IT BEGAN.
SIGH
IT'S ACTUALLY A GREAT STORY...

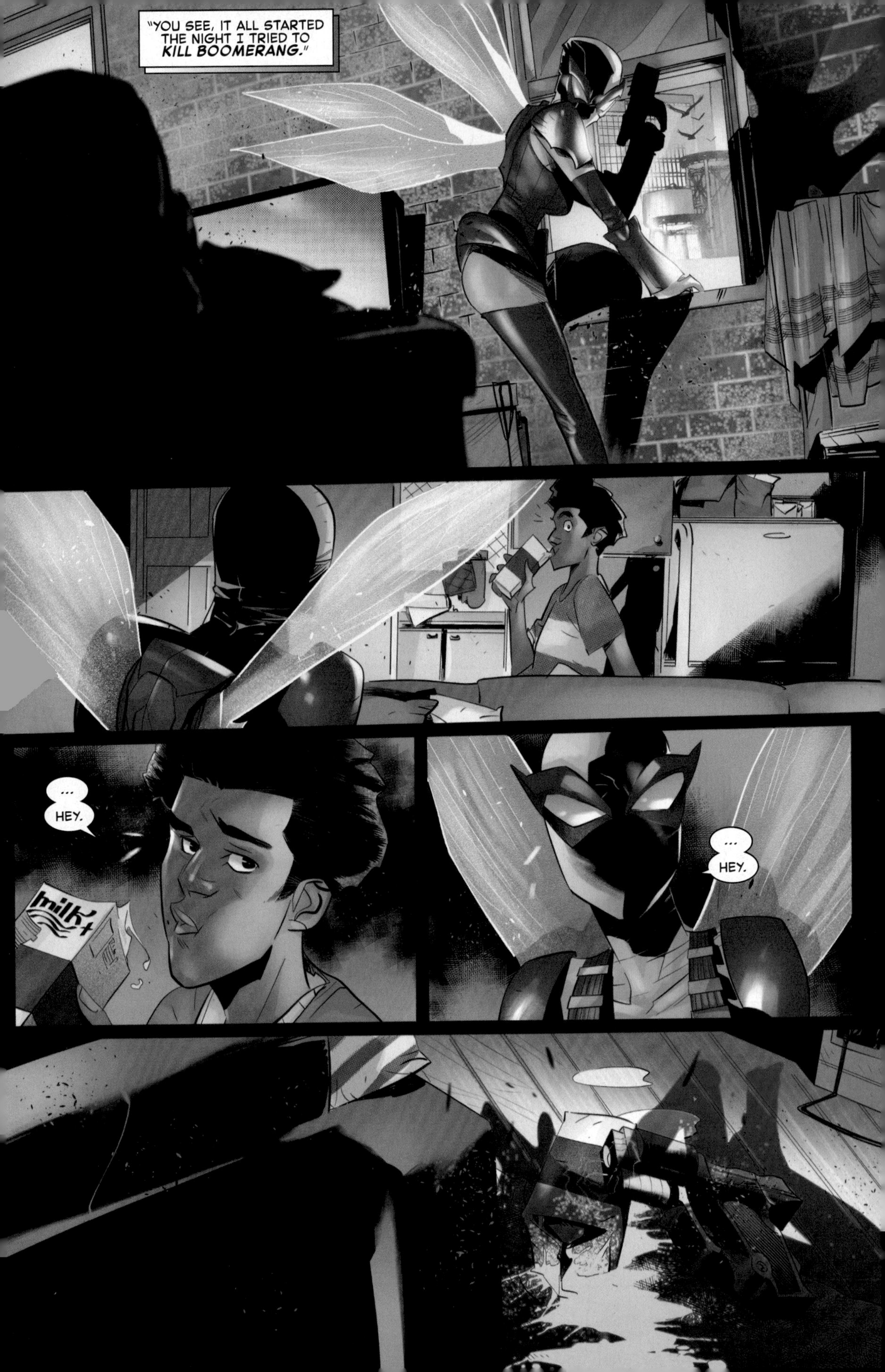
"YOU SEE, IT ALL STARTED THE NIGHT I TRIED TO KILL BOOMERANG."
...
HEY.
...
HEY.
milk

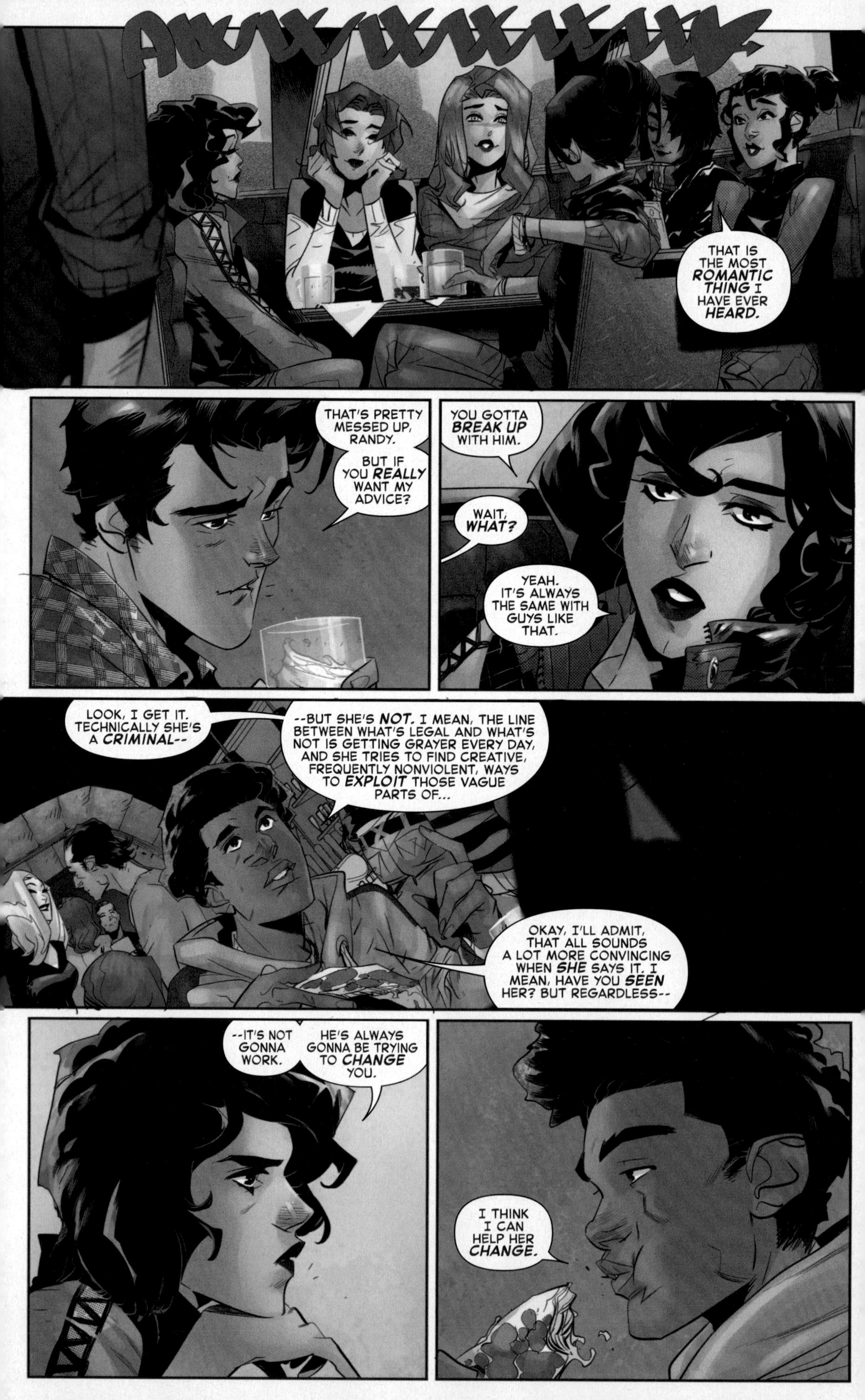
AWWWWWWWWW
THAT IS THE MOST ROMANTIC THING I HAVE EVER HEARD.
THAT'S PRETTY MESSED UP, RANDY.
BUT IF YOU REALLY WANT MY ADVICE?
YOU GOTTA BREAK UP WITH HIM.
WAIT, WHAT?
YEAH. IT'S ALWAYS THE SAME WITH GUYS LIKE THAT.
LOOK, I GET IT. TECHNICALLY SHE'S A CRIMINAL--
--BUT SHE'S NOT. I MEAN, THE LINE BETWEEN WHAT'S LEGAL AND WHAT'S NOT IS GETTING GRAYER EVERY DAY, AND SHE TRIES TO FIND CREATIVE, FREQUENTLY NONVIOLENT, WAYS TO EXPLOIT THOSE VAGUE PARTS OF...
OKAY, I'LL ADMIT, THAT ALL SOUNDS A LOT MORE CONVINCING WHEN SHE SAYS IT. I MEAN, HAVE YOU SEEN HER? BUT REGARDLESS--
--IT'S NOT GONNA WORK.
HE'S ALWAYS GONNA BE TRYING TO CHANGE YOU.
I THINK I CAN HELP HER CHANGE.

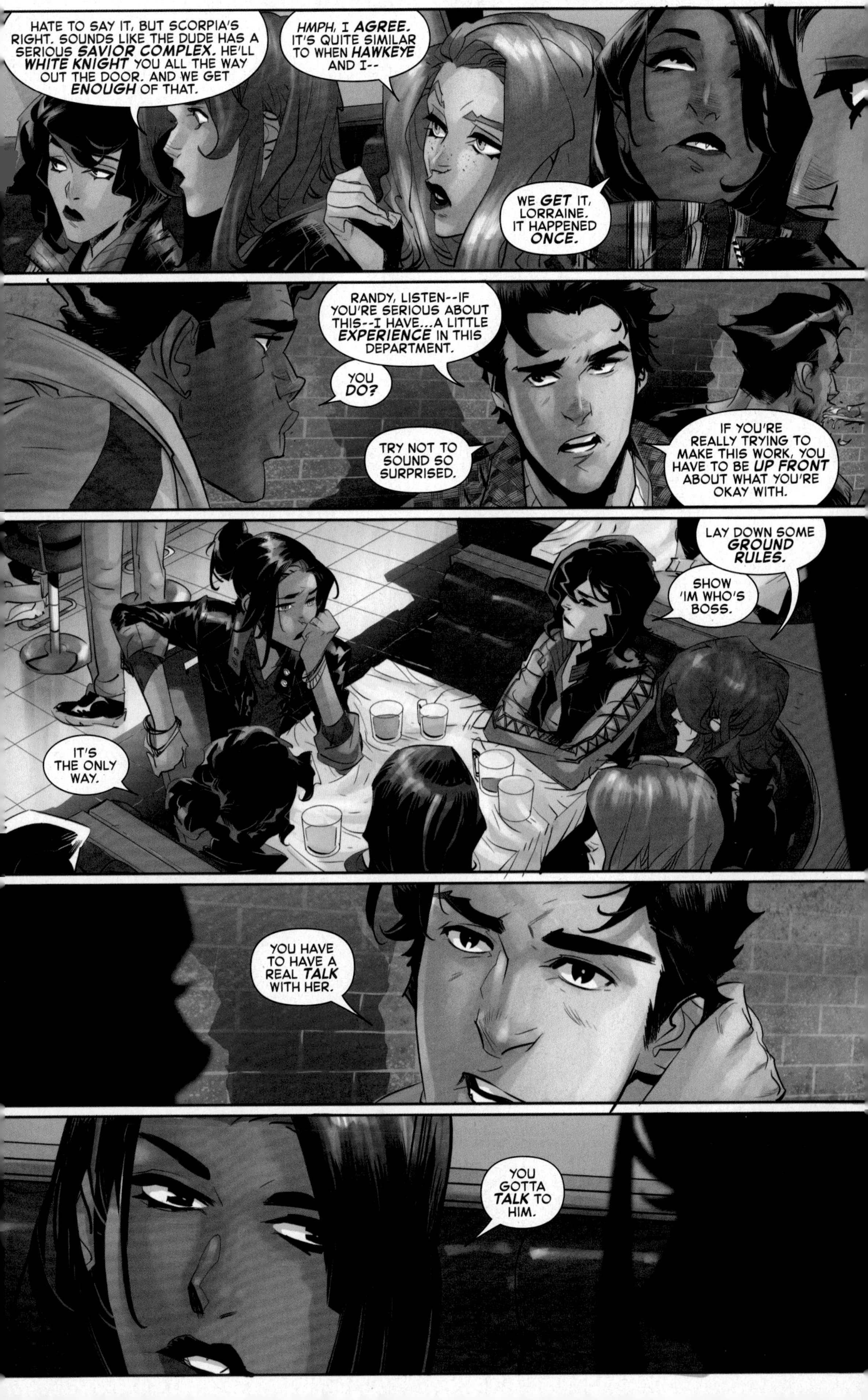

HATE TO SAY IT, BUT SCORPIA'S RIGHT. SOUNDS LIKE THE DUDE HAS A SERIOUS SAVIOR COMPLEX. HE'LL WHITE KNIGHT YOU ALL THE WAY OUT THE DOOR. AND WE GET ENOUGH OF THAT.
HMPH, I AGREE. IT'S QUITE SIMILAR TO WHEN HAWKEYE AND I--
WE GET IT, LORRAINE. IT HAPPENED ONCE.
RANDY, LISTEN--IF YOU'RE SERIOUS ABOUT THIS--I HAVE...A LITTLE EXPERIENCE IN THIS DEPARTMENT.
YOU DO?
TRY NOT TO SOUND SO SURPRISED.
IF YOU'RE REALLY TRYING TO MAKE THIS WORK, YOU HAVE TO BE UP FRONT ABOUT WHAT YOU'RE OKAY WITH.
LAY DOWN SOME GROUND RULES.
SHOW 'IM WHO'S BOSS.
IT'S THE ONLY WAY.
YOU HAVE TO HAVE A REAL TALK WITH HER.
YOU GOTTA TALK TO HIM.

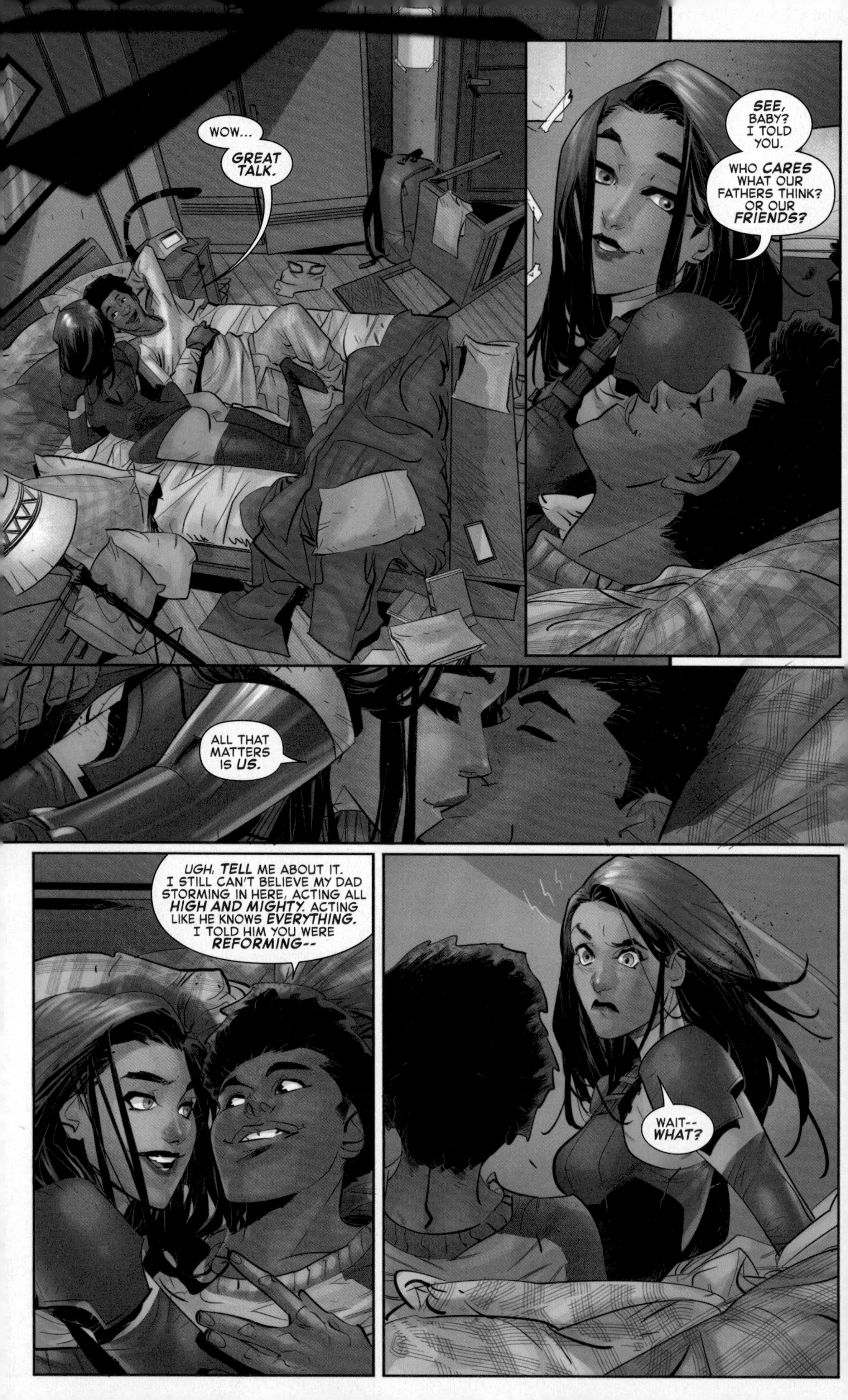
WOW...
GREAT TALK.
SEE, BABY? I TOLD YOU.
WHO CARES WHAT OUR FATHERS THINK? OR OUR FRIENDS?
ALL THAT MATTERS IS US.
UGH, TELL ME ABOUT IT. I STILL CAN'T BELIEVE MY DAD STORMING IN HERE, ACTING ALL HIGH AND MIGHTY. ACTING LIKE HE KNOWS EVERYTHING. I TOLD HIM YOU WERE REFORMING--
WAIT--WHAT?

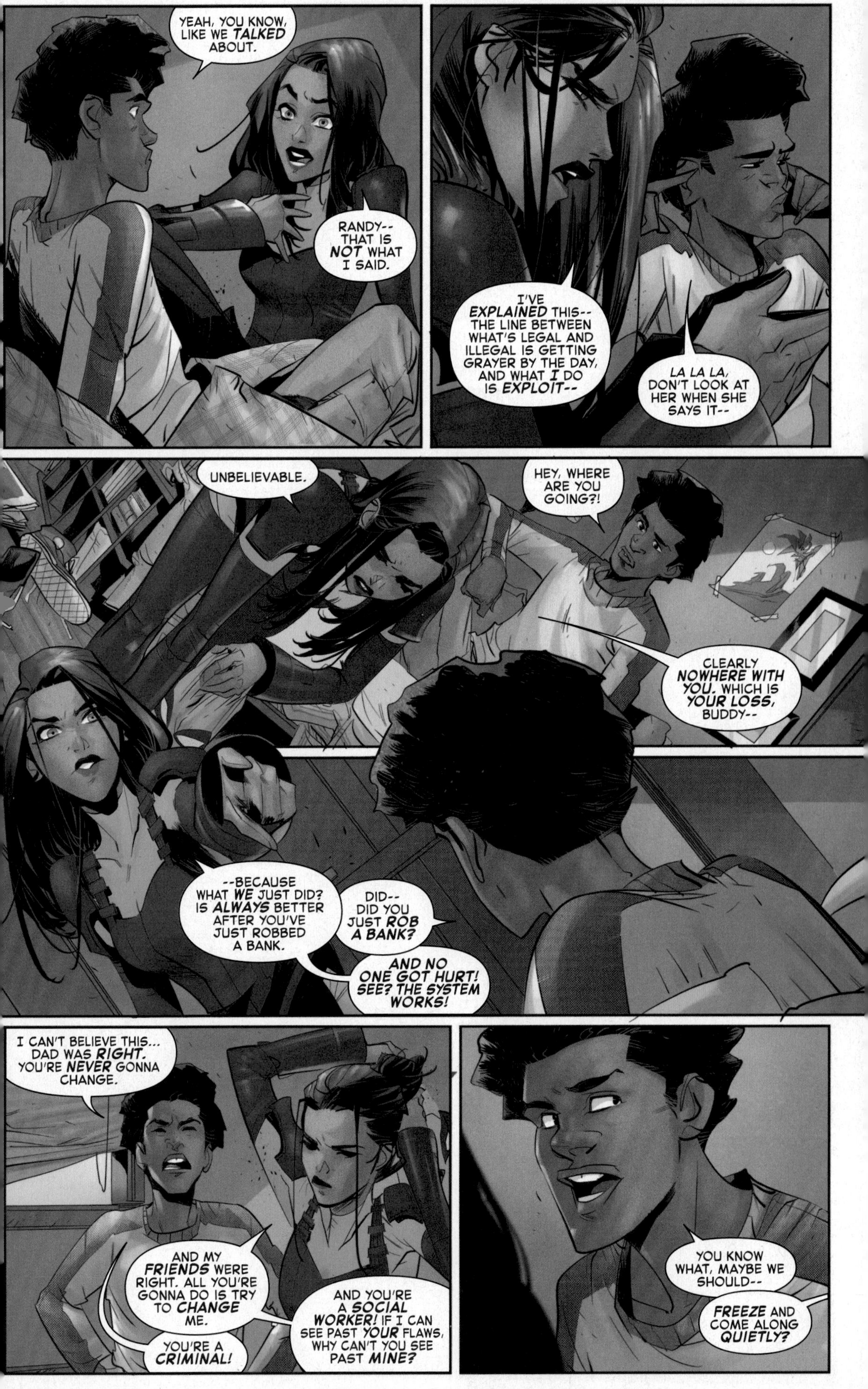
YEAH, YOU KNOW, LIKE WE TALKED ABOUT.
RANDY-- THAT IS NOT WHAT I SAID.
I'VE EXPLAINED THIS-- THE LINE BETWEEN WHAT'S LEGAL AND ILLEGAL IS GETTING GRAYER BY THE DAY, AND WHAT I DO IS EXPLOIT--
LA LA LA, DON'T LOOK AT HER WHEN SHE SAYS IT--
UNBELIEVABLE.
HEY, WHERE ARE YOU GOING?!
CLEARLY NOWHERE WITH YOU. WHICH IS YOUR LOSS, BUDDY--
--BECAUSE WHAT WE JUST DID? IS ALWAYS BETTER AFTER YOU'VE JUST ROBBED A BANK.
DID-- DID YOU JUST ROB A BANK?
AND NO ONE GOT HURT! SEE? THE SYSTEM WORKS!
I CAN'T BELIEVE THIS... DAD WAS RIGHT. YOU'RE NEVER GONNA CHANGE.
AND MY FRIENDS WERE RIGHT. ALL YOU'RE GONNA DO IS TRY TO CHANGE ME.
YOU'RE A CRIMINAL!
AND YOU'RE A SOCIAL WORKER! IF I CAN SEE PAST YOUR FLAWS, WHY CAN'T YOU SEE PAST MINE?
YOU KNOW WHAT, MAYBE WE SHOULD--
FREEZE AND COME ALONG QUIETLY?

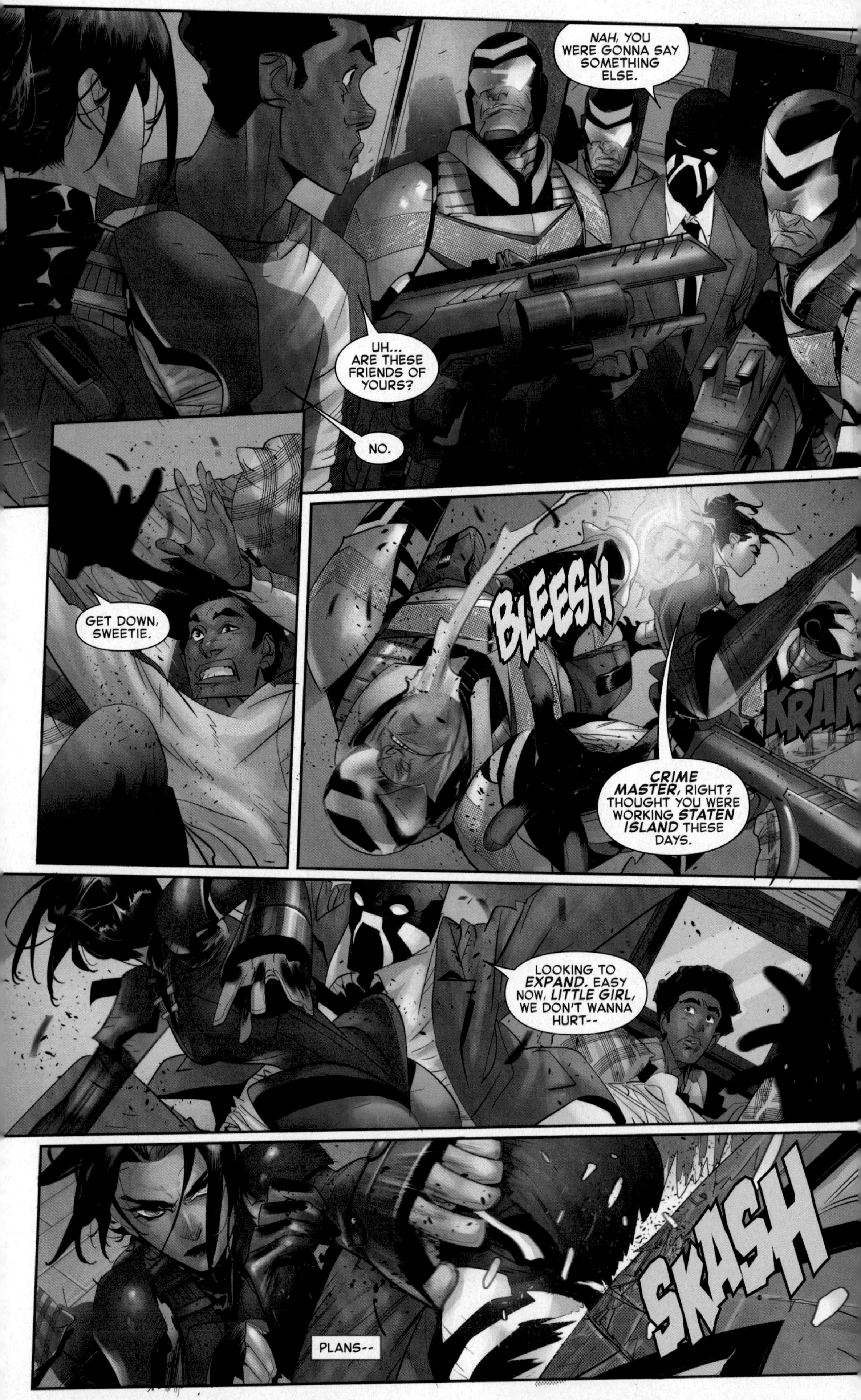
NAH, YOU WERE GONNA SAY SOMETHING ELSE.
UH... ARE THESE FRIENDS OF YOURS?
NO.
GET DOWN, SWEETIE.
BLEESH
KRAK
CRIME MASTER, RIGHT? THOUGHT YOU WERE WORKING STATEN ISLAND THESE DAYS.
LOOKING TO EXPAND. EASY NOW, LITTLE GIRL, WE DON'T WANNA HURT--
SKASH
PLANS--

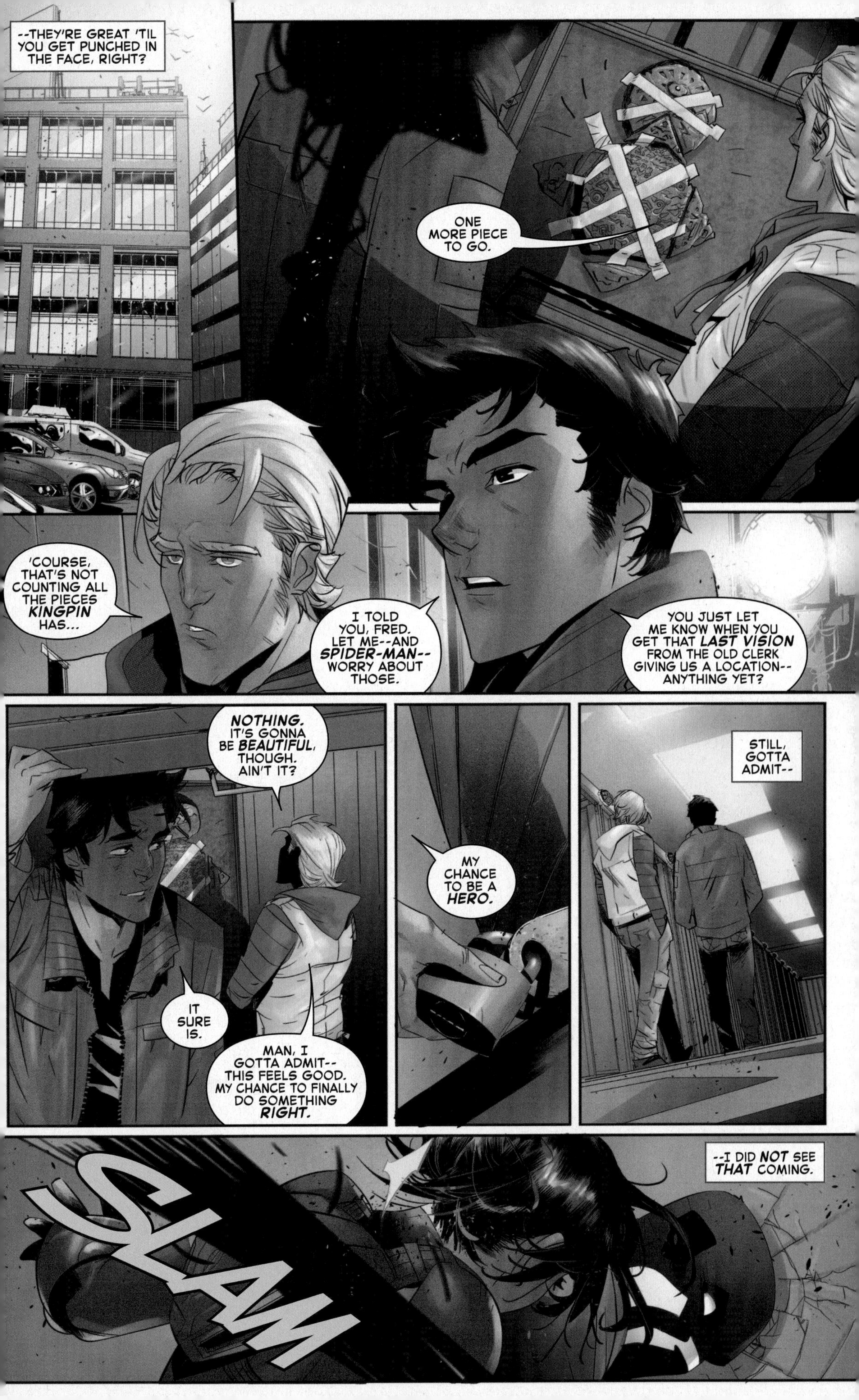
--THEY'RE GREAT 'TIL YOU GET PUNCHED IN THE FACE, RIGHT?
ONE MORE PIECE TO GO.
'COURSE, THAT'S NOT COUNTING ALL THE PIECES KINGPIN HAS...
I TOLD YOU, FRED. LET ME--AND SPIDER-MAN--WORRY ABOUT THOSE.
YOU JUST LET ME KNOW WHEN YOU GET THAT LAST VISION FROM THE OLD CLERK GIVING US A LOCATION--ANYTHING YET?
NOTHING. IT'S GONNA BE BEAUTIFUL, THOUGH. AIN'T IT?
IT SURE IS.
MAN, I GOTTA ADMIT--THIS FEELS GOOD. MY CHANCE TO FINALLY DO SOMETHING RIGHT.
MY CHANCE TO BE A HERO.
STILL, GOTTA ADMIT--
SLAM
--I DID NOT SEE THAT COMING.

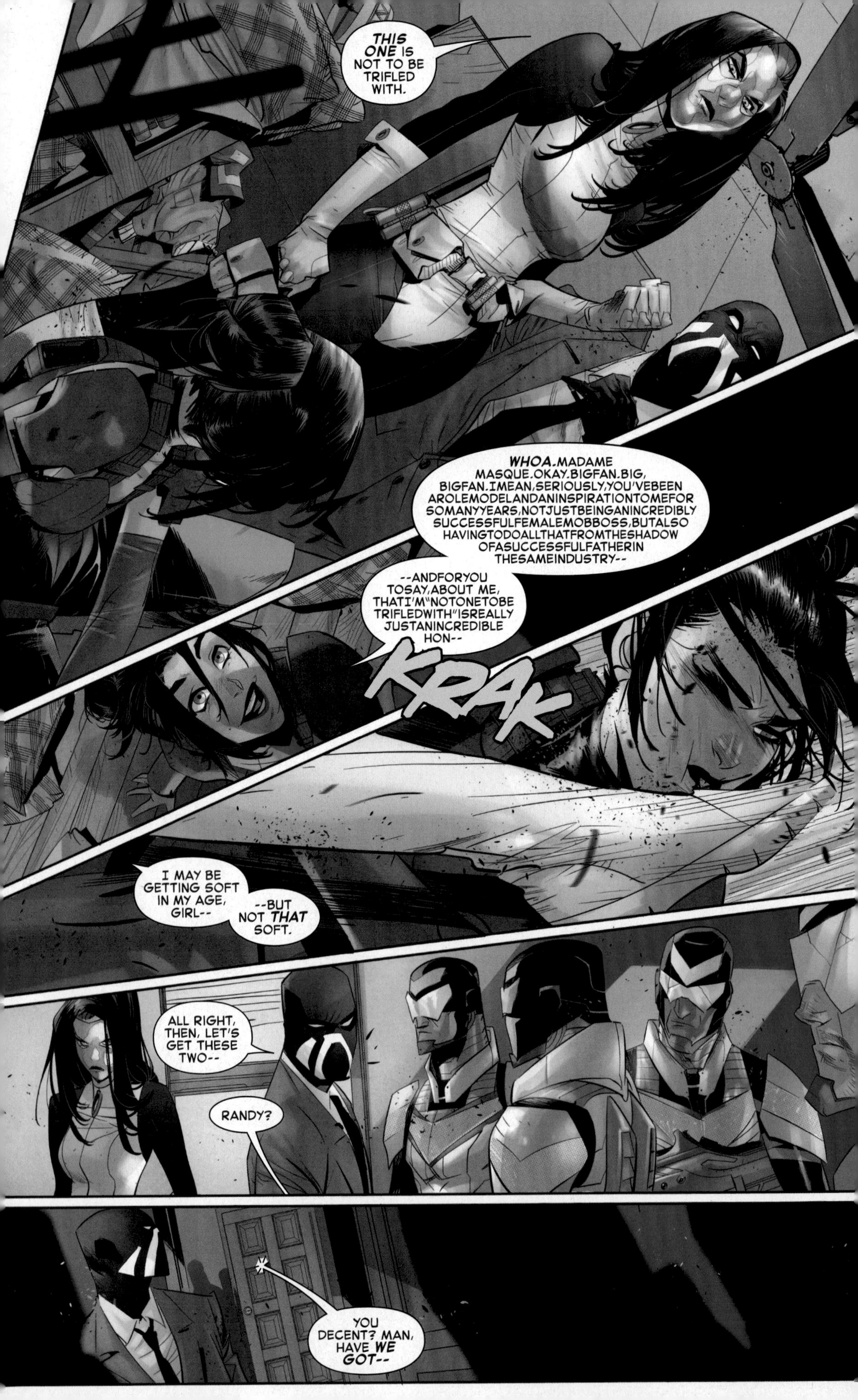
THIS ONE IS NOT TO BE TRIFLED WITH.
WHOA. MADAME MASQUE. OKAY. BIGFAN. BIG, BIGFAN. IMEAN, SERIOUSLY, YOU'VEBEEN AROLEMODELANDANINSPIRATIONTOMEFOR SOMANYYEARS, NOTJUSTBEINGANINCREDIBLY SUCCESSFULFEMALEMOBBOSS, BUTALSO HAVINGTODOALLTHATFROMTHESHADOW OFASUCCESSFULFATHERIN THESAMEINDUSTRY--
--ANDFORYOU TOSAY, ABOUT ME, THATI'M "NOTONETOBE TRIFLEDWITH" ISREALLY JUSTANINCREDIBLE HON--
KRAK
I MAY BE GETTING SOFT IN MY AGE, GIRL--
--BUT NOT THAT SOFT.
ALL RIGHT, THEN, LET'S GET THESE TWO--
RANDY?
YOU DECENT? MAN, HAVE WE GOT--

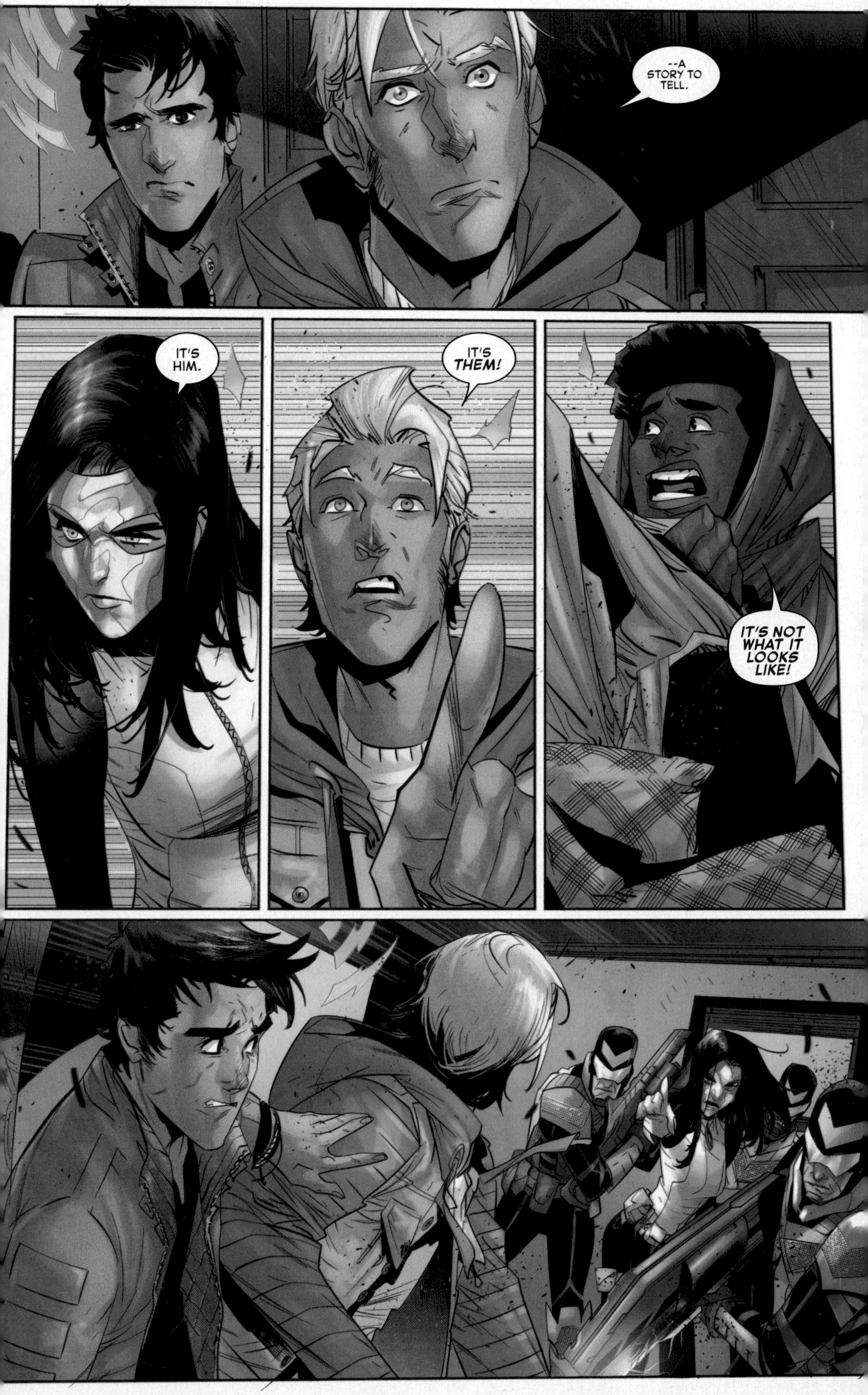
--A STORY TO TELL.
IT'S HIM.
IT'S *THEM!*
IT'S NOT WHAT IT LOOKS LIKE!

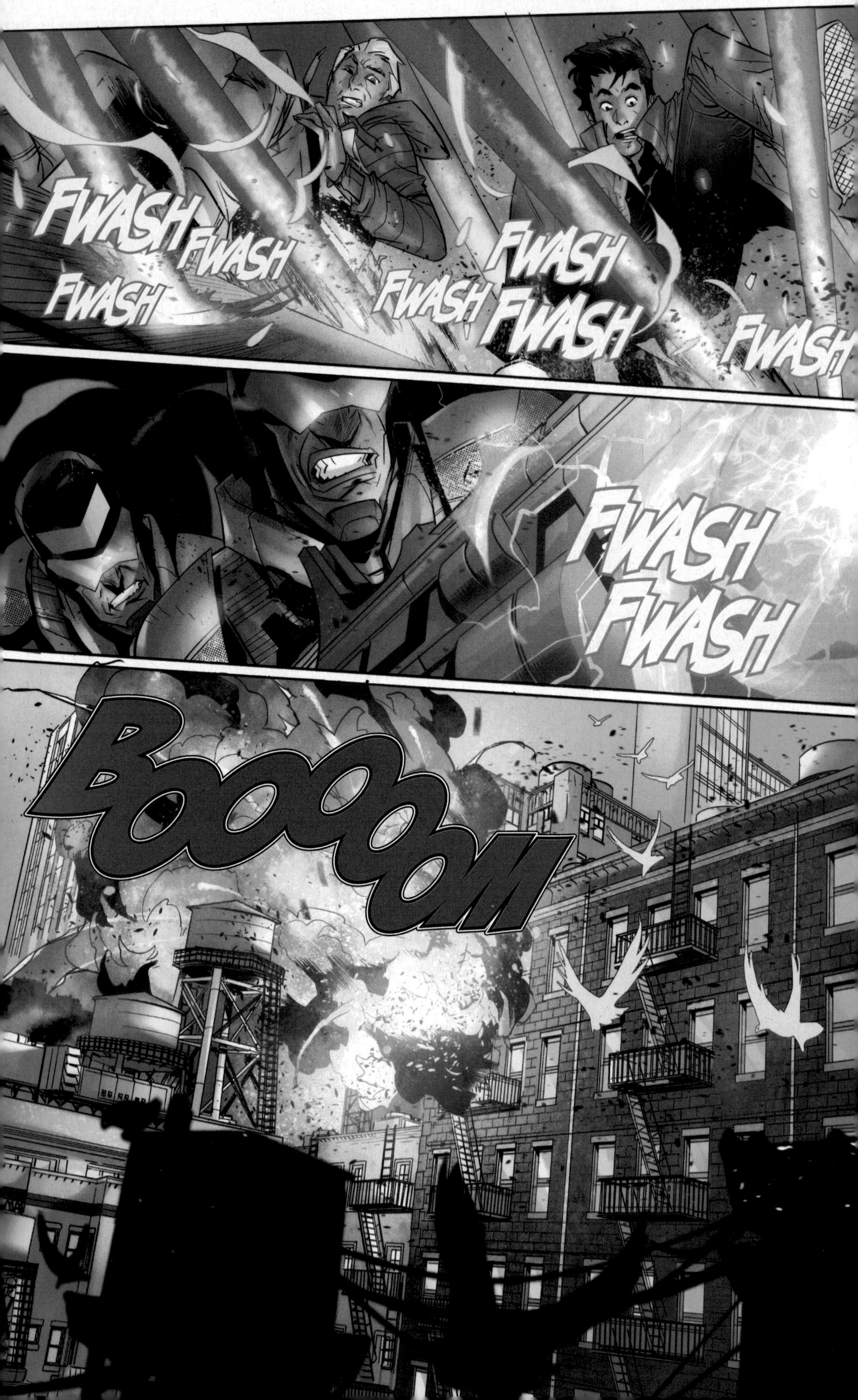
FWASH
FWASH
FWASH
FWASH
FWASH
FWASH
FWASH
FWASH
FWASH
BOOOOOM

64

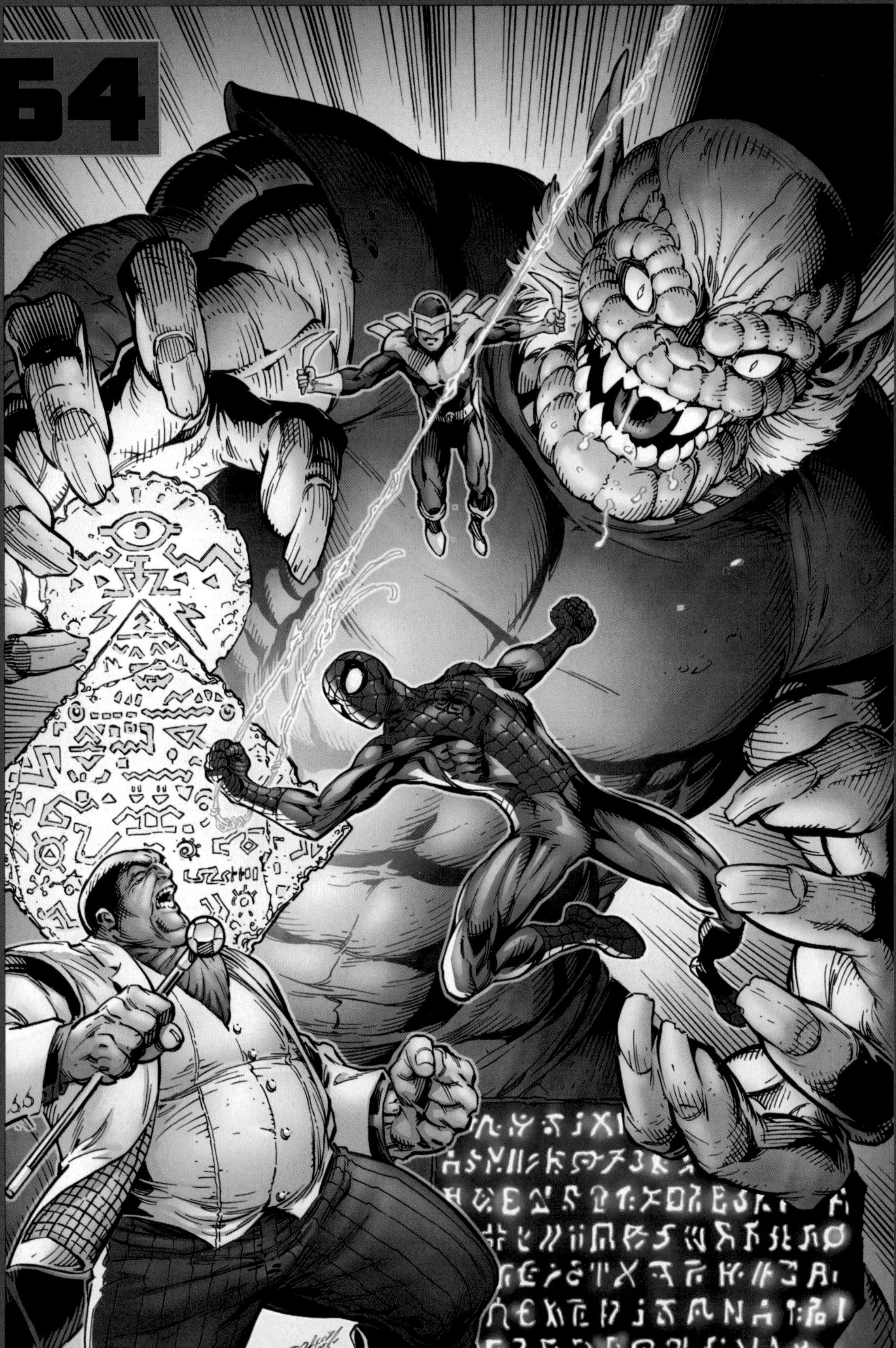

KING'S RANSOM PART 2

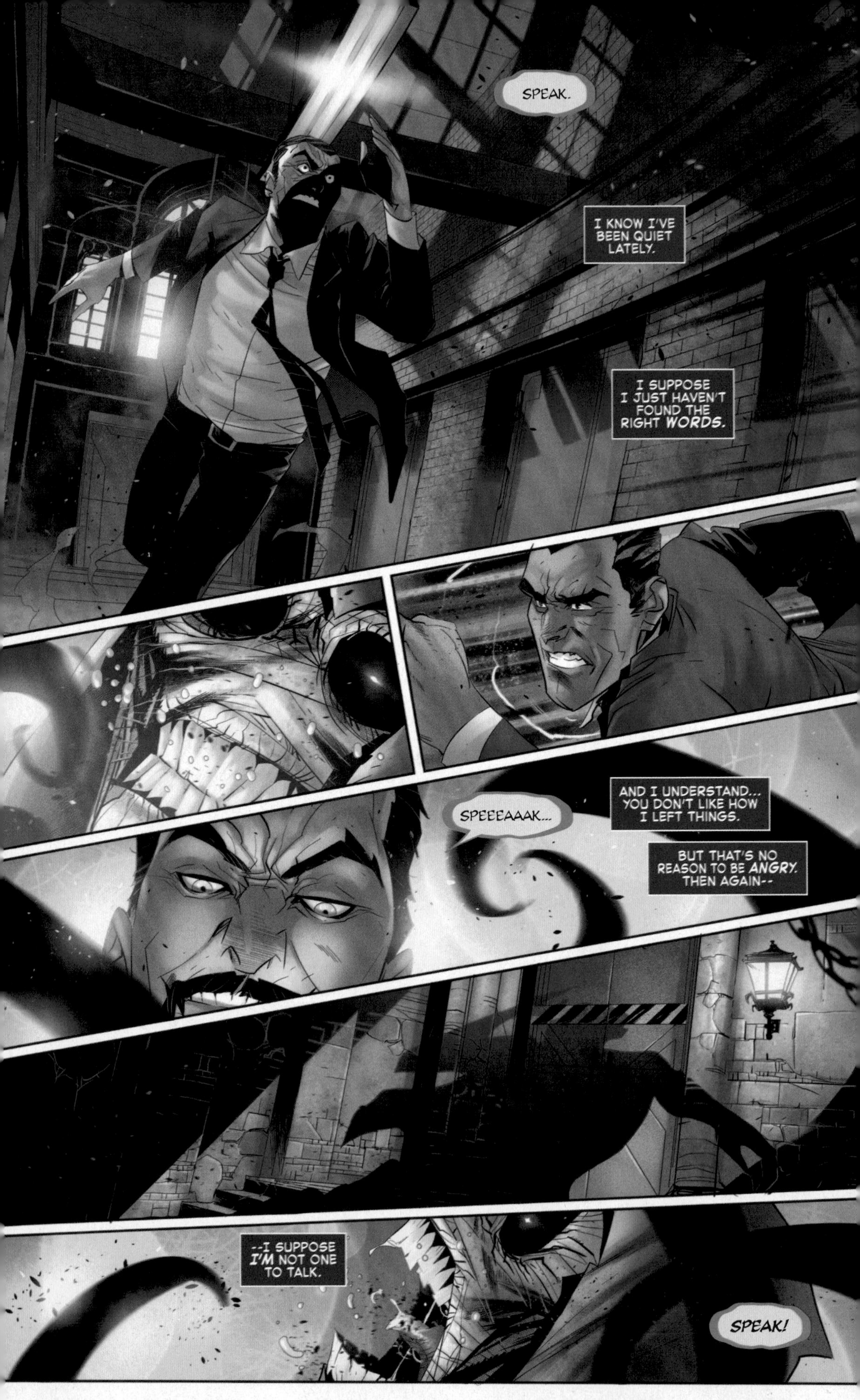
SPEAK.
I KNOW I'VE BEEN QUIET LATELY.
I SUPPOSE I JUST HAVEN'T FOUND THE RIGHT WORDS.
SPEEEAAAK...
AND I UNDERSTAND... YOU DON'T LIKE HOW I LEFT THINGS.
BUT THAT'S NO REASON TO BE ANGRY. THEN AGAIN--
--I SUPPOSE I'M NOT ONE TO TALK.
SPEAK!

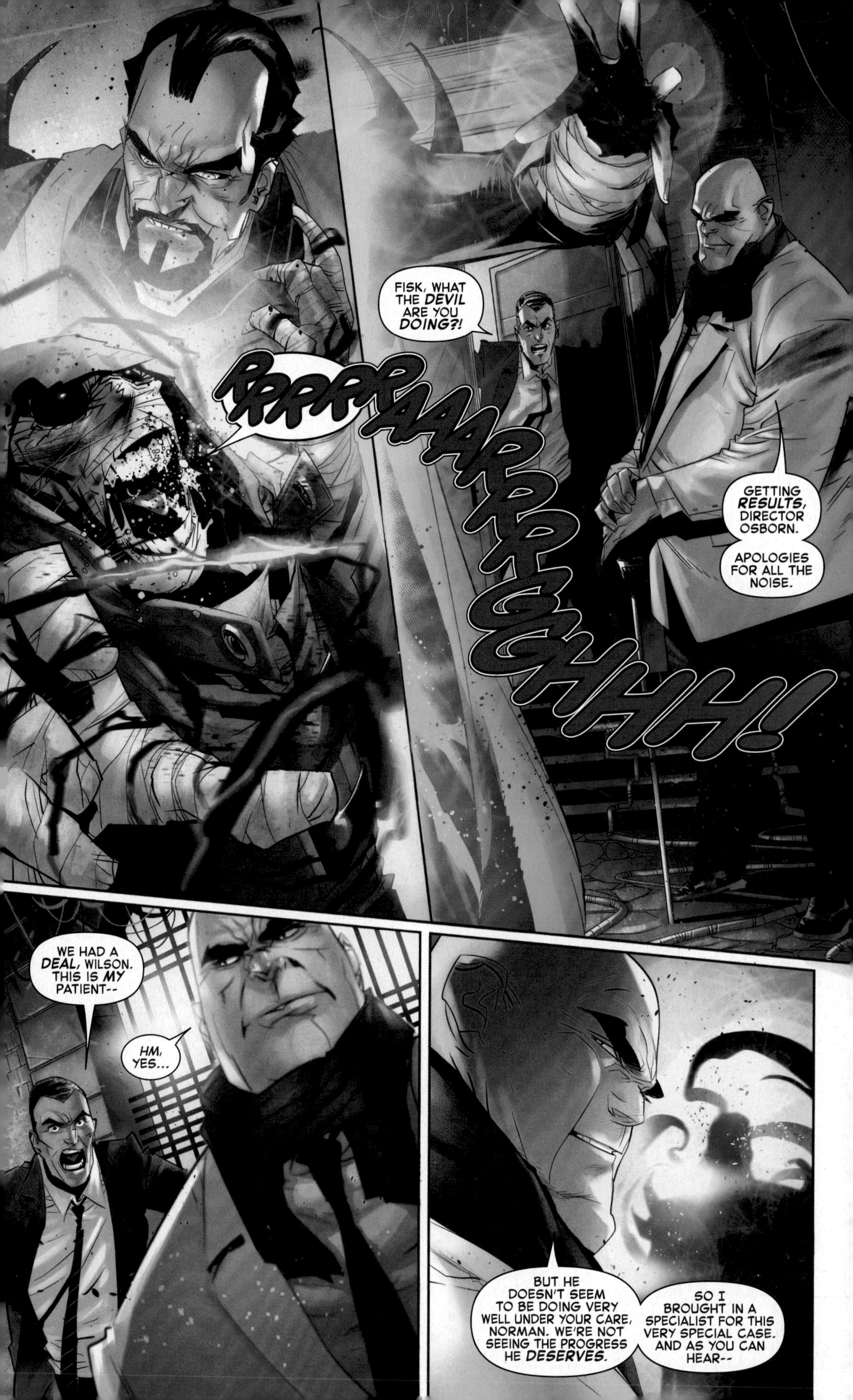

FISK, WHAT THE *DEVIL* ARE YOU *DOING?!*
RRRRRAAARRRGHHHH!
GETTING *RESULTS,* DIRECTOR OSBORN.
APOLOGIES FOR ALL THE NOISE.
WE HAD A *DEAL,* WILSON. THIS IS *MY* PATIENT--
HM, YES...
BUT HE DOESN'T SEEM TO BE DOING VERY WELL UNDER YOUR CARE, NORMAN. WE'RE NOT SEEING THE PROGRESS HE *DESERVES.*
SO I BROUGHT IN A SPECIALIST FOR THIS VERY SPECIAL CASE. AND AS YOU CAN HEAR--

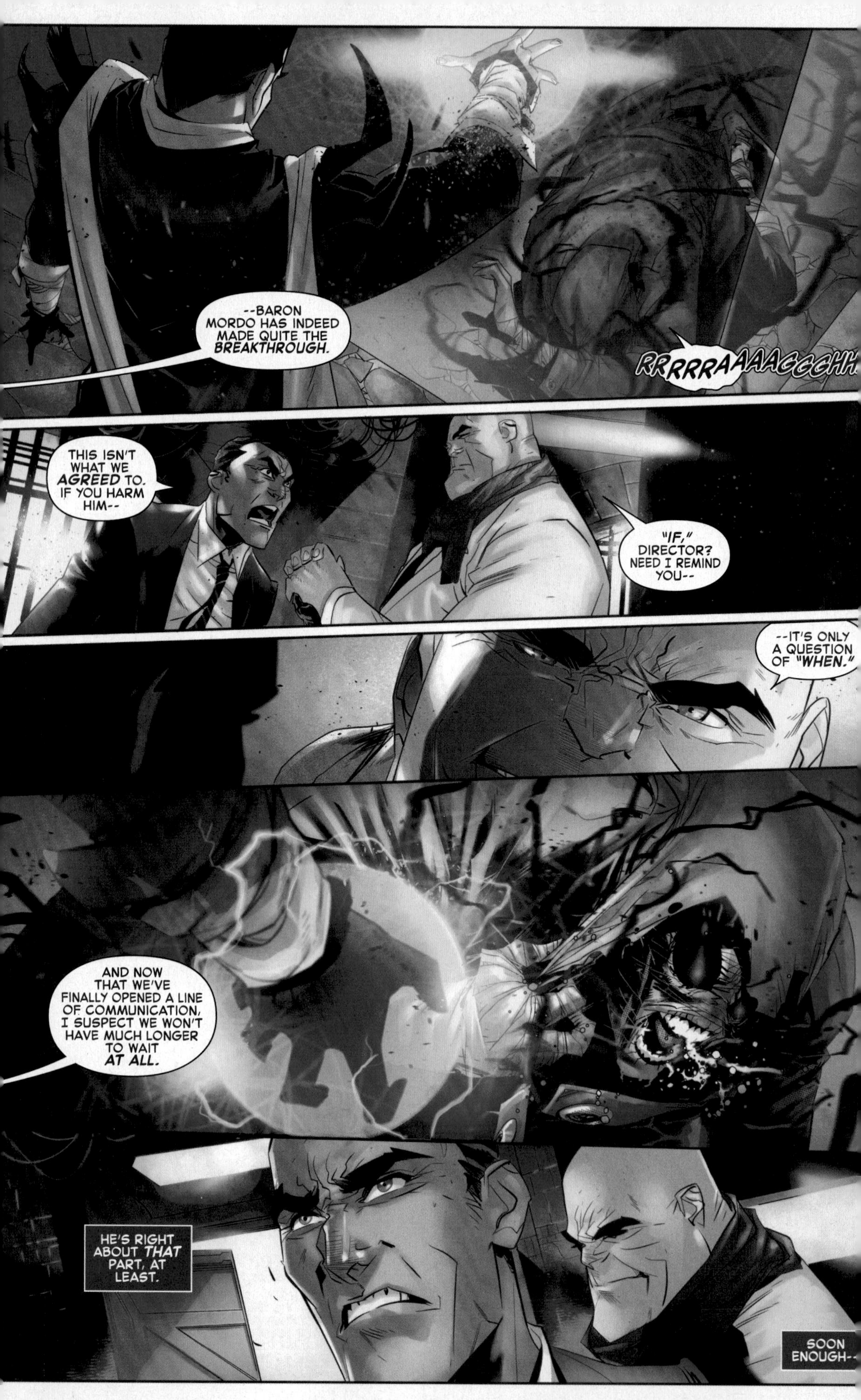
--BARON MORDO HAS INDEED MADE QUITE THE BREAKTHROUGH.
RRRRRAAAAGGGHH
THIS ISN'T WHAT WE AGREED TO. IF YOU HARM HIM--
"IF," DIRECTOR? NEED I REMIND YOU--
--IT'S ONLY A QUESTION OF "WHEN."
AND NOW THAT WE'VE FINALLY OPENED A LINE OF COMMUNICATION, I SUSPECT WE WON'T HAVE MUCH LONGER TO WAIT AT ALL.
HE'S RIGHT ABOUT THAT PART, AT LEAST.
SOON ENOUGH--

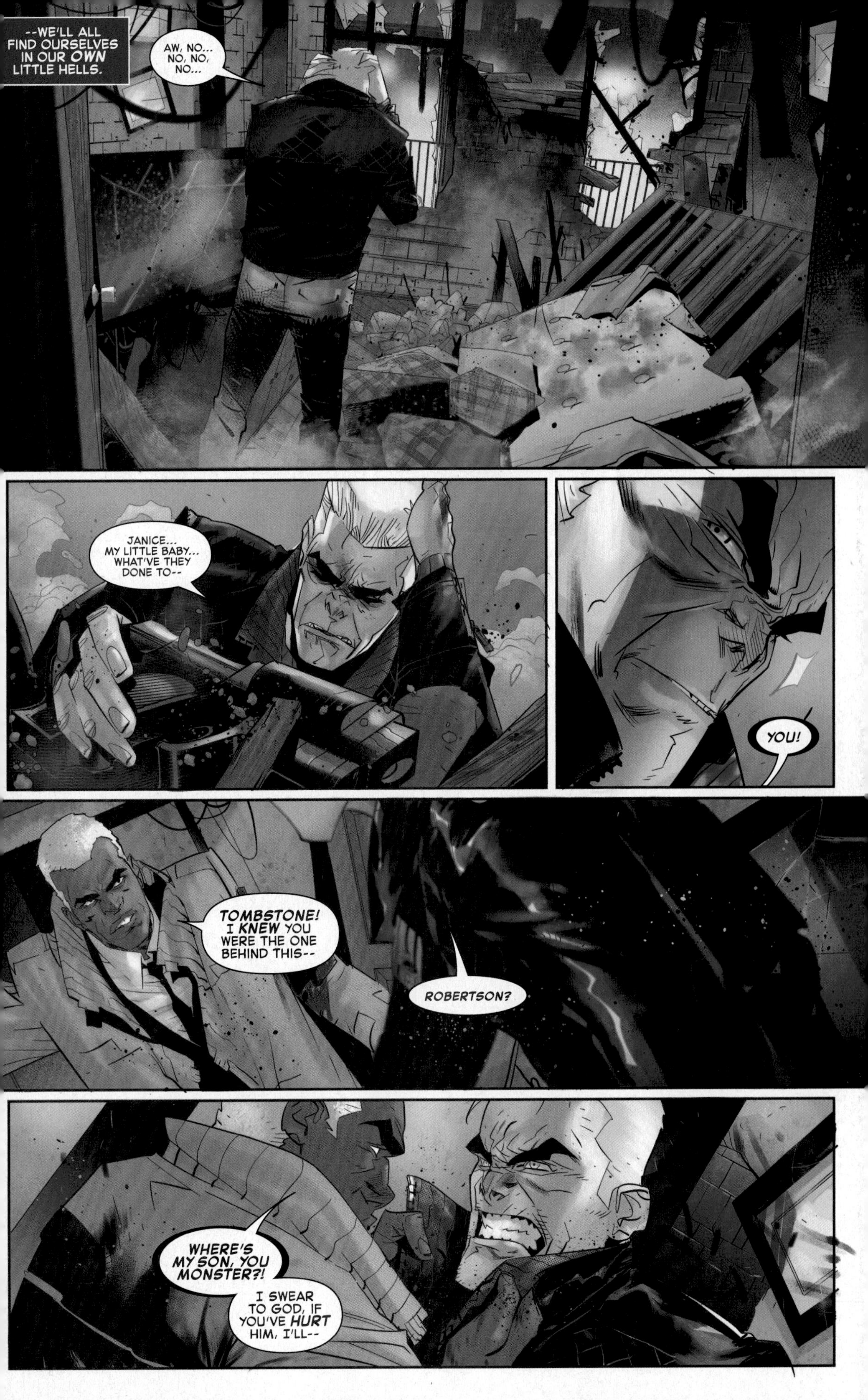
--WE'LL ALL FIND OURSELVES IN OUR OWN LITTLE HELLS.
AW, NO... NO, NO, NO...
JANICE... MY LITTLE BABY... WHAT'VE THEY DONE TO--
YOU!
TOMBSTONE! I KNEW YOU WERE THE ONE BEHIND THIS--
ROBERTSON?
WHERE'S MY SON, YOU MONSTER?!
I SWEAR TO GOD, IF YOU'VE HURT HIM, I'LL--

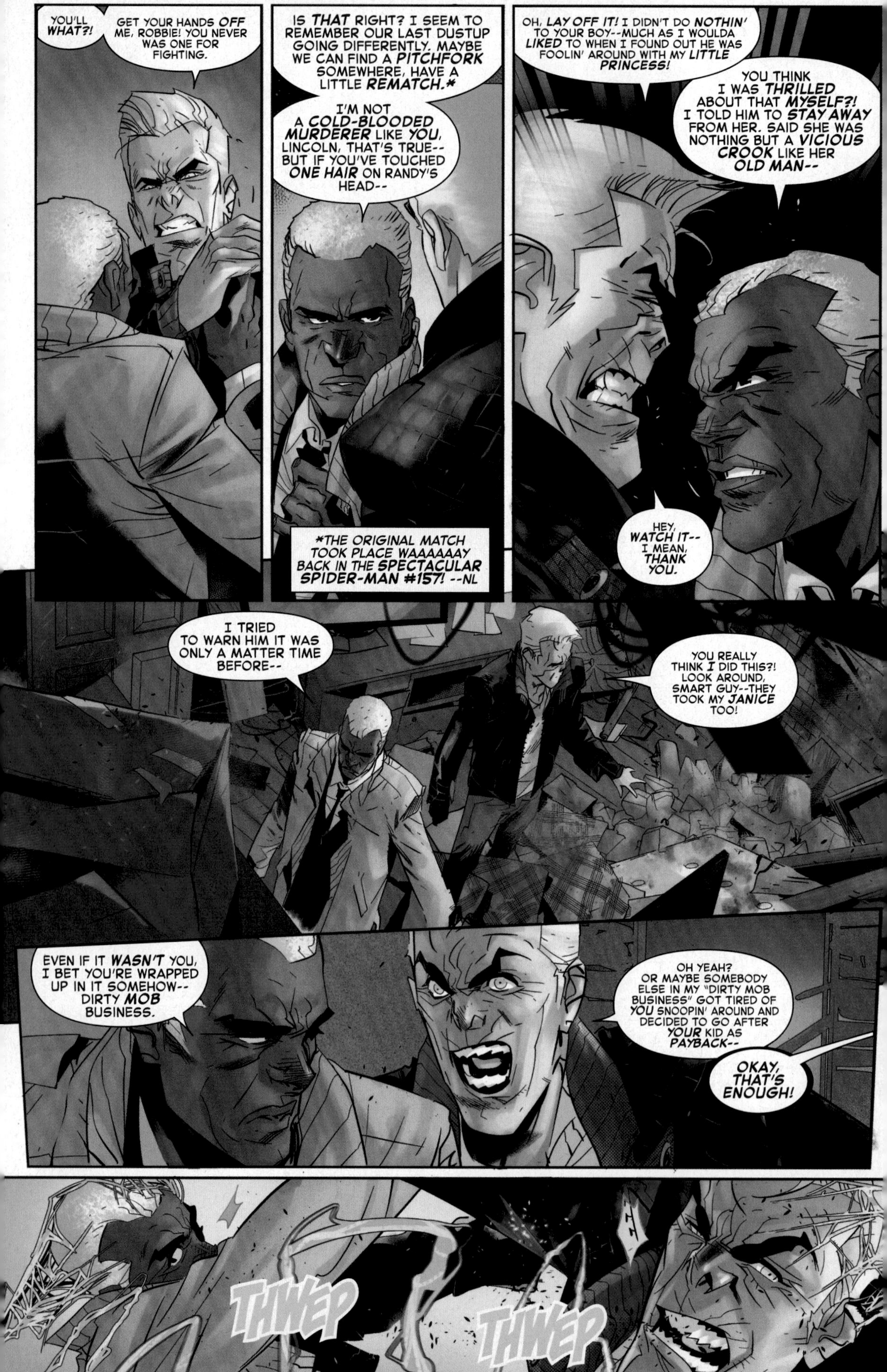
YOU'LL WHAT?!
GET YOUR HANDS OFF ME, ROBBIE! YOU NEVER WAS ONE FOR FIGHTING.
IS THAT RIGHT? I SEEM TO REMEMBER OUR LAST DUSTUP GOING DIFFERENTLY. MAYBE WE CAN FIND A PITCHFORK SOMEWHERE, HAVE A LITTLE REMATCH.*
I'M NOT A COLD-BLOODED MURDERER LIKE YOU, LINCOLN, THAT'S TRUE-- BUT IF YOU'VE TOUCHED ONE HAIR ON RANDY'S HEAD--
*THE ORIGINAL MATCH TOOK PLACE WAAAAAAY BACK IN THE SPECTACULAR SPIDER-MAN #157! --NL
OH, LAY OFF IT! I DIDN'T DO NOTHIN' TO YOUR BOY--MUCH AS I WOULDA LIKED TO WHEN I FOUND OUT HE WAS FOOLIN' AROUND WITH MY LITTLE PRINCESS!
YOU THINK I WAS THRILLED ABOUT THAT MYSELF?! I TOLD HIM TO STAY AWAY FROM HER. SAID SHE WAS NOTHING BUT A VICIOUS CROOK LIKE HER OLD MAN--
HEY, WATCH IT-- I MEAN, THANK YOU.
I TRIED TO WARN HIM IT WAS ONLY A MATTER TIME BEFORE--
YOU REALLY THINK I DID THIS?! LOOK AROUND, SMART GUY--THEY TOOK MY JANICE TOO!
EVEN IF IT WASN'T YOU, I BET YOU'RE WRAPPED UP IN IT SOMEHOW-- DIRTY MOB BUSINESS.
OH YEAH? OR MAYBE SOMEBODY ELSE IN MY "DIRTY MOB BUSINESS" GOT TIRED OF YOU SNOOPIN' AROUND AND DECIDED TO GO AFTER YOUR KID AS PAYBACK--
OKAY, THAT'S ENOUGH!
THWEP
THWEP

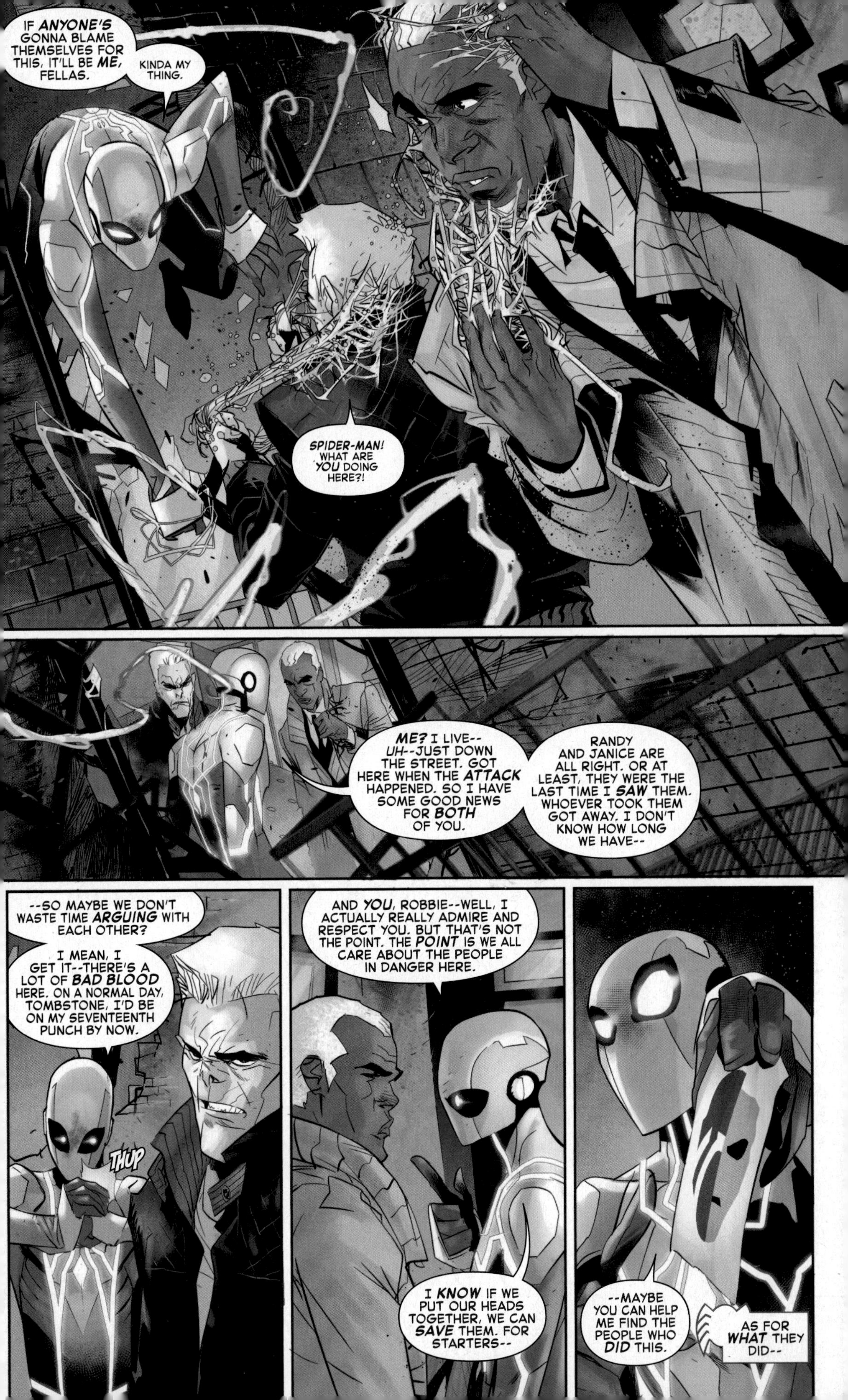
IF ANYONE'S GONNA BLAME THEMSELVES FOR THIS, IT'LL BE ME, FELLAS.
KINDA MY THING.
SPIDER-MAN! WHAT ARE YOU DOING HERE?!
ME? I LIVE-- UH--JUST DOWN THE STREET. GOT HERE WHEN THE ATTACK HAPPENED. SO I HAVE SOME GOOD NEWS FOR BOTH OF YOU.
RANDY AND JANICE ARE ALL RIGHT. OR AT LEAST, THEY WERE THE LAST TIME I SAW THEM. WHOEVER TOOK THEM GOT AWAY. I DON'T KNOW HOW LONG WE HAVE--
--SO MAYBE WE DON'T WASTE TIME ARGUING WITH EACH OTHER?
I MEAN, I GET IT--THERE'S A LOT OF BAD BLOOD HERE. ON A NORMAL DAY, TOMBSTONE, I'D BE ON MY SEVENTEENTH PUNCH BY NOW.
THUP
AND YOU, ROBBIE--WELL, I ACTUALLY REALLY ADMIRE AND RESPECT YOU. BUT THAT'S NOT THE POINT. THE POINT IS WE ALL CARE ABOUT THE PEOPLE IN DANGER HERE.
I KNOW IF WE PUT OUR HEADS TOGETHER, WE CAN SAVE THEM. FOR STARTERS--
--MAYBE YOU CAN HELP ME FIND THE PEOPLE WHO DID THIS.
AS FOR WHAT THEY DID--

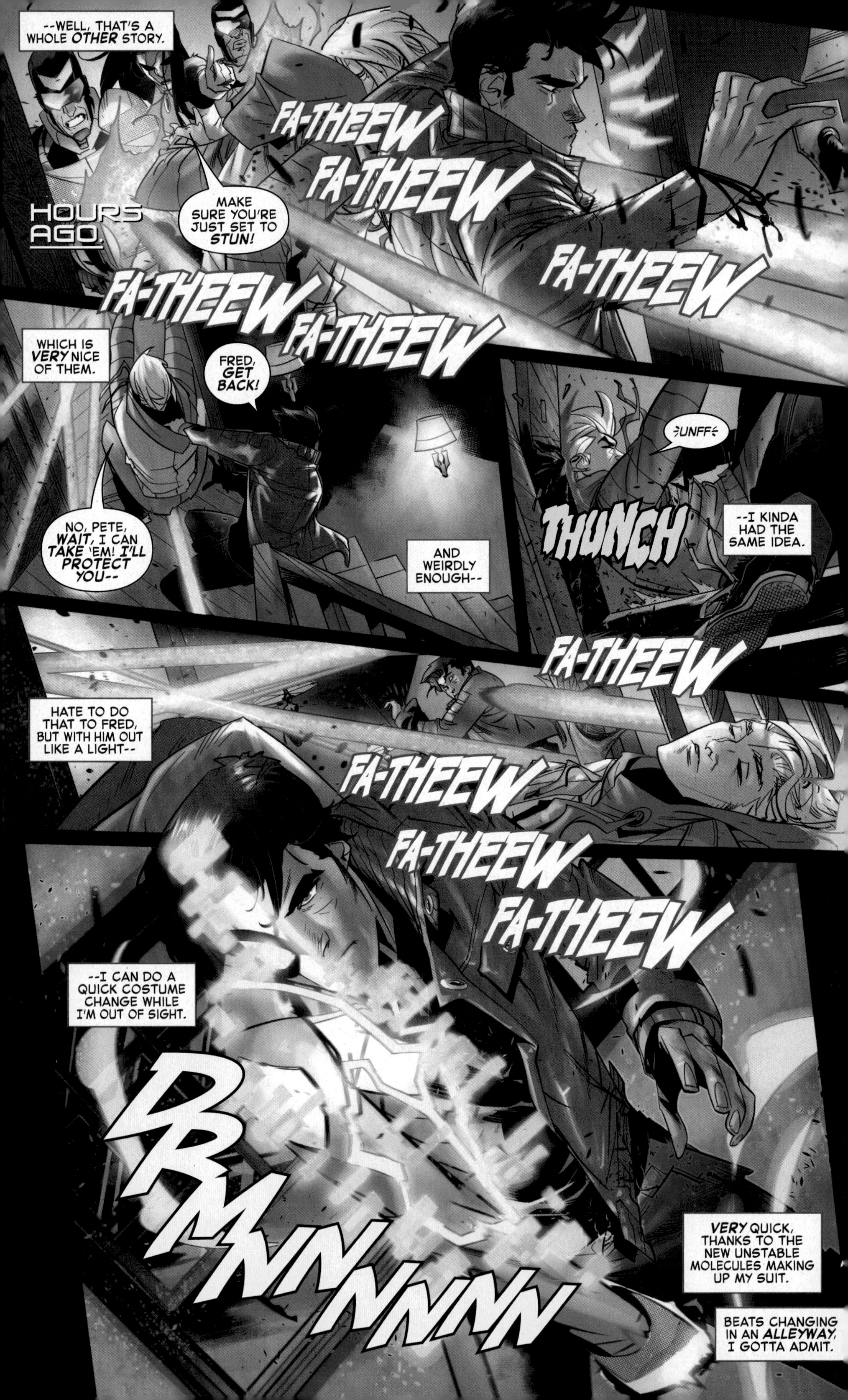

--WELL, THAT'S A WHOLE OTHER STORY.
HOURS AGO.
MAKE SURE YOU'RE JUST SET TO STUN!
FA-THEEW
FA-THEEW
FA-THEEW
FA-THEEW
FA-THEEW
WHICH IS VERY NICE OF THEM.
FRED, GET BACK!
NO, PETE, WAIT, I CAN TAKE 'EM! I'LL PROTECT YOU--
AND WEIRDLY ENOUGH--
UNFF
THUNCH
--I KINDA HAD THE SAME IDEA.
FA-THEEW
HATE TO DO THAT TO FRED, BUT WITH HIM OUT LIKE A LIGHT--
FA-THEEW
FA-THEEW
FA-THEEW
--I CAN DO A QUICK COSTUME CHANGE WHILE I'M OUT OF SIGHT.
DRMNNNNNNN
VERY QUICK, THANKS TO THE NEW UNSTABLE MOLECULES MAKING UP MY SUIT.
BEATS CHANGING IN AN ALLEYWAY, I GOTTA ADMIT.

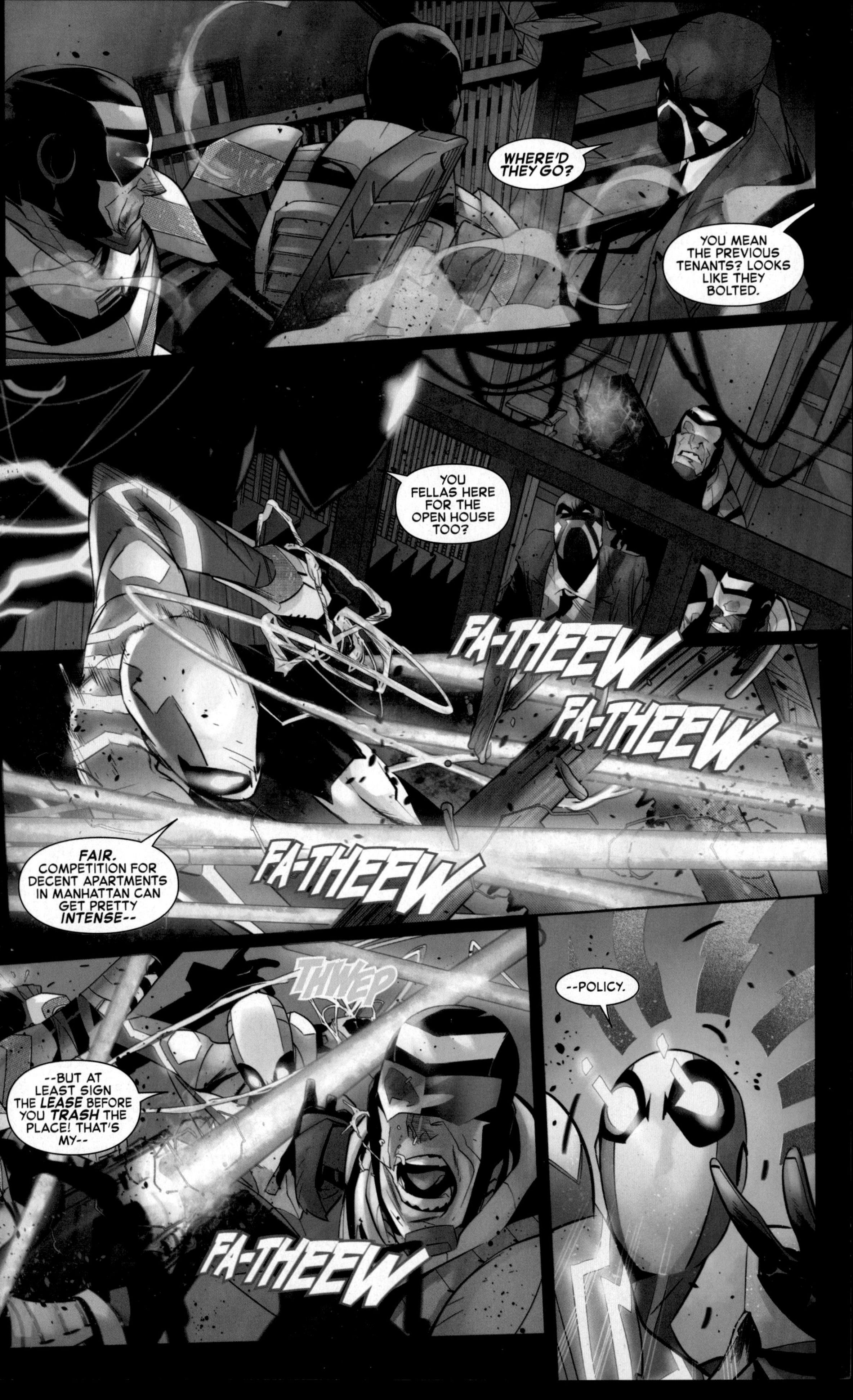
WHERE'D THEY GO?
YOU MEAN THE PREVIOUS TENANTS? LOOKS LIKE THEY BOLTED.
YOU FELLAS HERE FOR THE OPEN HOUSE TOO?
FA-THEEW
FA-THEEW
FAIR. COMPETITION FOR DECENT APARTMENTS IN MANHATTAN CAN GET PRETTY INTENSE--
FA-THEEW
THWEP
--BUT AT LEAST SIGN THE LEASE BEFORE YOU TRASH THE PLACE! THAT'S MY--
FA-THEEW
--POLICY.

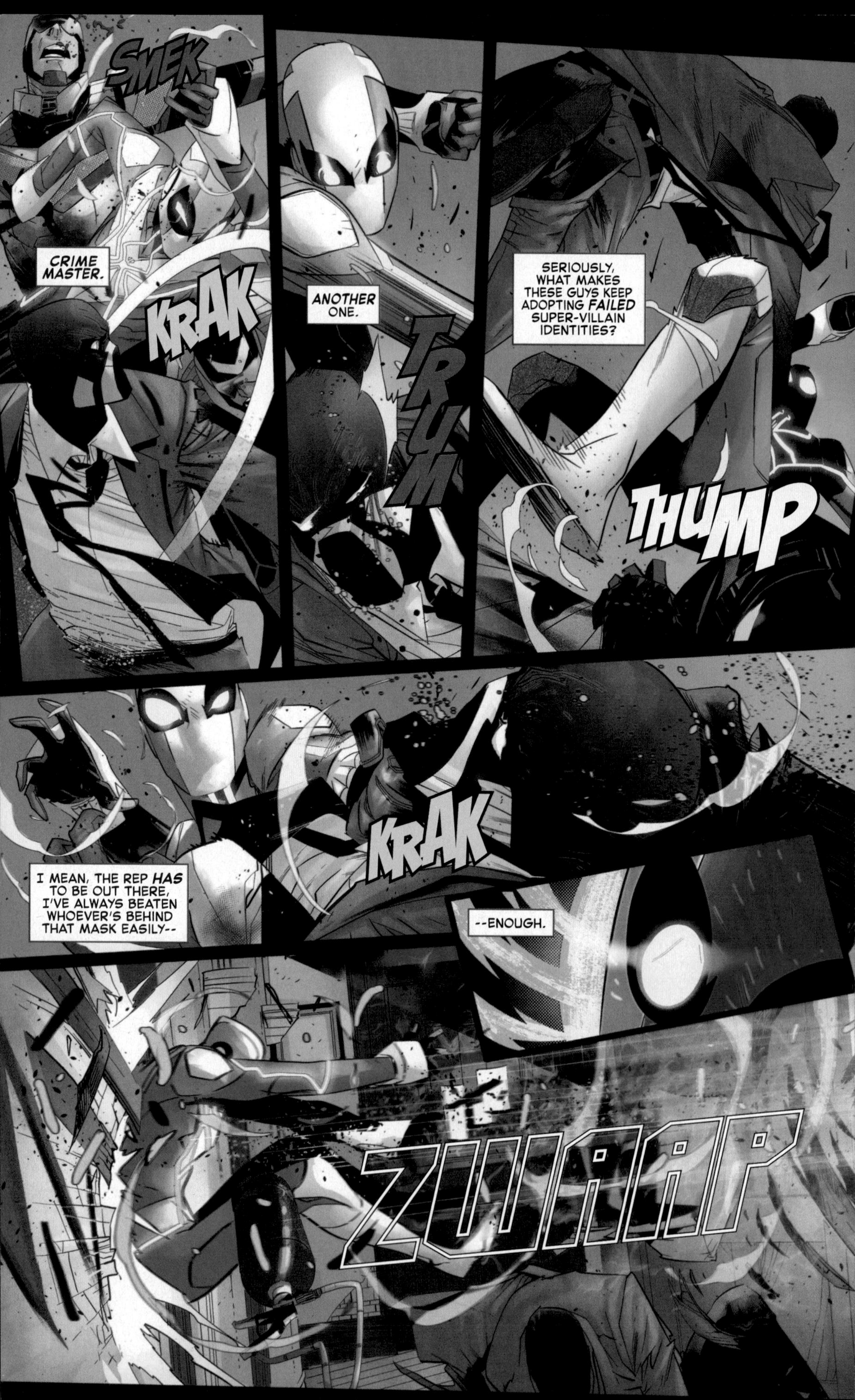
SMEK
CRIME MASTER.
KRAK
ANOTHER ONE.
TRUM
SERIOUSLY, WHAT MAKES THESE GUYS KEEP ADOPTING *FAILED* SUPER-VILLAIN IDENTITIES?
THUMP
I MEAN, THE REP *HAS* TO BE OUT THERE, I'VE ALWAYS BEATEN WHOEVER'S BEHIND THAT MASK EASILY--
KRAK
--ENOUGH.
ZUUAAP

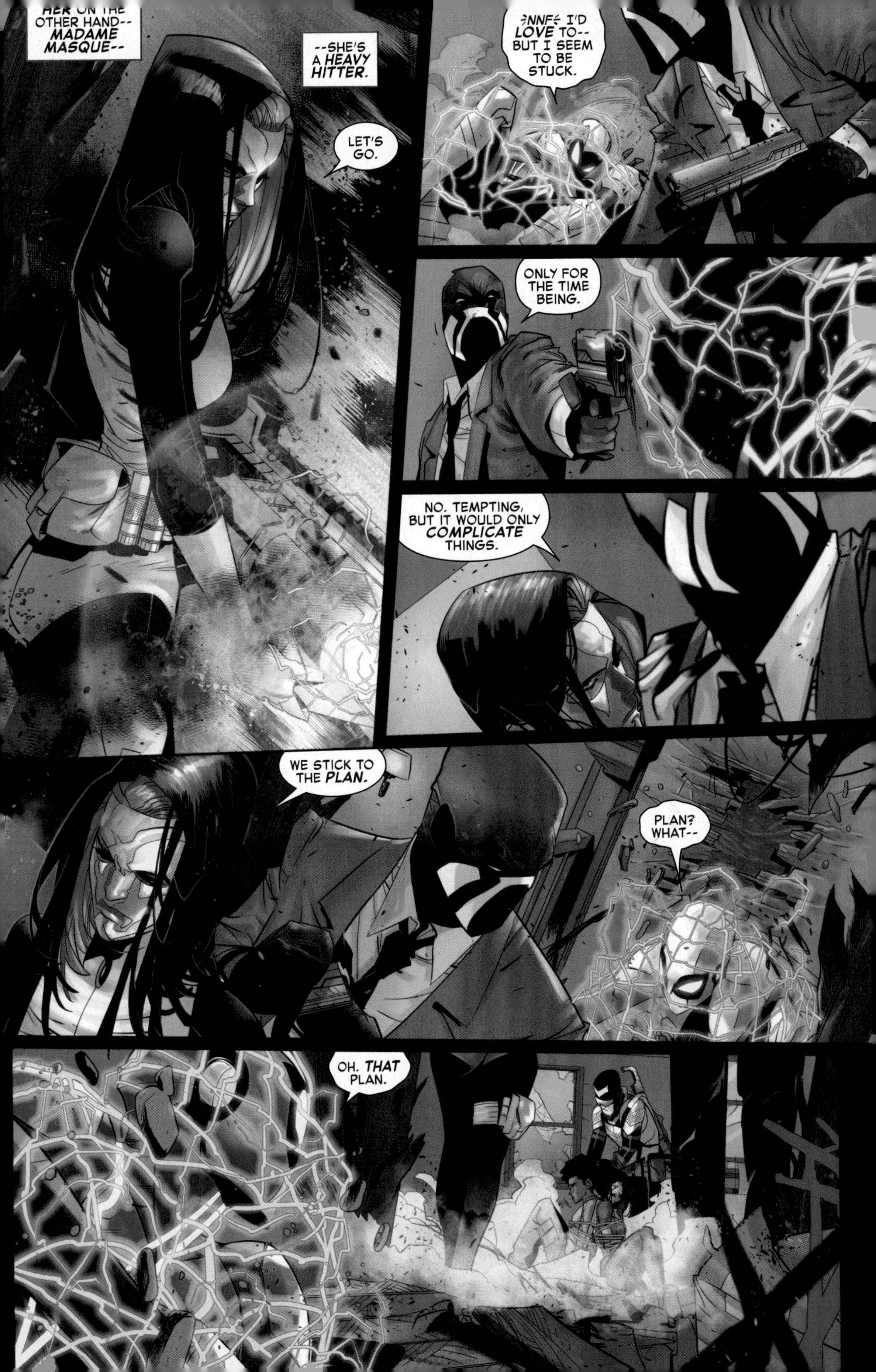
HER ON THE OTHER HAND-- MADAME MASQUE--
--SHE'S A HEAVY HITTER.
LET'S GO.
≶NNF≶ I'D LOVE TO-- BUT I SEEM TO BE STUCK.
ONLY FOR THE TIME BEING.
NO. TEMPTING, BUT IT WOULD ONLY COMPLICATE THINGS.
WE STICK TO THE PLAN.
PLAN? WHAT--
OH. THAT PLAN.

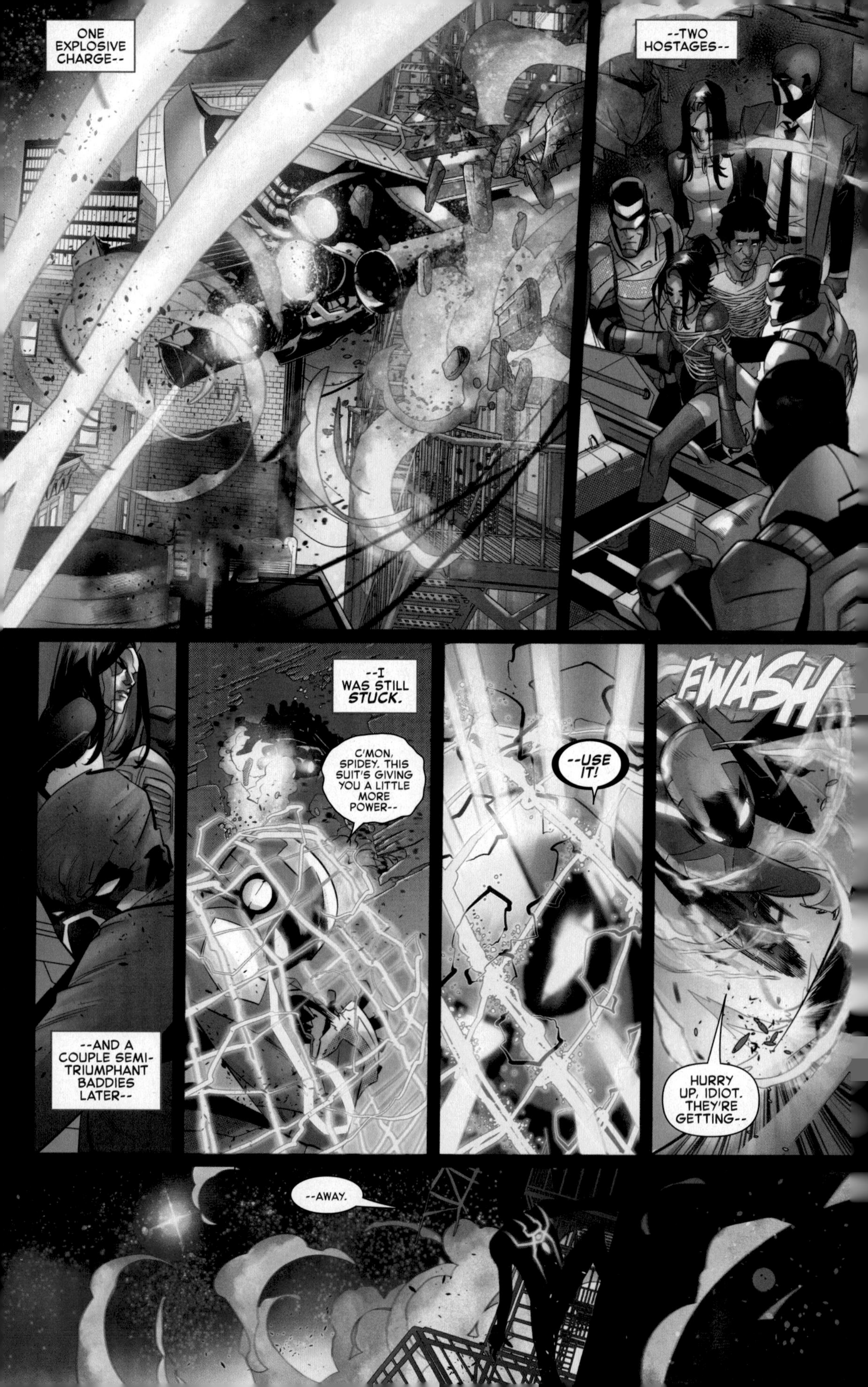

ONE EXPLOSIVE CHARGE--
--TWO HOSTAGES--
--AND A COUPLE SEMI-TRIUMPHANT BADDIES LATER--
--I WAS STILL STUCK.
C'MON, SPIDEY. THIS SUIT'S GIVING YOU A LITTLE MORE POWER--
--USE IT!
FWASH
HURRY UP, IDIOT. THEY'RE GETTING--
--AWAY.

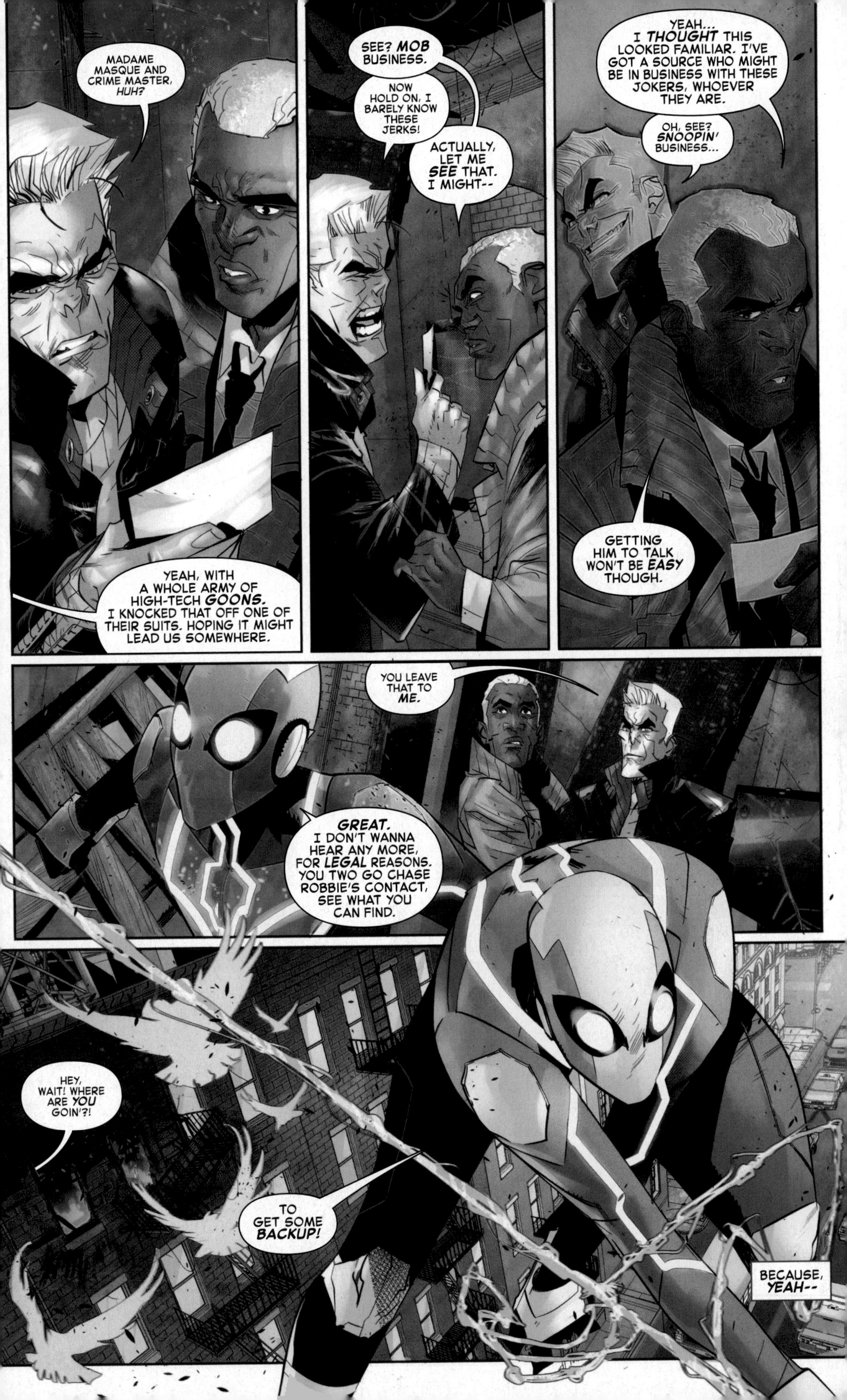
MADAME MASQUE AND CRIME MASTER, *HUH?*
YEAH, WITH A WHOLE ARMY OF HIGH-TECH ***GOONS.*** I KNOCKED THAT OFF ONE OF THEIR SUITS. HOPING IT MIGHT LEAD US SOMEWHERE.
SEE? ***MOB*** BUSINESS.
NOW HOLD ON, I BARELY KNOW THESE JERKS!
ACTUALLY, LET ME ***SEE*** THAT. I MIGHT--
YEAH... I ***THOUGHT*** THIS LOOKED FAMILIAR. I'VE GOT A SOURCE WHO MIGHT BE IN BUSINESS WITH THESE JOKERS, WHOEVER THEY ARE.
OH, SEE? ***SNOOPIN'*** BUSINESS...
GETTING HIM TO TALK WON'T BE ***EASY*** THOUGH.
YOU LEAVE THAT TO ***ME.***
GREAT. I DON'T WANNA HEAR ANY MORE, FOR ***LEGAL*** REASONS. YOU TWO GO CHASE ROBBIE'S CONTACT, SEE WHAT YOU CAN FIND.
HEY, WAIT! WHERE ARE ***YOU*** GOIN'?!
TO GET SOME ***BACKUP!***
BECAUSE, ***YEAH--***

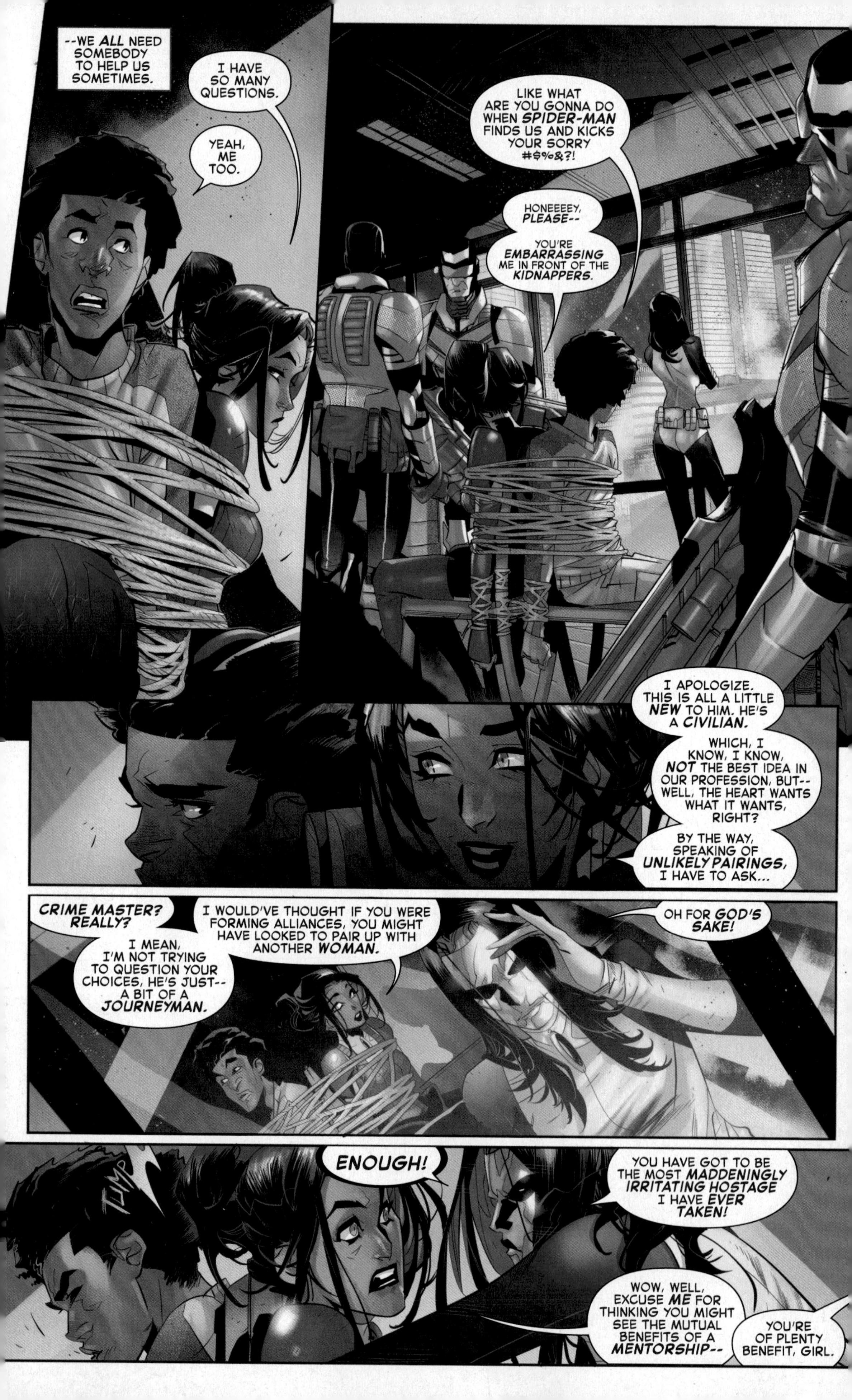
--WE ALL NEED SOMEBODY TO HELP US SOMETIMES.
I HAVE SO MANY QUESTIONS.
YEAH, ME TOO.
LIKE WHAT ARE YOU GONNA DO WHEN SPIDER-MAN FINDS US AND KICKS YOUR SORRY #$%&?!
HONEEEEY, PLEASE--
YOU'RE EMBARRASSING ME IN FRONT OF THE KIDNAPPERS.
I APOLOGIZE. THIS IS ALL A LITTLE NEW TO HIM. HE'S A CIVILIAN.
WHICH, I KNOW, I KNOW, NOT THE BEST IDEA IN OUR PROFESSION, BUT--WELL, THE HEART WANTS WHAT IT WANTS, RIGHT?
BY THE WAY, SPEAKING OF UNLIKELY PAIRINGS, I HAVE TO ASK...
CRIME MASTER? REALLY?
I MEAN, I'M NOT TRYING TO QUESTION YOUR CHOICES, HE'S JUST--A BIT OF A JOURNEYMAN.
I WOULD'VE THOUGHT IF YOU WERE FORMING ALLIANCES, YOU MIGHT HAVE LOOKED TO PAIR UP WITH ANOTHER WOMAN.
OH FOR GOD'S SAKE!
TUMP
ENOUGH!
YOU HAVE GOT TO BE THE MOST MADDENINGLY IRRITATING HOSTAGE I HAVE EVER TAKEN!
WOW, WELL, EXCUSE ME FOR THINKING YOU MIGHT SEE THE MUTUAL BENEFITS OF A MENTORSHIP--
YOU'RE OF PLENTY BENEFIT, GIRL.

THE TWO OF YOU REPRESENT QUITE THE *WINDFALL* FOR US, I'M HAPPY TO REPORT.

WELL, YOU GUYS ARE OUTTA LUCK. I AM COMPLETELY OUT OF THE LOOP ON FRED AND PETE'S WHOLE *TABLET SCAVENGER HUNT* THING.

WE DON'T CARE ABOUT THE TABLET.

WAIT--YOU *DON'T*?

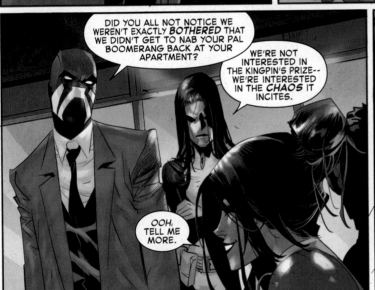

DID YOU ALL NOT NOTICE WE WEREN'T EXACTLY *BOTHERED* THAT WE DIDN'T GET TO NAB YOUR PAL BOOMERANG BACK AT YOUR APARTMENT?

WE'RE NOT INTERESTED IN THE KINGPIN'S PRIZE-- WE'RE INTERESTED IN THE *CHAOS* IT INCITES.

OOH, TELL ME MORE.

I MEAN-- *YOU'LL NEVER GET AWAY WITH THIS!*

ACTUALLY, THIS IS THE *ONE TIME* WE *WILL.* SEE, MAYOR FISK RUNS A TIGHT SHIP. NO TURF WARS OR POWER GRABS TOLERATED IN THE CRIMINAL UNDERWORLD.

WHICH IS A PROBLEM FOR AN UP-AND-COMER LIKE *ME.*

OR SOMEONE WHOSE FAMILY'S PRIMARY HOLDINGS ARE A BIT TOO FOCUSED ON THE *WEST COAST,* LIKE MYSELF.

BUT NOW THAT THE KINGPIN IS LETTING *EVERYBODY* IN ON THE CHASE, COMPETITIVE SPIRITS ARE GONNA RUN HIGH AND ALL.

AND *WITH* THEM, CONSIDERABLY MORE PERMISSIVENESS WHEN IT COMES TO *BLOODSHED.*

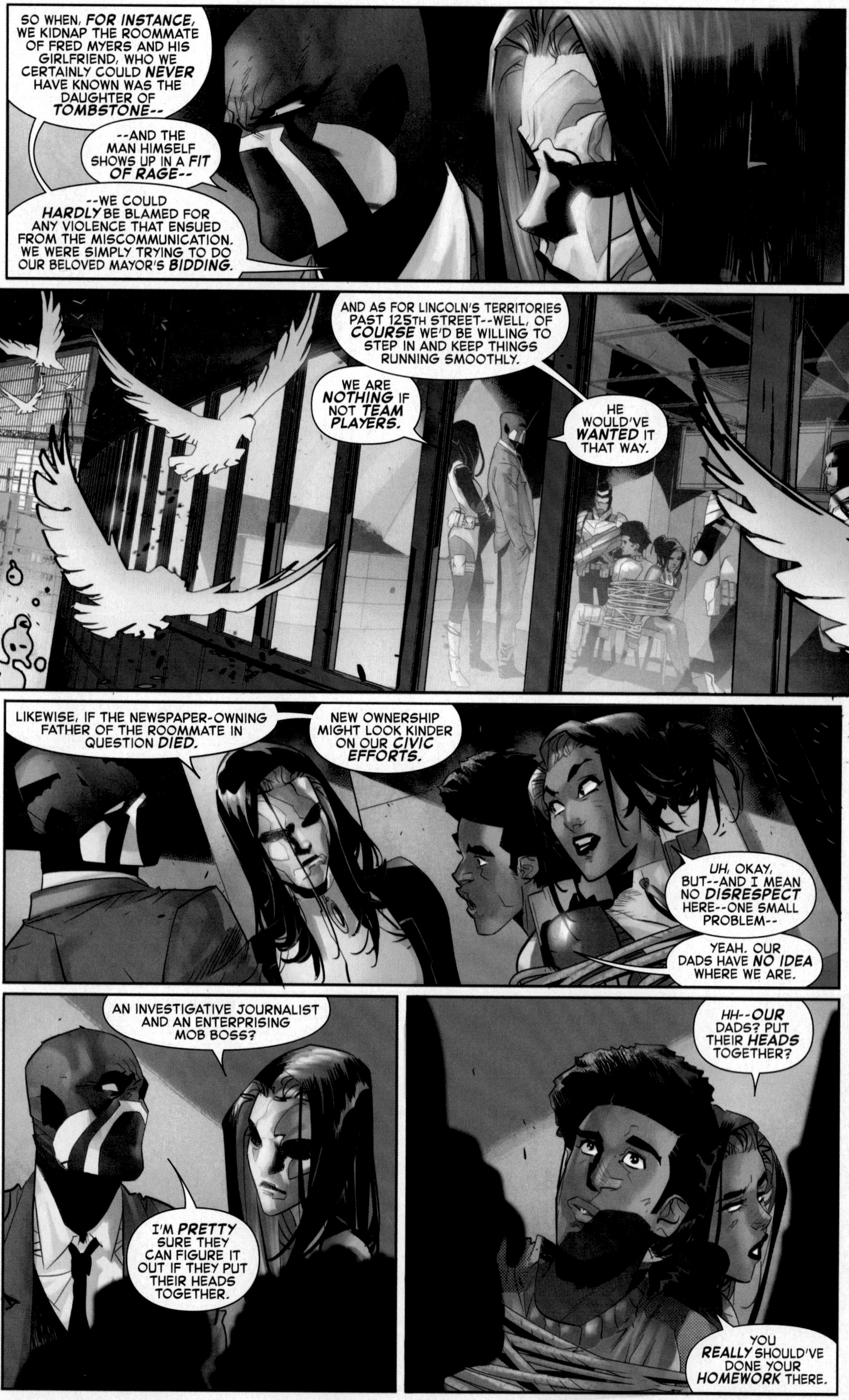
SO WHEN, FOR INSTANCE, WE KIDNAP THE ROOMMATE OF FRED MYERS AND HIS GIRLFRIEND, WHO WE CERTAINLY COULD NEVER HAVE KNOWN WAS THE DAUGHTER OF TOMBSTONE--
--AND THE MAN HIMSELF SHOWS UP IN A FIT OF RAGE--
--WE COULD HARDLY BE BLAMED FOR ANY VIOLENCE THAT ENSUED FROM THE MISCOMMUNICATION. WE WERE SIMPLY TRYING TO DO OUR BELOVED MAYOR'S BIDDING.
AND AS FOR LINCOLN'S TERRITORIES PAST 125TH STREET--WELL, OF COURSE WE'D BE WILLING TO STEP IN AND KEEP THINGS RUNNING SMOOTHLY.
WE ARE NOTHING IF NOT TEAM PLAYERS.
HE WOULD'VE WANTED IT THAT WAY.
LIKEWISE, IF THE NEWSPAPER-OWNING FATHER OF THE ROOMMATE IN QUESTION DIED.
NEW OWNERSHIP MIGHT LOOK KINDER ON OUR CIVIC EFFORTS.
UH, OKAY, BUT--AND I MEAN NO DISRESPECT HERE--ONE SMALL PROBLEM--
YEAH. OUR DADS HAVE NO IDEA WHERE WE ARE.
AN INVESTIGATIVE JOURNALIST AND AN ENTERPRISING MOB BOSS?
I'M PRETTY SURE THEY CAN FIGURE IT OUT IF THEY PUT THEIR HEADS TOGETHER.
HH--OUR DADS? PUT THEIR HEADS TOGETHER?
YOU REALLY SHOULD'VE DONE YOUR HOMEWORK THERE.

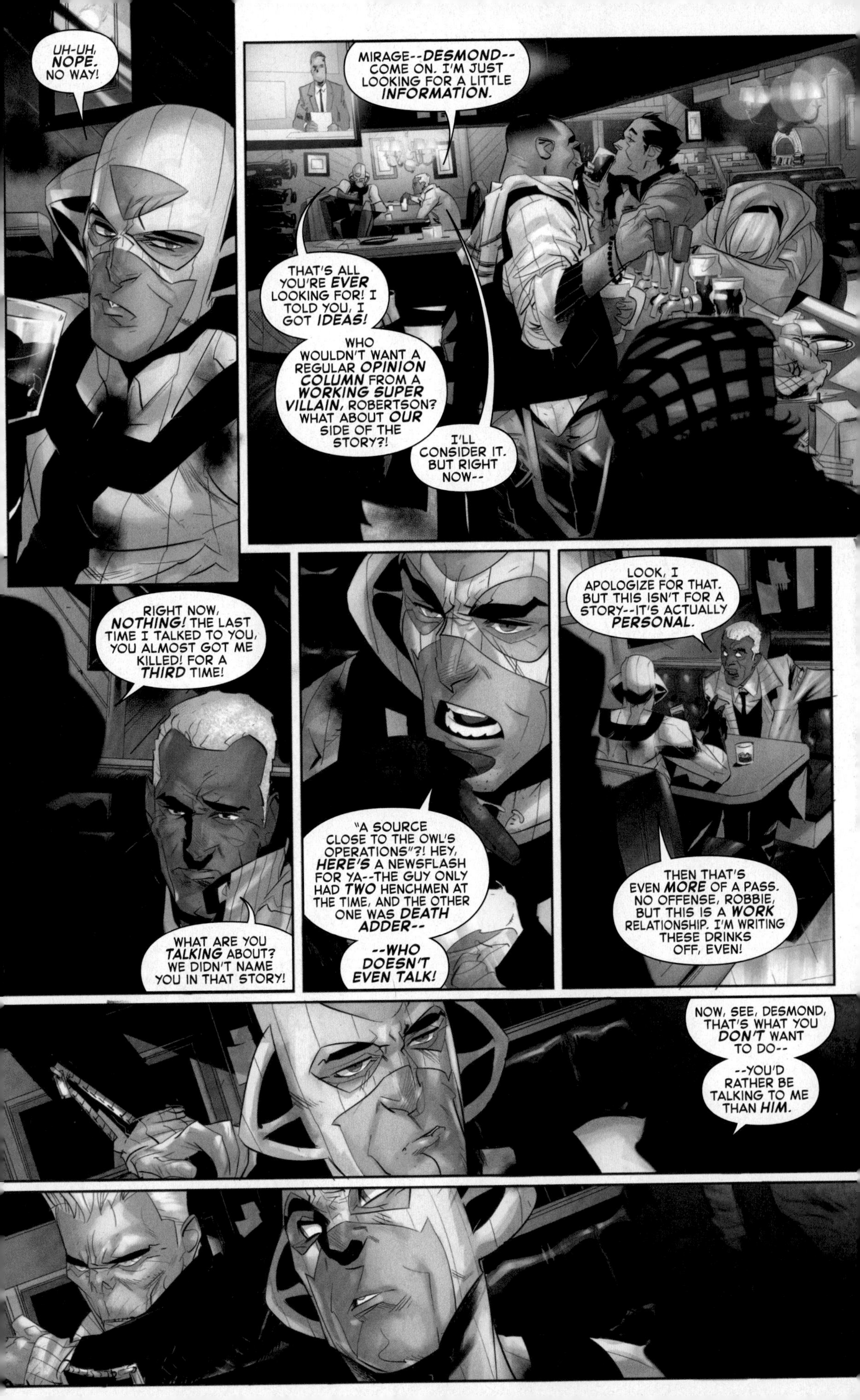
UH-UH, NOPE. NO WAY!
MIRAGE--DESMOND-- COME ON. I'M JUST LOOKING FOR A LITTLE INFORMATION.
THAT'S ALL YOU'RE EVER LOOKING FOR! I TOLD YOU, I GOT IDEAS!
WHO WOULDN'T WANT A REGULAR OPINION COLUMN FROM A WORKING SUPER VILLAIN, ROBERTSON? WHAT ABOUT OUR SIDE OF THE STORY?!
I'LL CONSIDER IT. BUT RIGHT NOW--
RIGHT NOW, NOTHING! THE LAST TIME I TALKED TO YOU, YOU ALMOST GOT ME KILLED! FOR A THIRD TIME!
WHAT ARE YOU TALKING ABOUT? WE DIDN'T NAME YOU IN THAT STORY!
"A SOURCE CLOSE TO THE OWL'S OPERATIONS"?! HEY, HERE'S A NEWSFLASH FOR YA--THE GUY ONLY HAD TWO HENCHMEN AT THE TIME, AND THE OTHER ONE WAS DEATH ADDER--
--WHO DOESN'T EVEN TALK!
LOOK, I APOLOGIZE FOR THAT. BUT THIS ISN'T FOR A STORY--IT'S ACTUALLY PERSONAL.
THEN THAT'S EVEN MORE OF A PASS. NO OFFENSE, ROBBIE, BUT THIS IS A WORK RELATIONSHIP. I'M WRITING THESE DRINKS OFF, EVEN!
NOW, SEE, DESMOND, THAT'S WHAT YOU DON'T WANT TO DO--
--YOU'D RATHER BE TALKING TO ME THAN HIM.

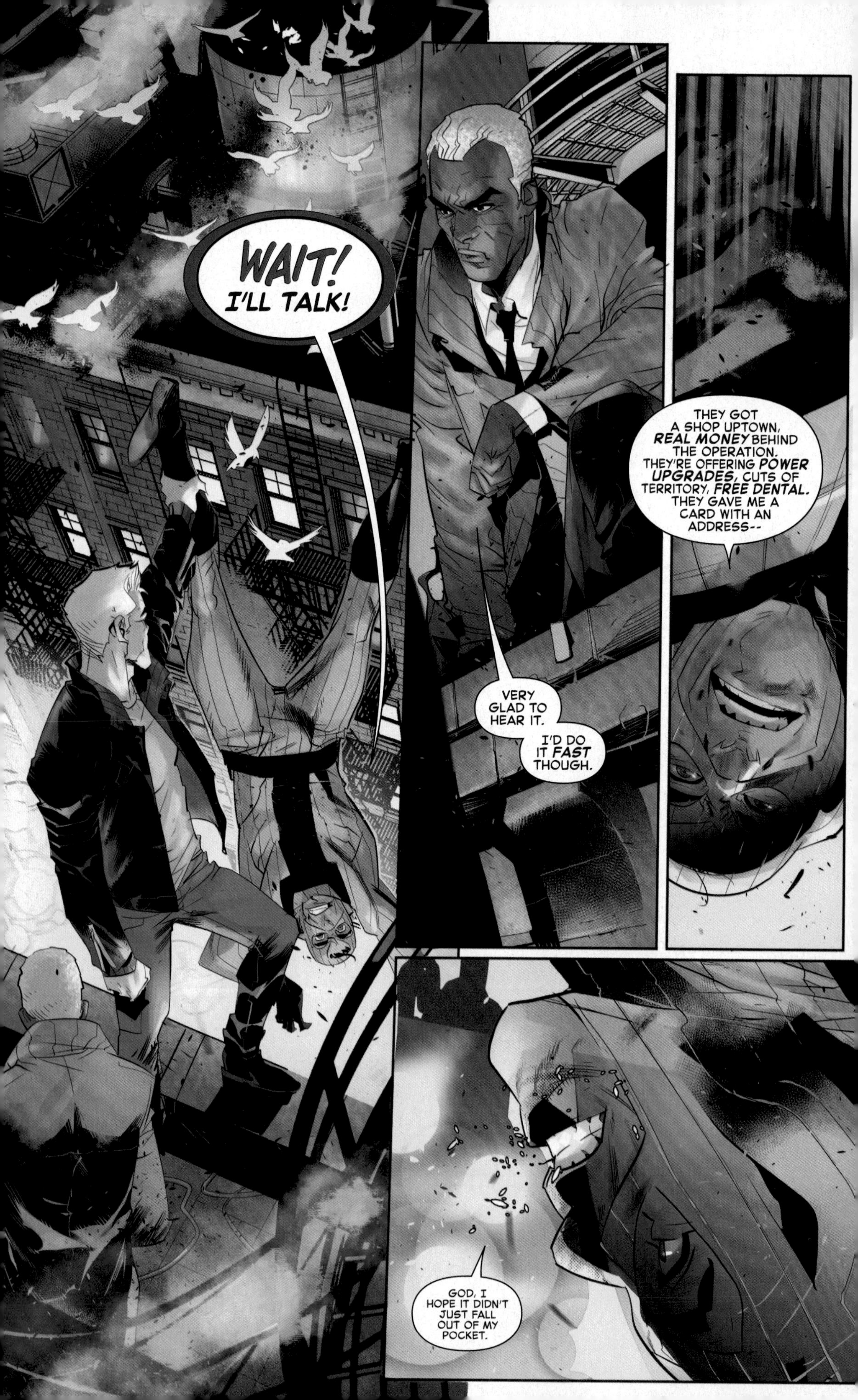
WAIT! I'LL TALK!
VERY GLAD TO HEAR IT.
I'D DO IT FAST THOUGH.
THEY GOT A SHOP UPTOWN, REAL MONEY BEHIND THE OPERATION. THEY'RE OFFERING POWER UPGRADES, CUTS OF TERRITORY, FREE DENTAL. THEY GAVE ME A CARD WITH AN ADDRESS--
GOD, I HOPE IT DIDN'T JUST FALL OUT OF MY POCKET.

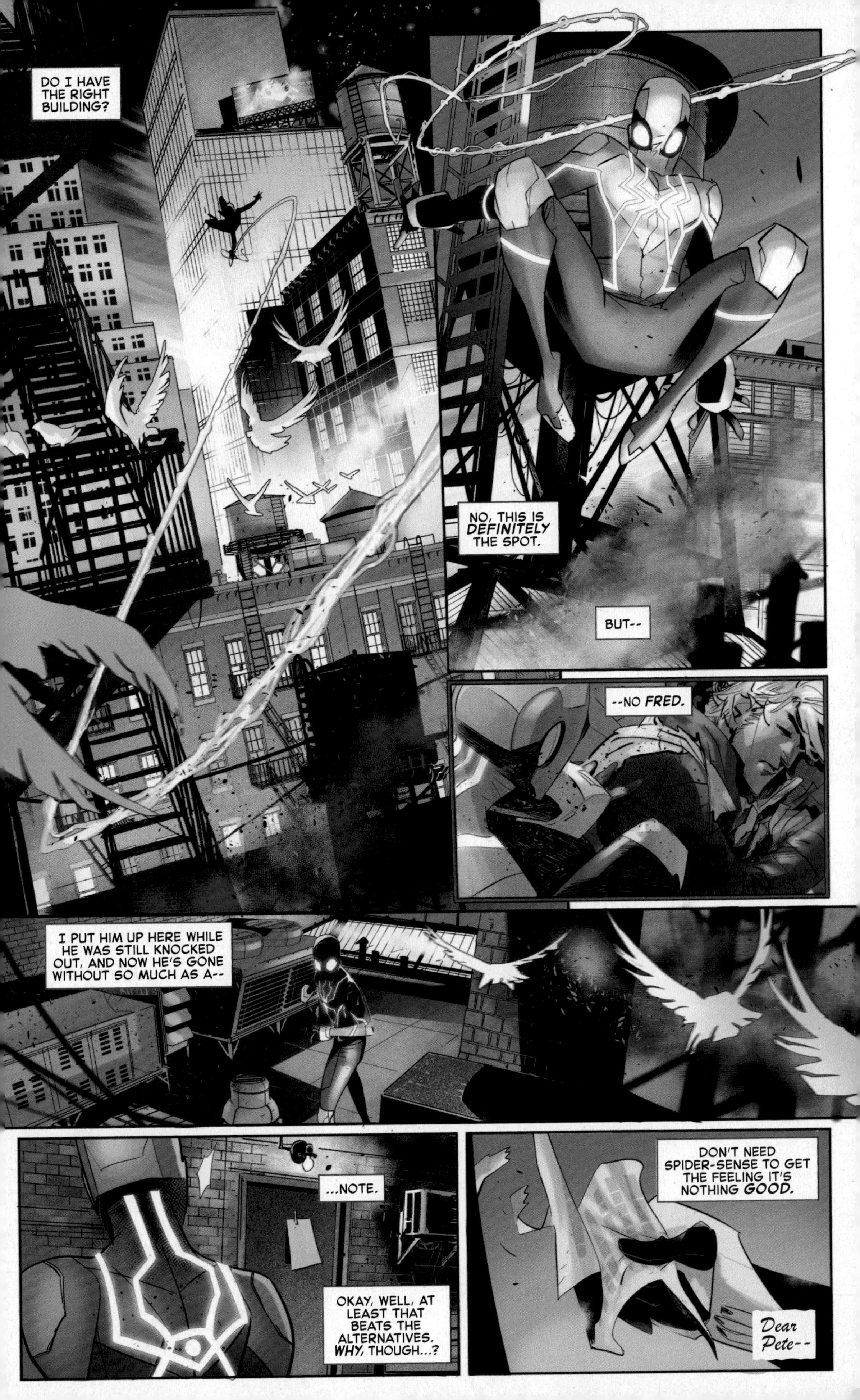
DO I HAVE THE RIGHT BUILDING?
NO, THIS IS DEFINITELY THE SPOT.
BUT--
--NO FRED.
I PUT HIM UP HERE WHILE HE WAS STILL KNOCKED OUT, AND NOW HE'S GONE WITHOUT SO MUCH AS A--
...NOTE.
OKAY, WELL, AT LEAST THAT BEATS THE ALTERNATIVES. WHY, THOUGH...?
DON'T NEED SPIDER-SENSE TO GET THE FEELING IT'S NOTHING GOOD.
Dear Pete--

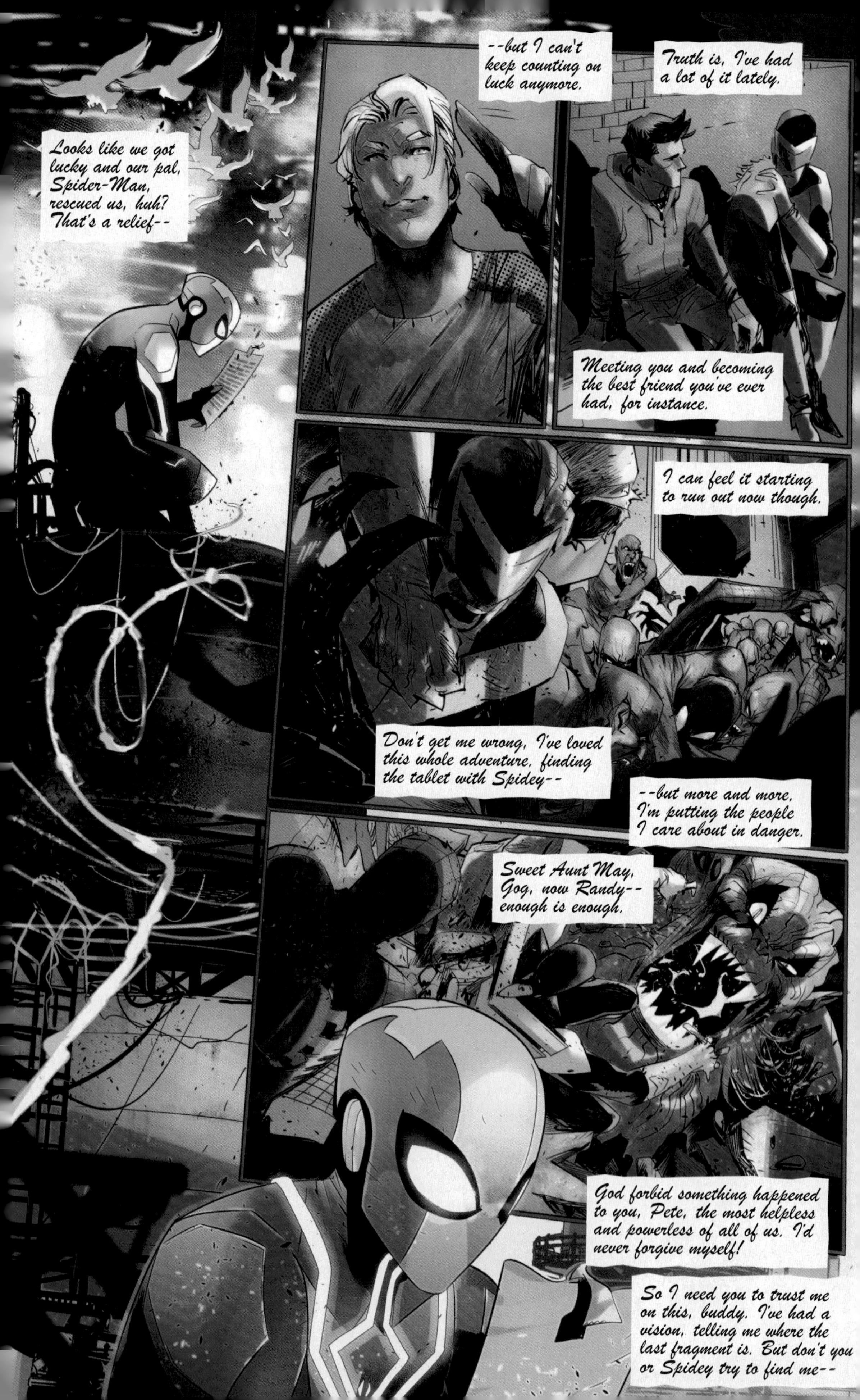

Looks like we got lucky and our pal, Spider-Man, rescued us, huh? That's a relief--
--but I can't keep counting on luck anymore.
Truth is, I've had a lot of it lately.
Meeting you and becoming the best friend you've ever had, for instance.
I can feel it starting to run out now though.
Don't get me wrong, I've loved this whole adventure, finding the tablet with Spidey--
--but more and more, I'm putting the people I care about in danger.
Sweet Aunt May, Gog, now Randy-- enough is enough.
God forbid something happened to you, Pete, the most helpless and powerless of all of us. I'd never forgive myself!
So I need you to trust me on this, buddy. I've had a vision, telling me where the last fragment is. But don't you or Spidey try to find me--

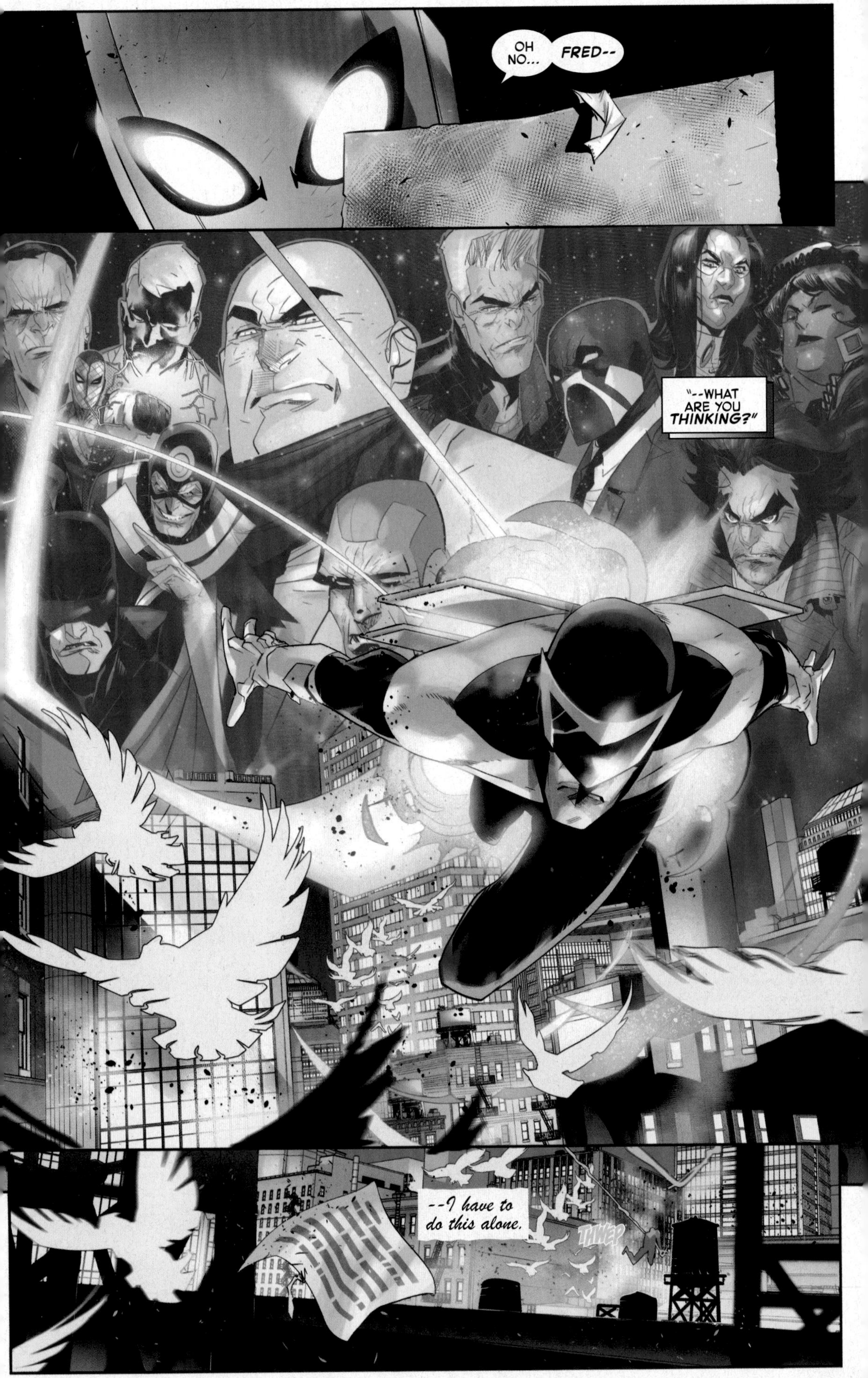
OH NO...
FRED--
"--WHAT ARE YOU THINKING?"
--I have to do this alone.
THWIP

65

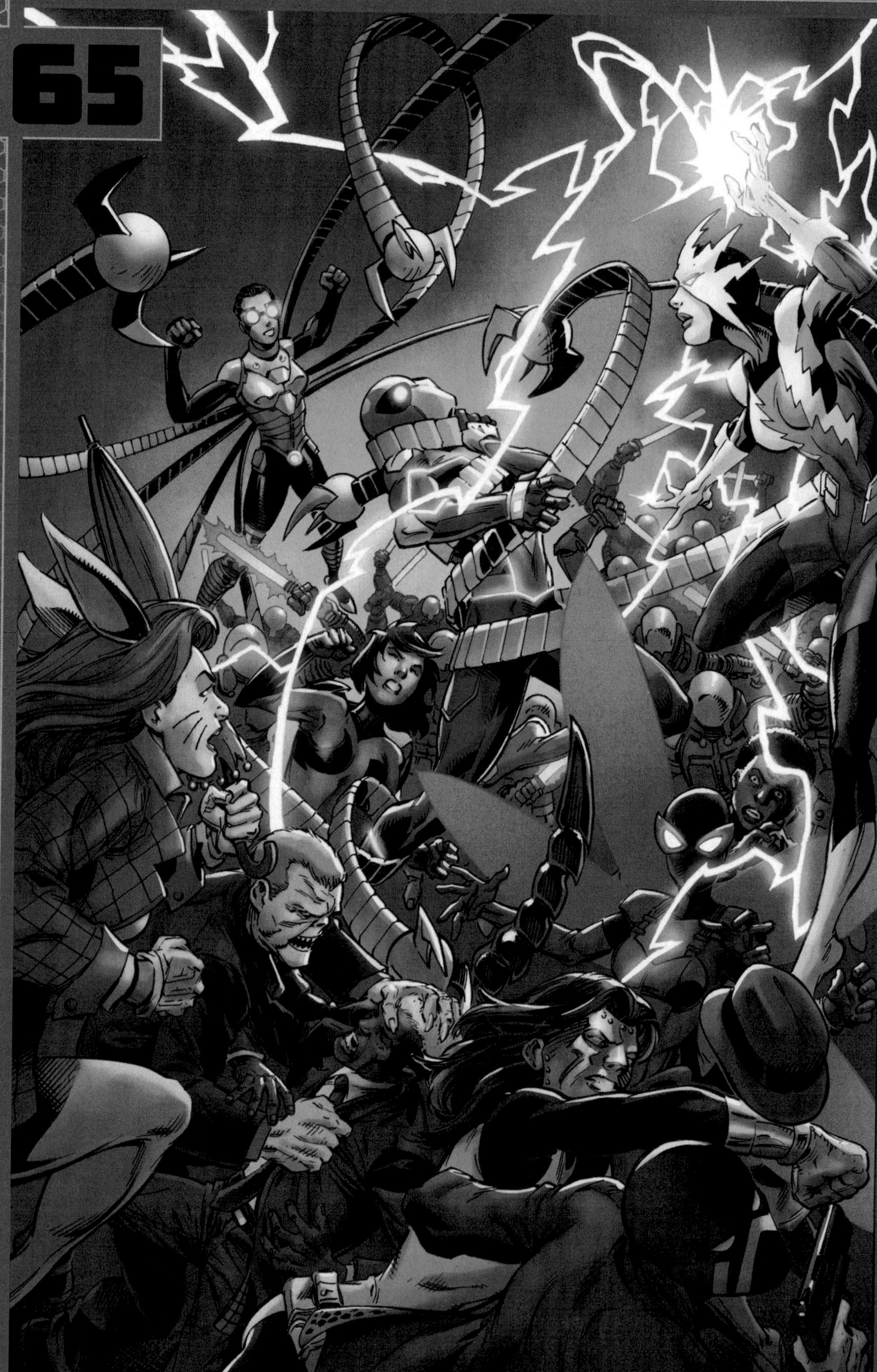

KING'S RANSOM PART 3

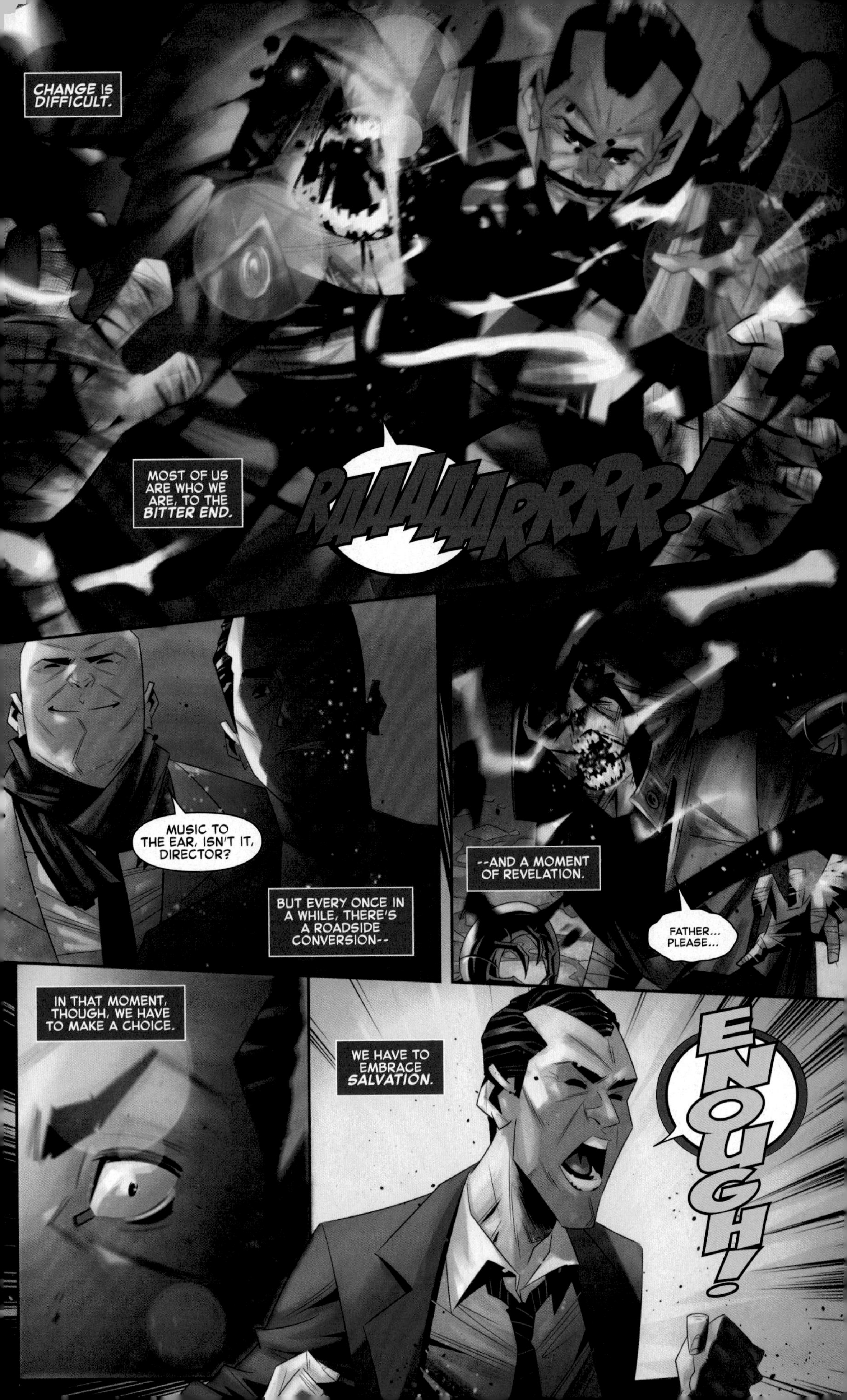
CHANGE IS DIFFICULT.
MOST OF US ARE WHO WE ARE, TO THE BITTER END.
RAAAAARRRR!
MUSIC TO THE EAR, ISN'T IT, DIRECTOR?
BUT EVERY ONCE IN A WHILE, THERE'S A ROADSIDE CONVERSION--
--AND A MOMENT OF REVELATION.
FATHER... PLEASE...
IN THAT MOMENT, THOUGH, WE HAVE TO MAKE A CHOICE.
WE HAVE TO EMBRACE SALVATION.
ENOUGH!

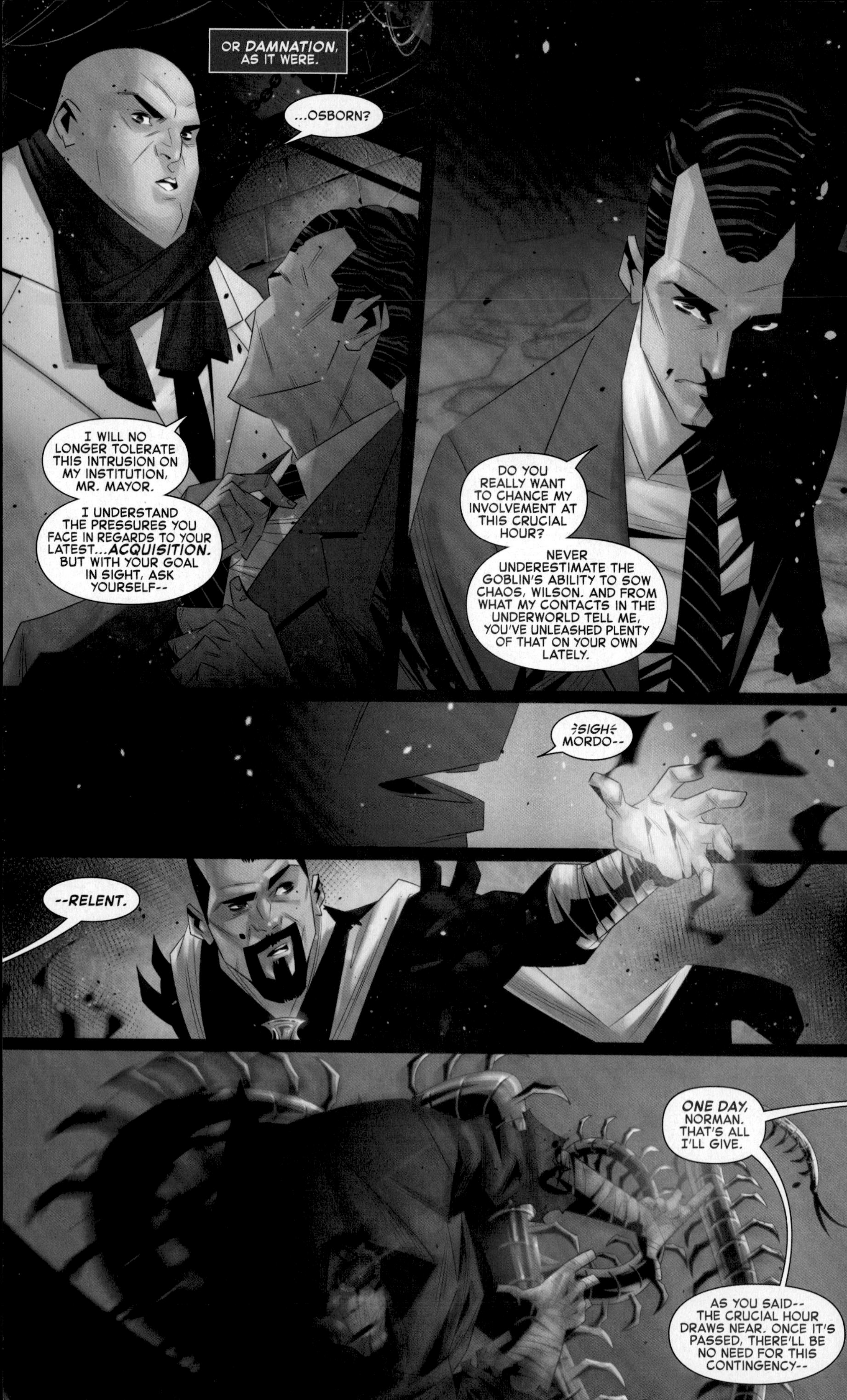

OR DAMNATION, AS IT WERE.
...OSBORN?
I WILL NO LONGER TOLERATE THIS INTRUSION ON MY INSTITUTION, MR. MAYOR.
I UNDERSTAND THE PRESSURES YOU FACE IN REGARDS TO YOUR LATEST...ACQUISITION. BUT WITH YOUR GOAL IN SIGHT, ASK YOURSELF--
DO YOU REALLY WANT TO CHANCE MY INVOLVEMENT AT THIS CRUCIAL HOUR?
NEVER UNDERESTIMATE THE GOBLIN'S ABILITY TO SOW CHAOS, WILSON. AND FROM WHAT MY CONTACTS IN THE UNDERWORLD TELL ME, YOU'VE UNLEASHED PLENTY OF THAT ON YOUR OWN LATELY.
SIGH MORDO--
--RELENT.
ONE DAY, NORMAN. THAT'S ALL I'LL GIVE.
AS YOU SAID-- THE CRUCIAL HOUR DRAWS NEAR. ONCE IT'S PASSED, THERE'LL BE NO NEED FOR THIS CONTINGENCY--

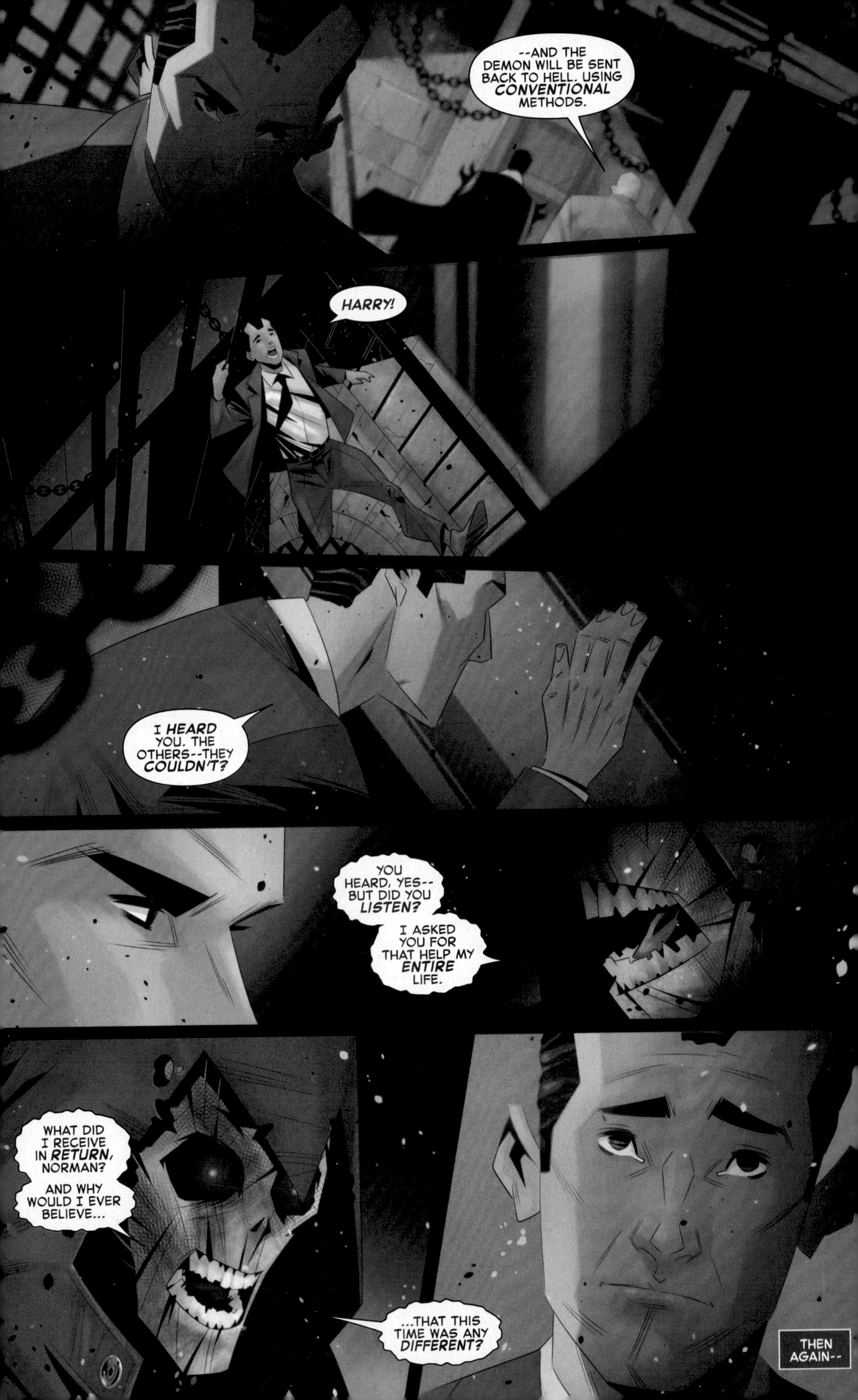
--AND THE DEMON WILL BE SENT BACK TO HELL. USING CONVENTIONAL METHODS.
HARRY!
I HEARD YOU. THE OTHERS--THEY COULDN'T?
YOU HEARD, YES--BUT DID YOU LISTEN?
I ASKED YOU FOR THAT HELP MY ENTIRE LIFE.
WHAT DID I RECEIVE IN RETURN, NORMAN?
AND WHY WOULD I EVER BELIEVE...
...THAT THIS TIME WAS ANY DIFFERENT?
THEN AGAIN--

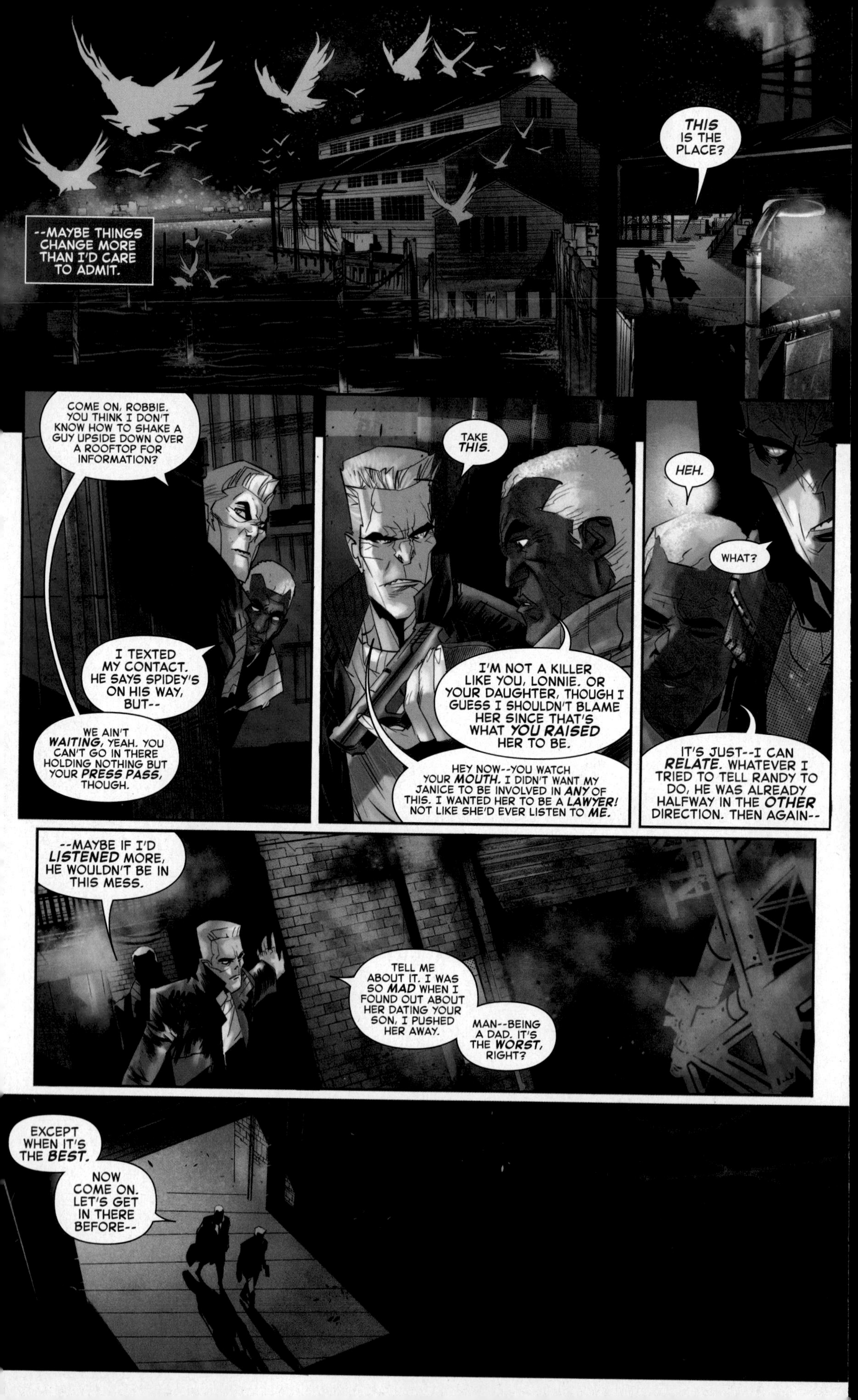
--MAYBE THINGS CHANGE MORE THAN I'D CARE TO ADMIT.
THIS IS THE PLACE?
COME ON, ROBBIE. YOU THINK I DON'T KNOW HOW TO SHAKE A GUY UPSIDE DOWN OVER A ROOFTOP FOR INFORMATION?
I TEXTED MY CONTACT. HE SAYS SPIDEY'S ON HIS WAY, BUT--
WE AIN'T WAITING, YEAH. YOU CAN'T GO IN THERE HOLDING NOTHING BUT YOUR PRESS PASS, THOUGH.
TAKE THIS.
I'M NOT A KILLER LIKE YOU, LONNIE. OR YOUR DAUGHTER, THOUGH I GUESS I SHOULDN'T BLAME HER SINCE THAT'S WHAT YOU RAISED HER TO BE.
HEY NOW--YOU WATCH YOUR MOUTH. I DIDN'T WANT MY JANICE TO BE INVOLVED IN ANY OF THIS. I WANTED HER TO BE A LAWYER! NOT LIKE SHE'D EVER LISTEN TO ME.
HEH.
WHAT?
IT'S JUST--I CAN RELATE. WHATEVER I TRIED TO TELL RANDY TO DO, HE WAS ALREADY HALFWAY IN THE OTHER DIRECTION. THEN AGAIN--
--MAYBE IF I'D LISTENED MORE, HE WOULDN'T BE IN THIS MESS.
TELL ME ABOUT IT. I WAS SO MAD WHEN I FOUND OUT ABOUT HER DATING YOUR SON, I PUSHED HER AWAY.
MAN--BEING A DAD. IT'S THE WORST, RIGHT?
EXCEPT WHEN IT'S THE BEST.
NOW COME ON. LET'S GET IN THERE BEFORE--

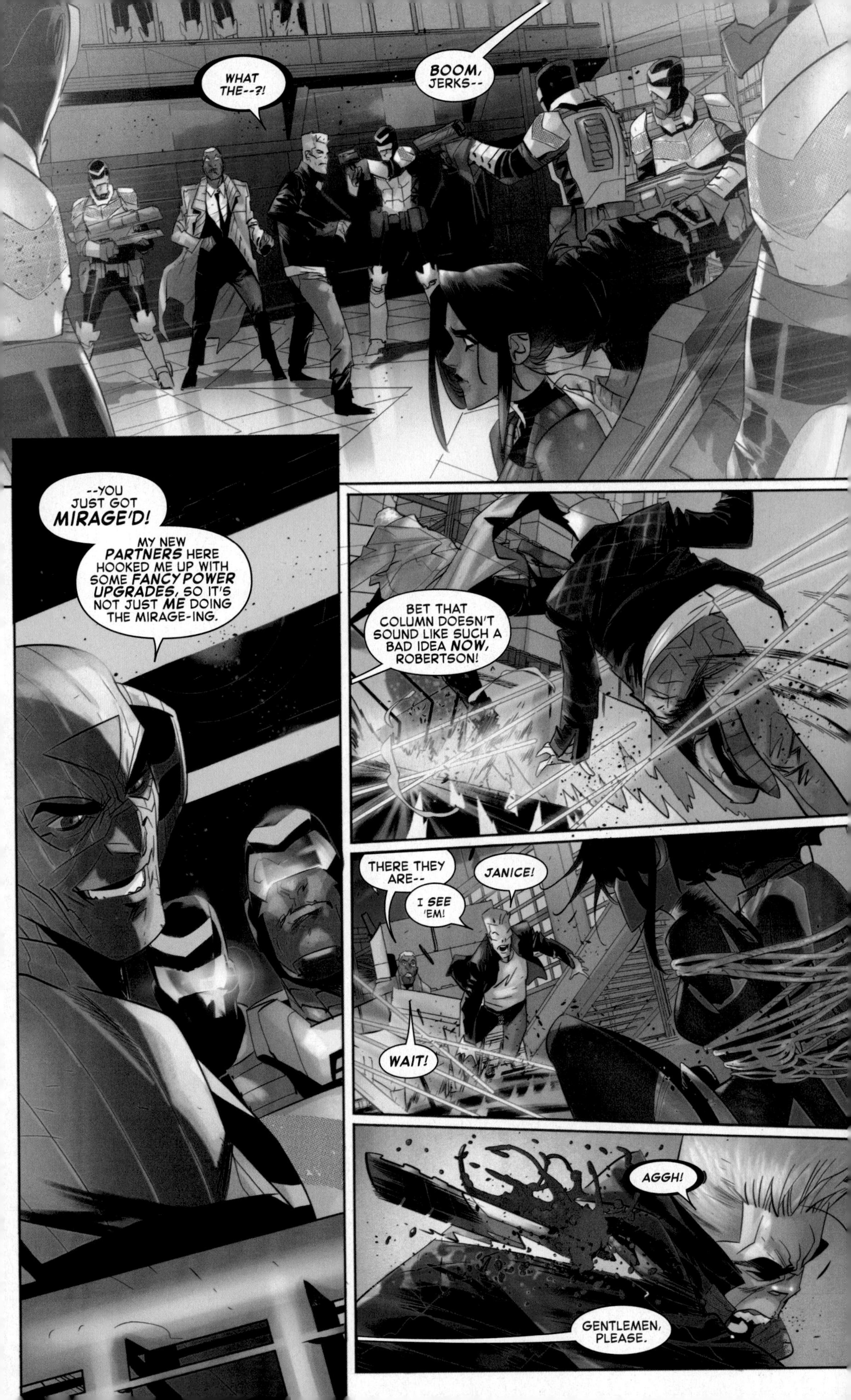
WHAT THE--?!
BOOM, JERKS--
--YOU JUST GOT MIRAGE'D!
MY NEW PARTNERS HERE HOOKED ME UP WITH SOME FANCY POWER UPGRADES, SO IT'S NOT JUST ME DOING THE MIRAGE-ING.
BET THAT COLUMN DOESN'T SOUND LIKE SUCH A BAD IDEA NOW, ROBERTSON!
THERE THEY ARE--
JANICE!
I SEE 'EM!
WAIT!
AGGH!
GENTLEMEN, PLEASE.

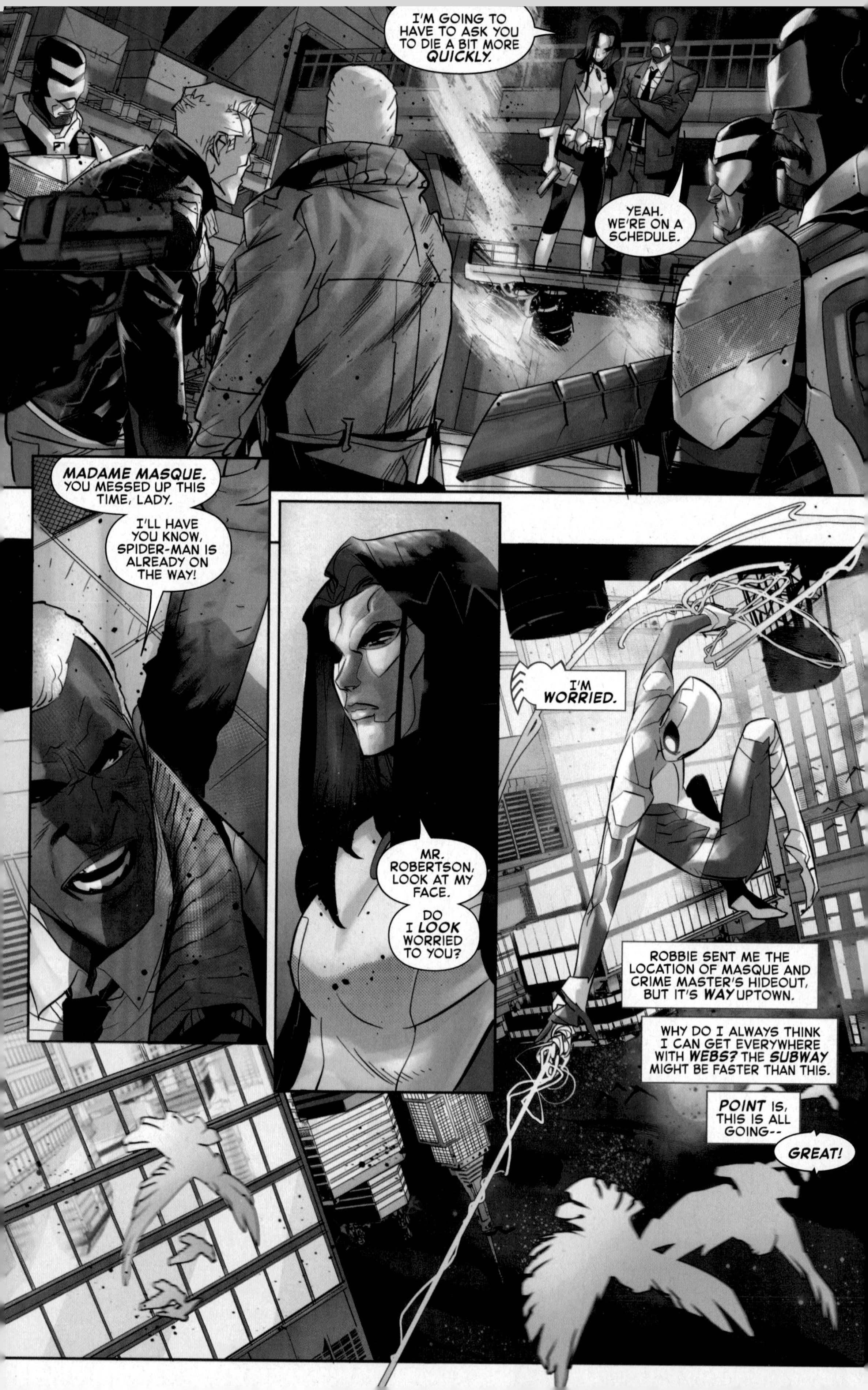
I'M GOING TO HAVE TO ASK YOU TO DIE A BIT MORE QUICKLY.
YEAH. WE'RE ON A SCHEDULE.
MADAME MASQUE. YOU MESSED UP THIS TIME, LADY.
I'LL HAVE YOU KNOW, SPIDER-MAN IS ALREADY ON THE WAY!
MR. ROBERTSON, LOOK AT MY FACE.
DO I LOOK WORRIED TO YOU?
I'M WORRIED.
ROBBIE SENT ME THE LOCATION OF MASQUE AND CRIME MASTER'S HIDEOUT, BUT IT'S WAY UPTOWN.
WHY DO I ALWAYS THINK I CAN GET EVERYWHERE WITH WEBS? THE SUBWAY MIGHT BE FASTER THAN THIS.
POINT IS, THIS IS ALL GOING--
GREAT!

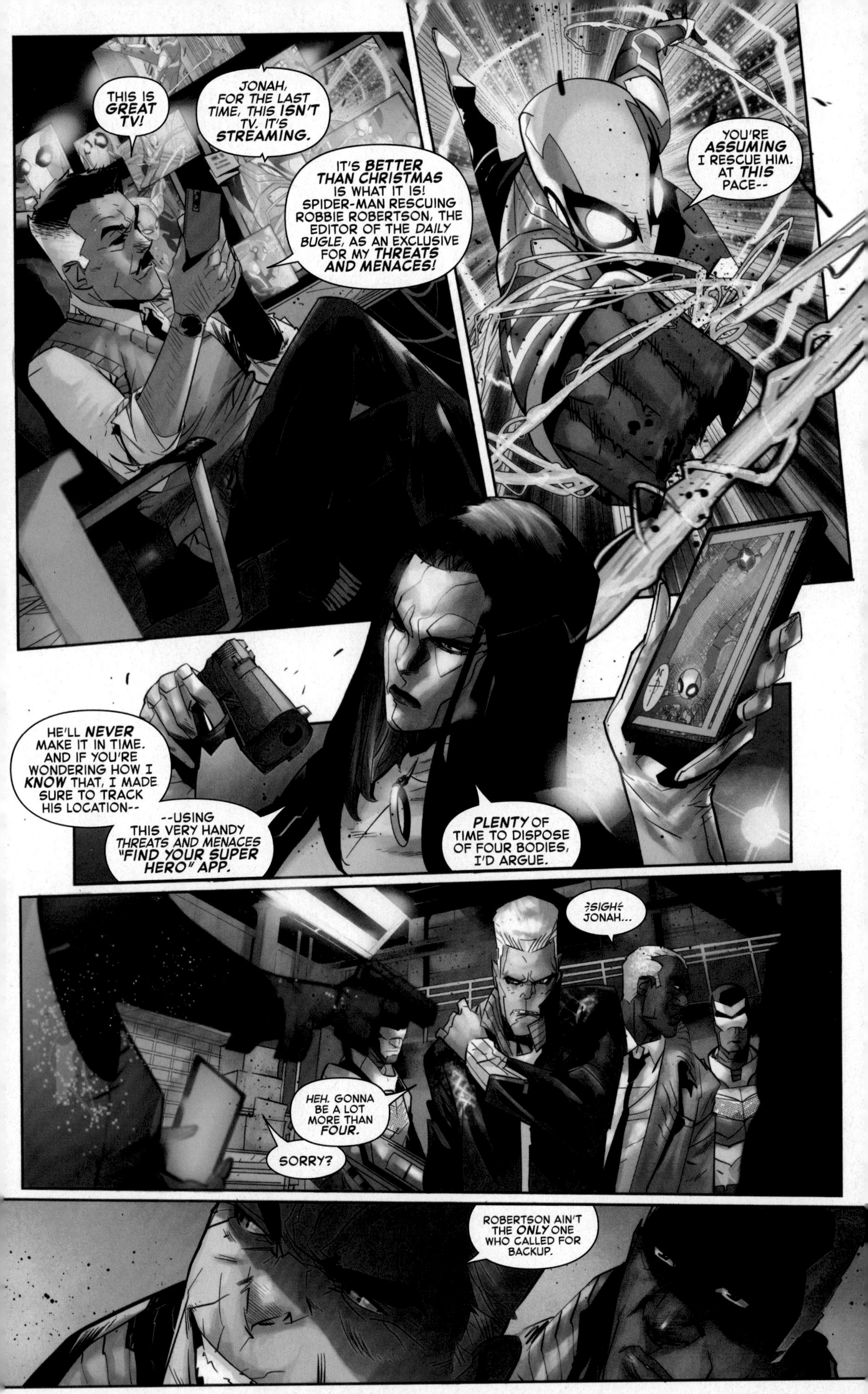
THIS IS GREAT TV!
JONAH, FOR THE LAST TIME, THIS ISN'T TV. IT'S STREAMING.
IT'S BETTER THAN CHRISTMAS IS WHAT IT IS! SPIDER-MAN RESCUING ROBBIE ROBERTSON, THE EDITOR OF THE DAILY BUGLE, AS AN EXCLUSIVE FOR MY THREATS AND MENACES!
YOU'RE ASSUMING I RESCUE HIM. AT THIS PACE--
HE'LL NEVER MAKE IT IN TIME. AND IF YOU'RE WONDERING HOW I KNOW THAT, I MADE SURE TO TRACK HIS LOCATION--
--USING THIS VERY HANDY THREATS AND MENACES "FIND YOUR SUPER HERO" APP.
PLENTY OF TIME TO DISPOSE OF FOUR BODIES, I'D ARGUE.
SIGH JONAH...
HEH. GONNA BE A LOT MORE THAN FOUR.
SORRY?
ROBERTSON AIN'T THE ONLY ONE WHO CALLED FOR BACKUP.

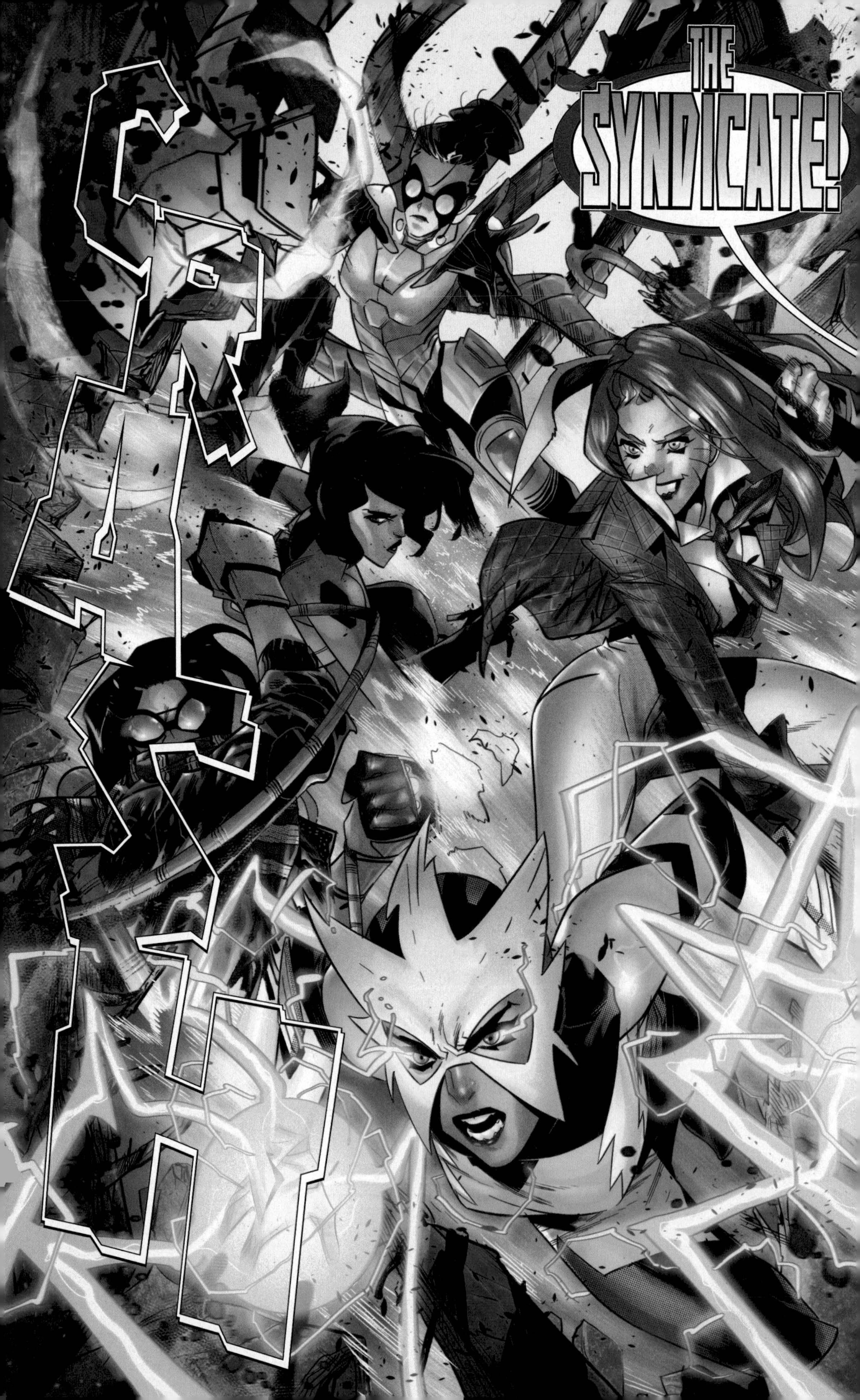
CRASH
THE SYNDICATE!

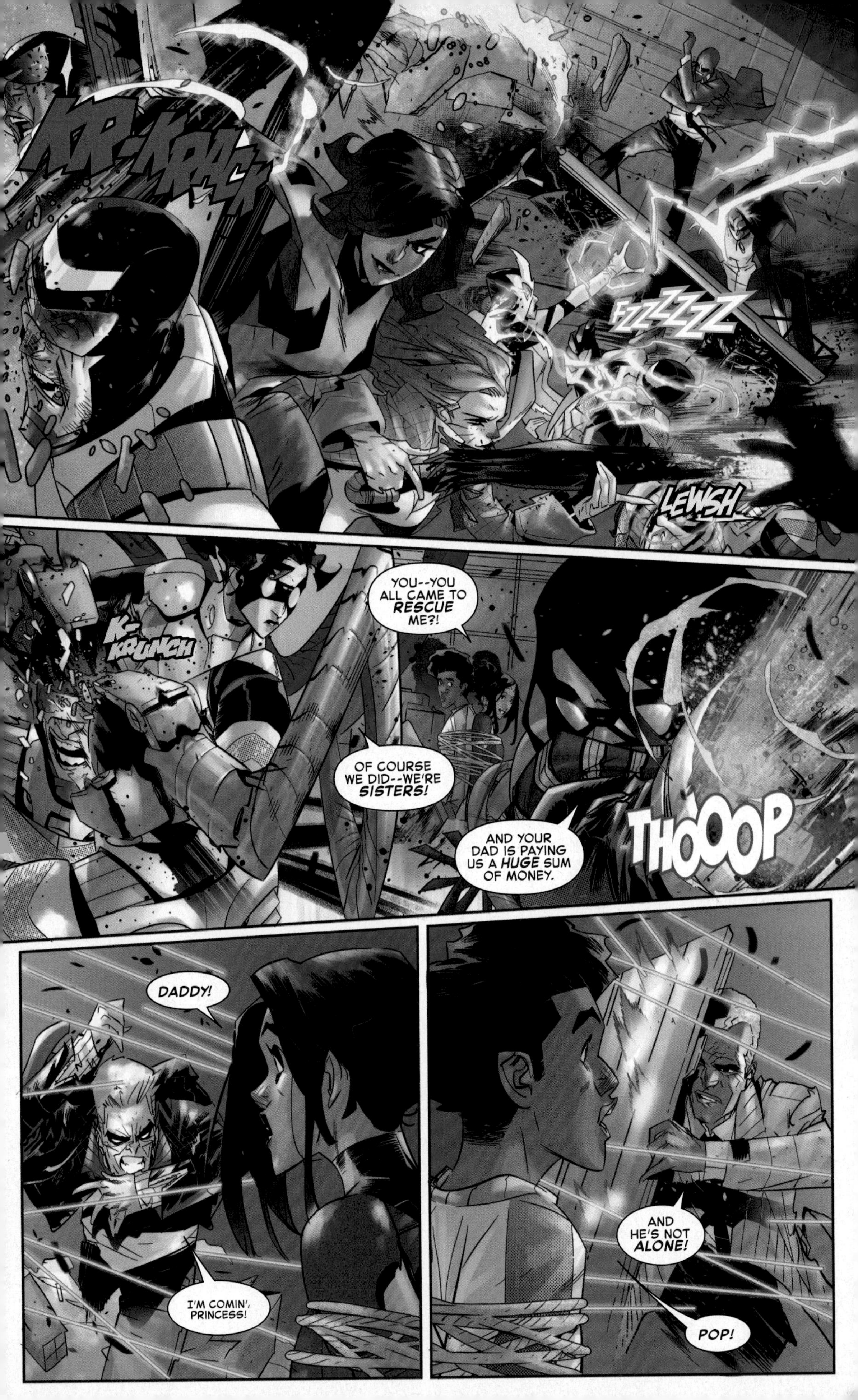
KRR-KRACK
FZZZZZZ
LEWSH
K-KRUNCH
YOU--YOU ALL CAME TO RESCUE ME?!
OF COURSE WE DID--WE'RE SISTERS!
AND YOUR DAD IS PAYING US A HUGE SUM OF MONEY.
THOOOP
DADDY!
I'M COMIN', PRINCESS!
AND HE'S NOT ALONE!
POP!

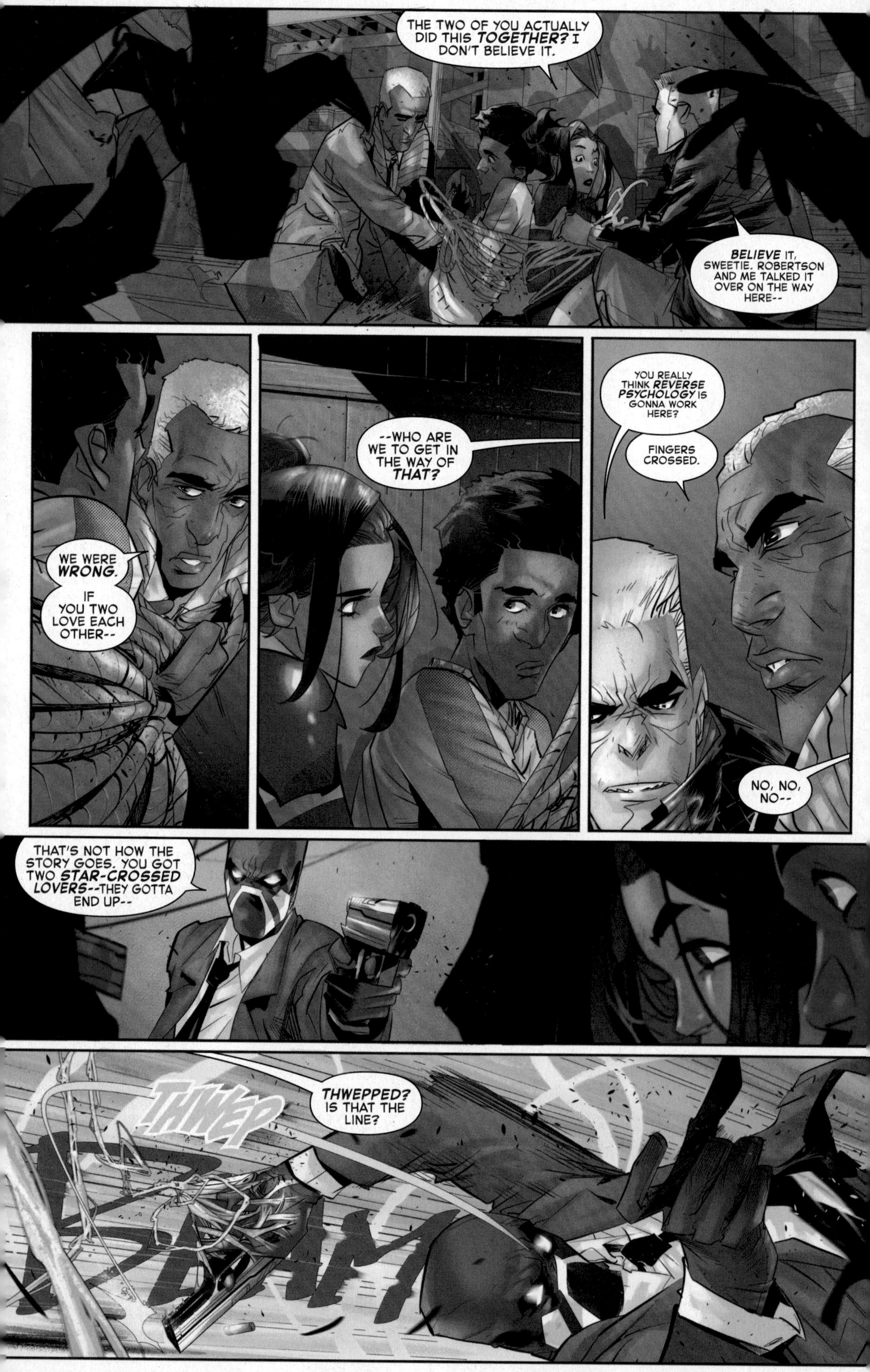
THE TWO OF YOU ACTUALLY DID THIS TOGETHER? I DON'T BELIEVE IT.
BELIEVE IT, SWEETIE. ROBERTSON AND ME TALKED IT OVER ON THE WAY HERE--
WE WERE WRONG.
IF YOU TWO LOVE EACH OTHER--
--WHO ARE WE TO GET IN THE WAY OF THAT?
YOU REALLY THINK REVERSE PSYCHOLOGY IS GONNA WORK HERE?
FINGERS CROSSED.
NO, NO, NO--
THAT'S NOT HOW THE STORY GOES. YOU GOT TWO STAR-CROSSED LOVERS--THEY GOTTA END UP--
THWEP
THWEPPED? IS THAT THE LINE?
SLAM

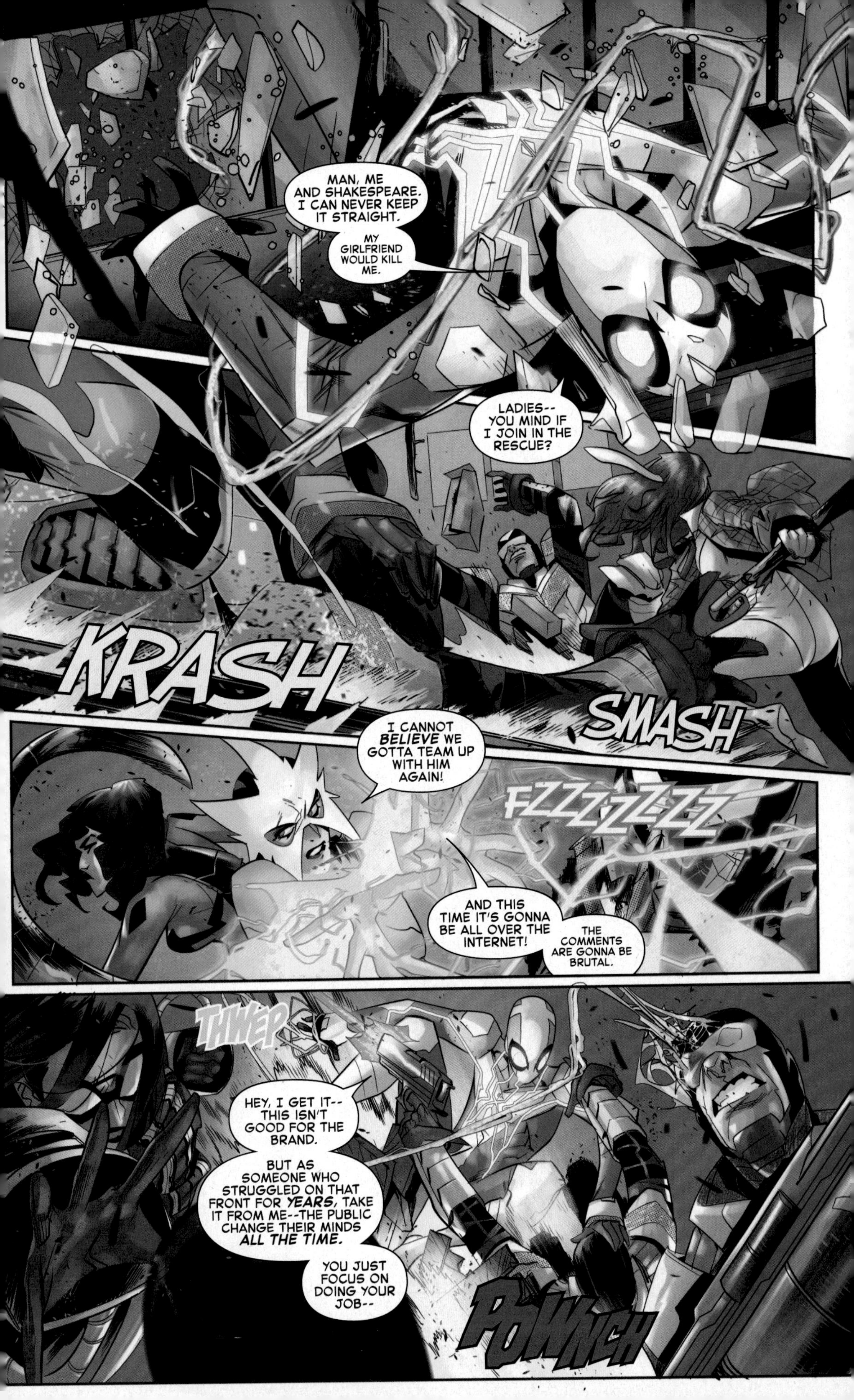

MAN, ME AND SHAKESPEARE. I CAN NEVER KEEP IT STRAIGHT.
MY GIRLFRIEND WOULD KILL ME.
LADIES-- YOU MIND IF I JOIN IN THE RESCUE?
KRASH
SMASH
I CANNOT *BELIEVE* WE GOTTA TEAM UP WITH HIM AGAIN!
FZZZZZZZ
AND THIS TIME IT'S GONNA BE ALL OVER THE INTERNET!
THE COMMENTS ARE GONNA BE BRUTAL.
THWEP
HEY, I GET IT-- THIS ISN'T GOOD FOR THE BRAND.
BUT AS SOMEONE WHO STRUGGLED ON THAT FRONT FOR *YEARS,* TAKE IT FROM ME--THE PUBLIC CHANGE THEIR MINDS *ALL THE TIME.*
YOU JUST FOCUS ON DOING YOUR JOB--
POWNCH

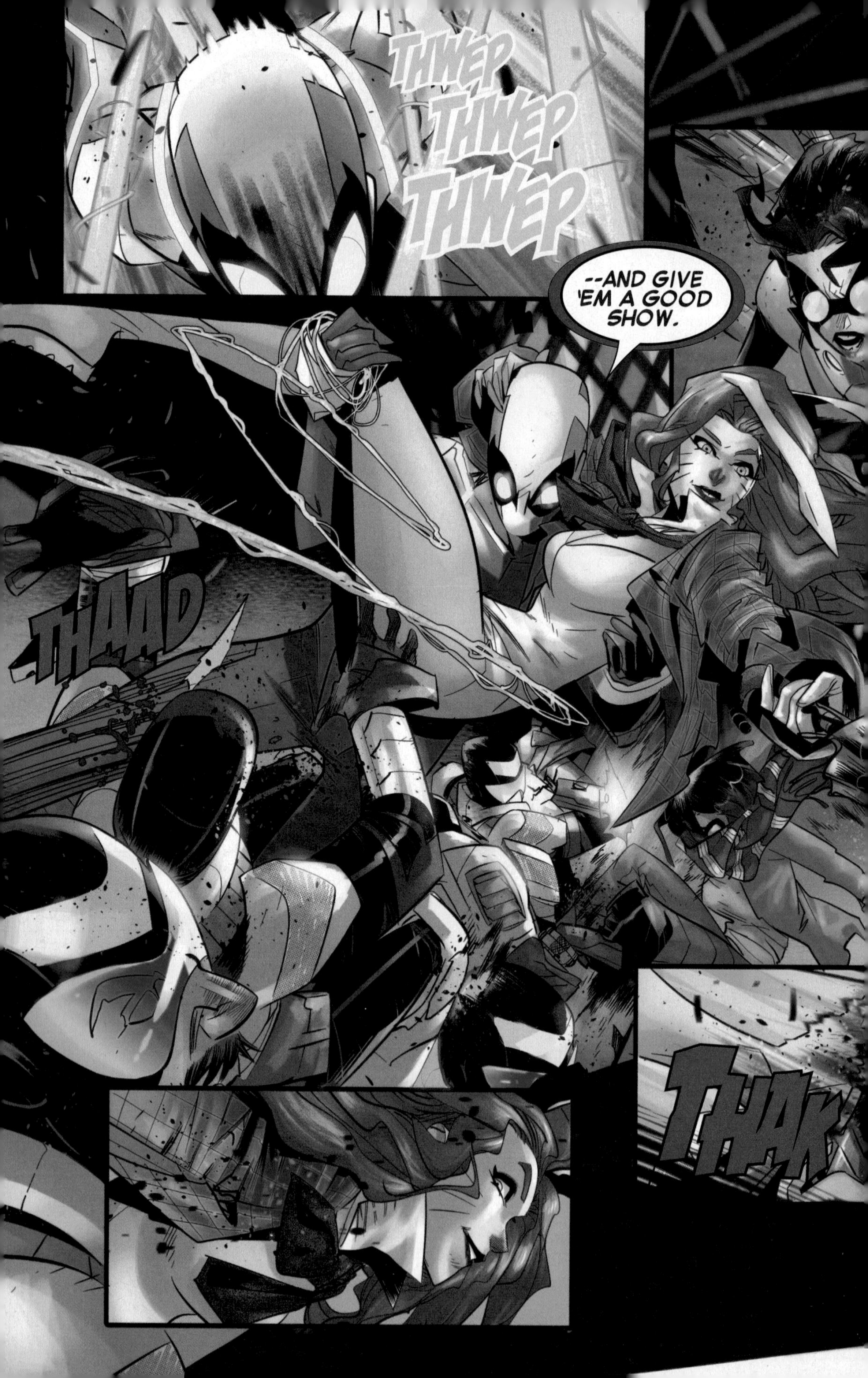
THWEP THWEP THWEP
--AND GIVE 'EM A GOOD SHOW.
THAAD
THAK

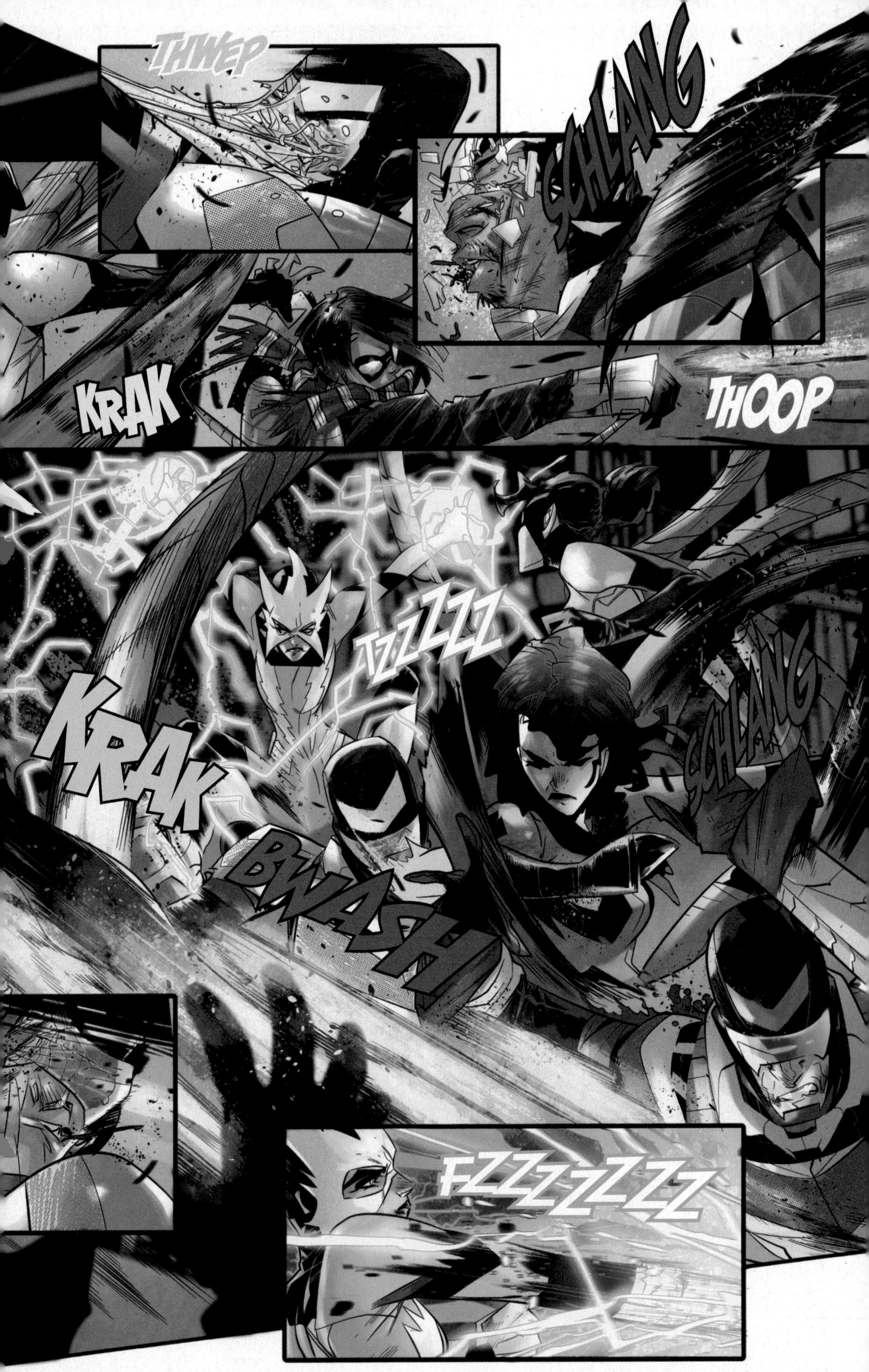
THWEP
SCHLANG
KRAK
THOOP
TZZZZZ
KRAK
SCHLANG
BWASH
FZZZZZZZZ

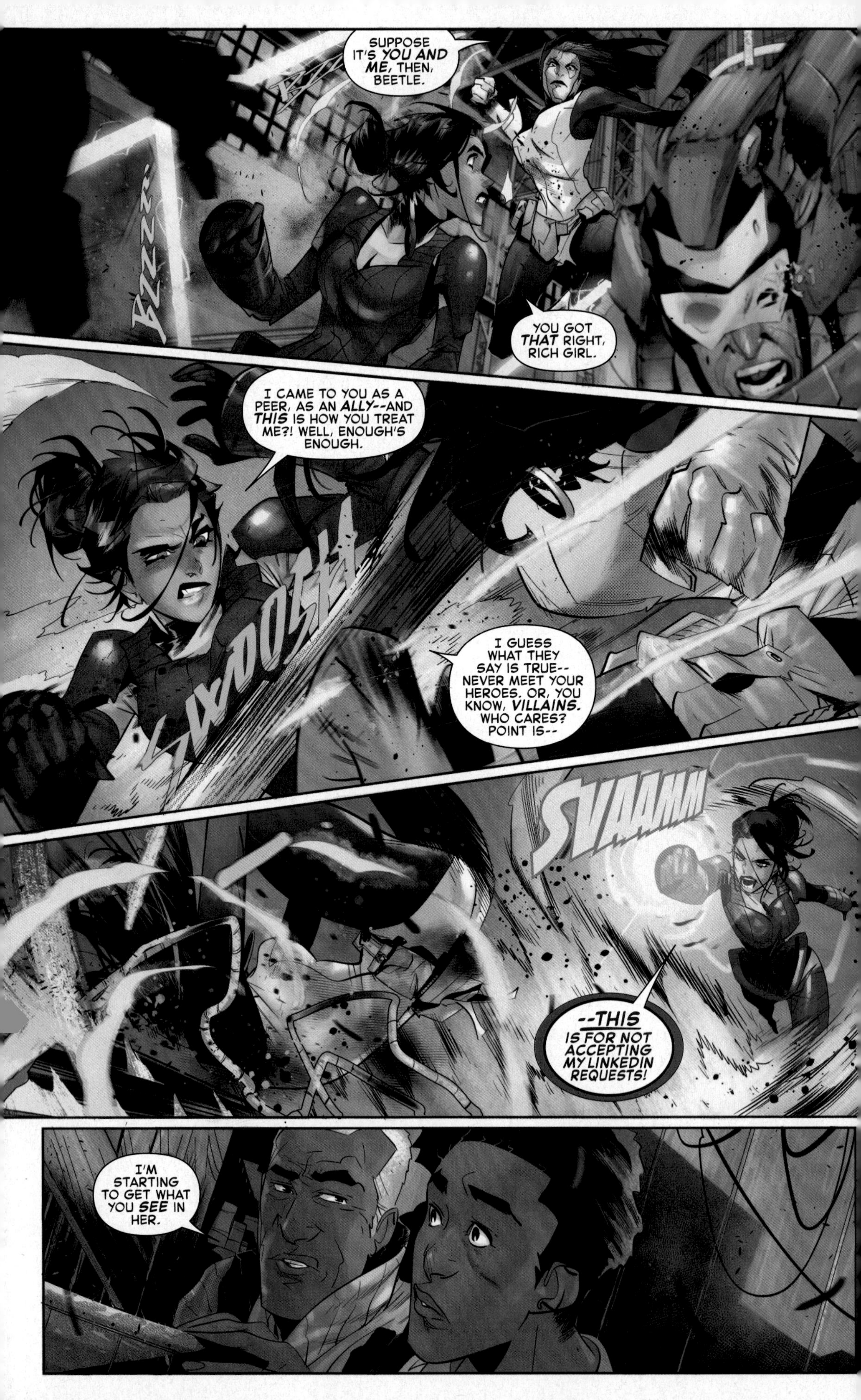
SUPPOSE IT'S *YOU AND ME,* THEN, BEETLE.
YOU GOT *THAT* RIGHT, RICH GIRL.
I CAME TO YOU AS A PEER, AS AN *ALLY*--AND *THIS* IS HOW YOU TREAT ME?! WELL, ENOUGH'S ENOUGH.
I GUESS WHAT THEY SAY IS TRUE--NEVER MEET YOUR HEROES. OR, YOU KNOW, *VILLAINS.* WHO CARES? POINT IS--
SVAAMM
--THIS IS FOR NOT ACCEPTING MY LINKEDIN REQUESTS!
I'M STARTING TO GET WHAT YOU *SEE* IN HER.

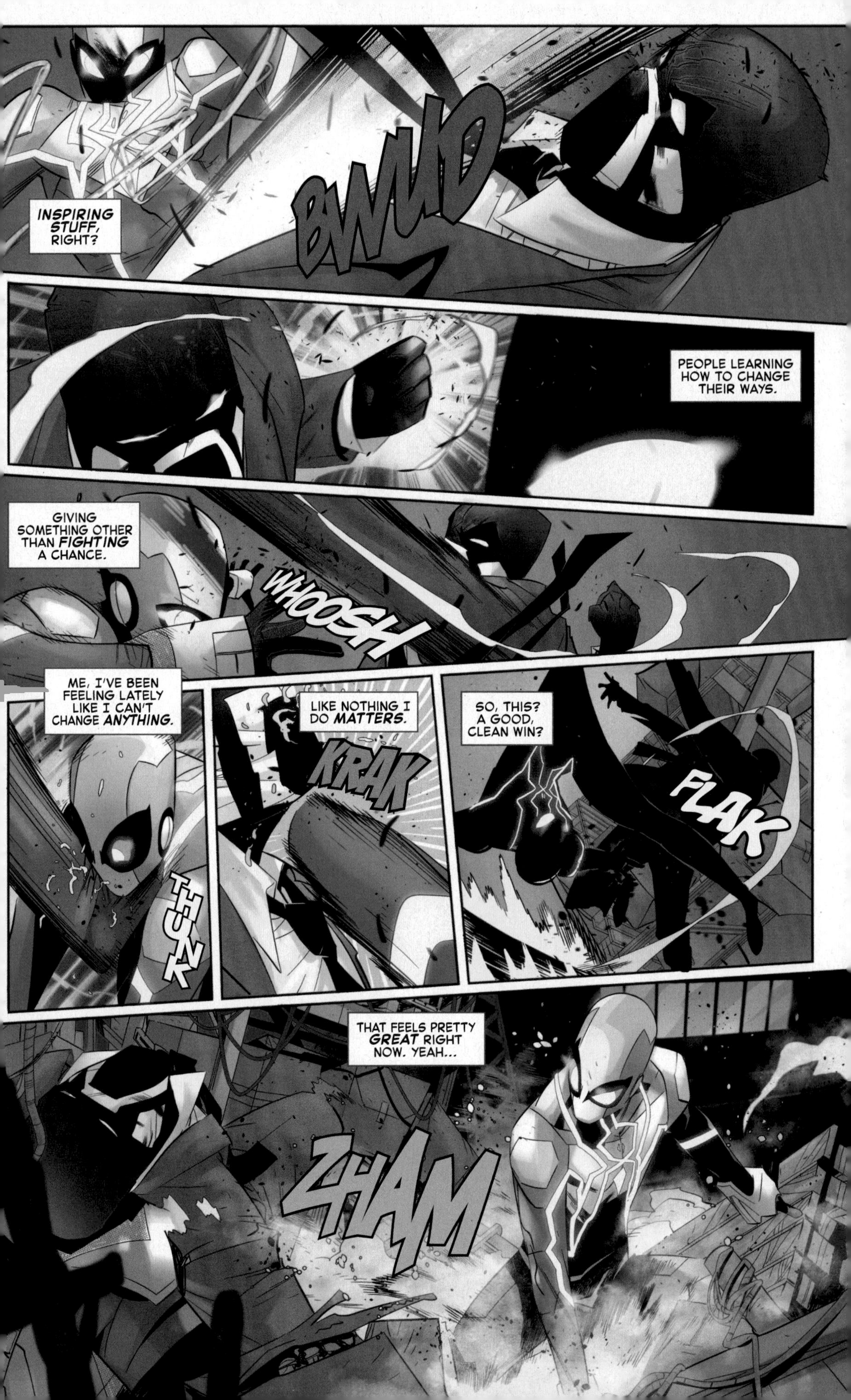
INSPIRING STUFF, RIGHT?
BWUMO
PEOPLE LEARNING HOW TO CHANGE THEIR WAYS.
GIVING SOMETHING OTHER THAN FIGHTING A CHANCE.
WHOOSH
ME, I'VE BEEN FEELING LATELY LIKE I CAN'T CHANGE ANYTHING.
THUNK
LIKE NOTHING I DO MATTERS.
KRAK
SO, THIS? A GOOD, CLEAN WIN?
FLAK
THAT FEELS PRETTY GREAT RIGHT NOW. YEAH...
ZHAM

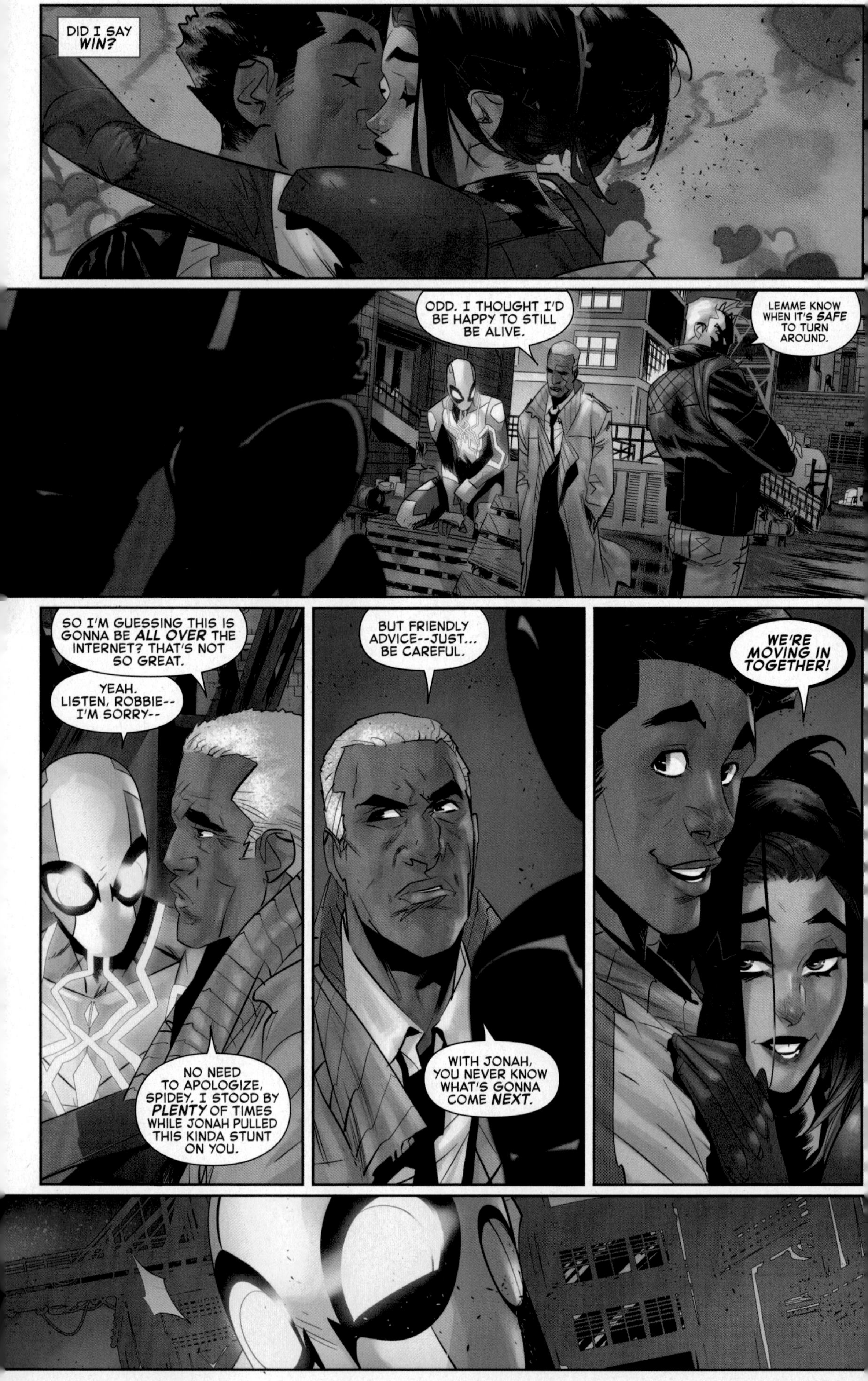
DID I SAY *WIN?*
ODD. I THOUGHT I'D BE HAPPY TO STILL BE ALIVE.
LEMME KNOW WHEN IT'S *SAFE* TO TURN AROUND.
SO I'M GUESSING THIS IS GONNA BE *ALL OVER* THE INTERNET? THAT'S NOT SO GREAT.
YEAH. LISTEN, ROBBIE-- I'M SORRY--
NO NEED TO APOLOGIZE, SPIDEY. I STOOD BY *PLENTY* OF TIMES WHILE JONAH PULLED THIS KINDA STUNT ON YOU.
BUT FRIENDLY ADVICE--JUST... BE CAREFUL.
WITH JONAH, YOU NEVER KNOW WHAT'S GONNA COME *NEXT.*
WE'RE MOVING IN TOGETHER!

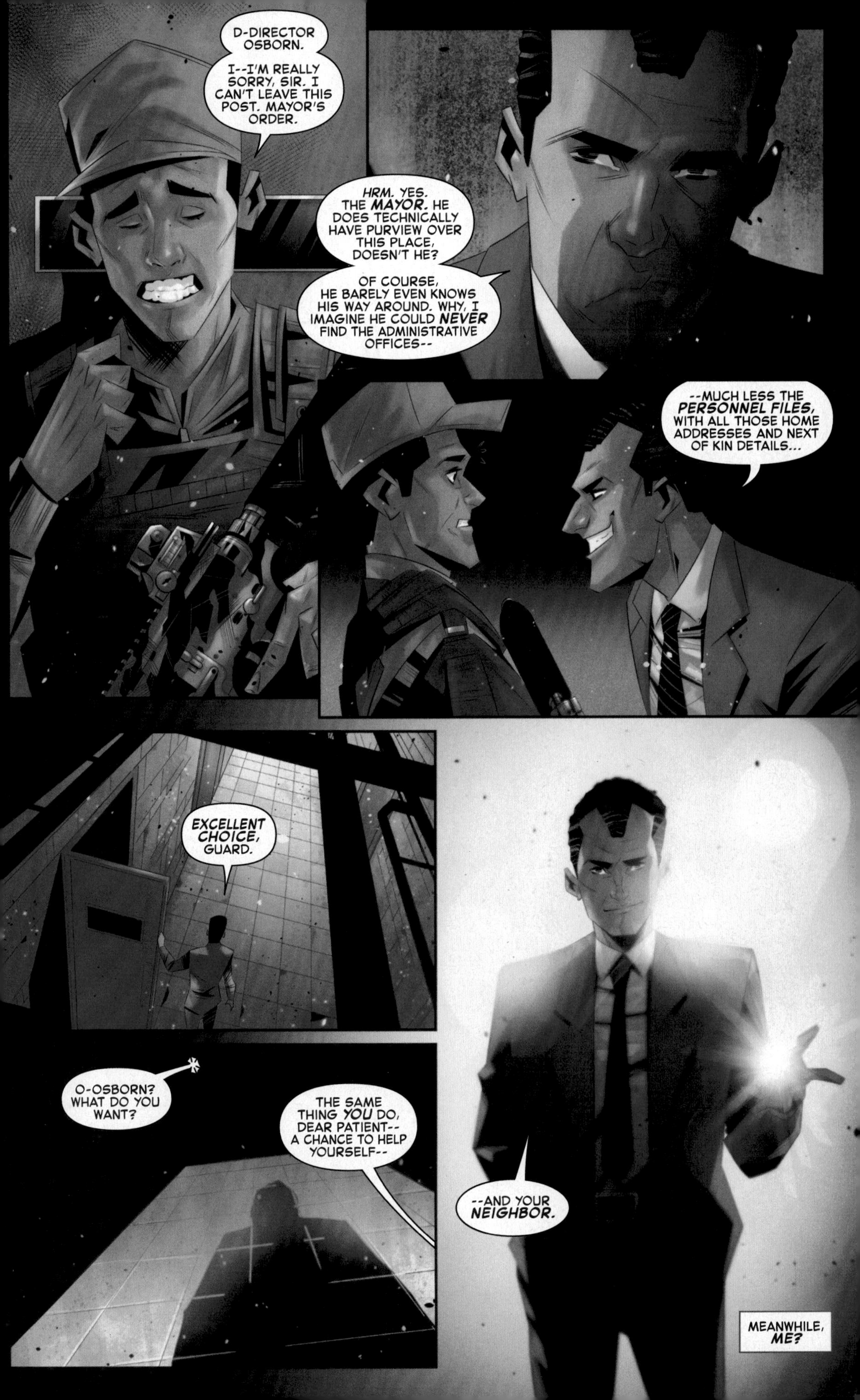
D-DIRECTOR OSBORN.
I--I'M REALLY SORRY, SIR. I CAN'T LEAVE THIS POST. MAYOR'S ORDER.
HRM. YES. THE MAYOR. HE DOES TECHNICALLY HAVE PURVIEW OVER THIS PLACE, DOESN'T HE?
OF COURSE, HE BARELY EVEN KNOWS HIS WAY AROUND. WHY, I IMAGINE HE COULD NEVER FIND THE ADMINISTRATIVE OFFICES--
--MUCH LESS THE PERSONNEL FILES, WITH ALL THOSE HOME ADDRESSES AND NEXT OF KIN DETAILS...
EXCELLENT CHOICE, GUARD.
O-OSBORN? WHAT DO YOU WANT?
THE SAME THING YOU DO, DEAR PATIENT-- A CHANCE TO HELP YOURSELF--
--AND YOUR NEIGHBOR.
MEANWHILE, ME?

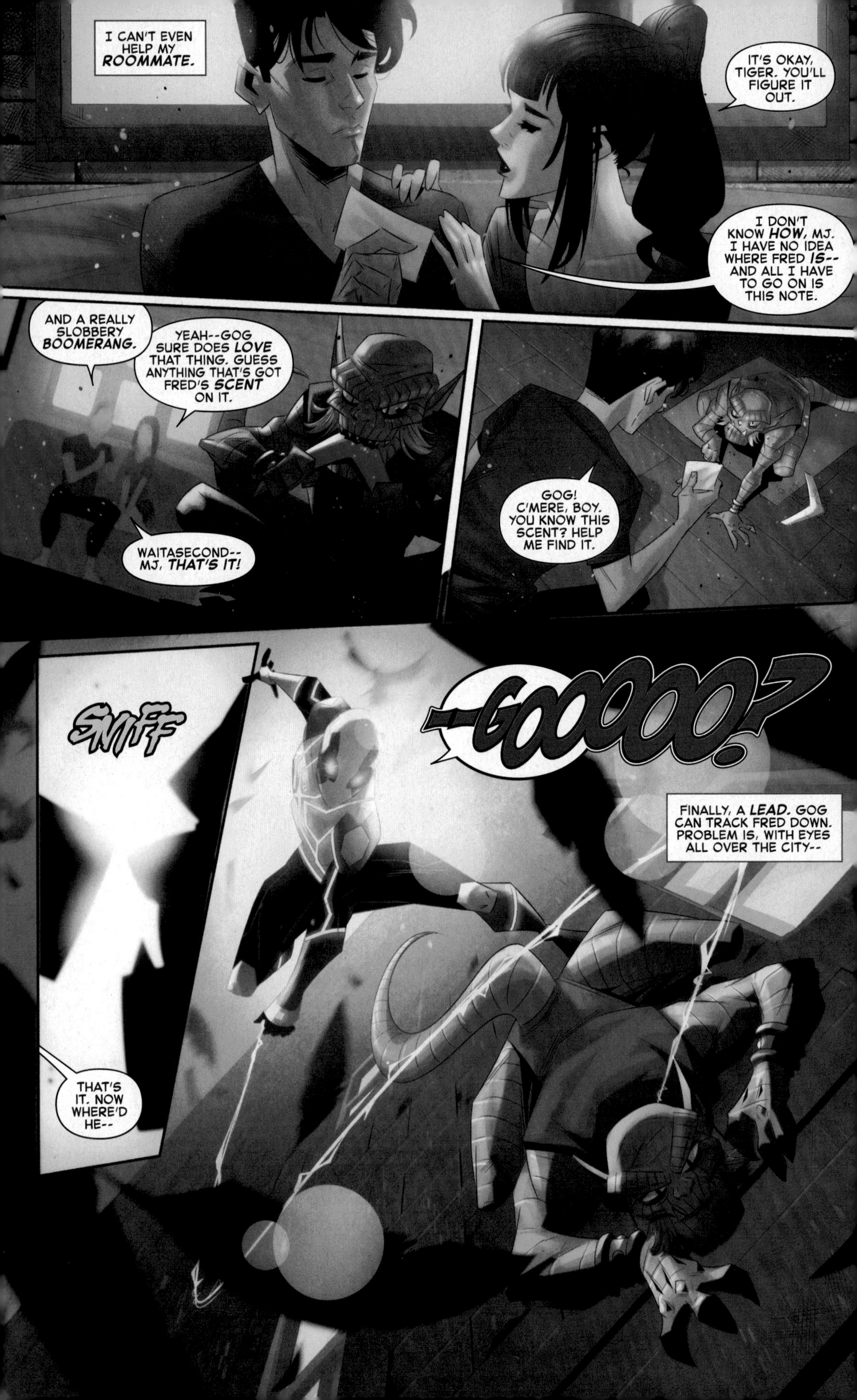
I CAN'T EVEN HELP MY ROOMMATE.
IT'S OKAY, TIGER. YOU'LL FIGURE IT OUT.
I DON'T KNOW HOW, MJ. I HAVE NO IDEA WHERE FRED IS-- AND ALL I HAVE TO GO ON IS THIS NOTE.
AND A REALLY SLOBBERY BOOMERANG.
YEAH--GOG SURE DOES LOVE THAT THING. GUESS ANYTHING THAT'S GOT FRED'S SCENT ON IT.
WAITASECOND-- MJ, THAT'S IT!
GOG! C'MERE, BOY. YOU KNOW THIS SCENT? HELP ME FIND IT.
SNIFF
-GOOOOO?
FINALLY, A LEAD. GOG CAN TRACK FRED DOWN. PROBLEM IS, WITH EYES ALL OVER THE CITY--
THAT'S IT. NOW WHERE'D HE--

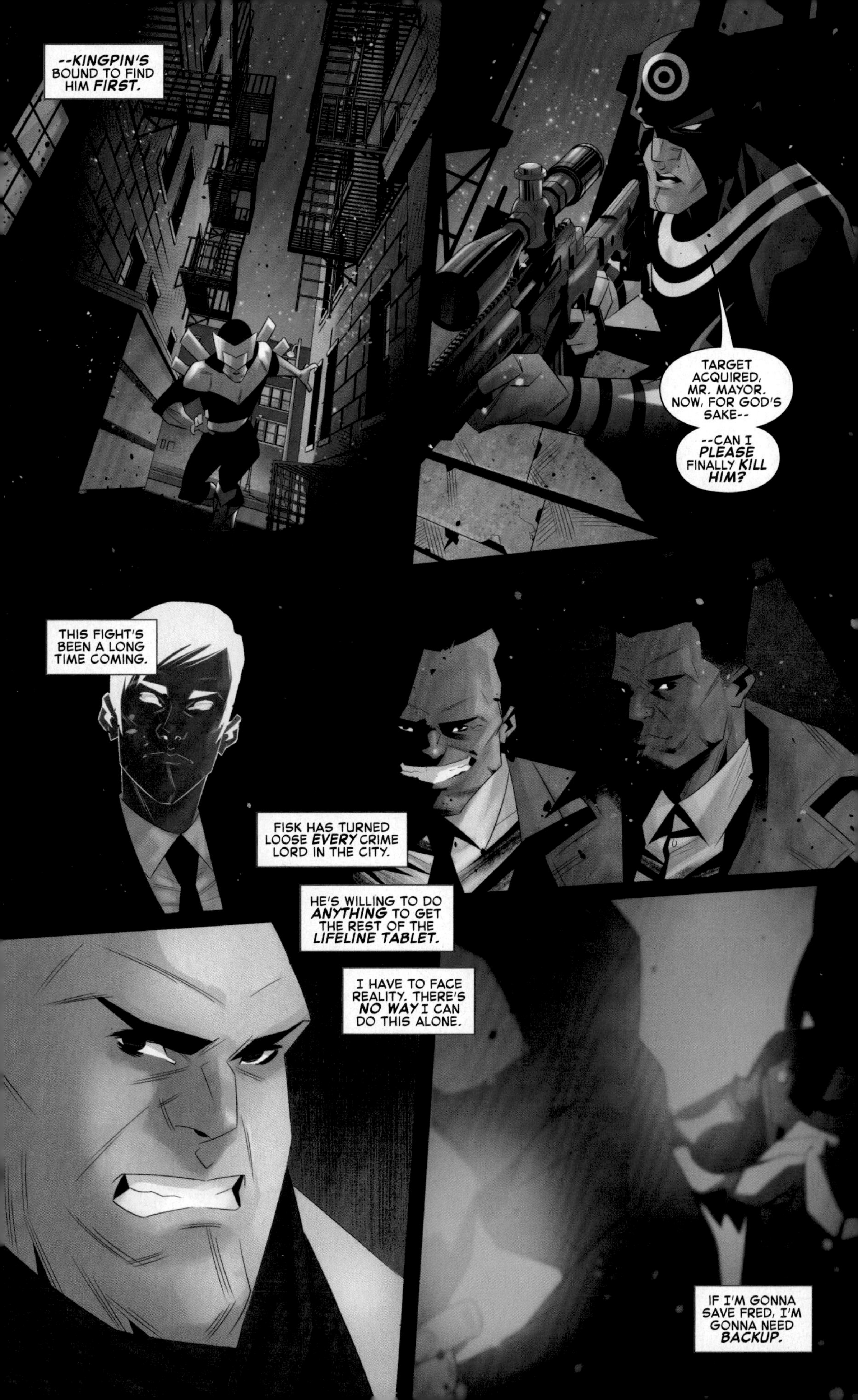
--KINGPIN'S BOUND TO FIND HIM FIRST.
TARGET ACQUIRED, MR. MAYOR. NOW, FOR GOD'S SAKE--
--CAN I PLEASE FINALLY KILL HIM?
THIS FIGHT'S BEEN A LONG TIME COMING.
FISK HAS TURNED LOOSE EVERY CRIME LORD IN THE CITY.
HE'S WILLING TO DO ANYTHING TO GET THE REST OF THE LIFELINE TABLET.
I HAVE TO FACE REALITY. THERE'S NO WAY I CAN DO THIS ALONE.
IF I'M GONNA SAVE FRED, I'M GONNA NEED BACKUP.

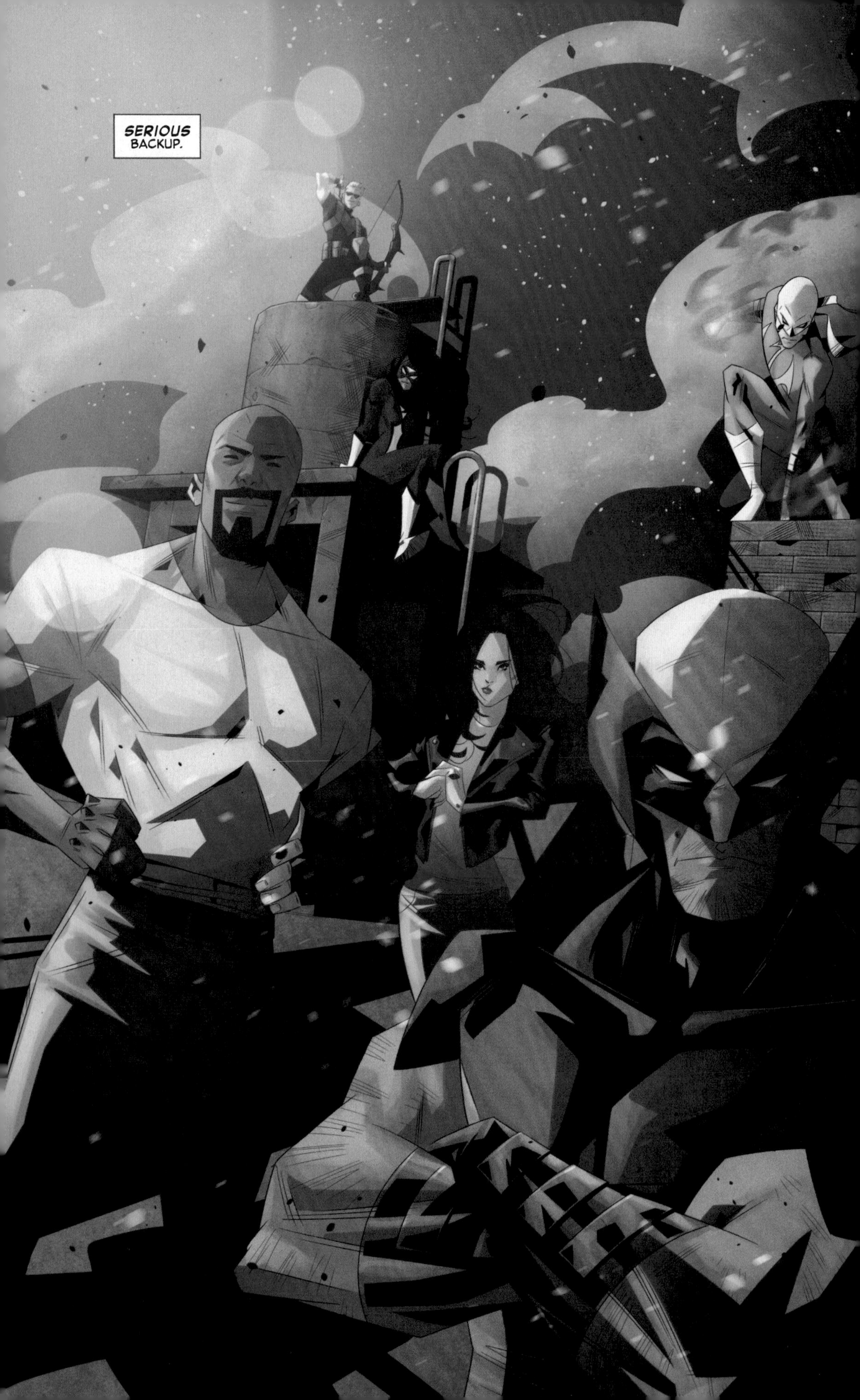
SERIOUS BACKUP.

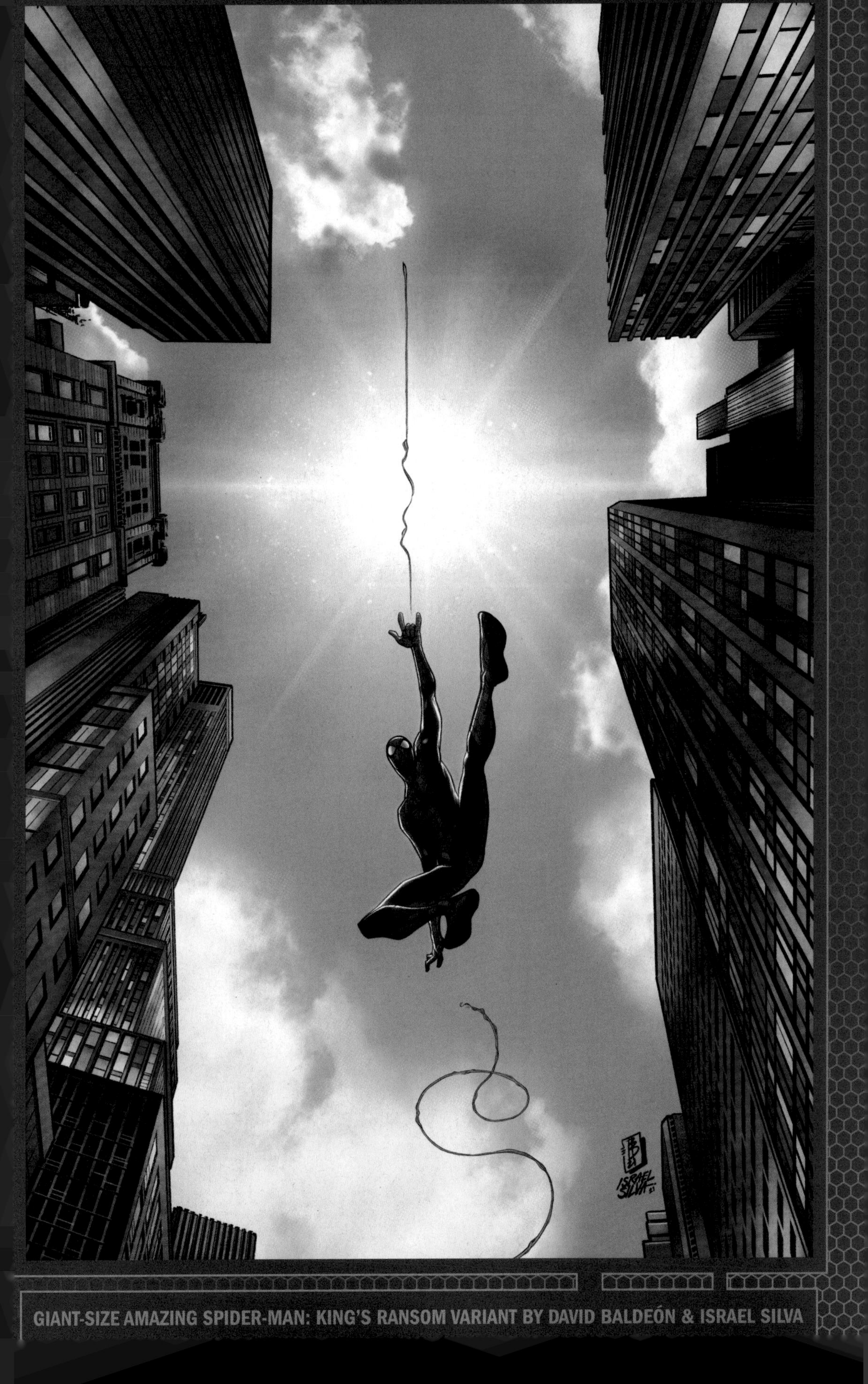
ISRAEL SILVA

GIANT-SIZE AMAZING SPIDER-MAN: KING'S RANSOM VARIANT BY DAVID BALDEÓN & ISRAEL SILVA

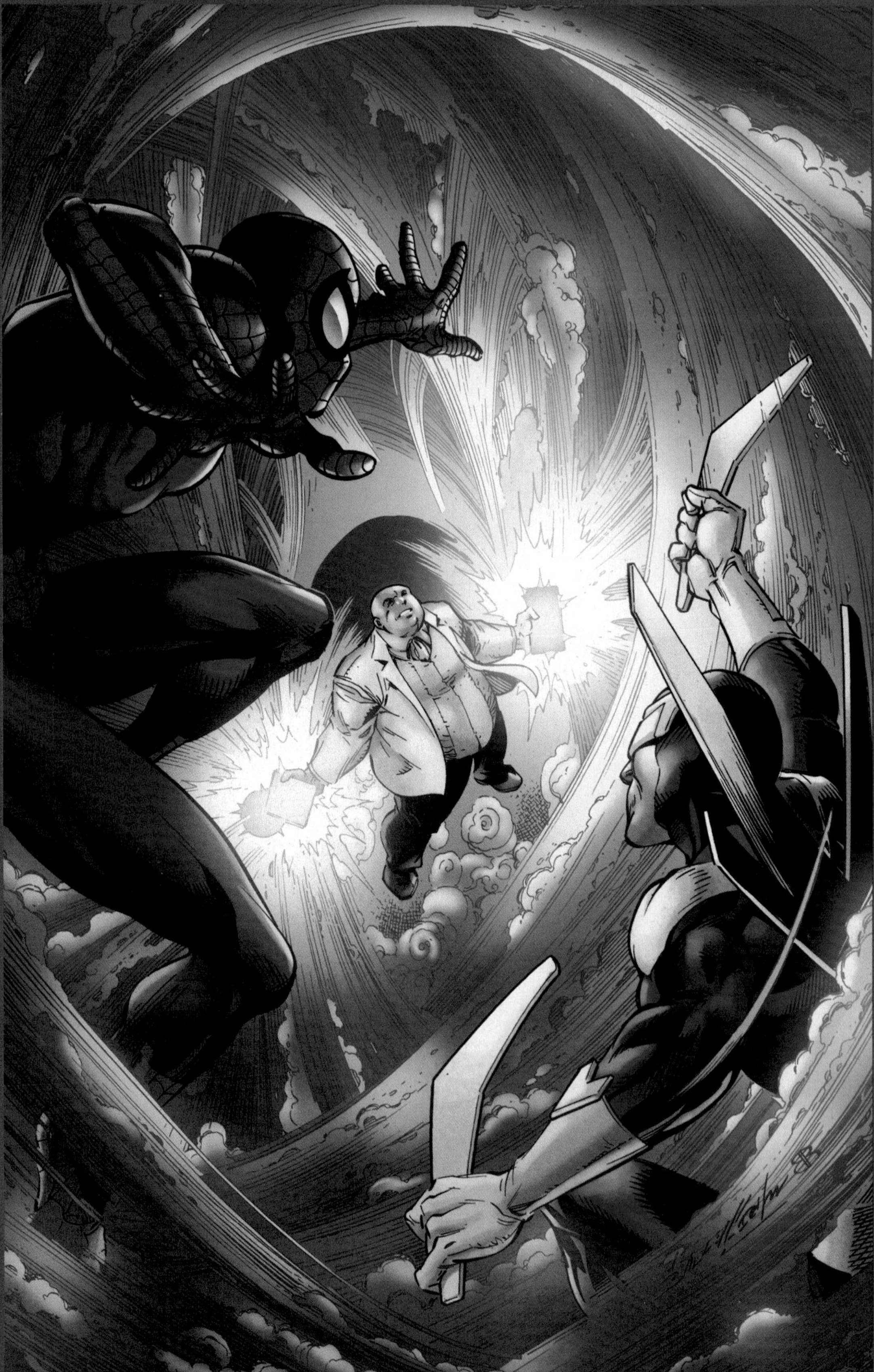

GIANT-SIZE AMAZING SPIDER-MAN **KING'S RANSOM** CONCLUSION

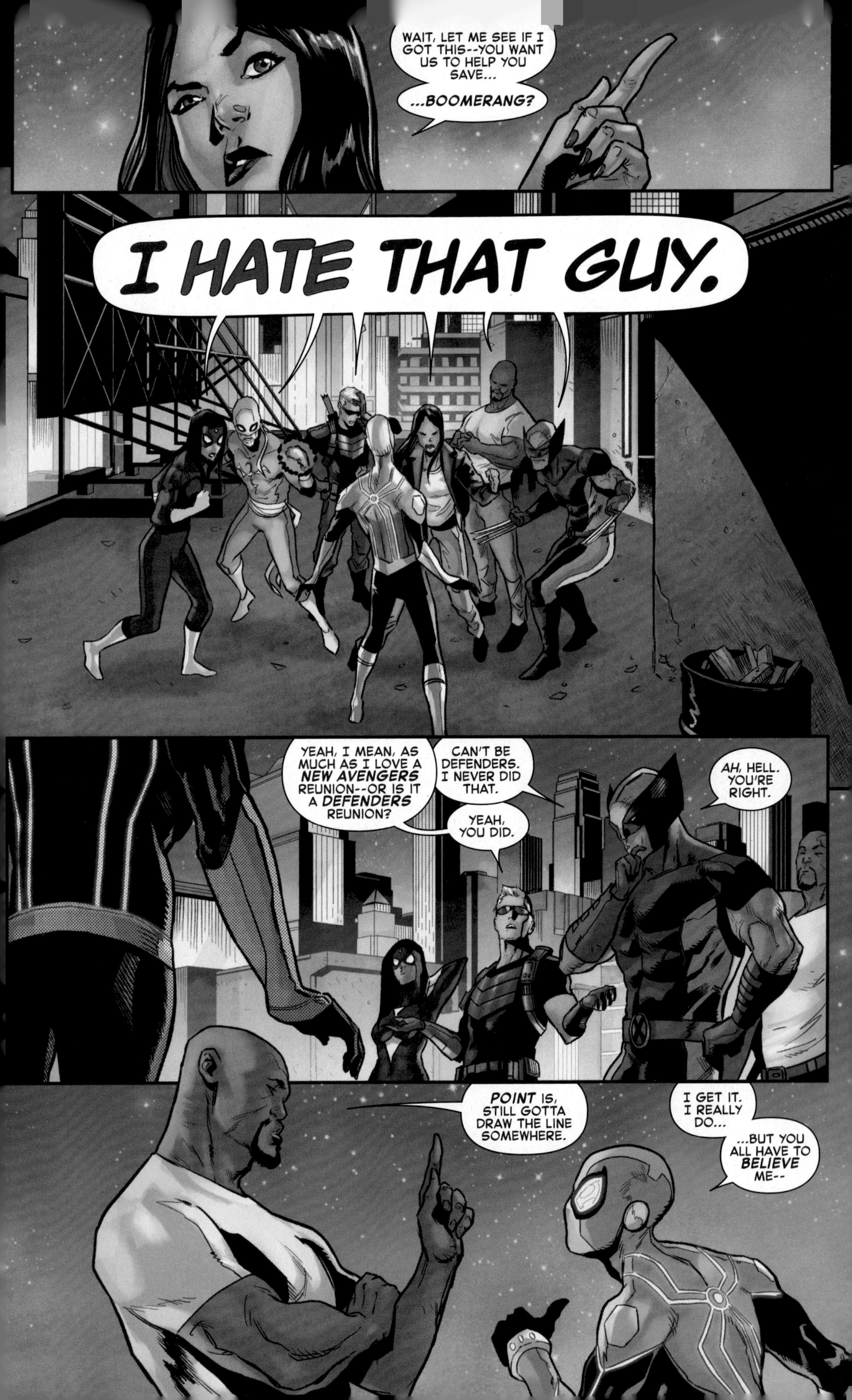
WAIT, LET ME SEE IF I GOT THIS--YOU WANT US TO HELP YOU SAVE...
...BOOMERANG?
I HATE THAT GUY.
YEAH, I MEAN, AS MUCH AS I LOVE A *NEW AVENGERS* REUNION--OR IS IT A *DEFENDERS* REUNION?
CAN'T BE DEFENDERS. I NEVER DID THAT.
YEAH, YOU DID.
AH, HELL. YOU'RE RIGHT.
POINT IS, STILL GOTTA DRAW THE LINE SOMEWHERE.
I GET IT. I REALLY DO...
...BUT YOU ALL HAVE TO *BELIEVE* ME--

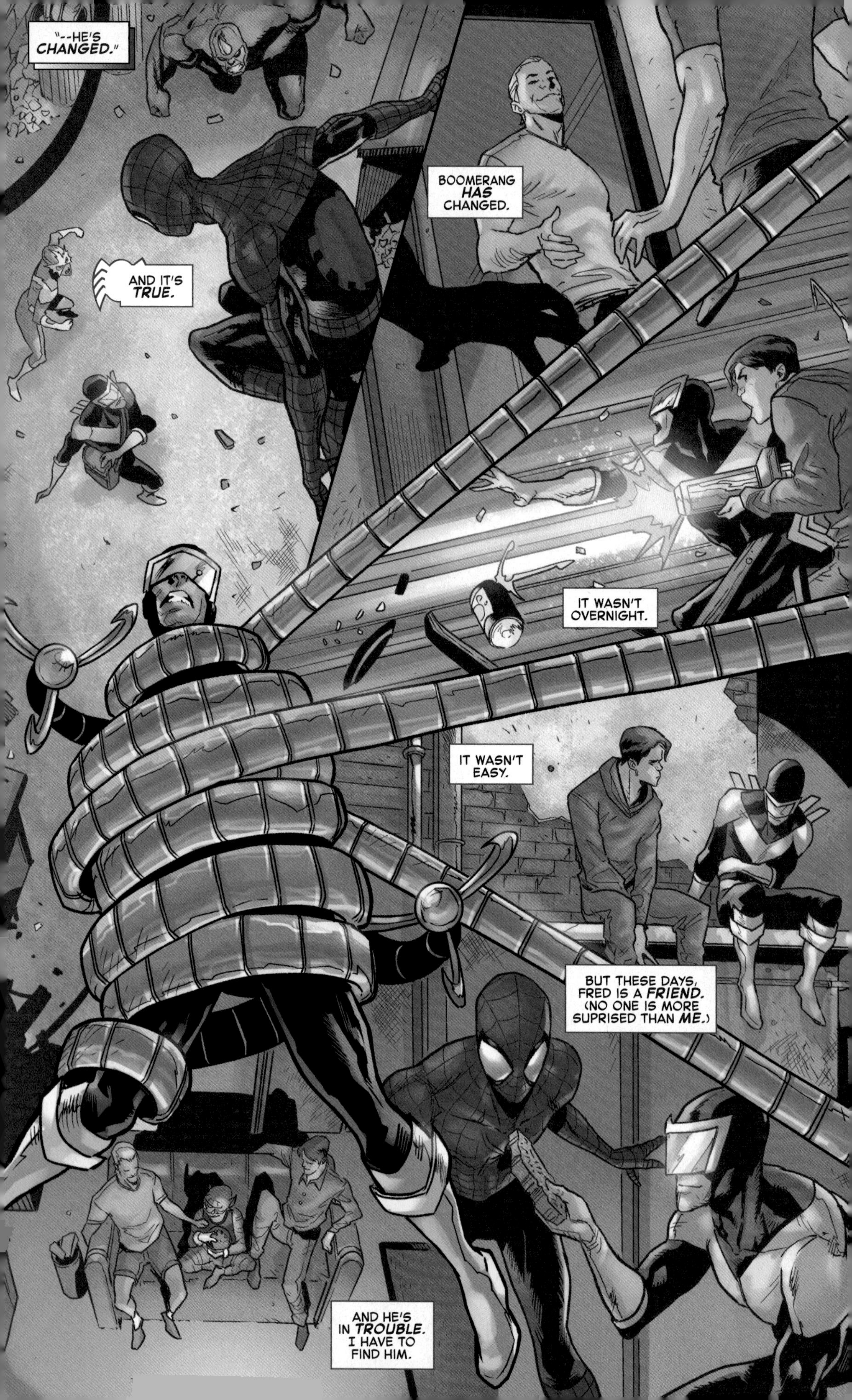
"--HE'S CHANGED."
BOOMERANG HAS CHANGED.
AND IT'S TRUE.
IT WASN'T OVERNIGHT.
IT WASN'T EASY.
BUT THESE DAYS, FRED IS A FRIEND. (NO ONE IS MORE SUPRISED THAN ME.)
AND HE'S IN TROUBLE. I HAVE TO FIND HIM.

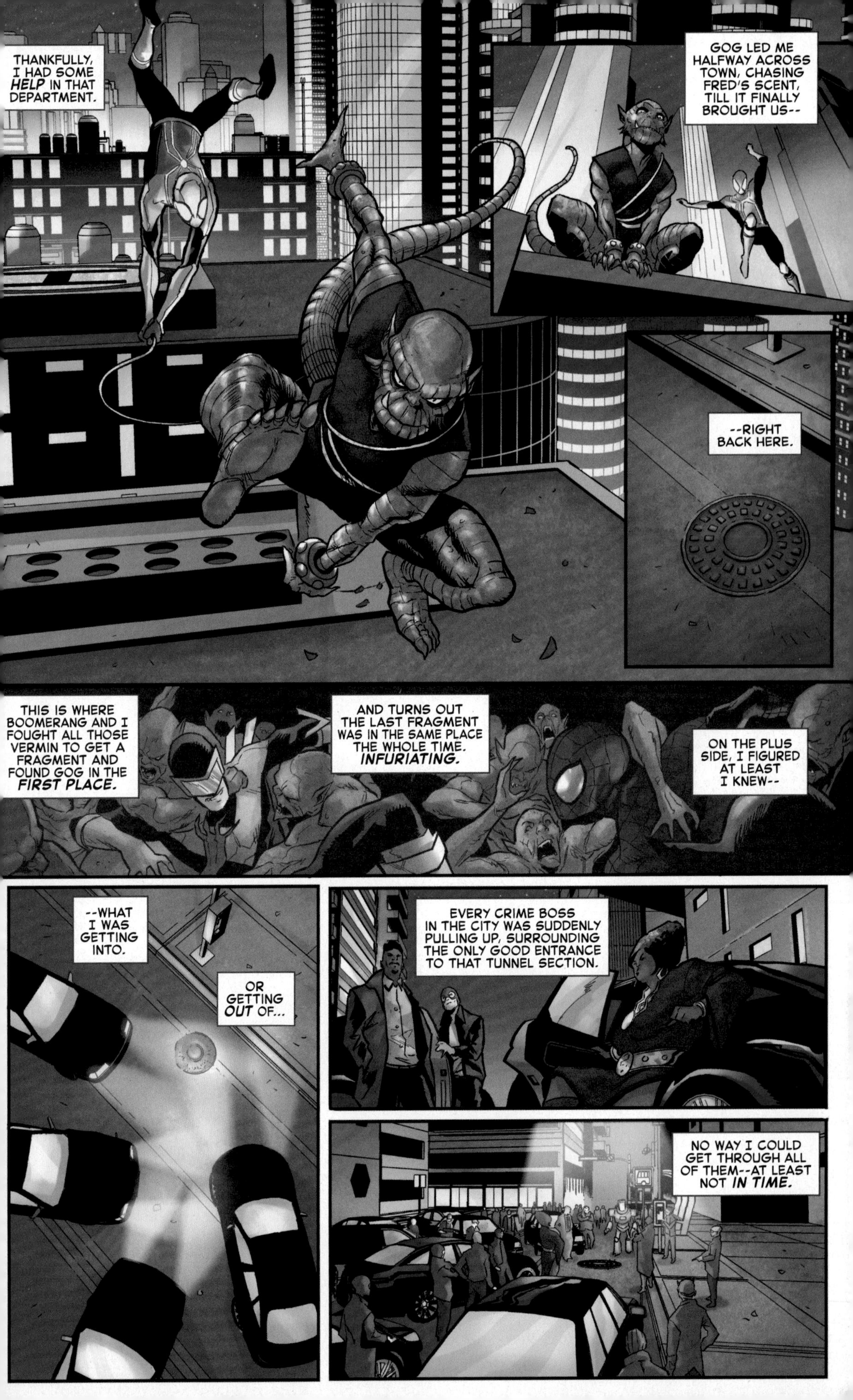
THANKFULLY, I HAD SOME HELP IN THAT DEPARTMENT.
GOG LED ME HALFWAY ACROSS TOWN, CHASING FRED'S SCENT, TILL IT FINALLY BROUGHT US--
--RIGHT BACK HERE.
THIS IS WHERE BOOMERANG AND I FOUGHT ALL THOSE VERMIN TO GET A FRAGMENT AND FOUND GOG IN THE FIRST PLACE.
AND TURNS OUT THE LAST FRAGMENT WAS IN THE SAME PLACE THE WHOLE TIME. INFURIATING.
ON THE PLUS SIDE, I FIGURED AT LEAST I KNEW--
--WHAT I WAS GETTING INTO.
OR GETTING OUT OF...
EVERY CRIME BOSS IN THE CITY WAS SUDDENLY PULLING UP, SURROUNDING THE ONLY GOOD ENTRANCE TO THAT TUNNEL SECTION.
NO WAY I COULD GET THROUGH ALL OF THEM--AT LEAST NOT IN TIME.

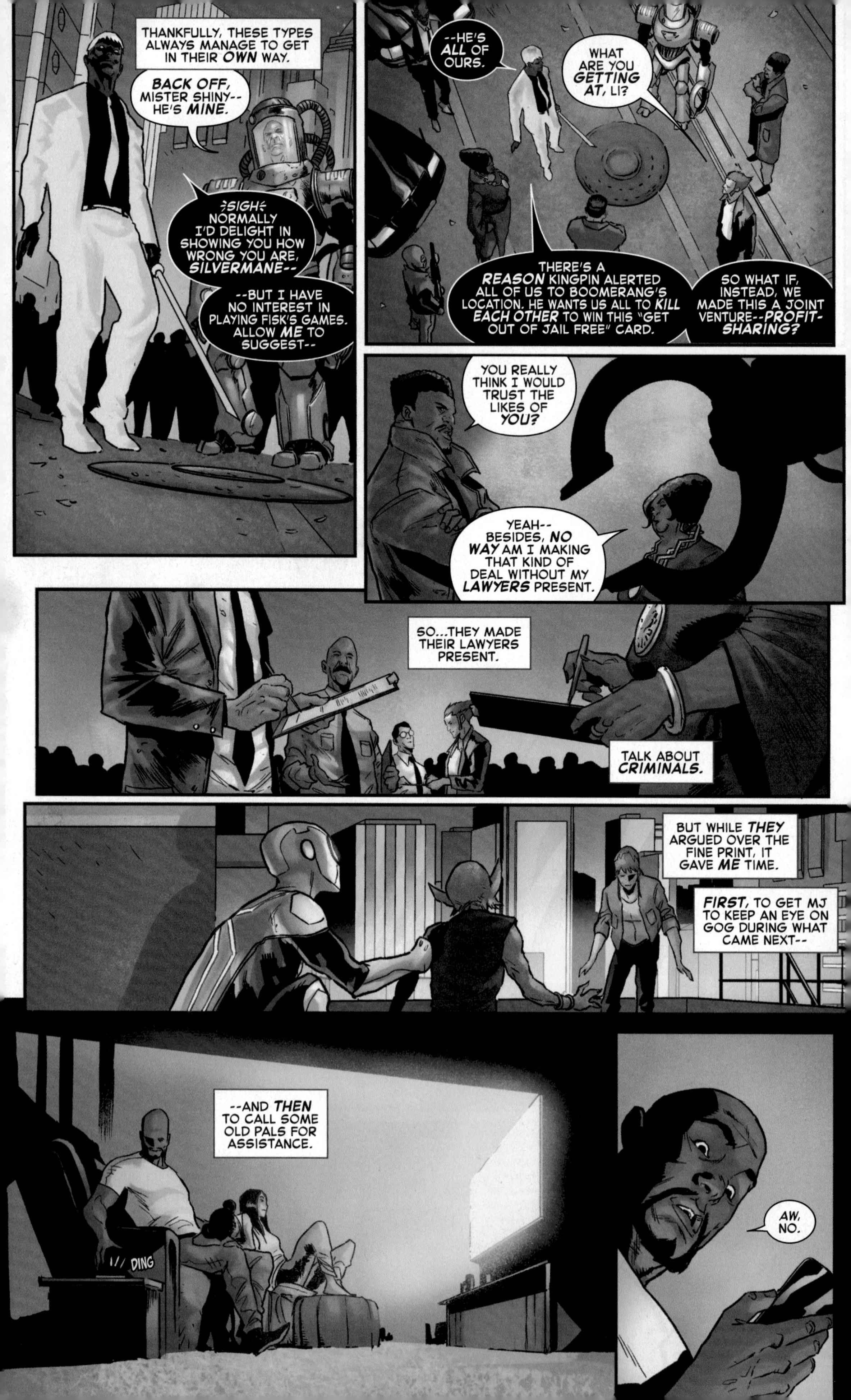
THANKFULLY, THESE TYPES ALWAYS MANAGE TO GET IN THEIR OWN WAY.
BACK OFF, MISTER SHINY-- HE'S MINE.
SIGH NORMALLY I'D DELIGHT IN SHOWING YOU HOW WRONG YOU ARE, SILVERMANE--
--BUT I HAVE NO INTEREST IN PLAYING FISK'S GAMES. ALLOW ME TO SUGGEST--
--HE'S ALL OF OURS.
WHAT ARE YOU GETTING AT, LI?
THERE'S A REASON KINGPIN ALERTED ALL OF US TO BOOMERANG'S LOCATION. HE WANTS US ALL TO KILL EACH OTHER TO WIN THIS "GET OUT OF JAIL FREE" CARD.
SO WHAT IF, INSTEAD, WE MADE THIS A JOINT VENTURE--PROFIT-SHARING?
YOU REALLY THINK I WOULD TRUST THE LIKES OF YOU?
YEAH-- BESIDES, NO WAY AM I MAKING THAT KIND OF DEAL WITHOUT MY LAWYERS PRESENT.
SO...THEY MADE THEIR LAWYERS PRESENT.
TALK ABOUT CRIMINALS.
BUT WHILE THEY ARGUED OVER THE FINE PRINT, IT GAVE ME TIME.
FIRST, TO GET MJ TO KEEP AN EYE ON GOG DURING WHAT CAME NEXT--
--AND THEN TO CALL SOME OLD PALS FOR ASSISTANCE.
DING
AW, NO.

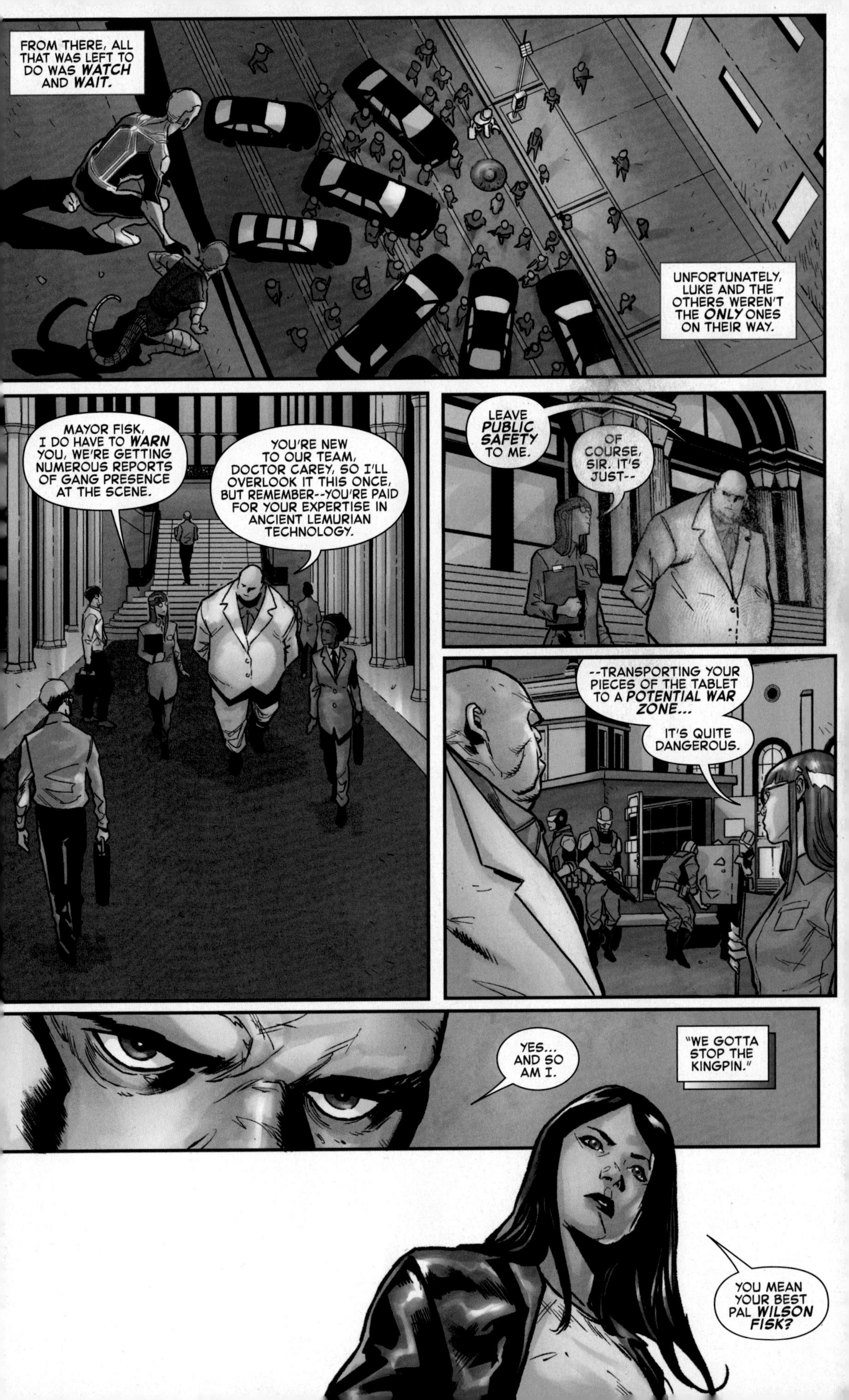
FROM THERE, ALL THAT WAS LEFT TO DO WAS WATCH AND WAIT.
UNFORTUNATELY, LUKE AND THE OTHERS WEREN'T THE ONLY ONES ON THEIR WAY.
MAYOR FISK, I DO HAVE TO WARN YOU, WE'RE GETTING NUMEROUS REPORTS OF GANG PRESENCE AT THE SCENE.
YOU'RE NEW TO OUR TEAM, DOCTOR CAREY, SO I'LL OVERLOOK IT THIS ONCE, BUT REMEMBER--YOU'RE PAID FOR YOUR EXPERTISE IN ANCIENT LEMURIAN TECHNOLOGY.
LEAVE PUBLIC SAFETY TO ME.
OF COURSE, SIR. IT'S JUST--
--TRANSPORTING YOUR PIECES OF THE TABLET TO A POTENTIAL WAR ZONE...
IT'S QUITE DANGEROUS.
YES... AND SO AM I.
"WE GOTTA STOP THE KINGPIN."
YOU MEAN YOUR BEST PAL WILSON FISK?

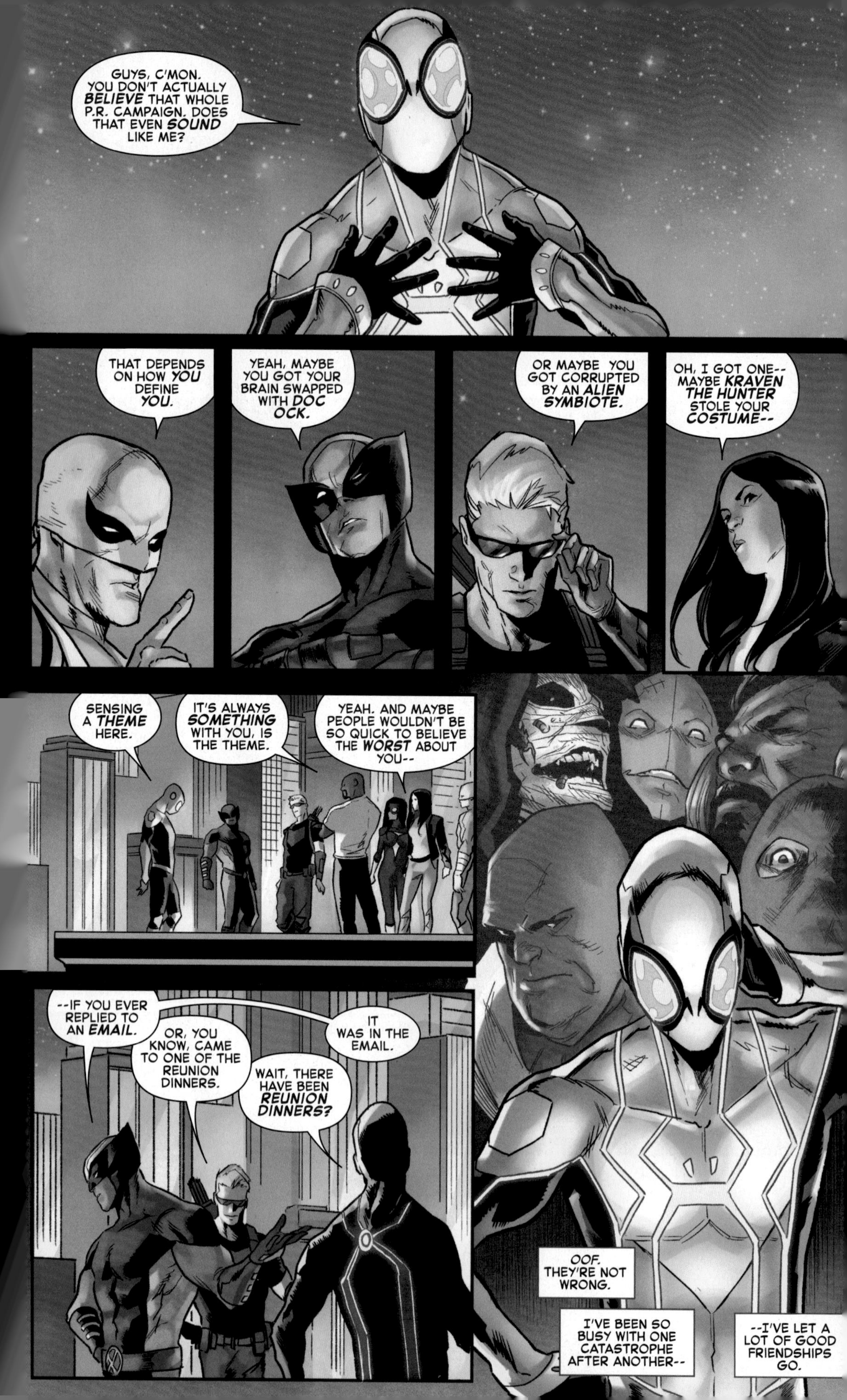

GUYS, C'MON. YOU DON'T ACTUALLY BELIEVE THAT WHOLE P.R. CAMPAIGN. DOES THAT EVEN SOUND LIKE ME?
THAT DEPENDS ON HOW YOU DEFINE YOU.
YEAH, MAYBE YOU GOT YOUR BRAIN SWAPPED WITH DOC OCK.
OR MAYBE YOU GOT CORRUPTED BY AN ALIEN SYMBIOTE.
OH, I GOT ONE-- MAYBE KRAVEN THE HUNTER STOLE YOUR COSTUME--
SENSING A THEME HERE.
IT'S ALWAYS SOMETHING WITH YOU, IS THE THEME.
YEAH. AND MAYBE PEOPLE WOULDN'T BE SO QUICK TO BELIEVE THE WORST ABOUT YOU--
--IF YOU EVER REPLIED TO AN EMAIL.
OR, YOU KNOW, CAME TO ONE OF THE REUNION DINNERS.
IT WAS IN THE EMAIL.
WAIT, THERE HAVE BEEN REUNION DINNERS?
OOF. THEY'RE NOT WRONG.
I'VE BEEN SO BUSY WITH ONE CATASTROPHE AFTER ANOTHER--
--I'VE LET A LOT OF GOOD FRIENDSHIPS GO.

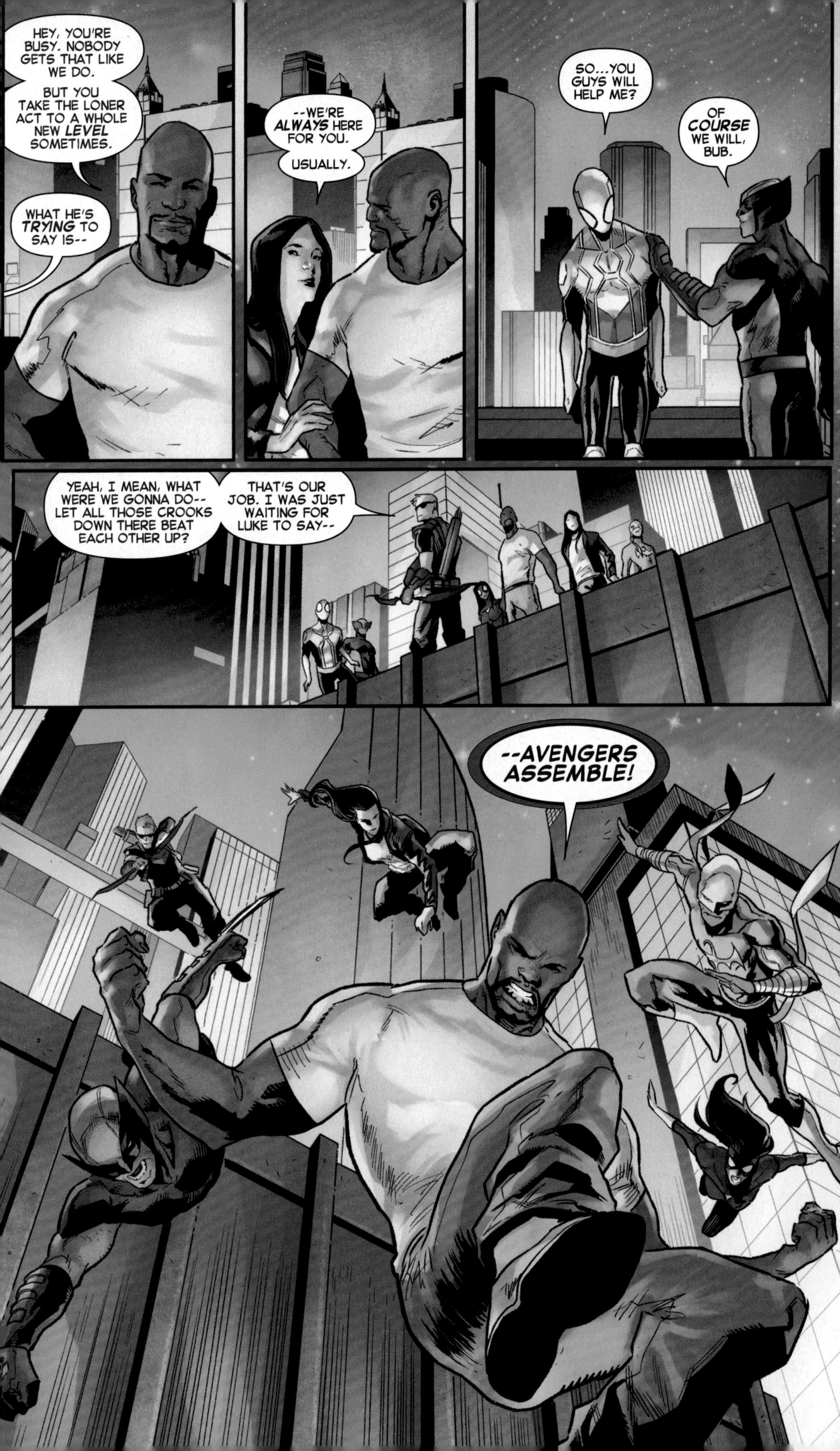
HEY, YOU'RE BUSY. NOBODY GETS THAT LIKE WE DO.
BUT YOU TAKE THE LONER ACT TO A WHOLE NEW LEVEL SOMETIMES.
WHAT HE'S TRYING TO SAY IS--
--WE'RE ALWAYS HERE FOR YOU.
USUALLY.
SO...YOU GUYS WILL HELP ME?
OF COURSE WE WILL, BUB.
YEAH, I MEAN, WHAT WERE WE GONNA DO-- LET ALL THOSE CROOKS DOWN THERE BEAT EACH OTHER UP?
THAT'S OUR JOB. I WAS JUST WAITING FOR LUKE TO SAY--
--AVENGERS ASSEMBLE!

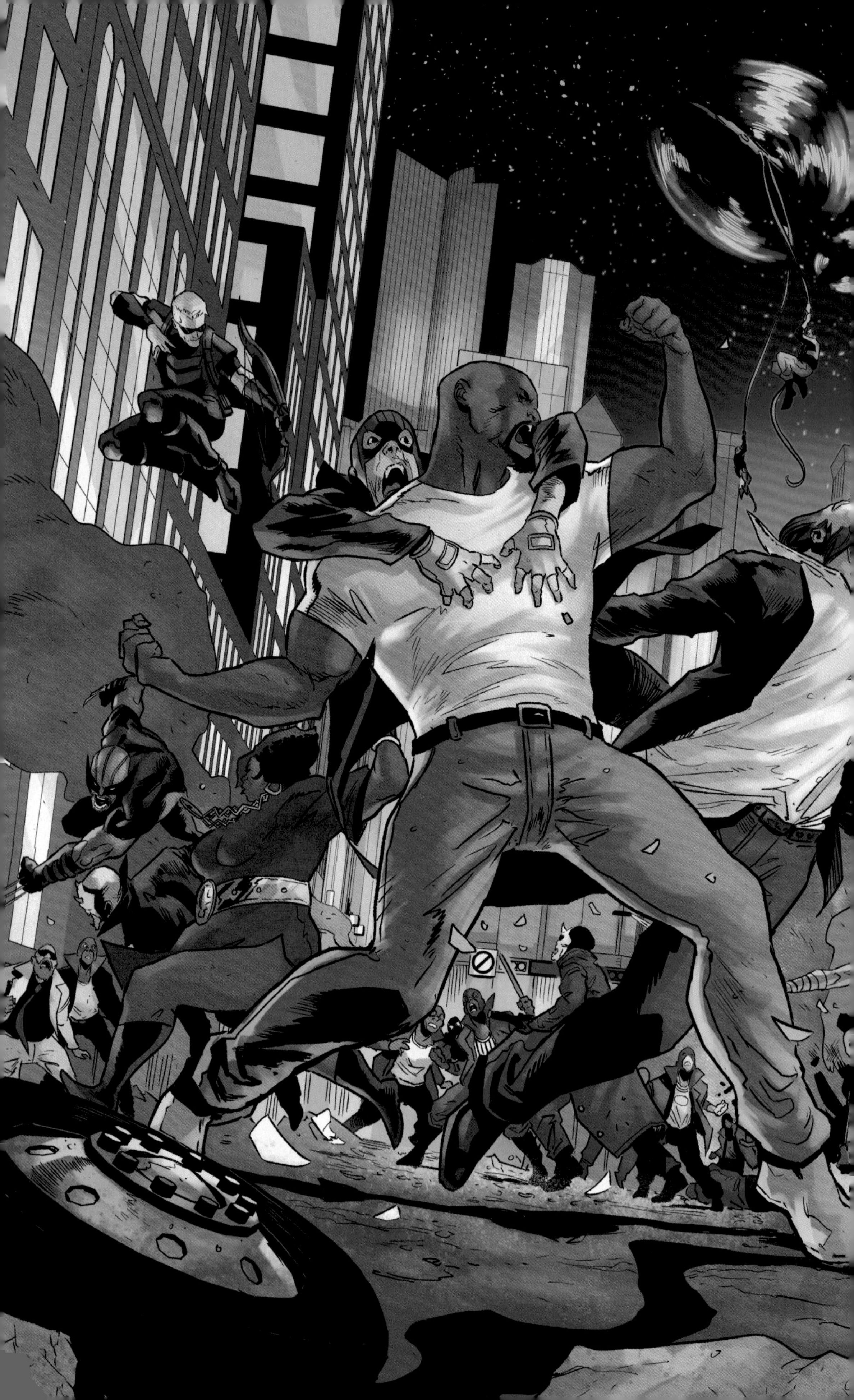

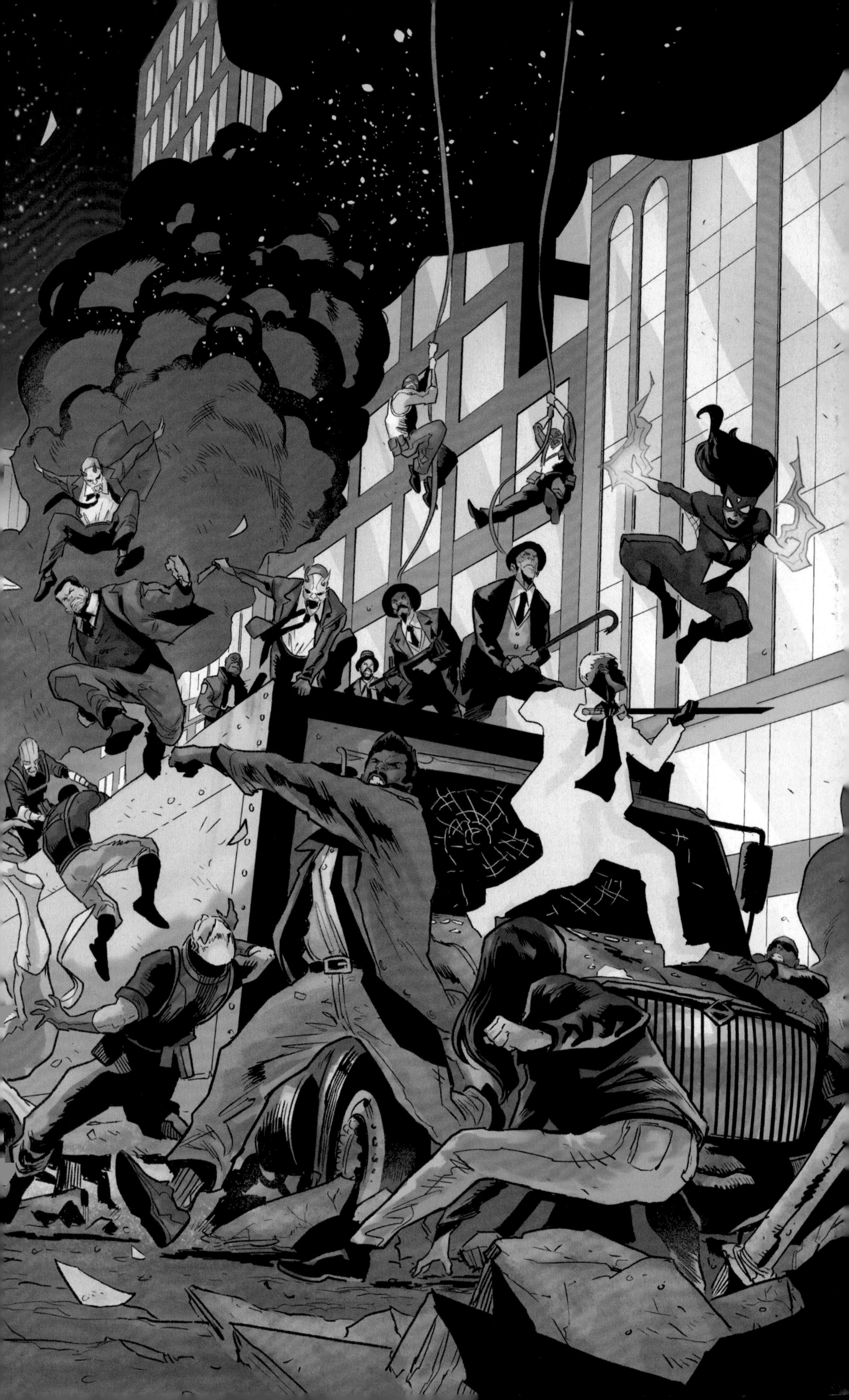

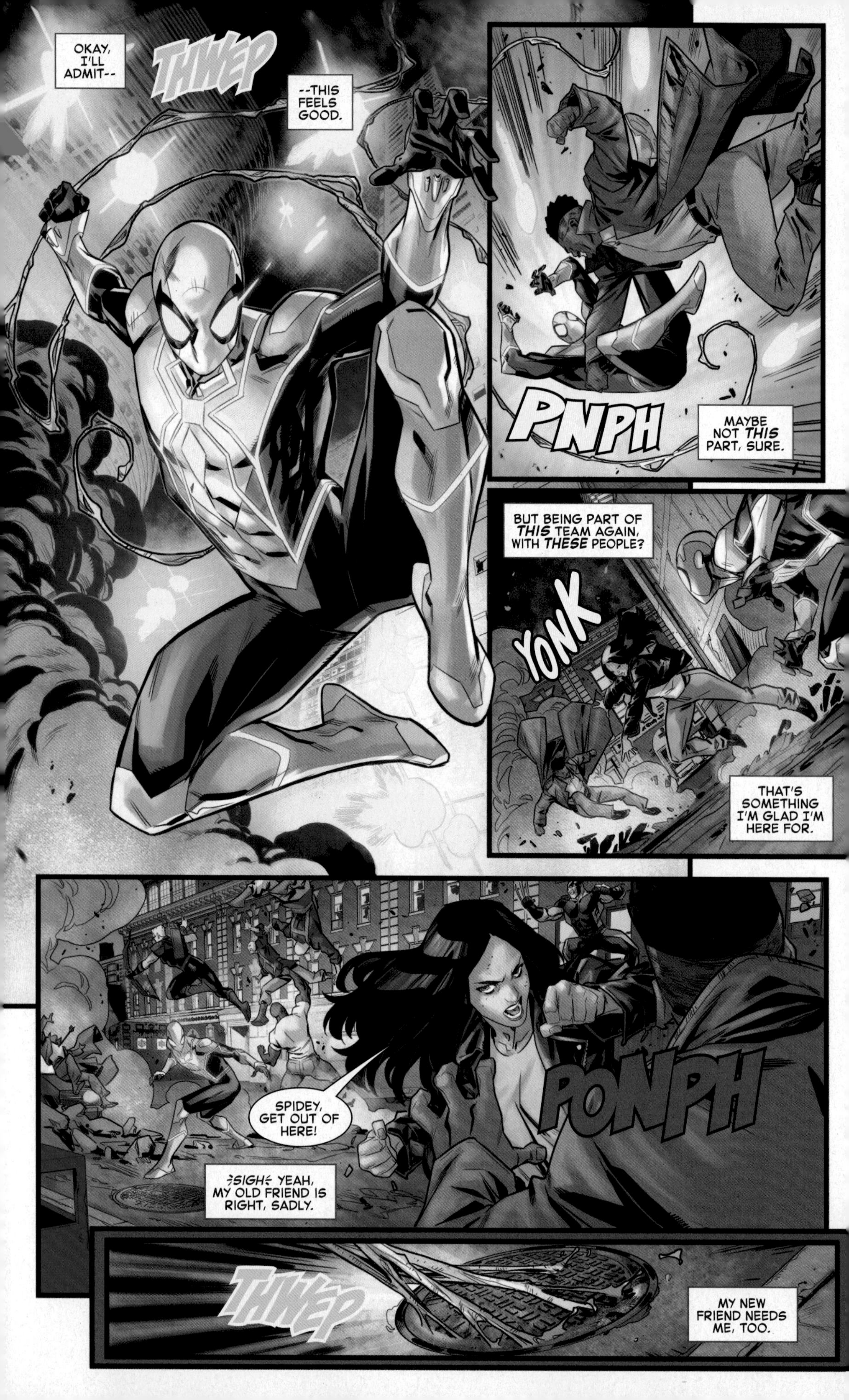

OKAY, I'LL ADMIT--
THWEP
--THIS FEELS GOOD.
PNPH
MAYBE NOT THIS PART, SURE.
BUT BEING PART OF THIS TEAM AGAIN, WITH THESE PEOPLE?
YONK
THAT'S SOMETHING I'M GLAD I'M HERE FOR.
SPIDEY, GET OUT OF HERE!
PONPH
SIGH YEAH, MY OLD FRIEND IS RIGHT, SADLY.
THWEP
MY NEW FRIEND NEEDS ME, TOO.

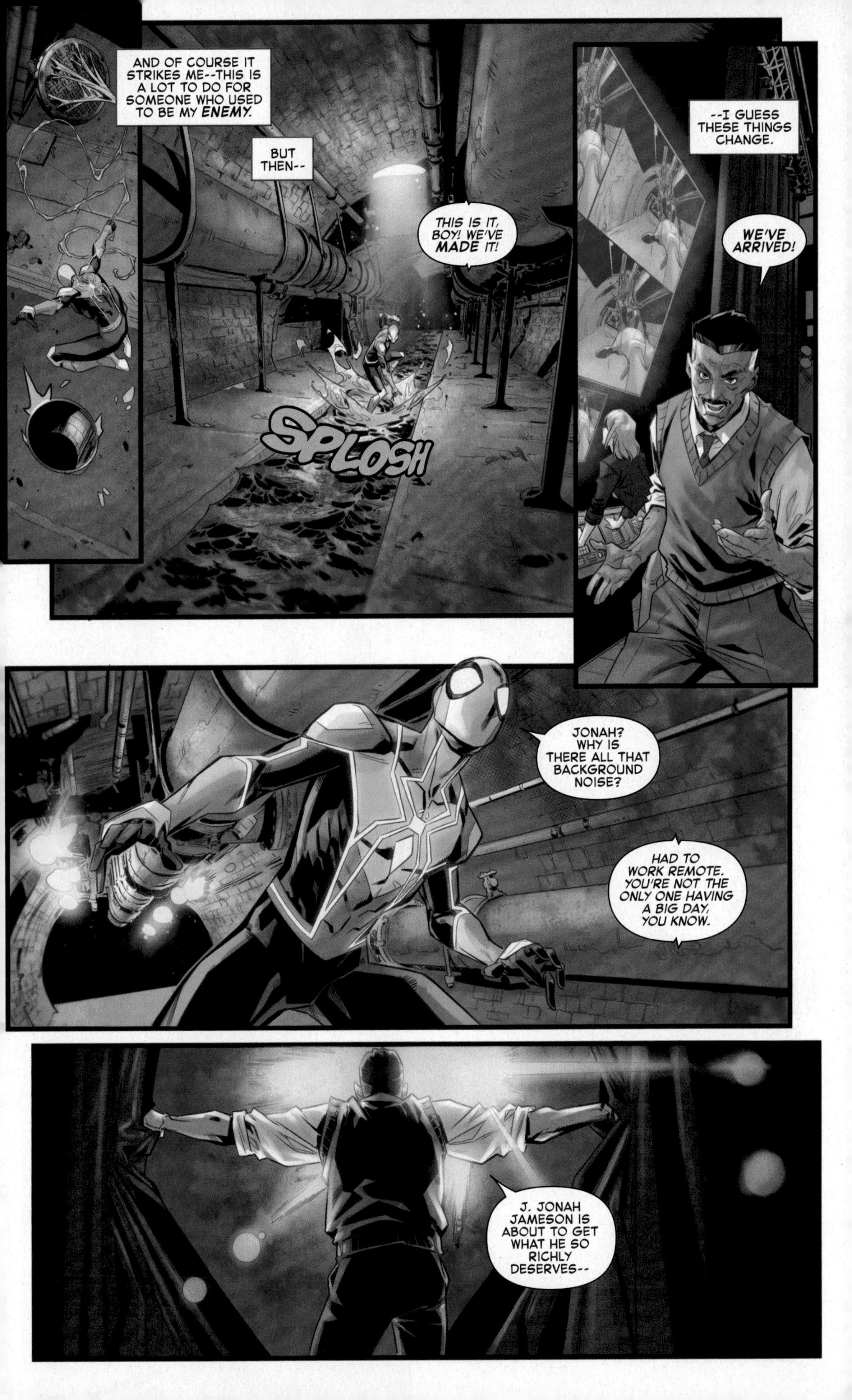
AND OF COURSE IT STRIKES ME--THIS IS A LOT TO DO FOR SOMEONE WHO USED TO BE MY ENEMY.
BUT THEN--
THIS IS IT, BOY! WE'VE MADE IT!
SPLOSH
--I GUESS THESE THINGS CHANGE.
WE'VE ARRIVED!
JONAH? WHY IS THERE ALL THAT BACKGROUND NOISE?
HAD TO WORK REMOTE. YOU'RE NOT THE ONLY ONE HAVING A BIG DAY, YOU KNOW.
J. JONAH JAMESON IS ABOUT TO GET WHAT HE SO RICHLY DESERVES--

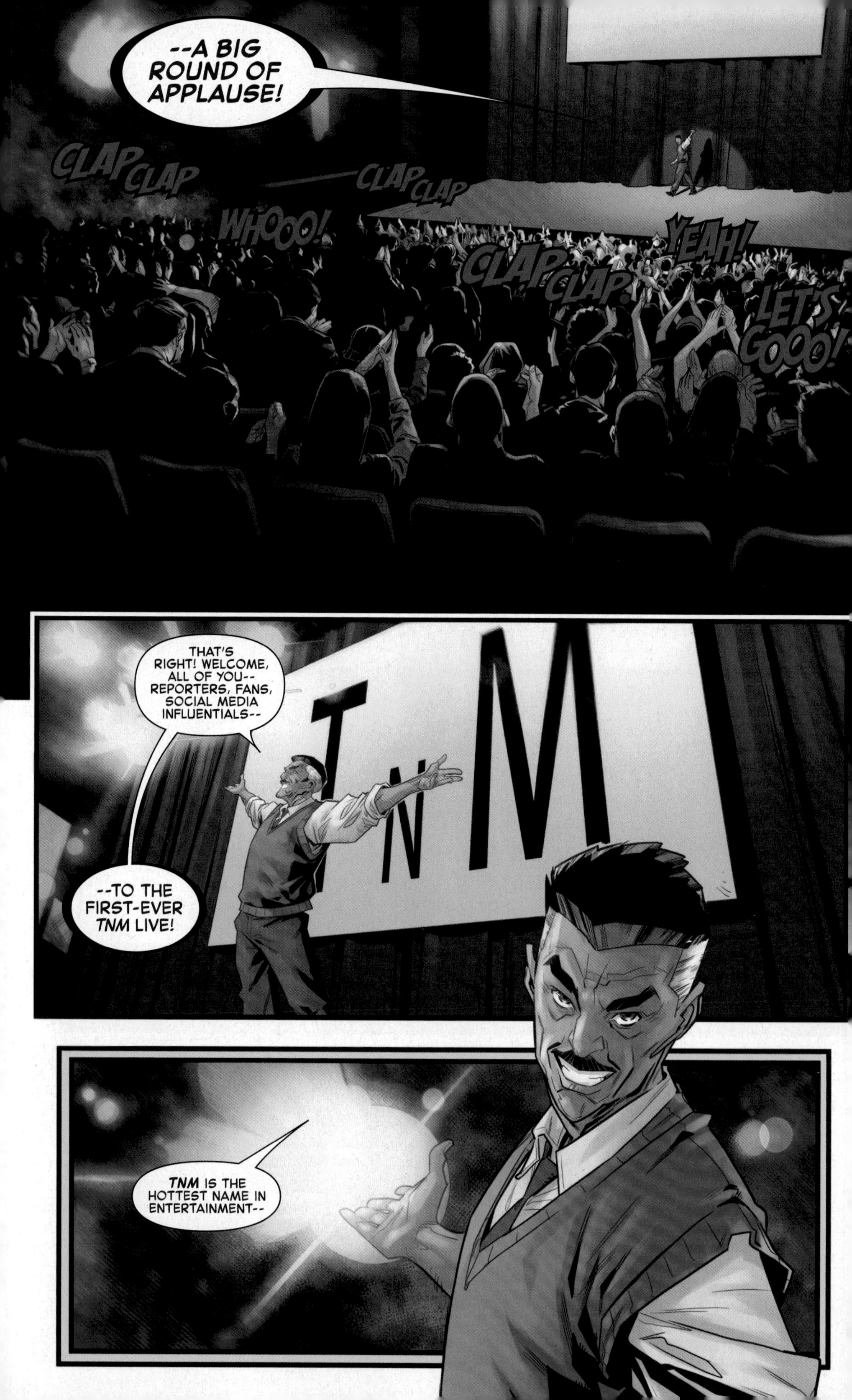
--A BIG ROUND OF APPLAUSE!
CLAP CLAP
CLAP CLAP
WHOOO!
YEAH!
CLAP CLAP
LET'S GOOO!
THAT'S RIGHT! WELCOME, ALL OF YOU-- REPORTERS, FANS, SOCIAL MEDIA INFLUENTIALS--
--TO THE FIRST-EVER *TNM* LIVE!
TNM
TNM IS THE HOTTEST NAME IN ENTERTAINMENT--

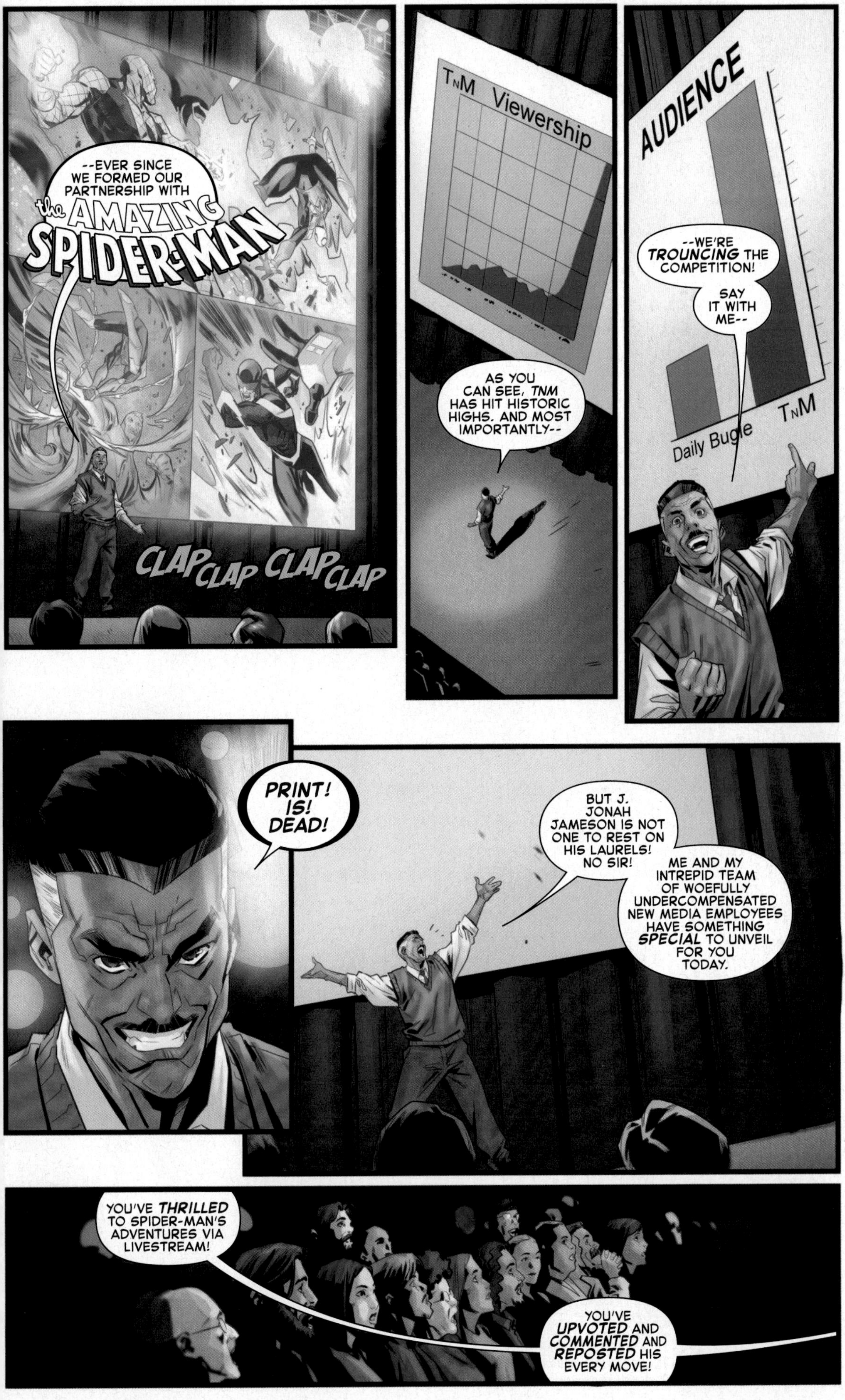
--EVER SINCE WE FORMED OUR PARTNERSHIP WITH the AMAZING SPIDER-MAN
CLAP CLAP CLAP CLAP
TNM Viewership
AS YOU CAN SEE, TNM HAS HIT HISTORIC HIGHS. AND MOST IMPORTANTLY--
AUDIENCE
Daily Bugle
TNM
--WE'RE TROUNCING THE COMPETITION!
SAY IT WITH ME--
PRINT! IS! DEAD!
BUT J. JONAH JAMESON IS NOT ONE TO REST ON HIS LAURELS! NO SIR!
ME AND MY INTREPID TEAM OF WOEFULLY UNDERCOMPENSATED NEW MEDIA EMPLOYEES HAVE SOMETHING SPECIAL TO UNVEIL FOR YOU TODAY.
YOU'VE THRILLED TO SPIDER-MAN'S ADVENTURES VIA LIVESTREAM!
YOU'VE UPVOTED AND COMMENTED AND REPOSTED HIS EVERY MOVE!

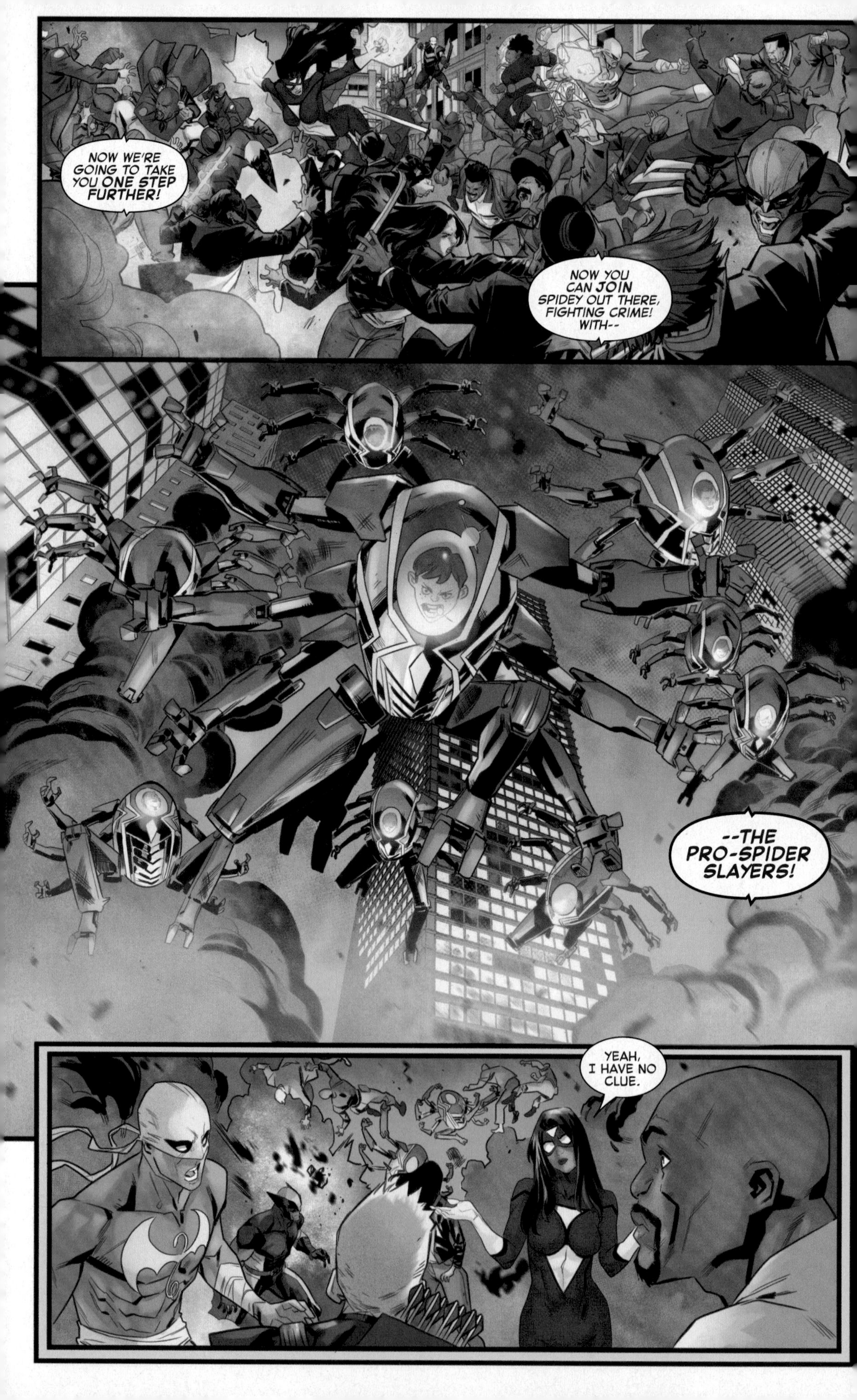
NOW WE'RE GOING TO TAKE YOU ONE STEP FURTHER!
NOW YOU CAN JOIN SPIDEY OUT THERE, FIGHTING CRIME! WITH--
--THE PRO-SPIDER SLAYERS!
YEAH, I HAVE NO CLUE.

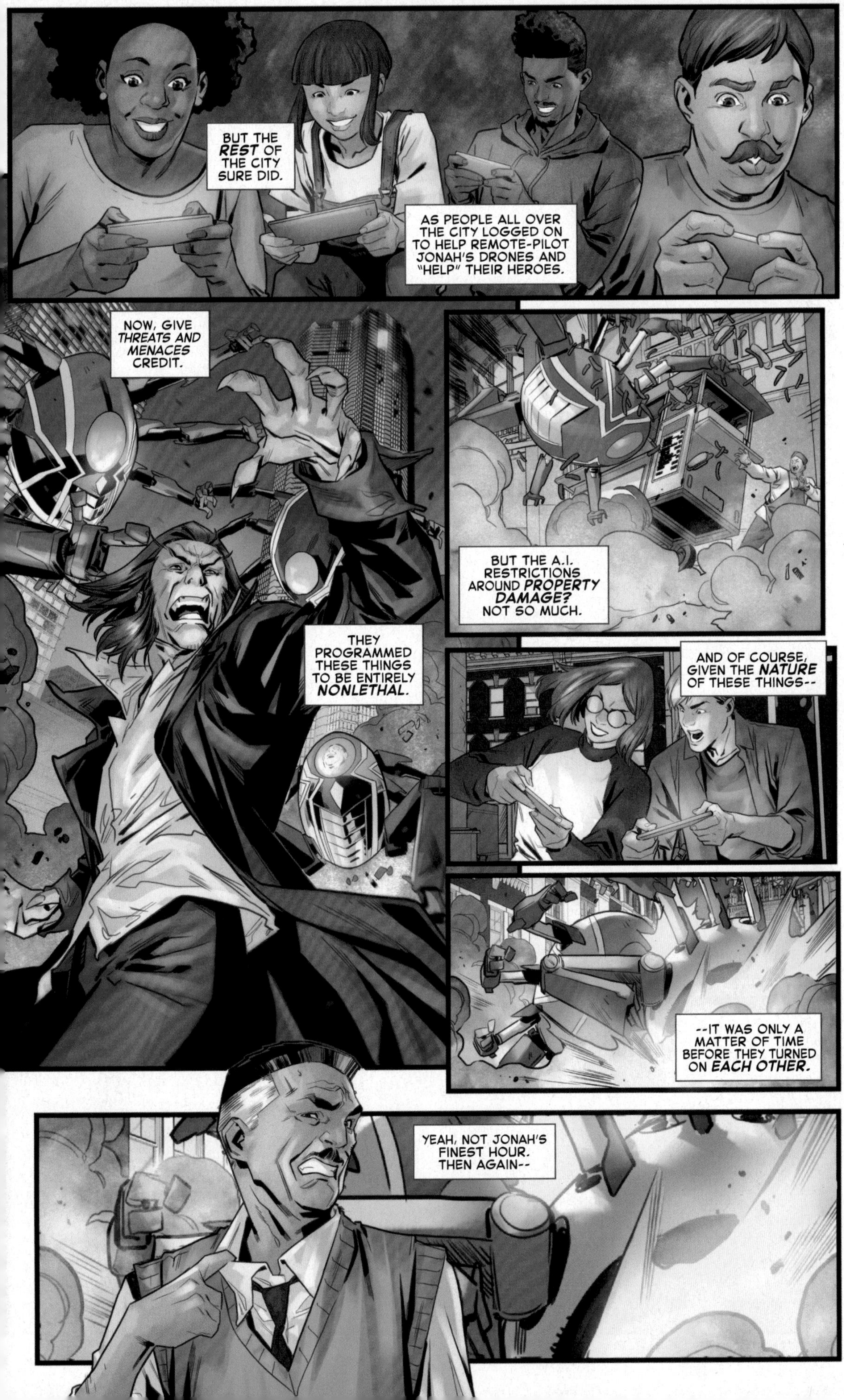
BUT THE REST OF THE CITY SURE DID.
AS PEOPLE ALL OVER THE CITY LOGGED ON TO HELP REMOTE-PILOT JONAH'S DRONES AND "HELP" THEIR HEROES.
NOW, GIVE THREATS AND MENACES CREDIT.
THEY PROGRAMMED THESE THINGS TO BE ENTIRELY NONLETHAL.
BUT THE A.I. RESTRICTIONS AROUND PROPERTY DAMAGE? NOT SO MUCH.
AND OF COURSE, GIVEN THE NATURE OF THESE THINGS--
--IT WAS ONLY A MATTER OF TIME BEFORE THEY TURNED ON EACH OTHER.
YEAH, NOT JONAH'S FINEST HOUR. THEN AGAIN--

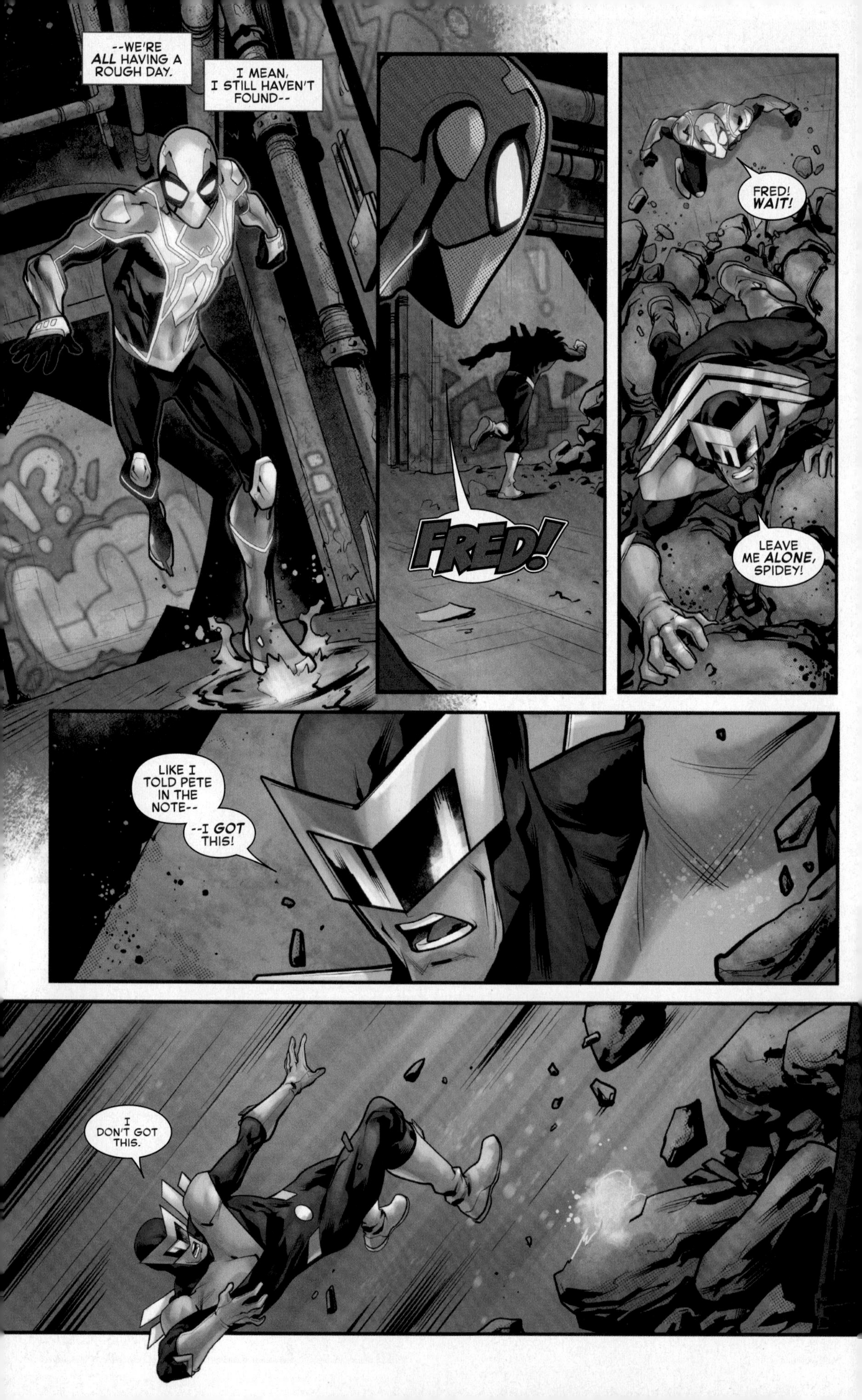
--WE'RE ALL HAVING A ROUGH DAY.
I MEAN, I STILL HAVEN'T FOUND--
FRED!
FRED! WAIT!
LEAVE ME ALONE, SPIDEY!
LIKE I TOLD PETE IN THE NOTE--
--I GOT THIS!
I DON'T GOT THIS.

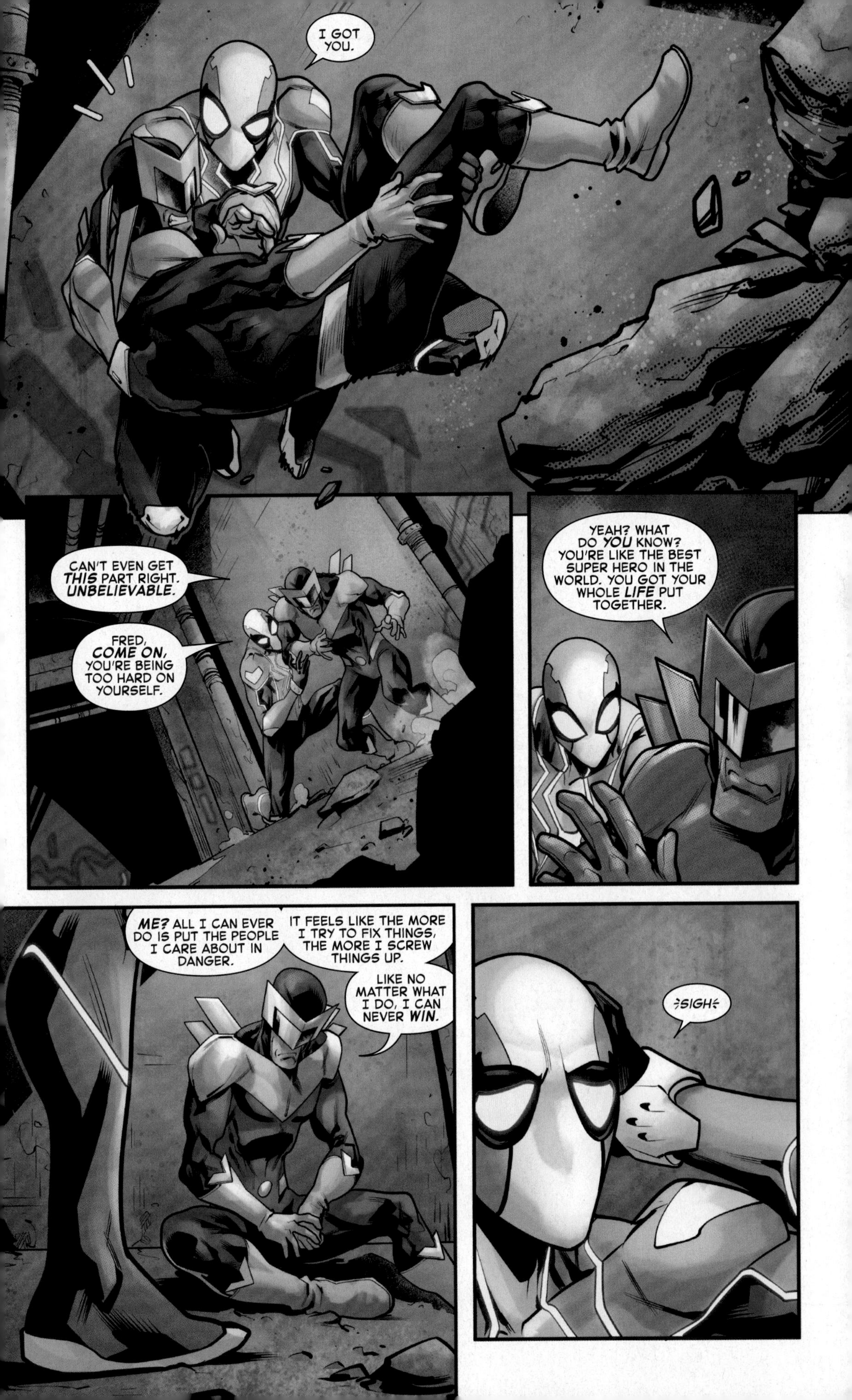
I GOT YOU.
CAN'T EVEN GET *THIS* PART RIGHT. ***UNBELIEVABLE.***
FRED, ***COME ON,*** YOU'RE BEING TOO HARD ON YOURSELF.
YEAH? WHAT DO *YOU* KNOW? YOU'RE LIKE THE BEST SUPER HERO IN THE WORLD. YOU GOT YOUR WHOLE *LIFE* PUT TOGETHER.
ME? ALL I CAN EVER DO IS PUT THE PEOPLE I CARE ABOUT IN DANGER.
IT FEELS LIKE THE MORE I TRY TO FIX THINGS, THE MORE I SCREW THINGS UP.
LIKE NO MATTER WHAT I DO, I CAN NEVER ***WIN.***
SIGH

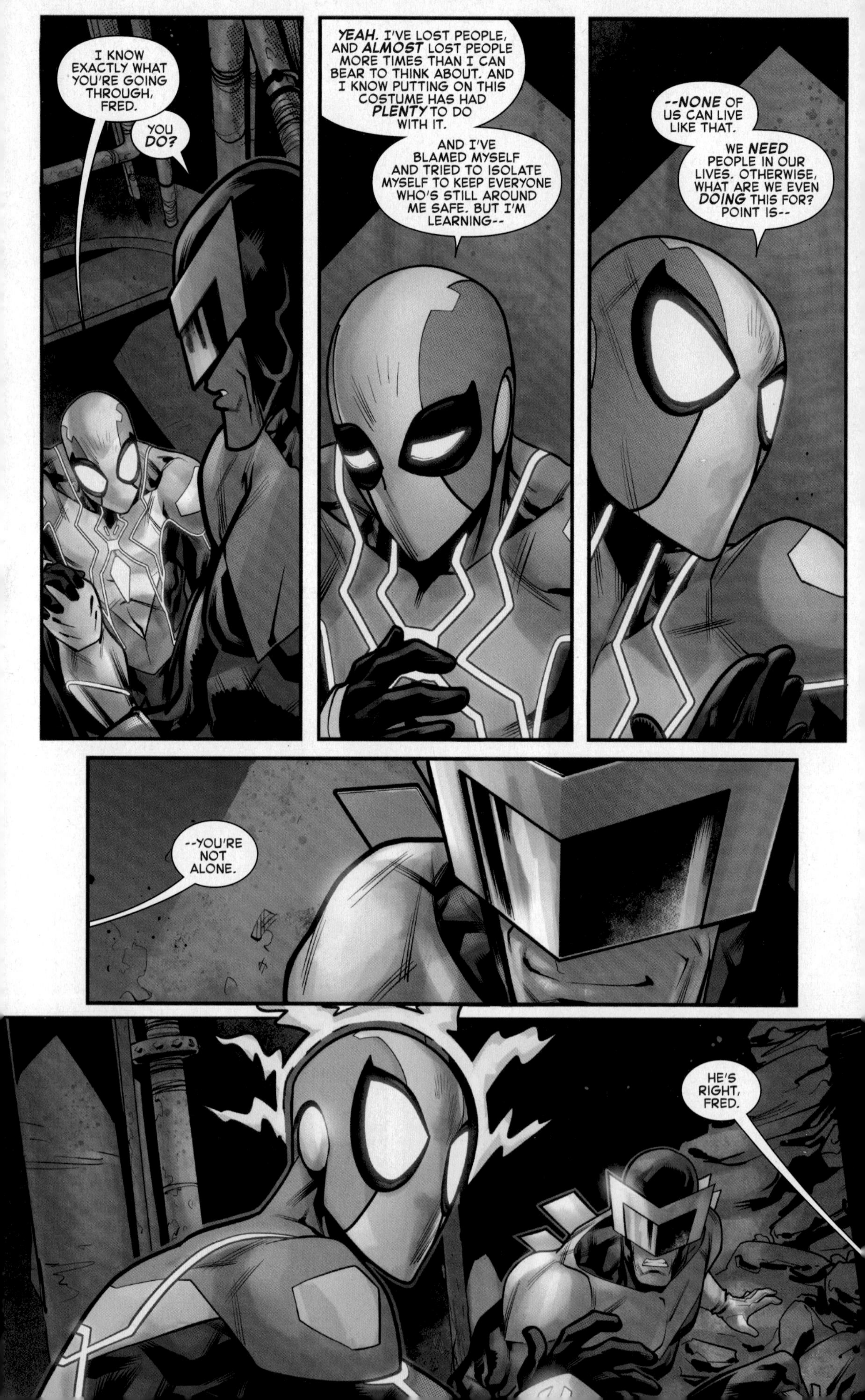
I KNOW EXACTLY WHAT YOU'RE GOING THROUGH, FRED.
YOU DO?
YEAH. I'VE LOST PEOPLE, AND ALMOST LOST PEOPLE MORE TIMES THAN I CAN BEAR TO THINK ABOUT. AND I KNOW PUTTING ON THIS COSTUME HAS HAD PLENTY TO DO WITH IT.
AND I'VE BLAMED MYSELF AND TRIED TO ISOLATE MYSELF TO KEEP EVERYONE WHO'S STILL AROUND ME SAFE. BUT I'M LEARNING--
--NONE OF US CAN LIVE LIKE THAT.
WE NEED PEOPLE IN OUR LIVES. OTHERWISE, WHAT ARE WE EVEN DOING THIS FOR? POINT IS--
--YOU'RE NOT ALONE.
HE'S RIGHT, FRED.

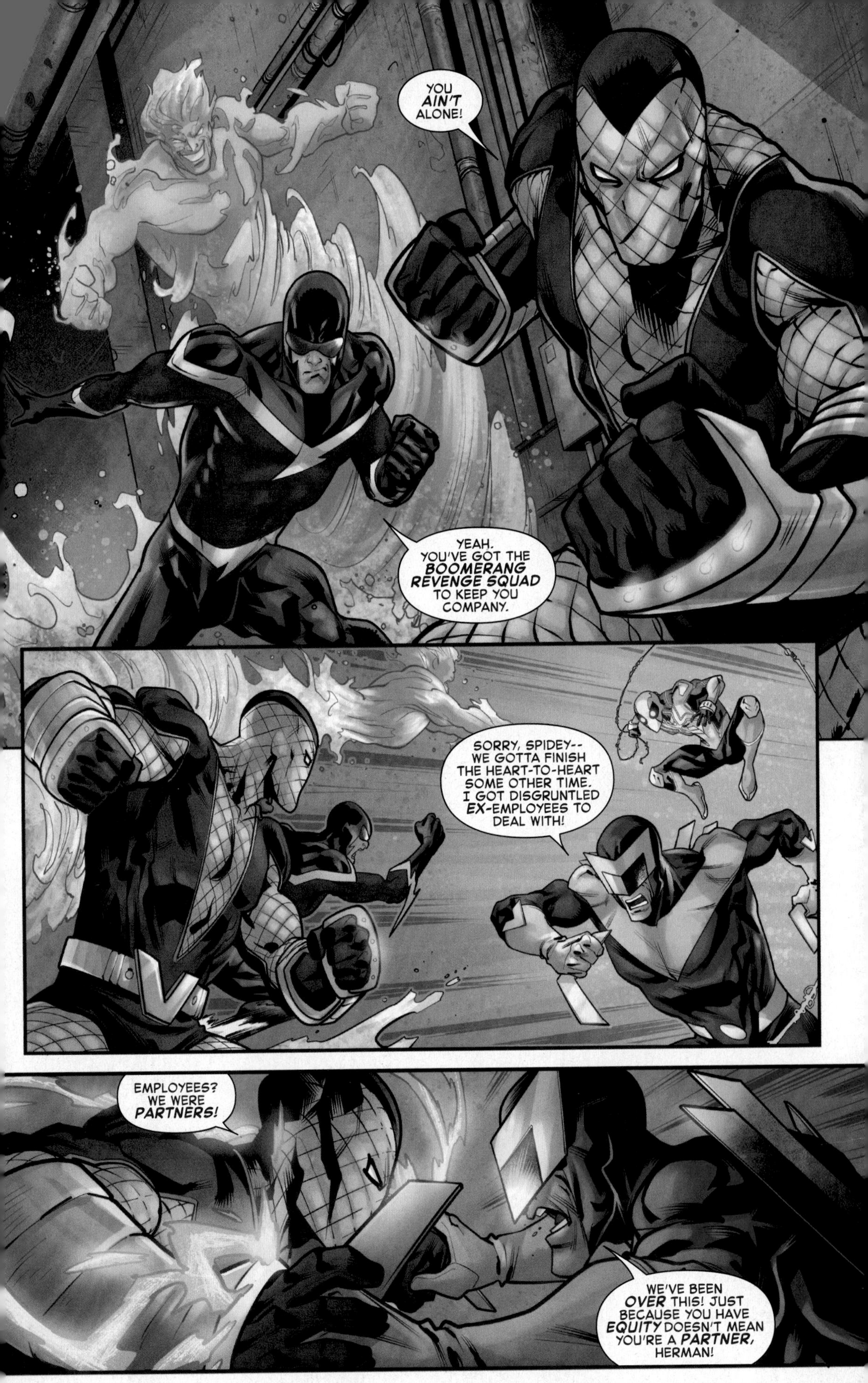

YOU AIN'T ALONE!
YEAH. YOU'VE GOT THE BOOMERANG REVENGE SQUAD TO KEEP YOU COMPANY.
SORRY, SPIDEY-- WE GOTTA FINISH THE HEART-TO-HEART SOME OTHER TIME. I GOT DISGRUNTLED EX-EMPLOYEES TO DEAL WITH!
EMPLOYEES? WE WERE PARTNERS!
WE'VE BEEN OVER THIS! JUST BECAUSE YOU HAVE EQUITY DOESN'T MEAN YOU'RE A PARTNER, HERMAN!

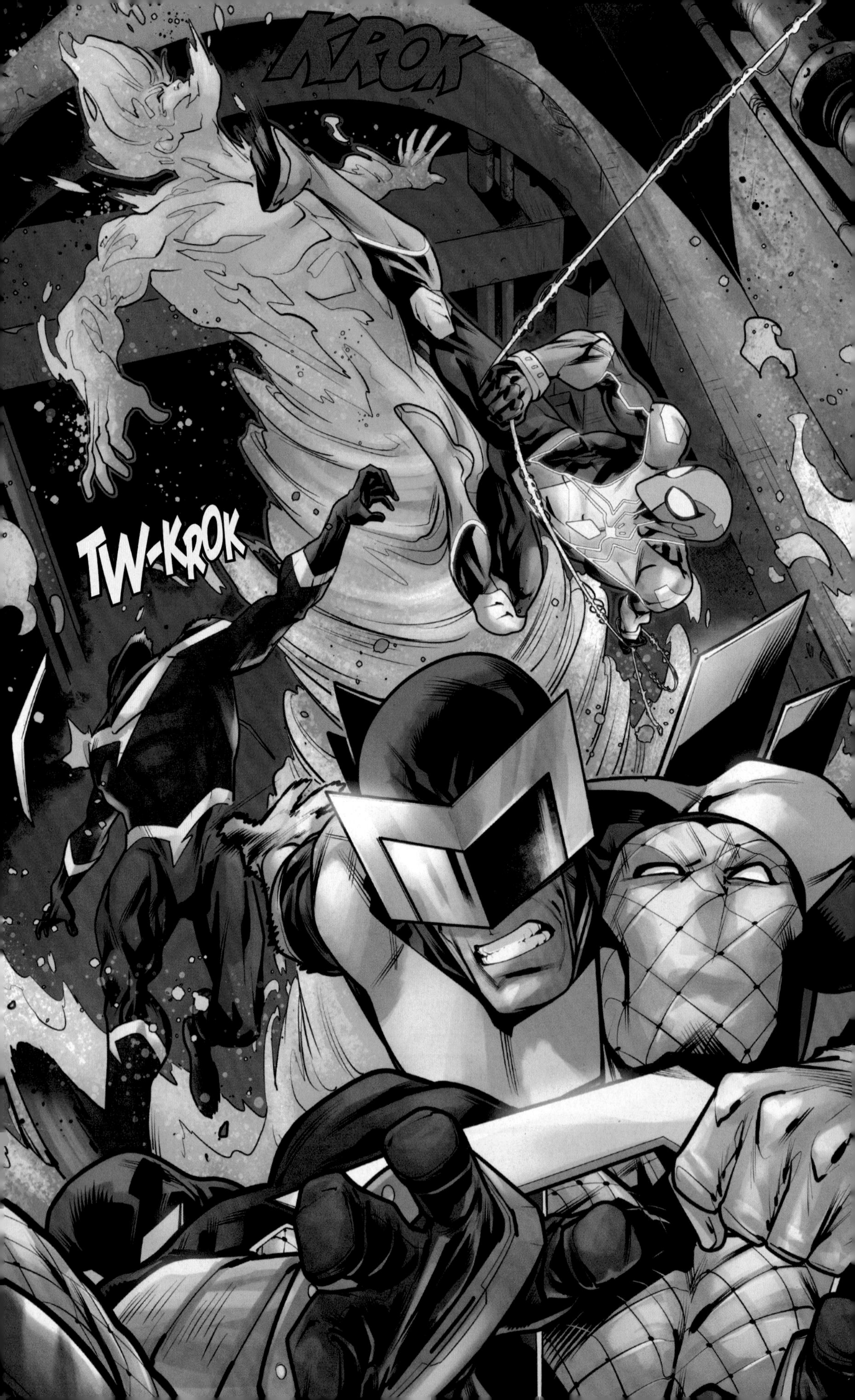
KROK
TW-KROK

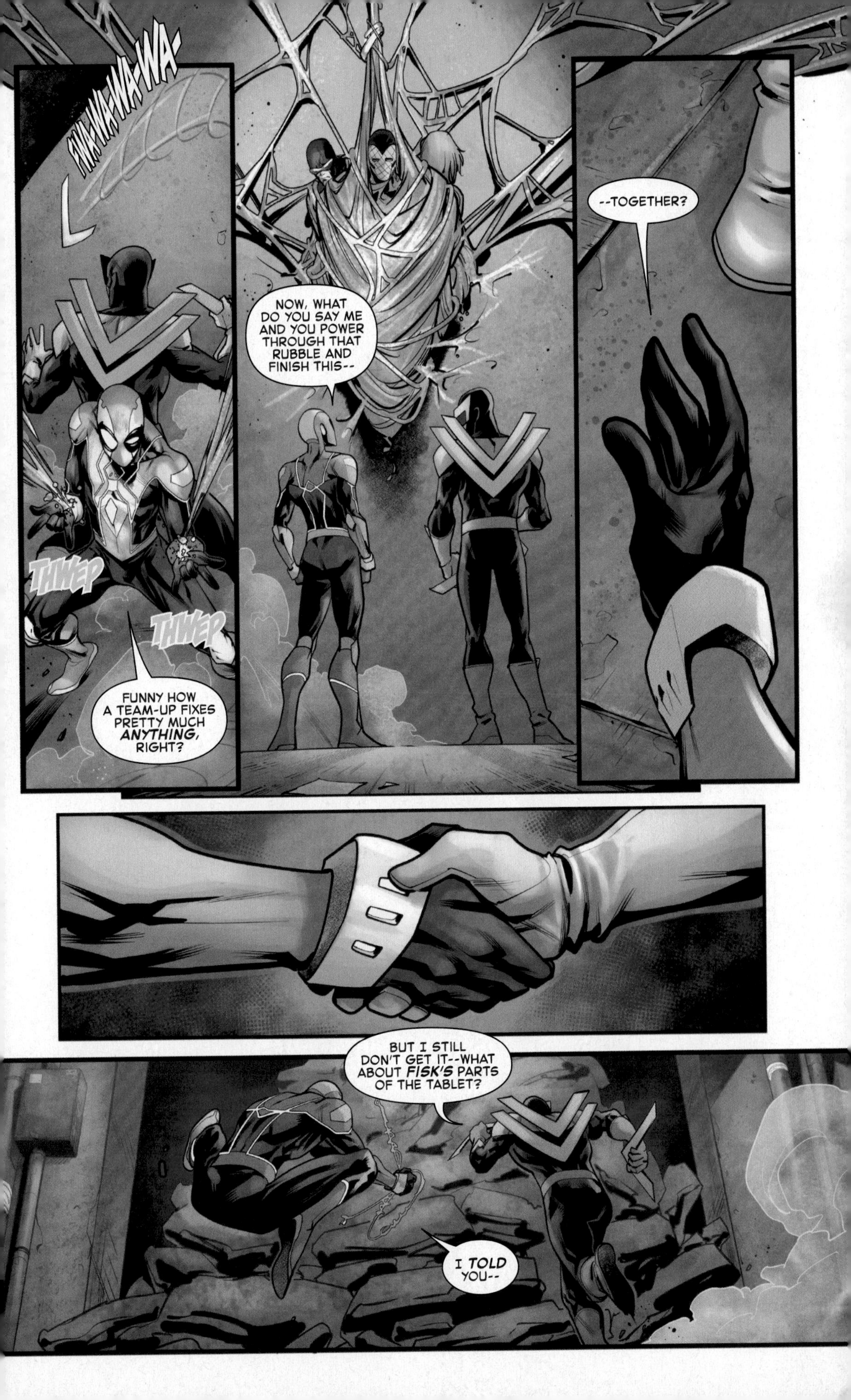
FWA-WA-WA-WA-
THWEP
THWEP
FUNNY HOW A TEAM-UP FIXES PRETTY MUCH *ANYTHING*, RIGHT?
NOW, WHAT DO YOU SAY ME AND YOU POWER THROUGH THAT RUBBLE AND FINISH THIS--
--TOGETHER?
BUT I STILL DON'T GET IT--WHAT ABOUT *FISK'S* PARTS OF THE TABLET?
I *TOLD* YOU--

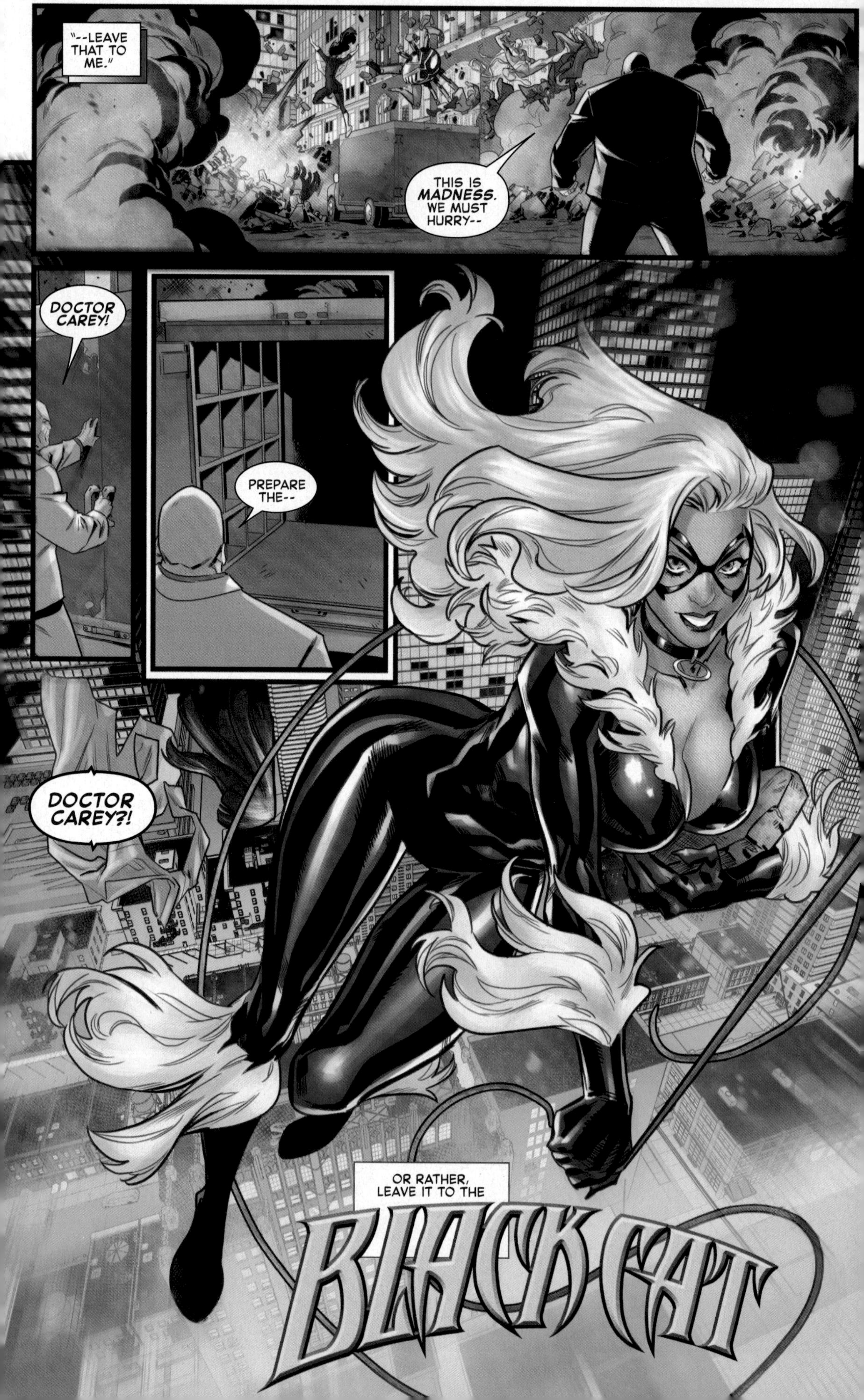
"--LEAVE THAT TO ME."
THIS IS MADNESS. WE MUST HURRY--
DOCTOR CAREY!
PREPARE THE--
DOCTOR CAREY?!
OR RATHER, LEAVE IT TO THE
BLACK CAT

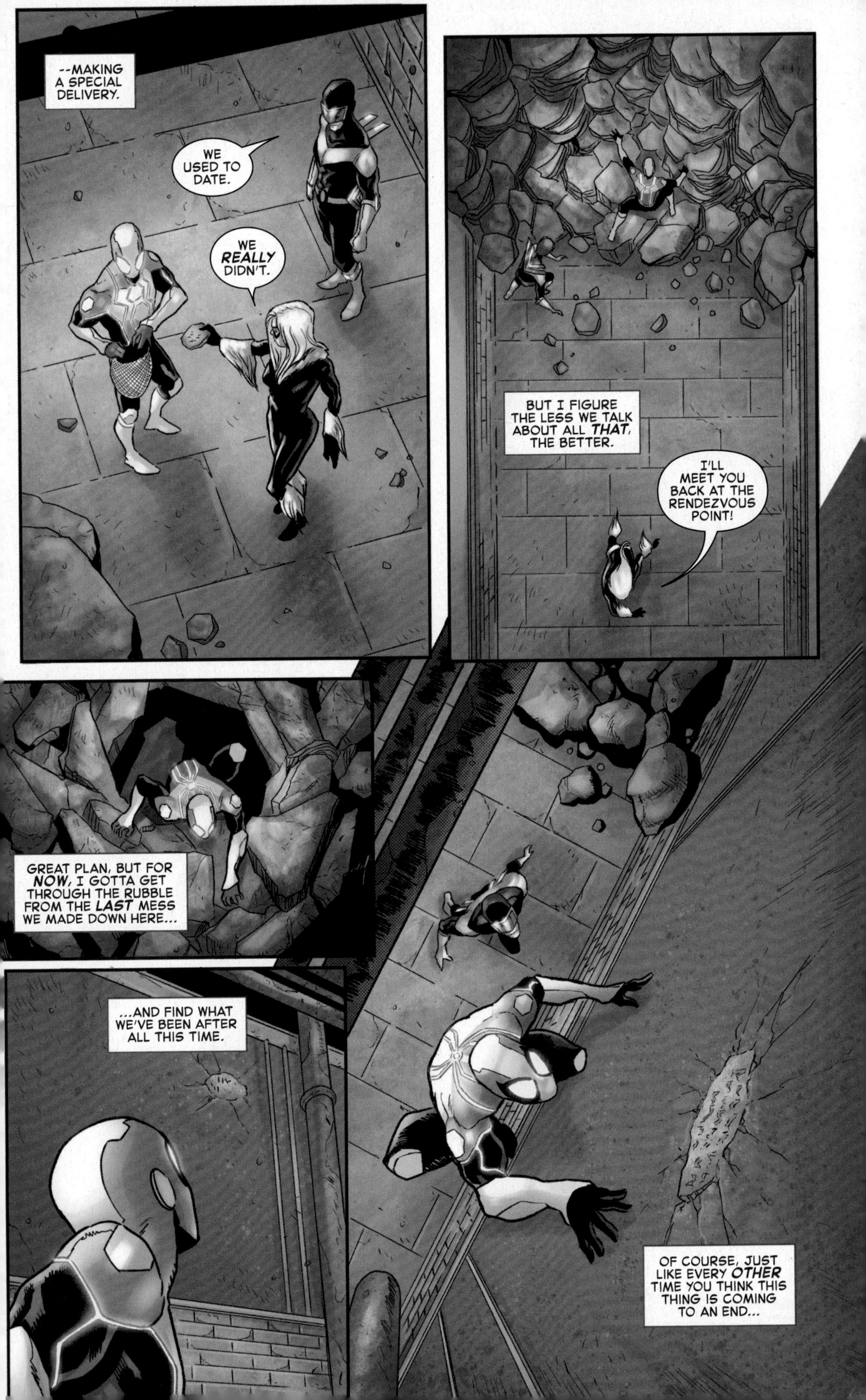
--MAKING A SPECIAL DELIVERY.
WE USED TO DATE.
WE REALLY DIDN'T.
BUT I FIGURE THE LESS WE TALK ABOUT ALL THAT, THE BETTER.
I'LL MEET YOU BACK AT THE RENDEZVOUS POINT!
GREAT PLAN, BUT FOR NOW, I GOTTA GET THROUGH THE RUBBLE FROM THE LAST MESS WE MADE DOWN HERE...
...AND FIND WHAT WE'VE BEEN AFTER ALL THIS TIME.
OF COURSE, JUST LIKE EVERY OTHER TIME YOU THINK THIS THING IS COMING TO AN END...

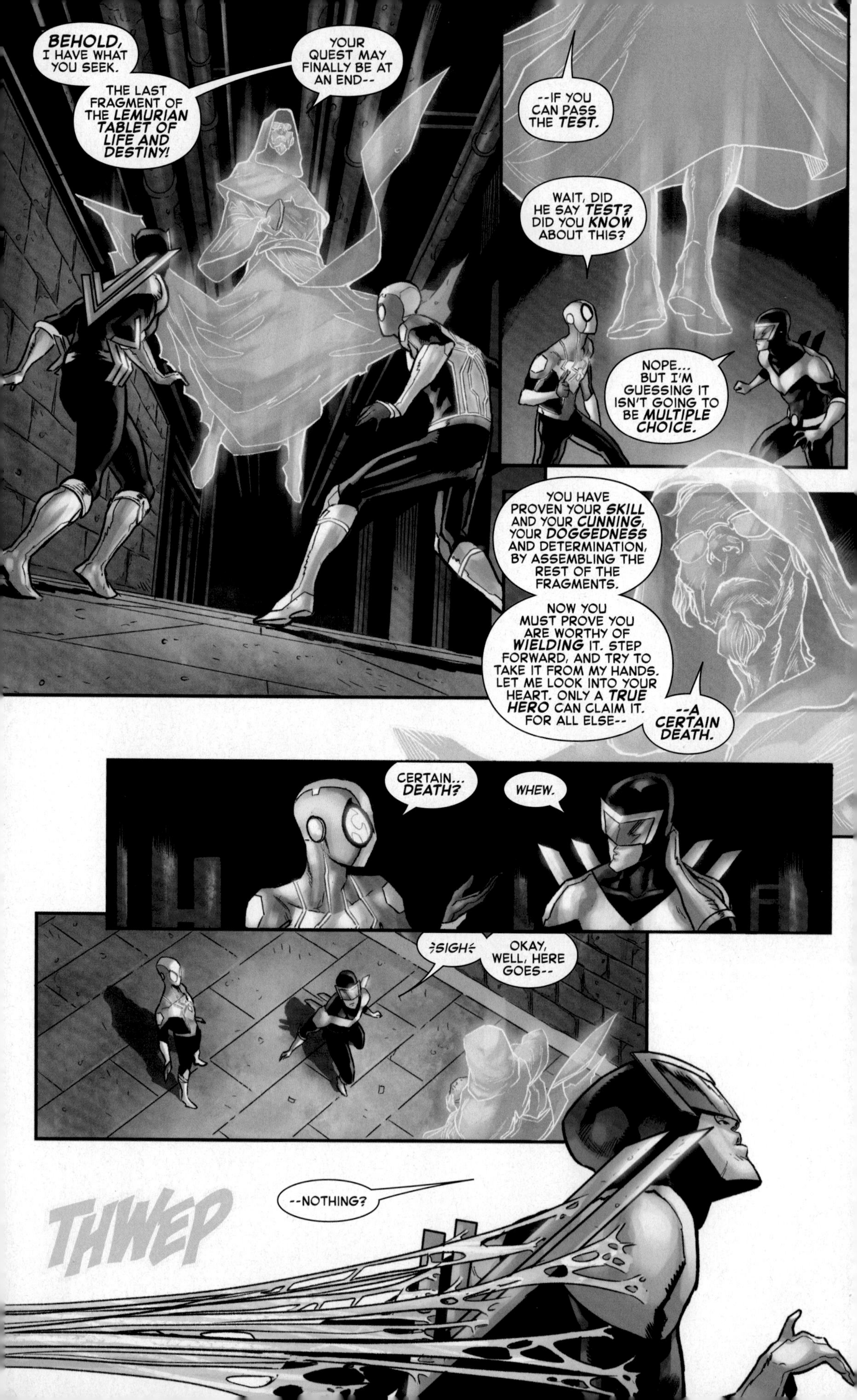
BEHOLD, I HAVE WHAT YOU SEEK.
THE LAST FRAGMENT OF THE LEMURIAN TABLET OF LIFE AND DESTINY!
YOUR QUEST MAY FINALLY BE AT AN END--
--IF YOU CAN PASS THE TEST.
WAIT, DID HE SAY TEST? DID YOU KNOW ABOUT THIS?
NOPE... BUT I'M GUESSING IT ISN'T GOING TO BE MULTIPLE CHOICE.
YOU HAVE PROVEN YOUR SKILL AND YOUR CUNNING, YOUR DOGGEDNESS AND DETERMINATION, BY ASSEMBLING THE REST OF THE FRAGMENTS.
NOW YOU MUST PROVE YOU ARE WORTHY OF WIELDING IT. STEP FORWARD, AND TRY TO TAKE IT FROM MY HANDS. LET ME LOOK INTO YOUR HEART. ONLY A TRUE HERO CAN CLAIM IT. FOR ALL ELSE--
--A CERTAIN DEATH.
CERTAIN... DEATH?
WHEW.
SIGH
OKAY, WELL, HERE GOES--
--NOTHING?
THWEP

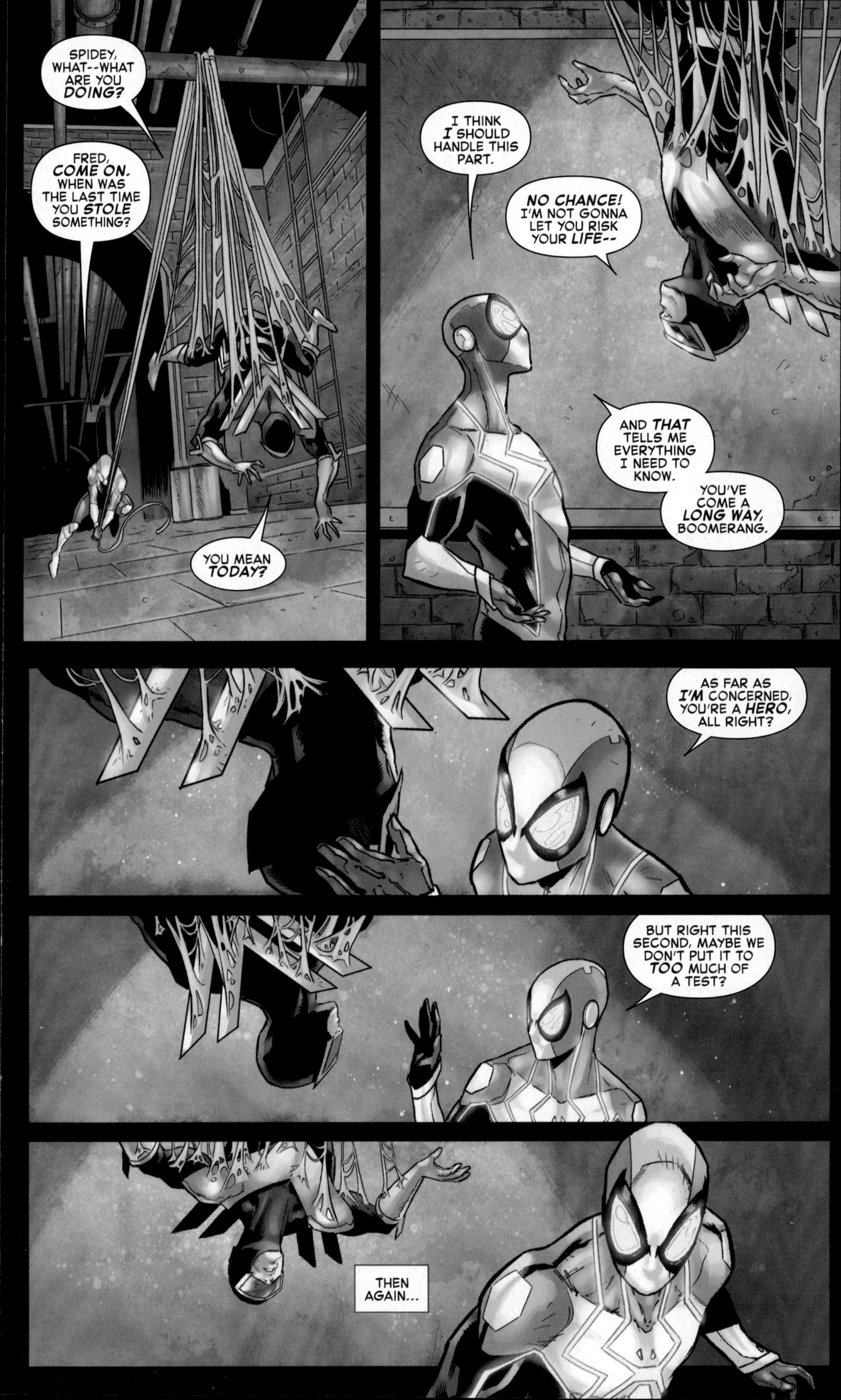

SPIDEY, WHAT--WHAT ARE YOU DOING?
FRED, COME ON. WHEN WAS THE LAST TIME YOU STOLE SOMETHING?
YOU MEAN TODAY?
I THINK I SHOULD HANDLE THIS PART.
NO CHANCE! I'M NOT GONNA LET YOU RISK YOUR LIFE--
AND THAT TELLS ME EVERYTHING I NEED TO KNOW.
YOU'VE COME A LONG WAY, BOOMERANG.
AS FAR AS I'M CONCERNED, YOU'RE A HERO, ALL RIGHT?
BUT RIGHT THIS SECOND, MAYBE WE DON'T PUT IT TO TOO MUCH OF A TEST?
THEN AGAIN...

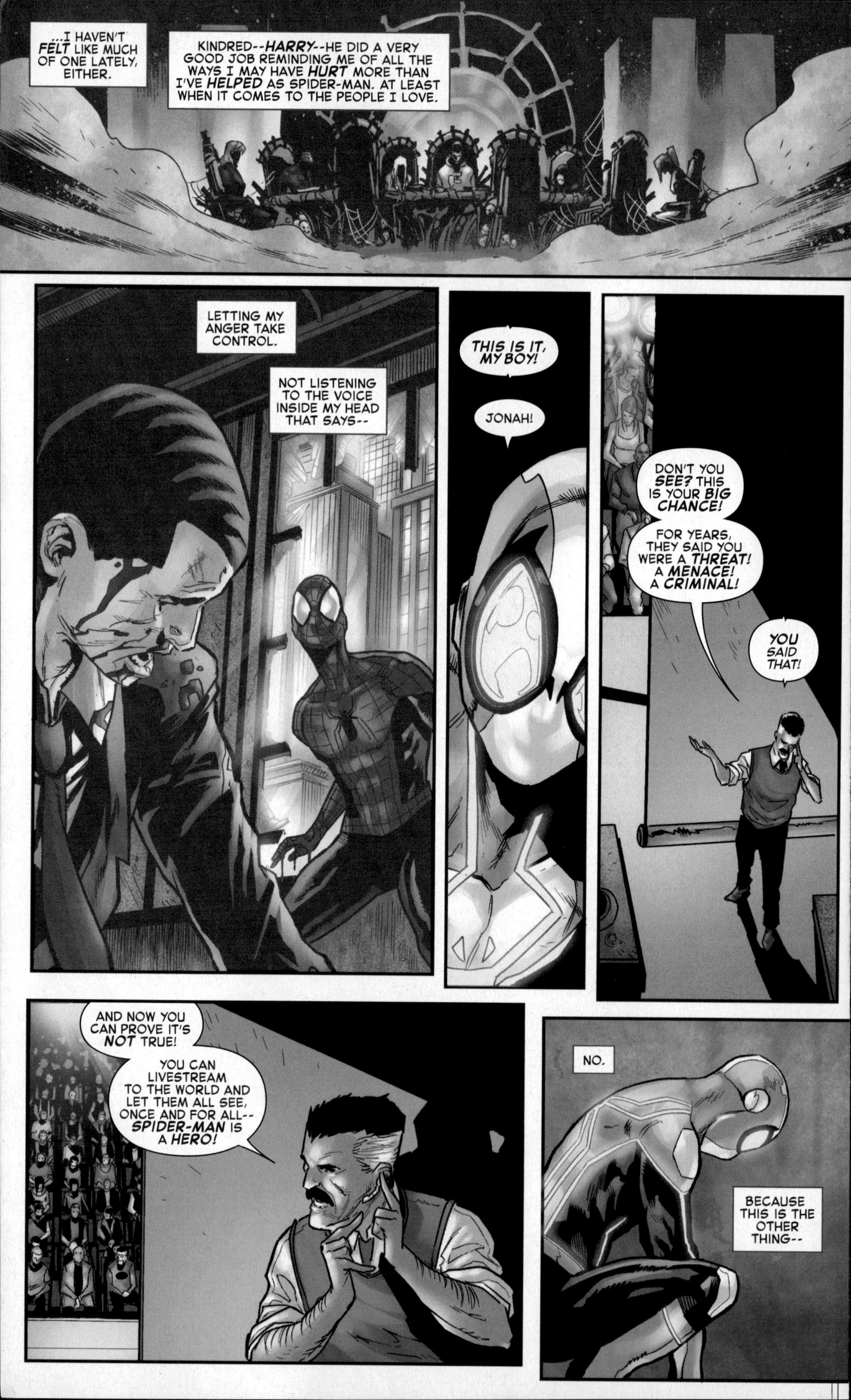
...I HAVEN'T FELT LIKE MUCH OF ONE LATELY, EITHER.
KINDRED--HARRY--HE DID A VERY GOOD JOB REMINDING ME OF ALL THE WAYS I MAY HAVE HURT MORE THAN I'VE HELPED AS SPIDER-MAN. AT LEAST WHEN IT COMES TO THE PEOPLE I LOVE.
LETTING MY ANGER TAKE CONTROL.
NOT LISTENING TO THE VOICE INSIDE MY HEAD THAT SAYS--
THIS IS IT, MY BOY!
JONAH!
DON'T YOU SEE? THIS IS YOUR BIG CHANCE!
FOR YEARS, THEY SAID YOU WERE A THREAT! A MENACE! A CRIMINAL!
YOU SAID THAT!
AND NOW YOU CAN PROVE IT'S NOT TRUE!
YOU CAN LIVESTREAM TO THE WORLD AND LET THEM ALL SEE, ONCE AND FOR ALL-- SPIDER-MAN IS A HERO!
NO.
BECAUSE THIS IS THE OTHER THING--

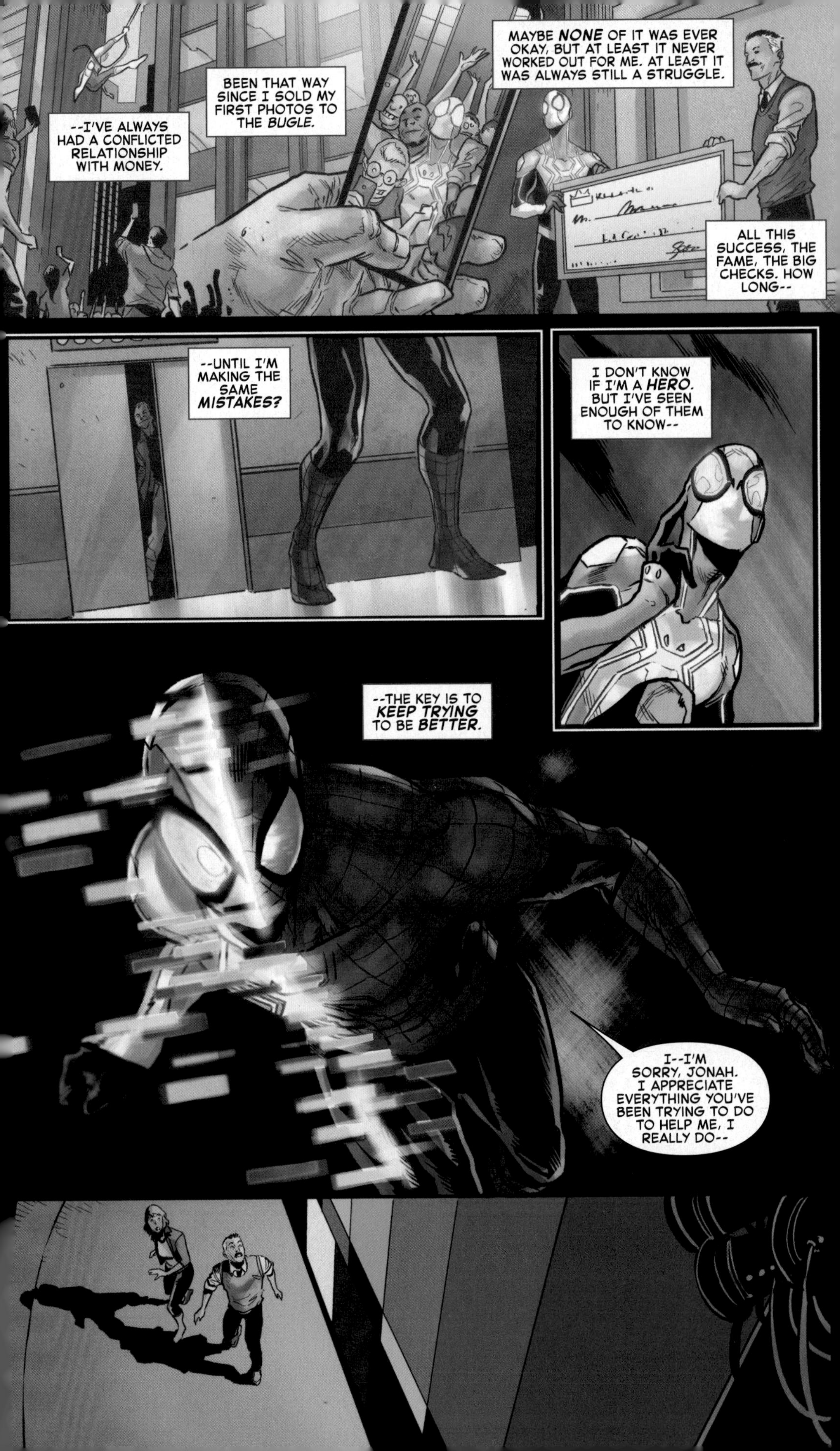
--I'VE ALWAYS HAD A CONFLICTED RELATIONSHIP WITH MONEY.
BEEN THAT WAY SINCE I SOLD MY FIRST PHOTOS TO THE BUGLE.
MAYBE NONE OF IT WAS EVER OKAY, BUT AT LEAST IT NEVER WORKED OUT FOR ME. AT LEAST IT WAS ALWAYS STILL A STRUGGLE.
ALL THIS SUCCESS, THE FAME, THE BIG CHECKS. HOW LONG--
--UNTIL I'M MAKING THE SAME MISTAKES?
I DON'T KNOW IF I'M A HERO. BUT I'VE SEEN ENOUGH OF THEM TO KNOW--
--THE KEY IS TO KEEP TRYING TO BE BETTER.
I--I'M SORRY, JONAH. I APPRECIATE EVERYTHING YOU'VE BEEN TRYING TO DO TO HELP ME, I REALLY DO--

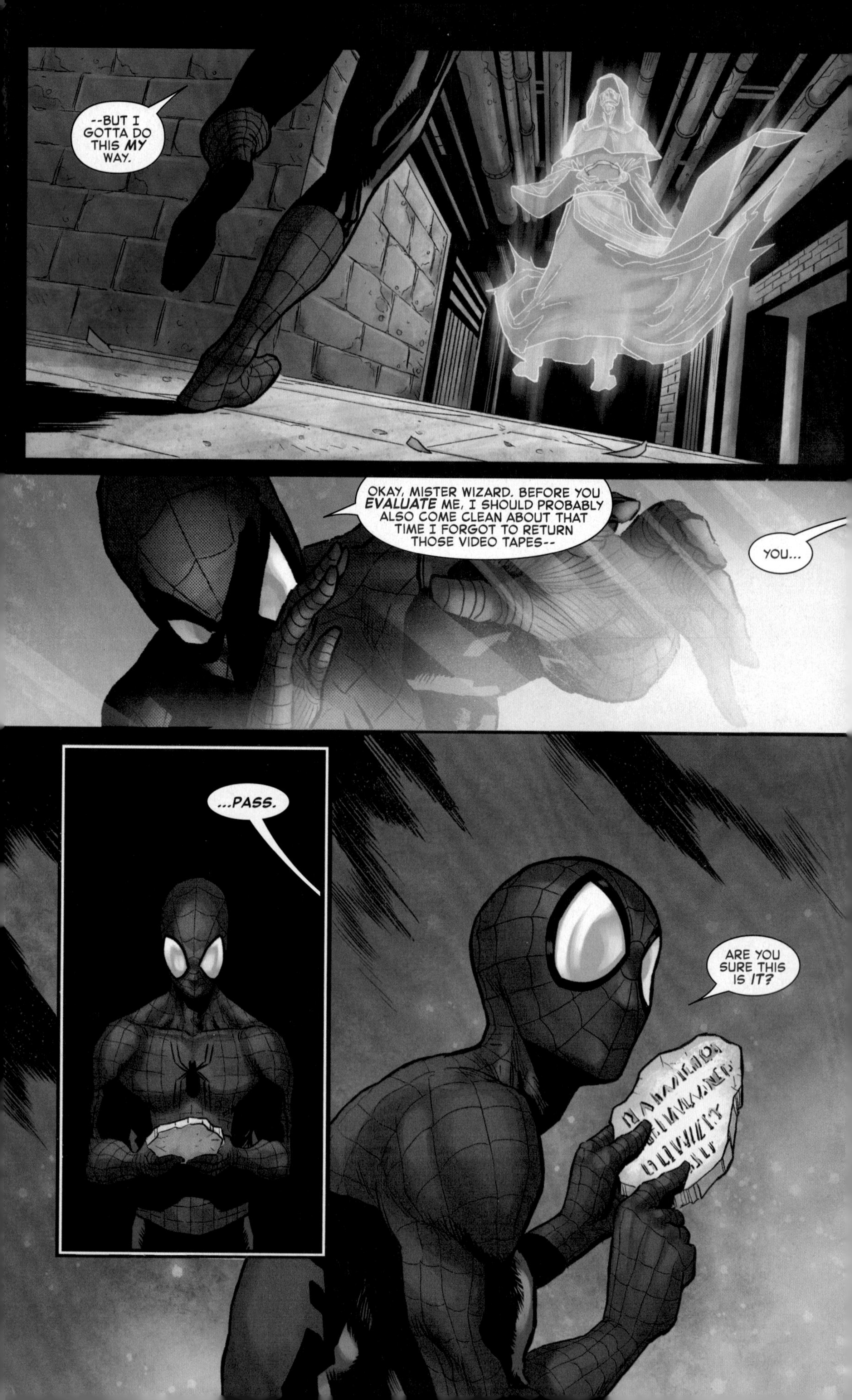
--BUT I GOTTA DO THIS MY WAY.
OKAY, MISTER WIZARD. BEFORE YOU EVALUATE ME, I SHOULD PROBABLY ALSO COME CLEAN ABOUT THAT TIME I FORGOT TO RETURN THOSE VIDEO TAPES--
YOU...
...PASS.
ARE YOU SURE THIS IS IT?

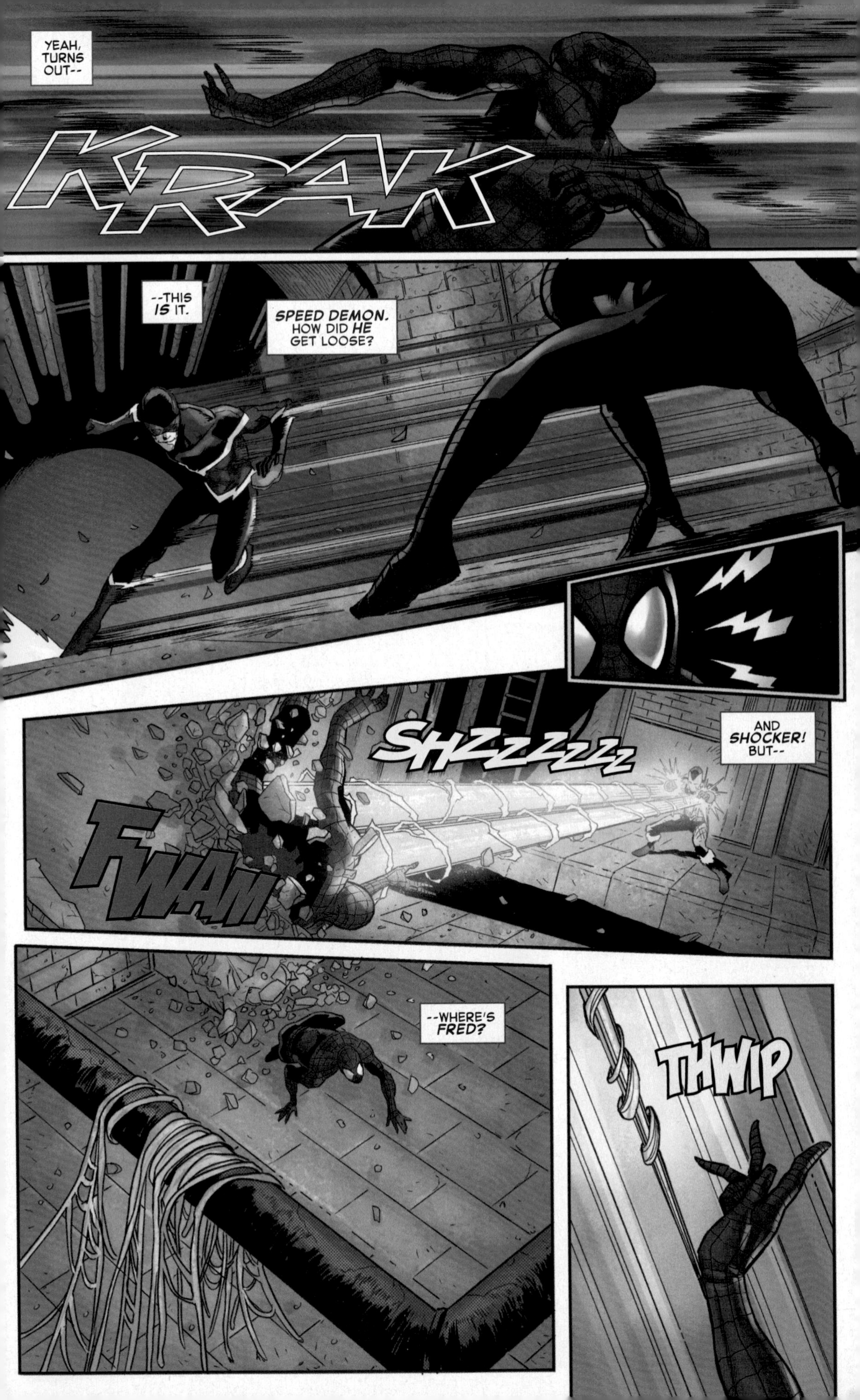

YEAH, TURNS OUT--
KRAK
--THIS IS IT.
SPEED DEMON. HOW DID HE GET LOOSE?
SHZZZZZZZ
FWAM
AND SHOCKER! BUT--
--WHERE'S FRED?
THWIP

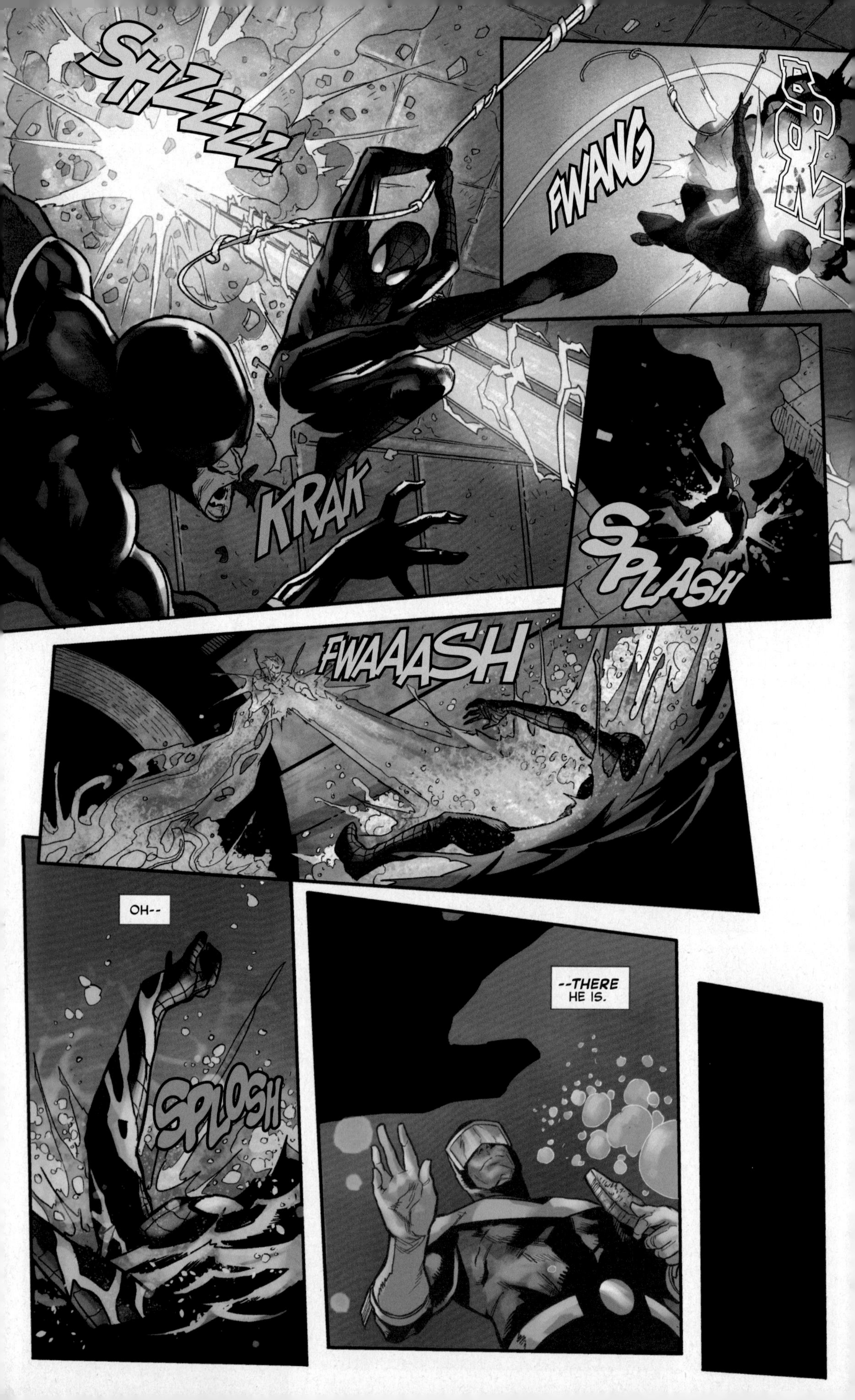
SHZZZZZ
KRAK
FWANG
BOOM
SPLASH
FWAAASH
OH--
SPLOSH
--THERE HE IS.

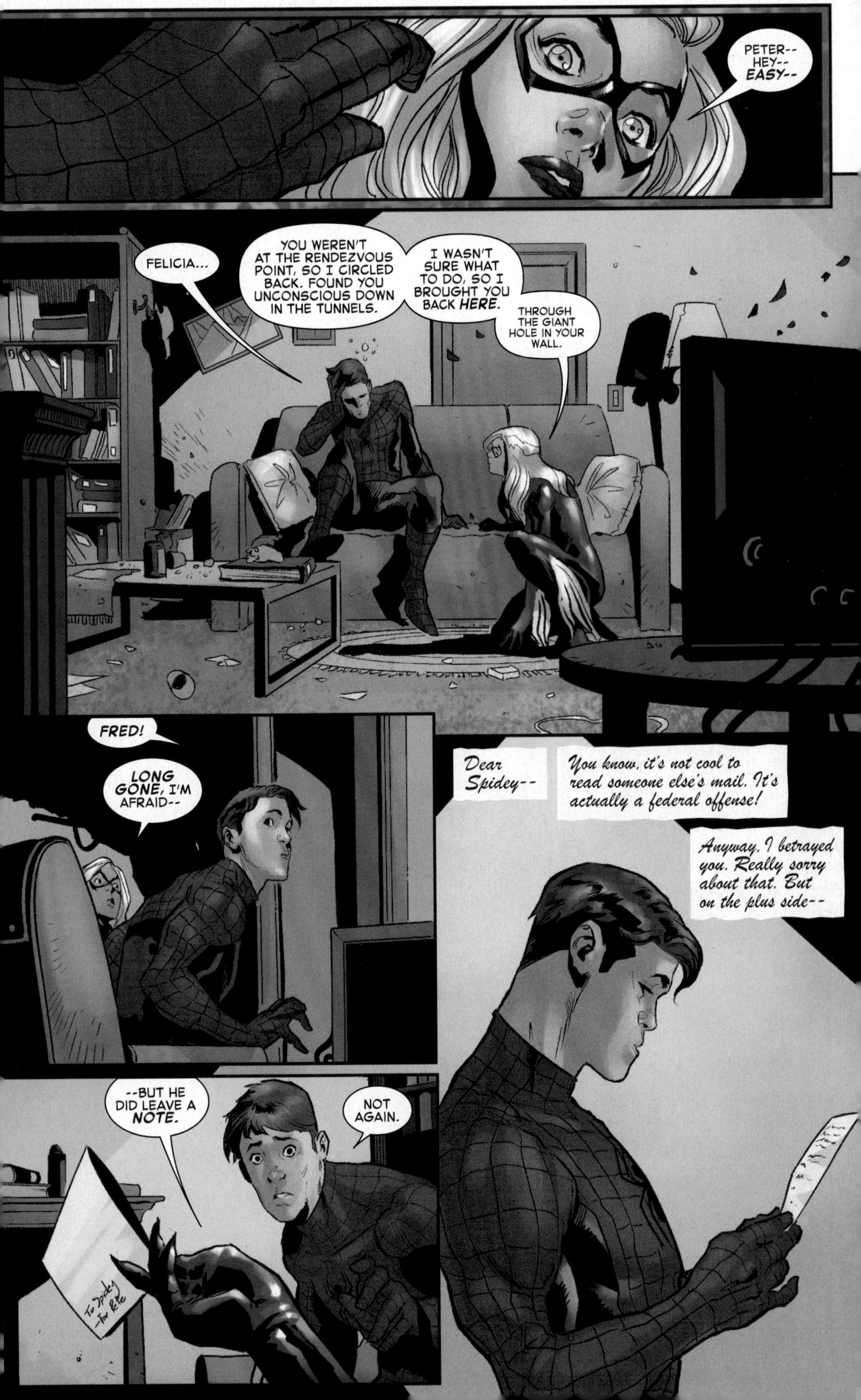
PETER-- HEY-- EASY--
FELICIA...
YOU WEREN'T AT THE RENDEZVOUS POINT, SO I CIRCLED BACK. FOUND YOU UNCONSCIOUS DOWN IN THE TUNNELS.
I WASN'T SURE WHAT TO DO, SO I BROUGHT YOU BACK HERE.
THROUGH THE GIANT HOLE IN YOUR WALL.
FRED!
LONG GONE, I'M AFRAID--
--BUT HE DID LEAVE A NOTE.
NOT AGAIN.
Dear Spidey--
You know, it's not cool to read someone else's mail. It's actually a federal offense!
Anyway, I betrayed you. Really sorry about that. But on the plus side--

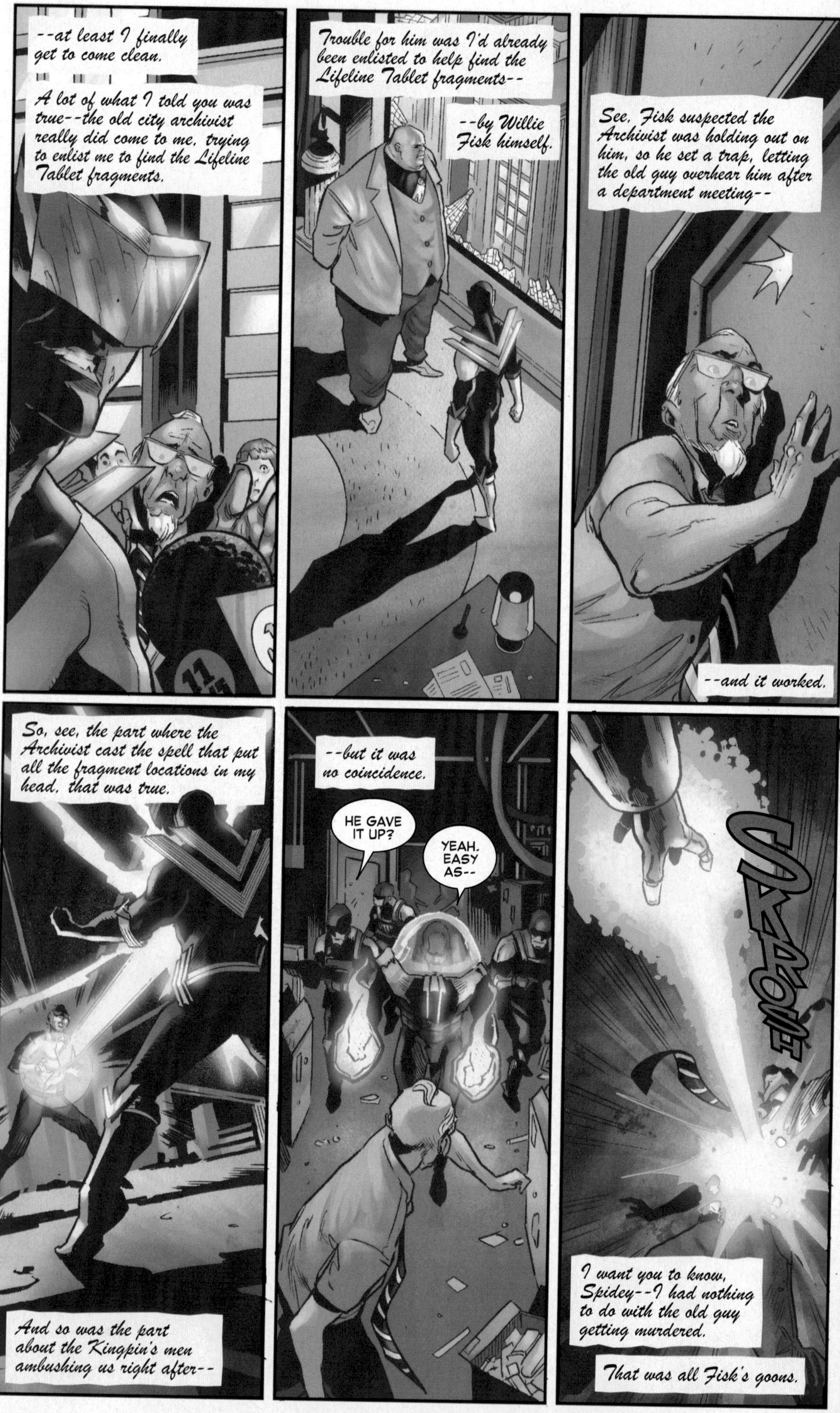
--at least I finally get to come clean.
A lot of what I told you was true--the old city archivist really did come to me, trying to enlist me to find the Lifeline Tablet fragments.
Trouble for him was I'd already been enlisted to help find the Lifeline Tablet fragments--
--by Willie Fisk himself.
See, Fisk suspected the Archivist was holding out on him, so he set a trap, letting the old guy overhear him after a department meeting--
--and it worked.
So, see, the part where the Archivist cast the spell that put all the fragment locations in my head, that was true.
And so was the part about the Kingpin's men ambushing us right after--
--but it was no coincidence.
HE GAVE IT UP?
YEAH, EASY AS--
SKROOM
I want you to know, Spidey--I had nothing to do with the old guy getting murdered.
That was all Fisk's goons.

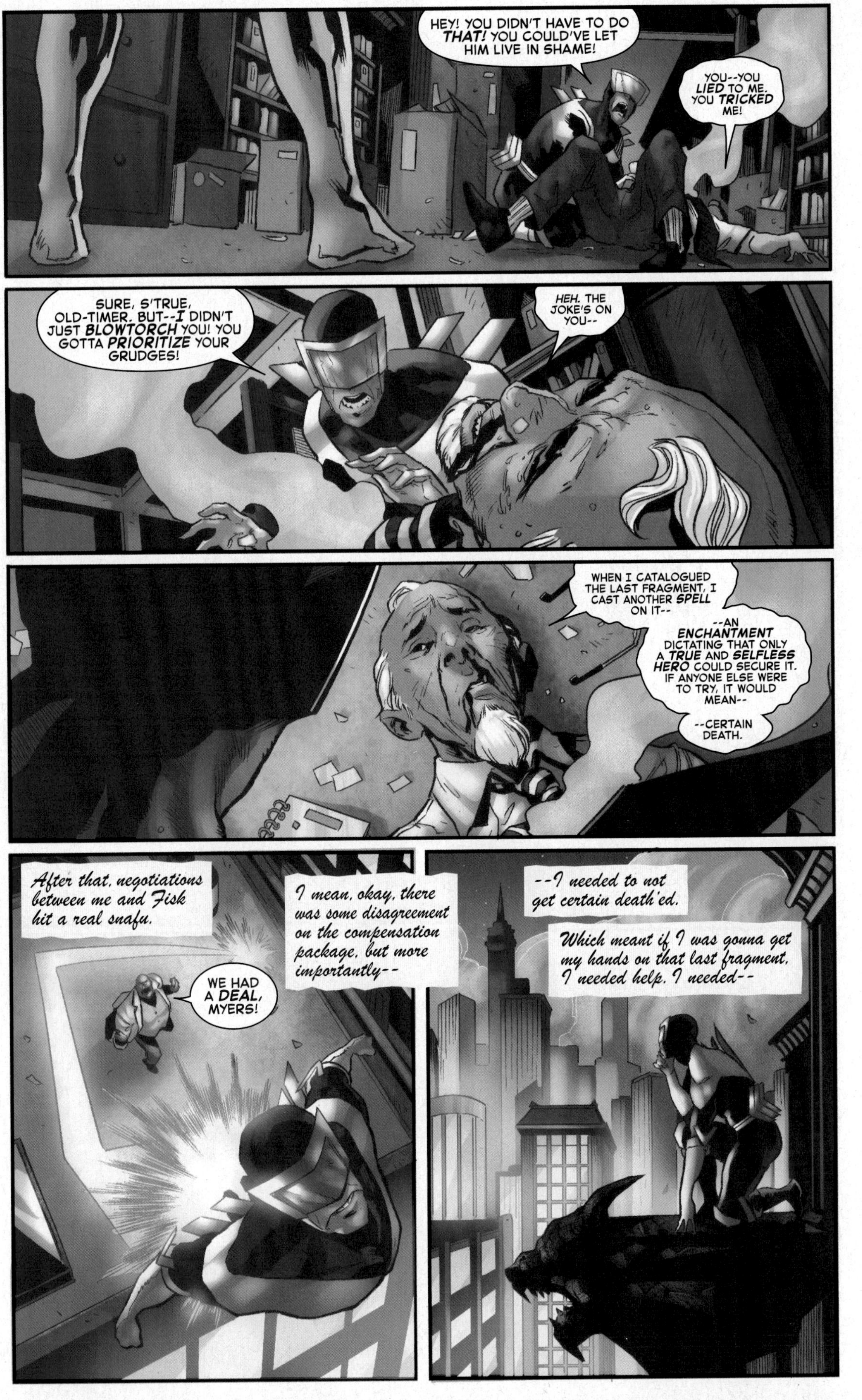
HEY! YOU DIDN'T HAVE TO DO THAT! YOU COULD'VE LET HIM LIVE IN SHAME!
YOU--YOU LIED TO ME. YOU TRICKED ME!
SURE, S'TRUE, OLD-TIMER. BUT--I DIDN'T JUST BLOWTORCH YOU! YOU GOTTA PRIORITIZE YOUR GRUDGES!
HEH. THE JOKE'S ON YOU--
WHEN I CATALOGUED THE LAST FRAGMENT, I CAST ANOTHER SPELL ON IT--
--AN ENCHANTMENT DICTATING THAT ONLY A TRUE AND SELFLESS HERO COULD SECURE IT. IF ANYONE ELSE WERE TO TRY, IT WOULD MEAN--
--CERTAIN DEATH.
After that, negotiations between me and Fisk hit a real snafu.
I mean, okay, there was some disagreement on the compensation package, but more importantly--
WE HAD A DEAL, MYERS!
--I needed to not get certain death'ed.
Which meant if I was gonna get my hands on that last fragment, I needed help. I needed--

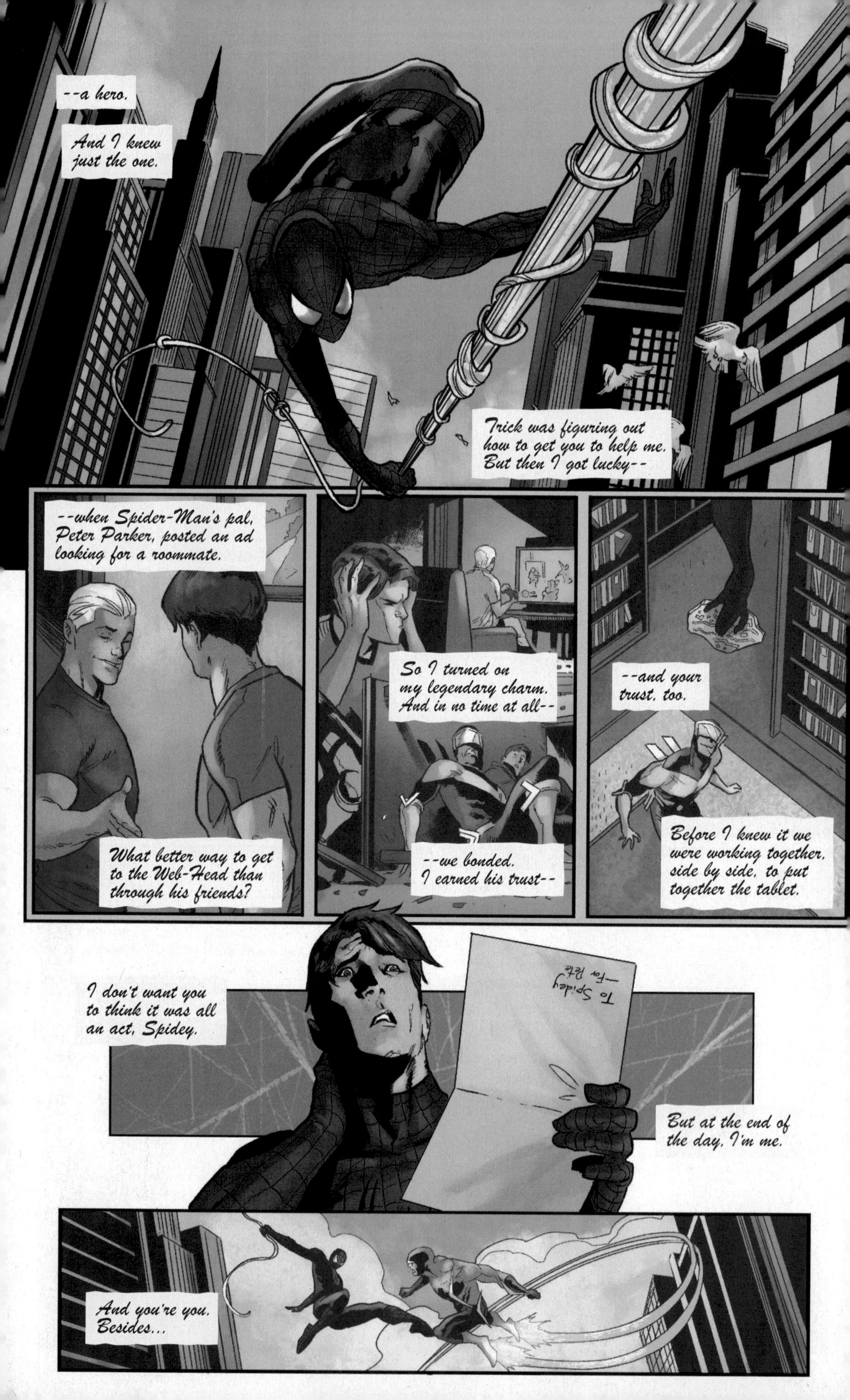
--a hero.
And I knew just the one.
Trick was figuring out how to get you to help me. But then I got lucky--
--when Spider-Man's pal, Peter Parker, posted an ad looking for a roommate.
What better way to get to the Web-Head than through his friends?
So I turned on my legendary charm. And in no time at all--
--we bonded. I earned his trust--
--and your trust, too.
Before I knew it we were working together, side by side, to put together the tablet.
I don't want you to think it was all an act, Spidey.
To Spidey
-For Pete
But at the end of the day, I'm me.
And you're you. Besides...

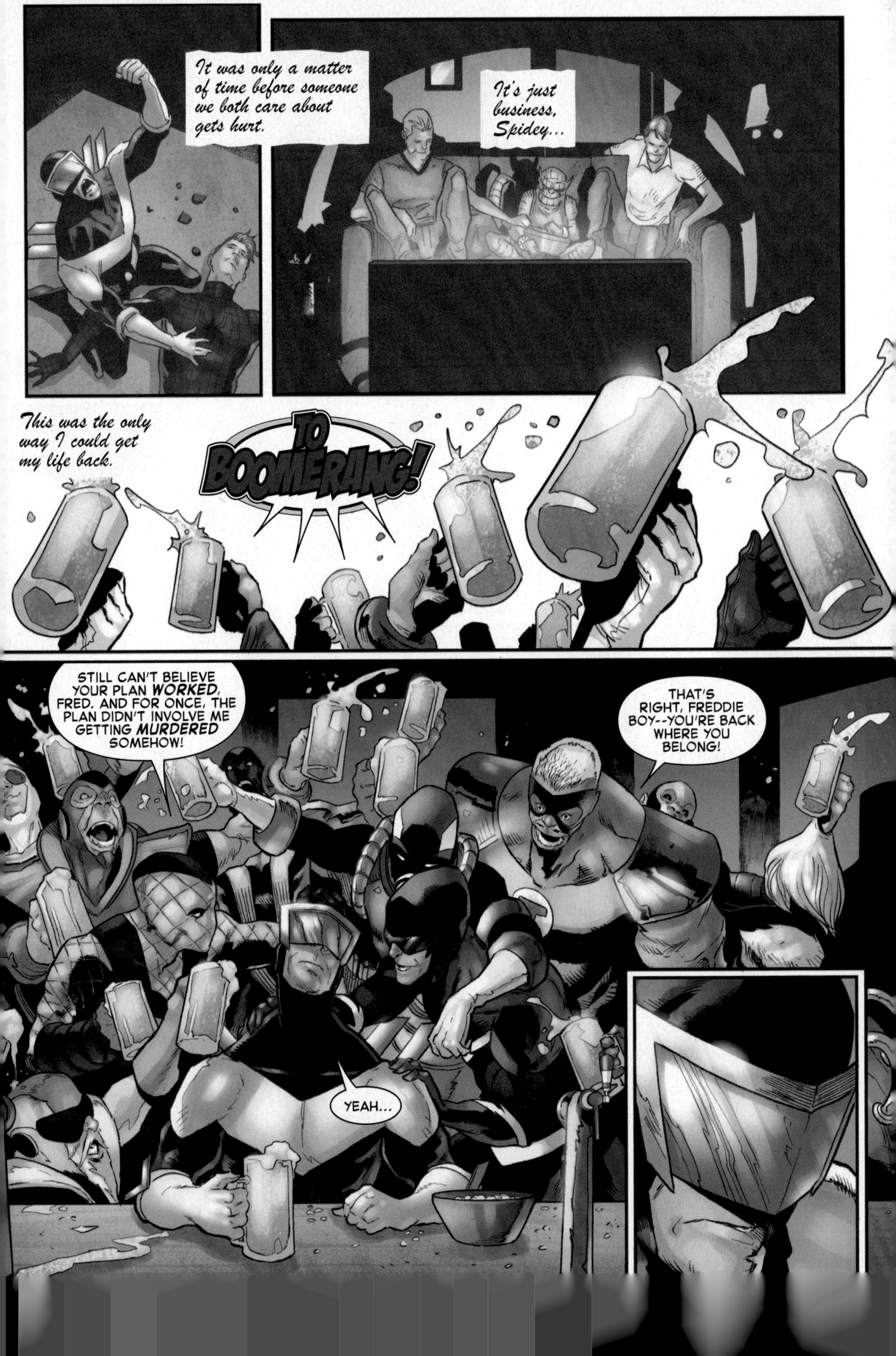
It was only a matter of time before someone we both care about gets hurt.
It's just business, Spidey...
This was the only way I could get my life back.
TO BOOMERANG!
STILL CAN'T BELIEVE YOUR PLAN WORKED, FRED. AND FOR ONCE, THE PLAN DIDN'T INVOLVE ME GETTING MURDERED SOMEHOW!
THAT'S RIGHT, FREDDIE BOY--YOU'RE BACK WHERE YOU BELONG!
YEAH...

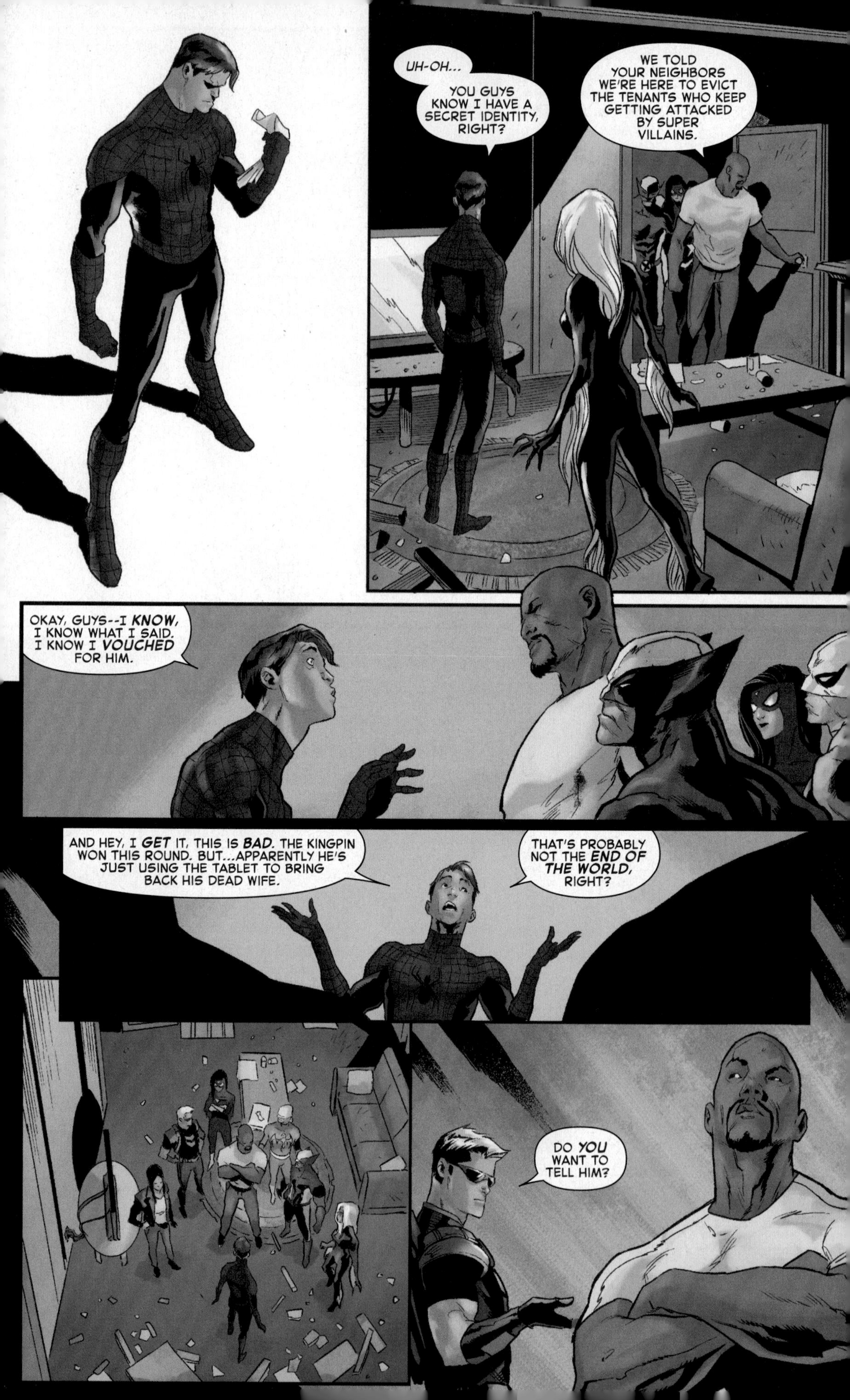
UH-OH...
YOU GUYS KNOW I HAVE A SECRET IDENTITY, RIGHT?
WE TOLD YOUR NEIGHBORS WE'RE HERE TO EVICT THE TENANTS WHO KEEP GETTING ATTACKED BY SUPER VILLAINS.
OKAY, GUYS--I KNOW, I KNOW WHAT I SAID. I KNOW I VOUCHED FOR HIM.
AND HEY, I GET IT, THIS IS BAD. THE KINGPIN WON THIS ROUND. BUT...APPARENTLY HE'S JUST USING THE TABLET TO BRING BACK HIS DEAD WIFE.
THAT'S PROBABLY NOT THE END OF THE WORLD, RIGHT?
DO YOU WANT TO TELL HIM?

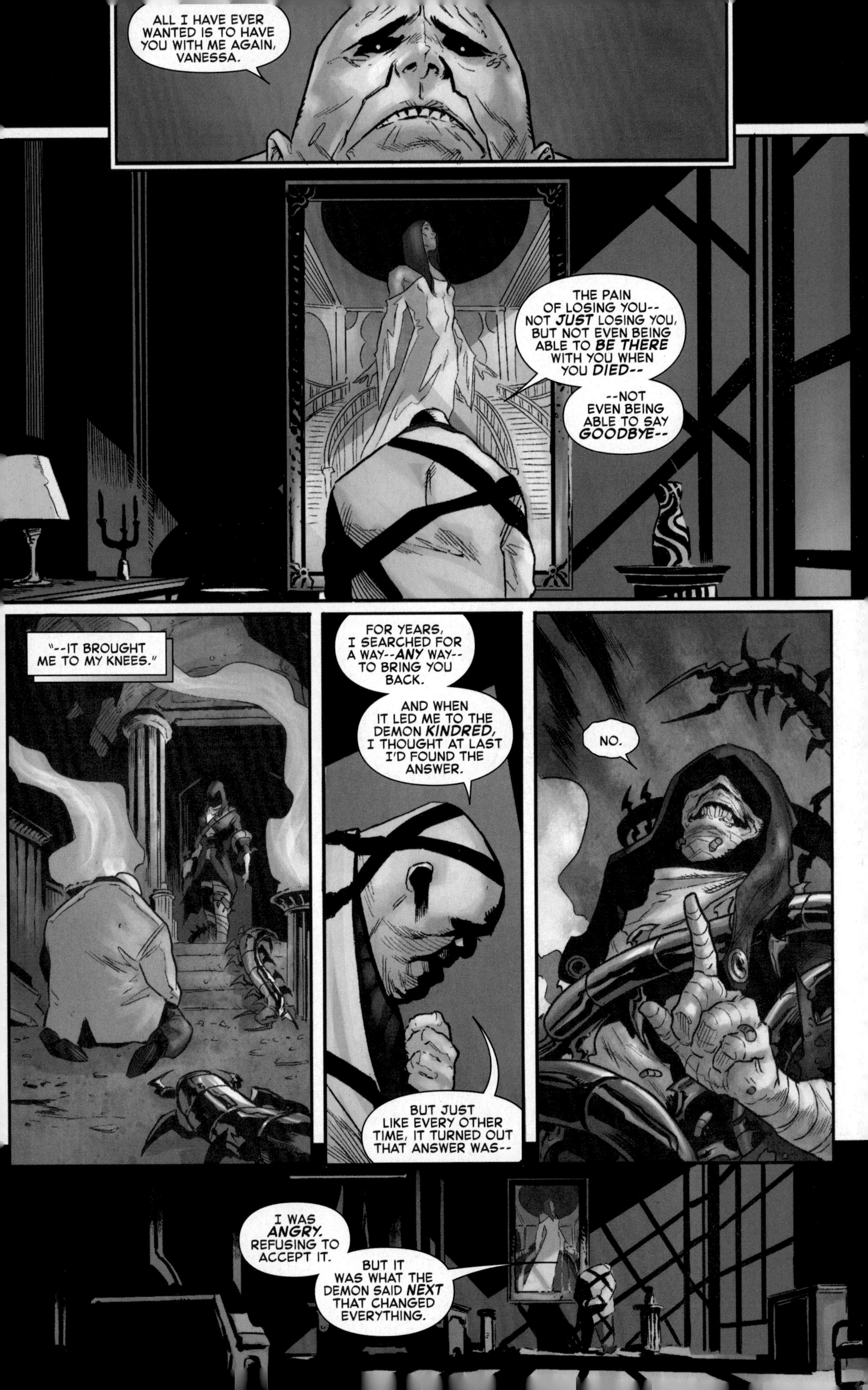
ALL I HAVE EVER WANTED IS TO HAVE YOU WITH ME AGAIN, VANESSA.
THE PAIN OF LOSING YOU-- NOT JUST LOSING YOU, BUT NOT EVEN BEING ABLE TO BE THERE WITH YOU WHEN YOU DIED--
--NOT EVEN BEING ABLE TO SAY GOODBYE--
"--IT BROUGHT ME TO MY KNEES."
FOR YEARS, I SEARCHED FOR A WAY--ANY WAY-- TO BRING YOU BACK.
AND WHEN IT LED ME TO THE DEMON KINDRED, I THOUGHT AT LAST I'D FOUND THE ANSWER.
BUT JUST LIKE EVERY OTHER TIME, IT TURNED OUT THAT ANSWER WAS--
NO.
I WAS ANGRY. REFUSING TO ACCEPT IT.
BUT IT WAS WHAT THE DEMON SAID NEXT THAT CHANGED EVERYTHING.

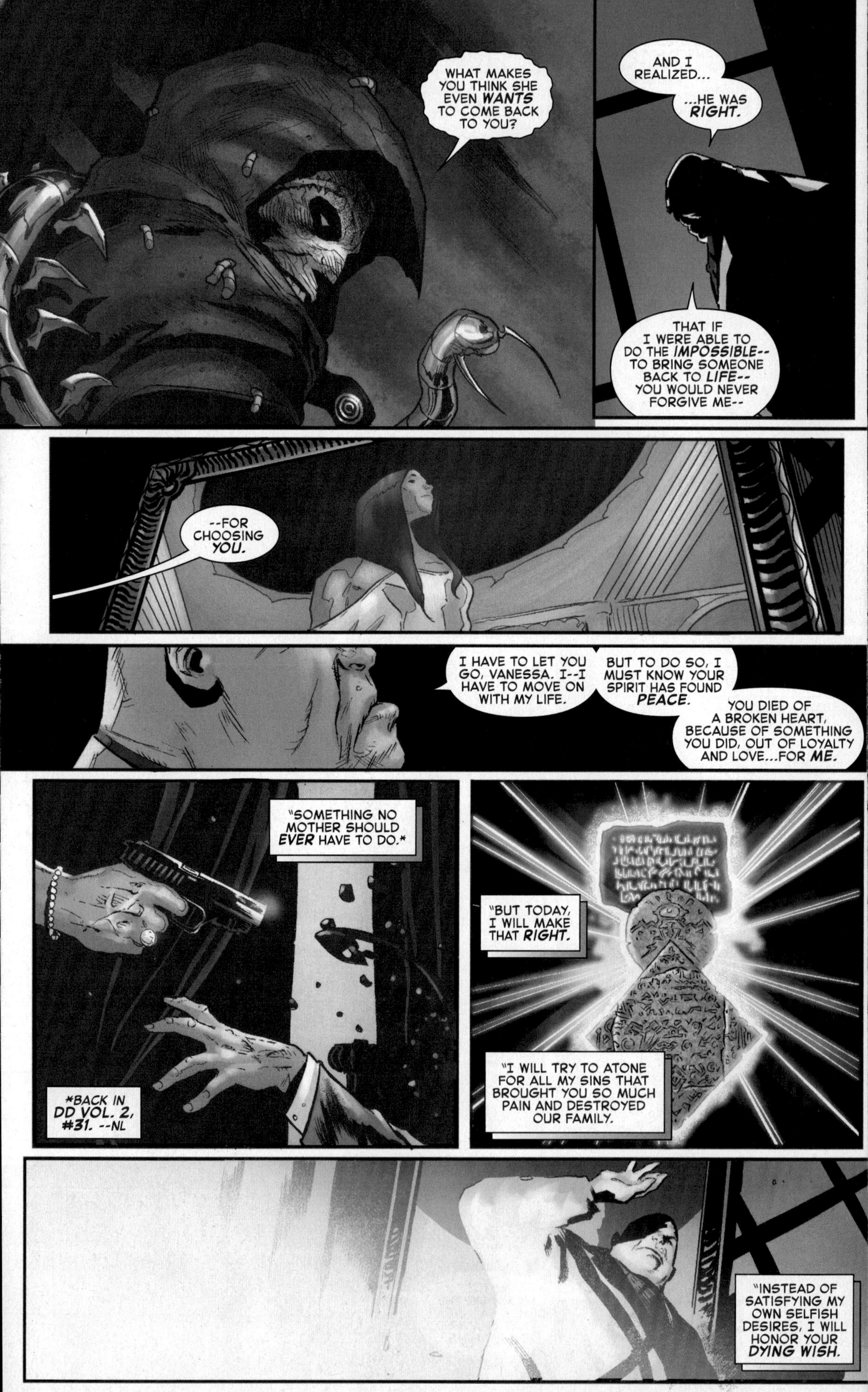
WHAT MAKES YOU THINK SHE EVEN WANTS TO COME BACK TO YOU?
AND I REALIZED...
...HE WAS RIGHT.
THAT IF I WERE ABLE TO DO THE IMPOSSIBLE-- TO BRING SOMEONE BACK TO LIFE-- YOU WOULD NEVER FORGIVE ME--
--FOR CHOOSING YOU.
I HAVE TO LET YOU GO, VANESSA. I--I HAVE TO MOVE ON WITH MY LIFE.
BUT TO DO SO, I MUST KNOW YOUR SPIRIT HAS FOUND PEACE.
YOU DIED OF A BROKEN HEART, BECAUSE OF SOMETHING YOU DID, OUT OF LOYALTY AND LOVE...FOR ME.
"SOMETHING NO MOTHER SHOULD EVER HAVE TO DO.*
*BACK IN DD VOL. 2, #31. --NL
"BUT TODAY, I WILL MAKE THAT RIGHT.
"I WILL TRY TO ATONE FOR ALL MY SINS THAT BROUGHT YOU SO MUCH PAIN AND DESTROYED OUR FAMILY.
"INSTEAD OF SATISFYING MY OWN SELFISH DESIRES, I WILL HONOR YOUR DYING WISH.

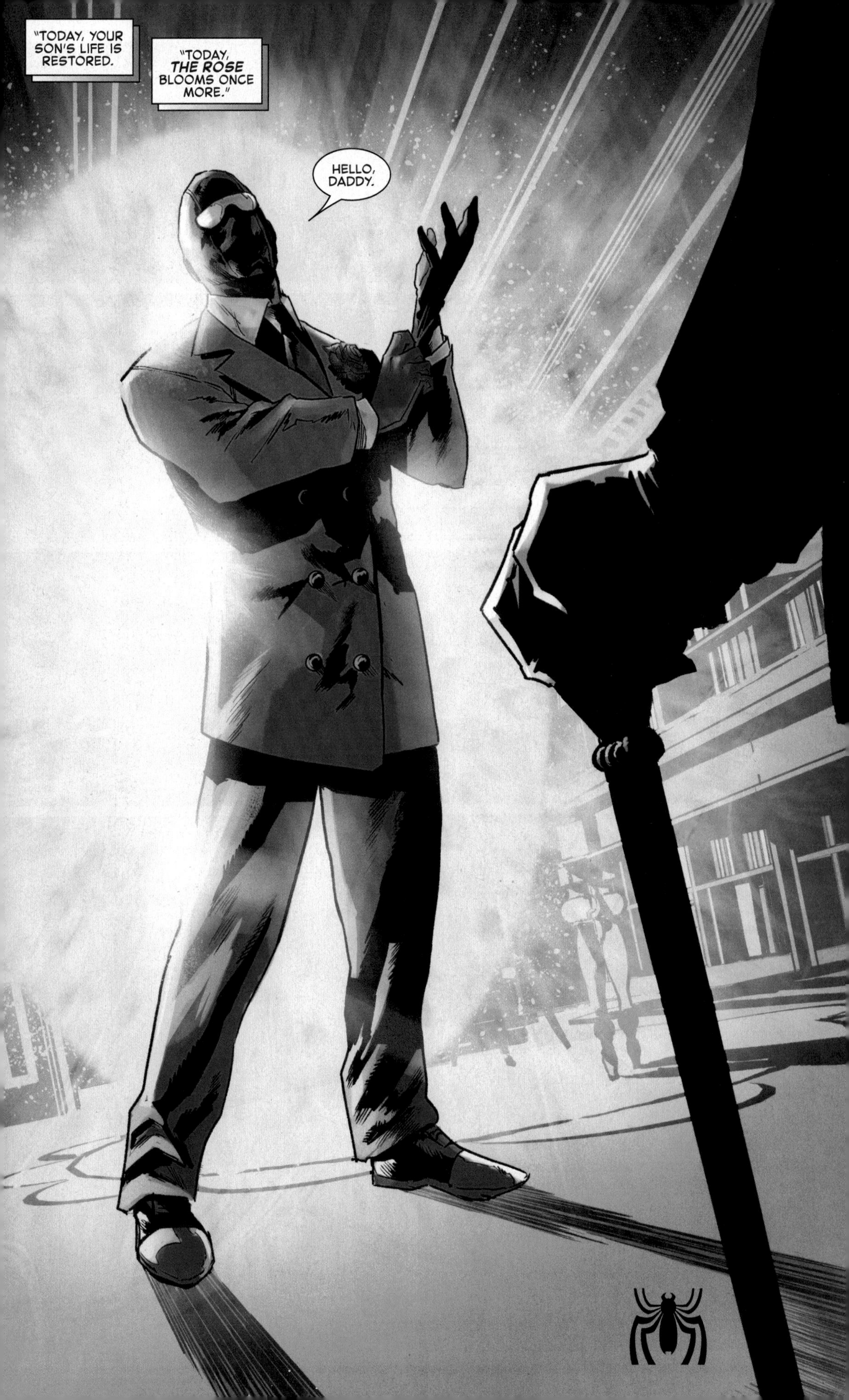
"TODAY, YOUR SON'S LIFE IS RESTORED.
"TODAY, THE ROSE BLOOMS ONCE MORE."
HELLO, DADDY.

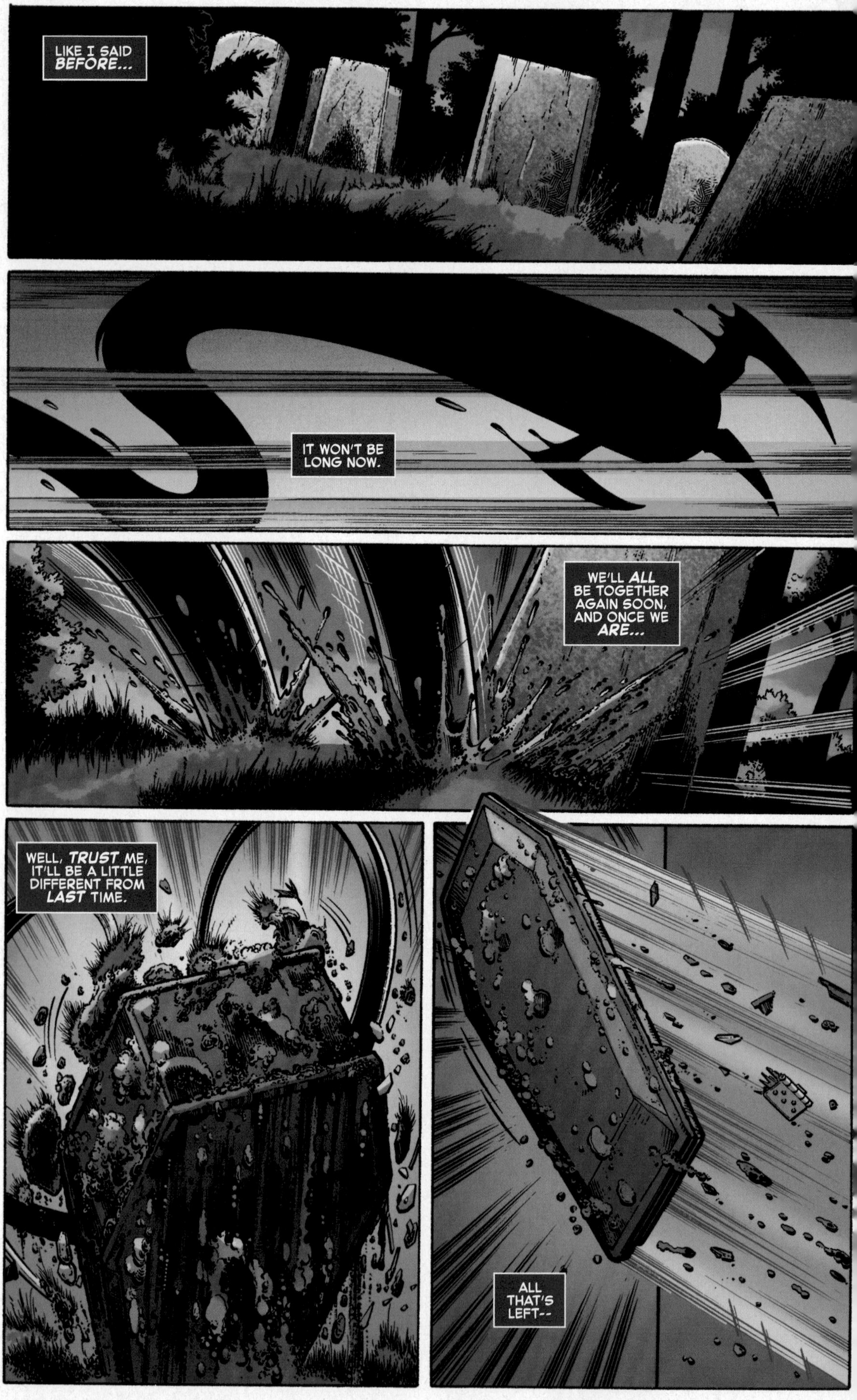
LIKE I SAID BEFORE...
IT WON'T BE LONG NOW.
WE'LL ALL BE TOGETHER AGAIN SOON, AND ONCE WE ARE...
WELL, TRUST ME, IT'LL BE A LITTLE DIFFERENT FROM LAST TIME.
ALL THAT'S LEFT--

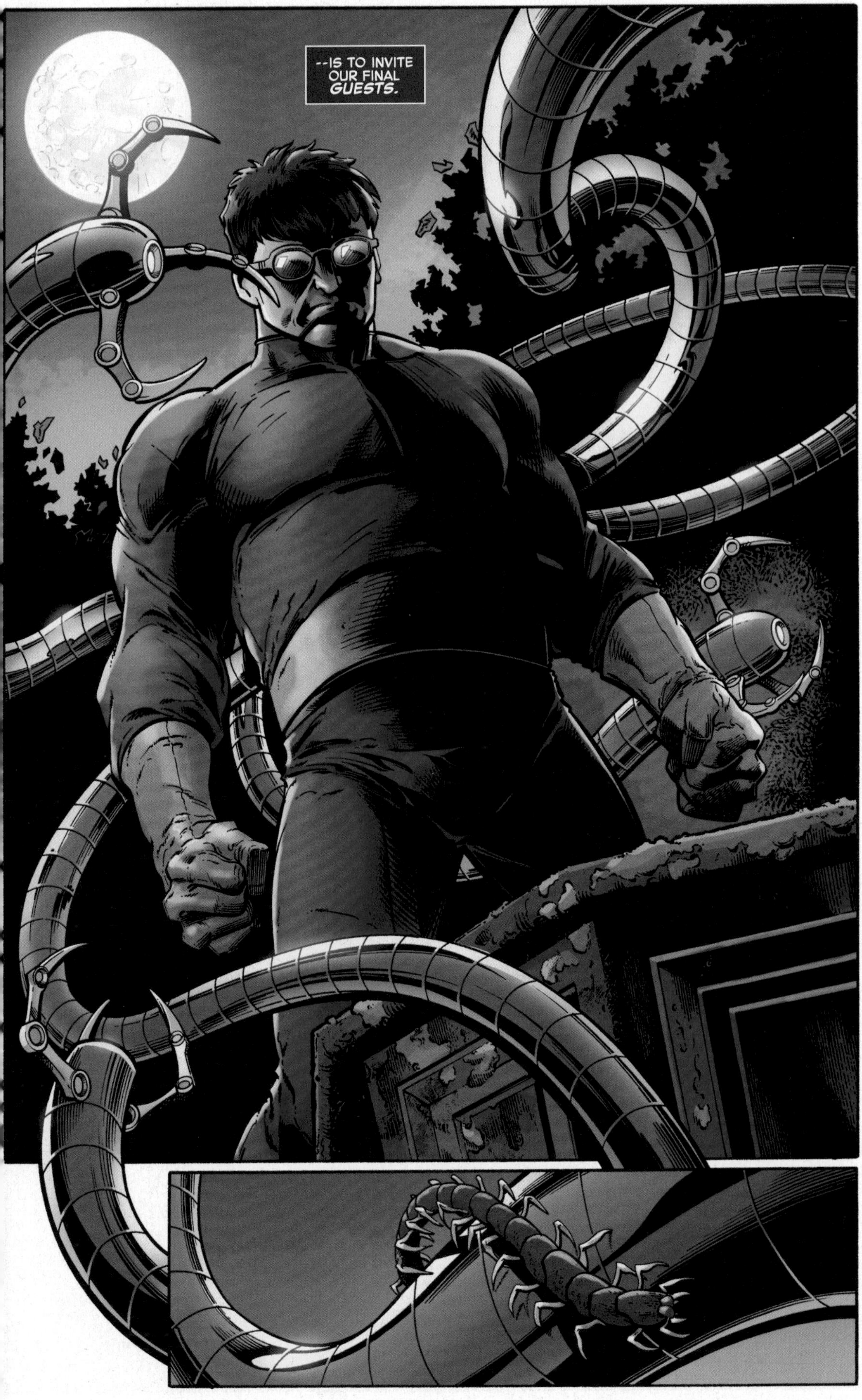
--IS TO INVITE OUR FINAL GUESTS.

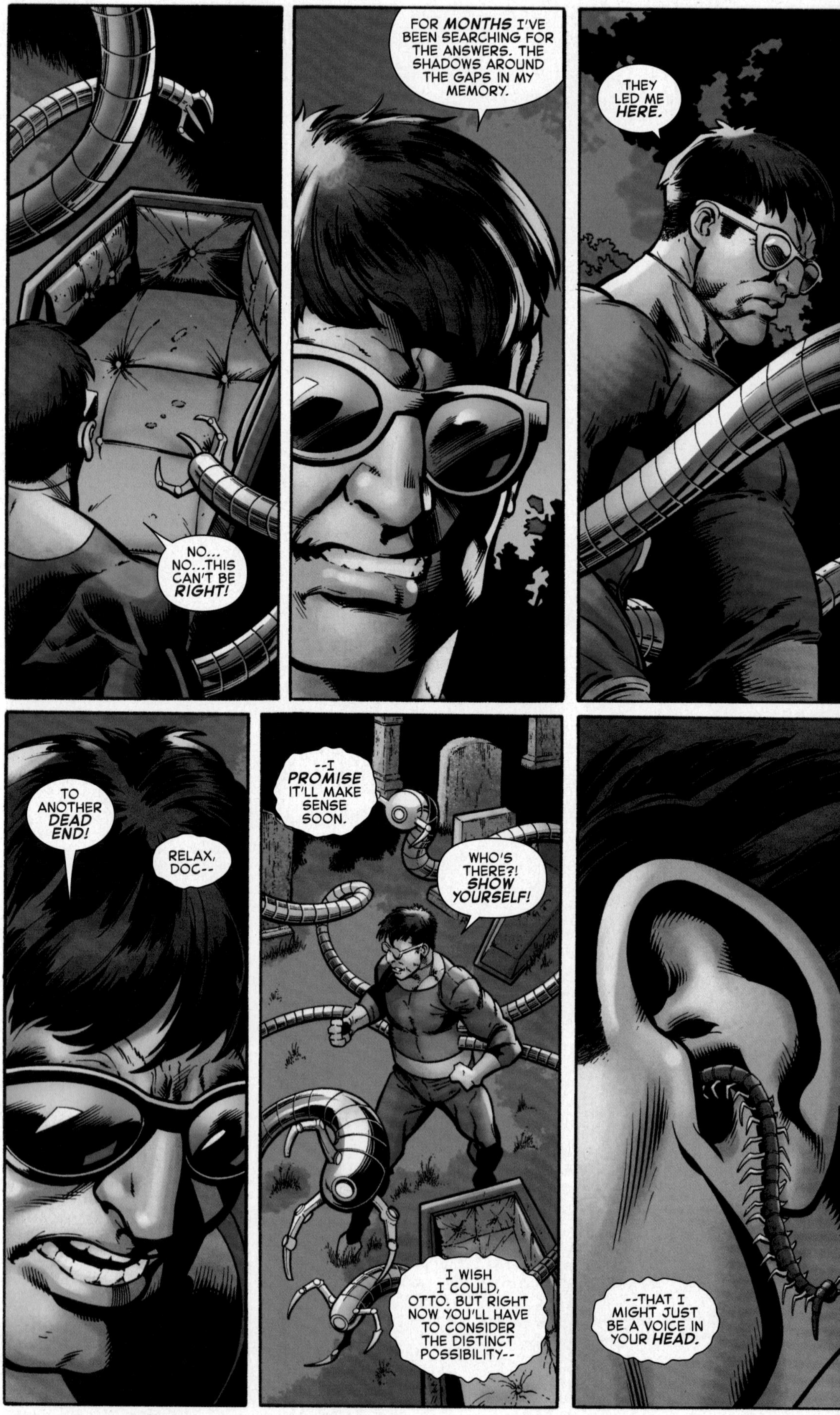
NO... NO...THIS CAN'T BE RIGHT!
FOR MONTHS I'VE BEEN SEARCHING FOR THE ANSWERS. THE SHADOWS AROUND THE GAPS IN MY MEMORY.
THEY LED ME HERE.
TO ANOTHER DEAD END!
RELAX, DOC--
--I PROMISE IT'LL MAKE SENSE SOON.
WHO'S THERE?! SHOW YOURSELF!
I WISH I COULD, OTTO. BUT RIGHT NOW YOU'LL HAVE TO CONSIDER THE DISTINCT POSSIBILITY--
--THAT I MIGHT JUST BE A VOICE IN YOUR HEAD.

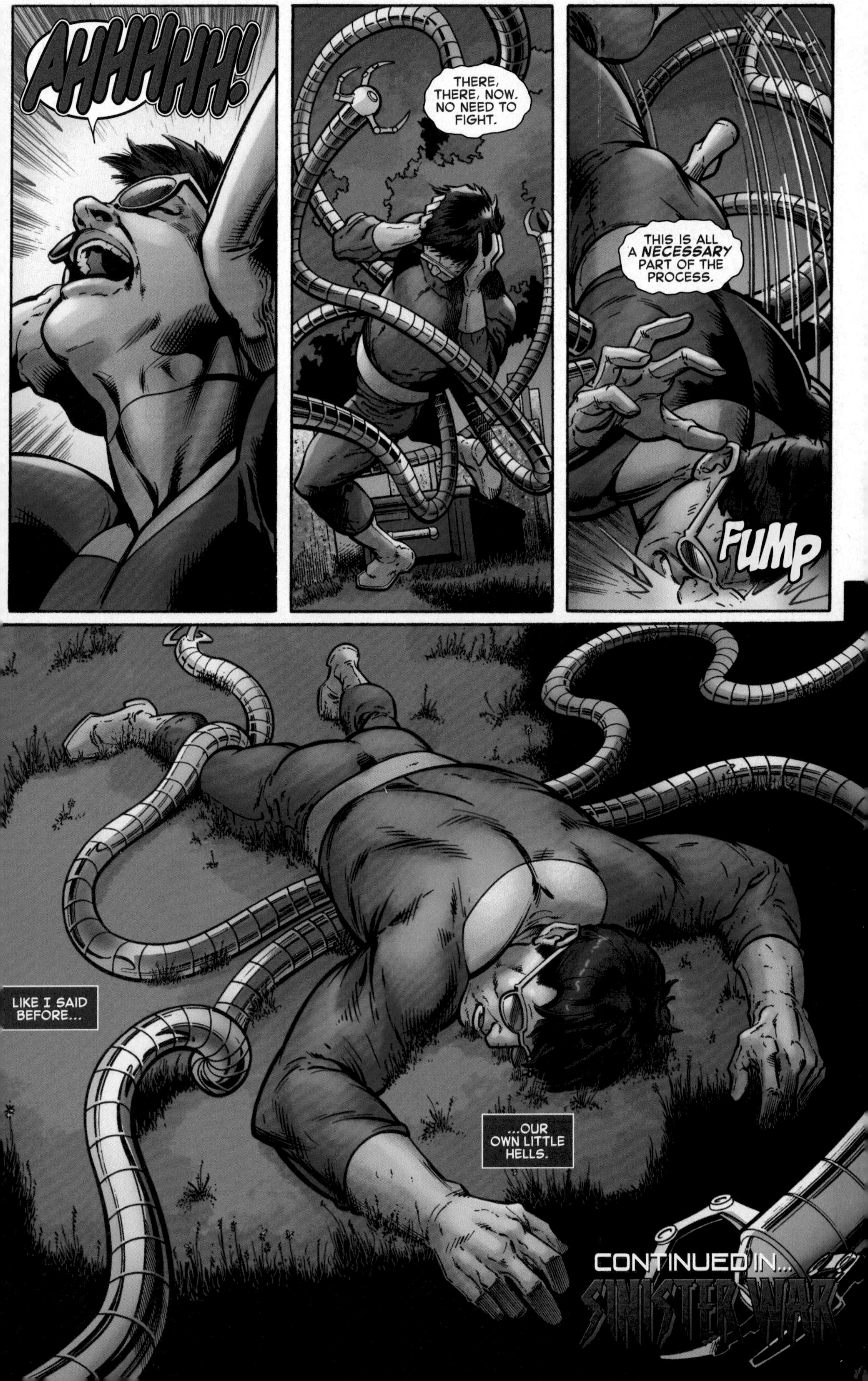
AHHHHH!
THERE, THERE, NOW. NO NEED TO FIGHT.
THIS IS ALL A NECESSARY PART OF THE PROCESS.
FUMP
LIKE I SAID BEFORE...
...OUR OWN LITTLE HELLS.
CONTINUED IN...
SINISTER WAR

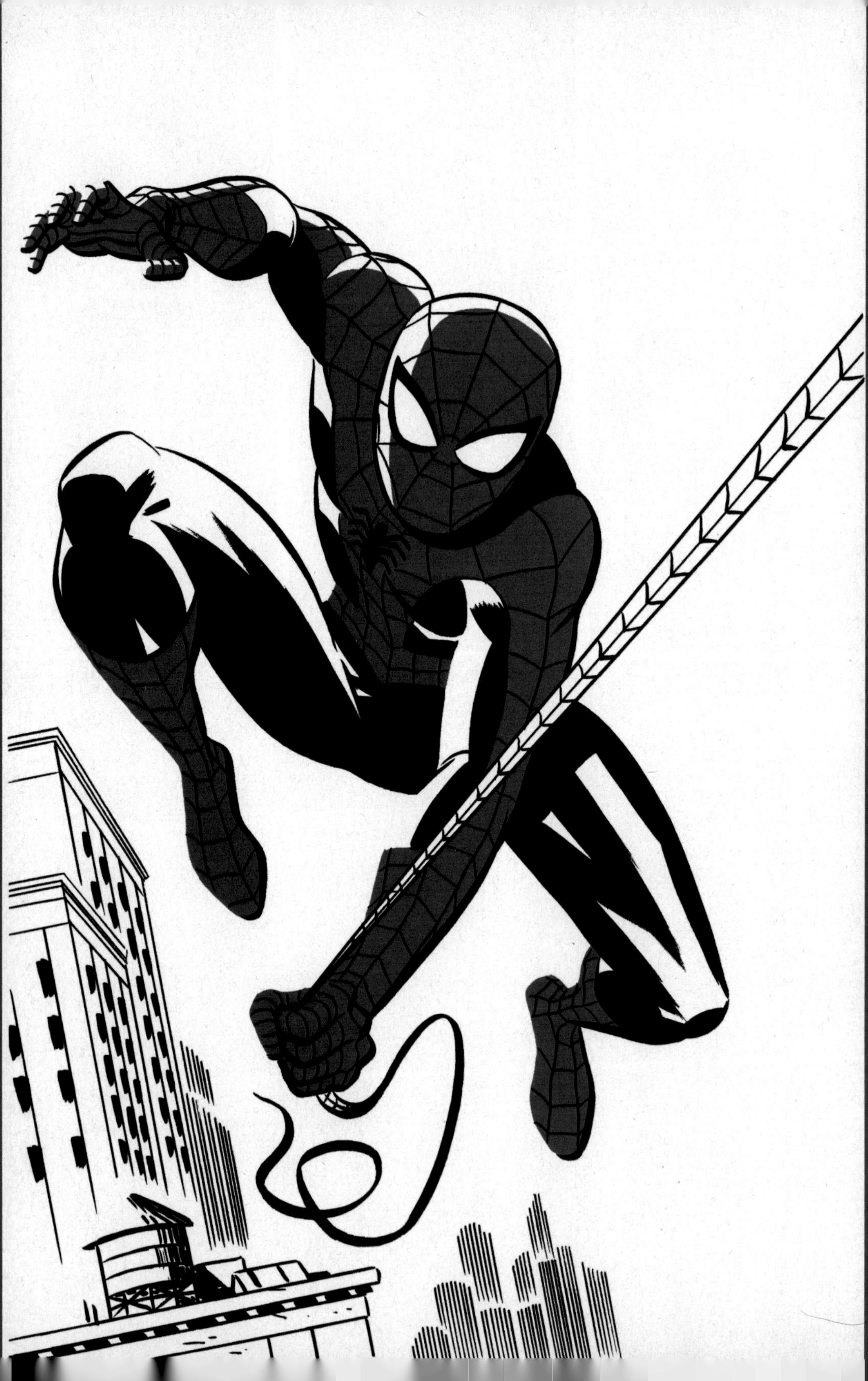

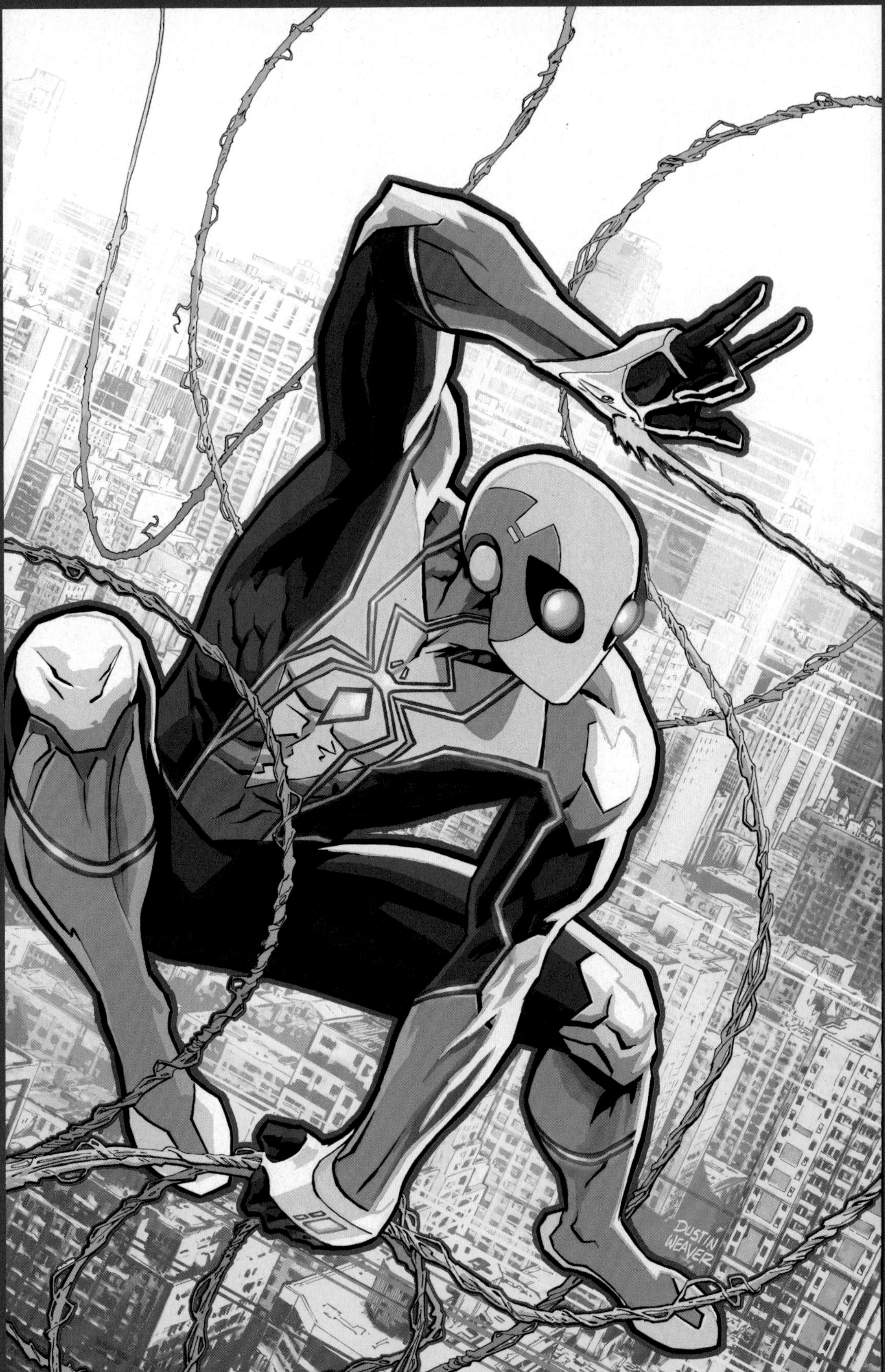
DUSTIN WEAVER

#62 VARIANT BY DUSTIN WEAVER

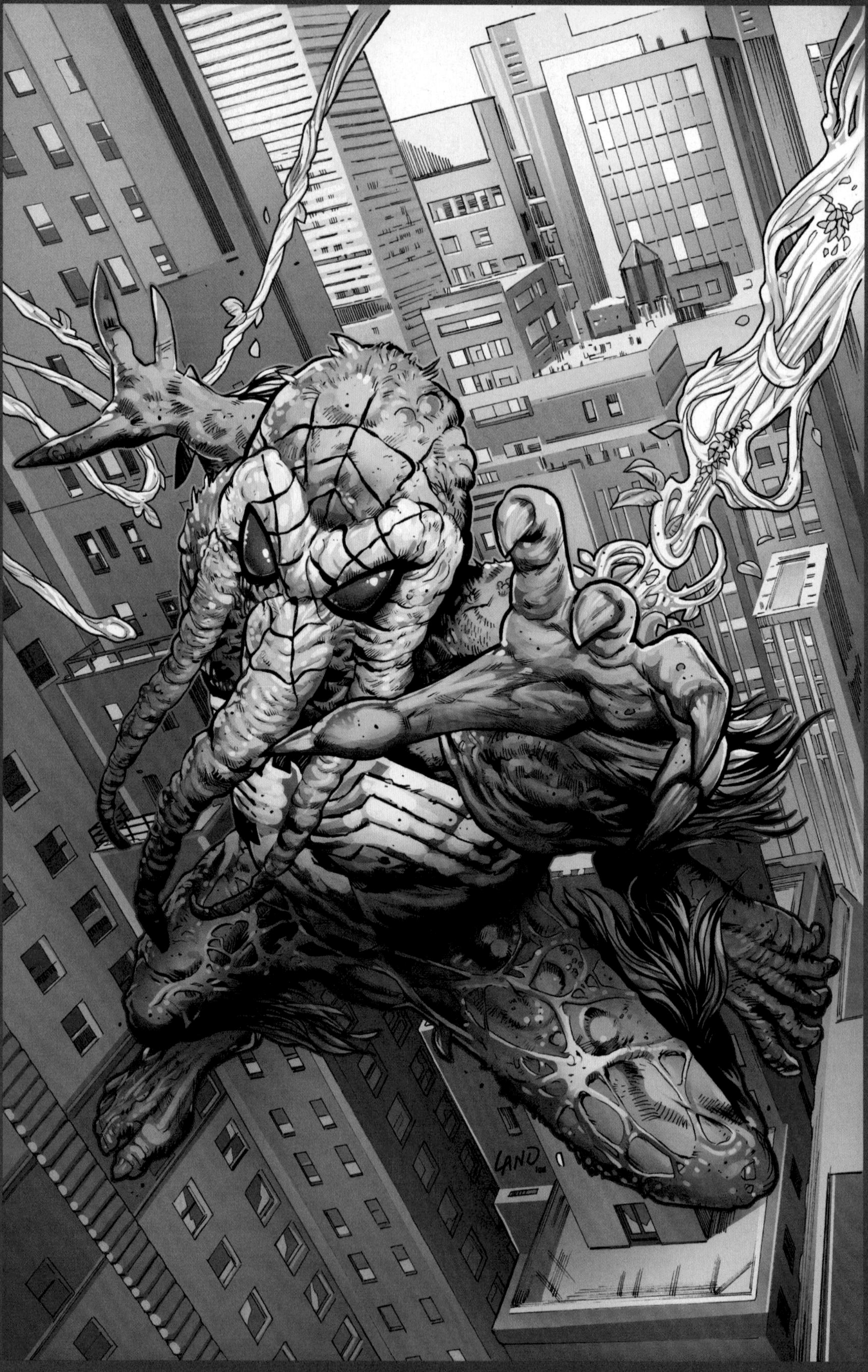
LAND

#62 MAN-THING 50TH ANNIVERSARY VARIANT BY GREG LAND & FRANK D'ARMATA

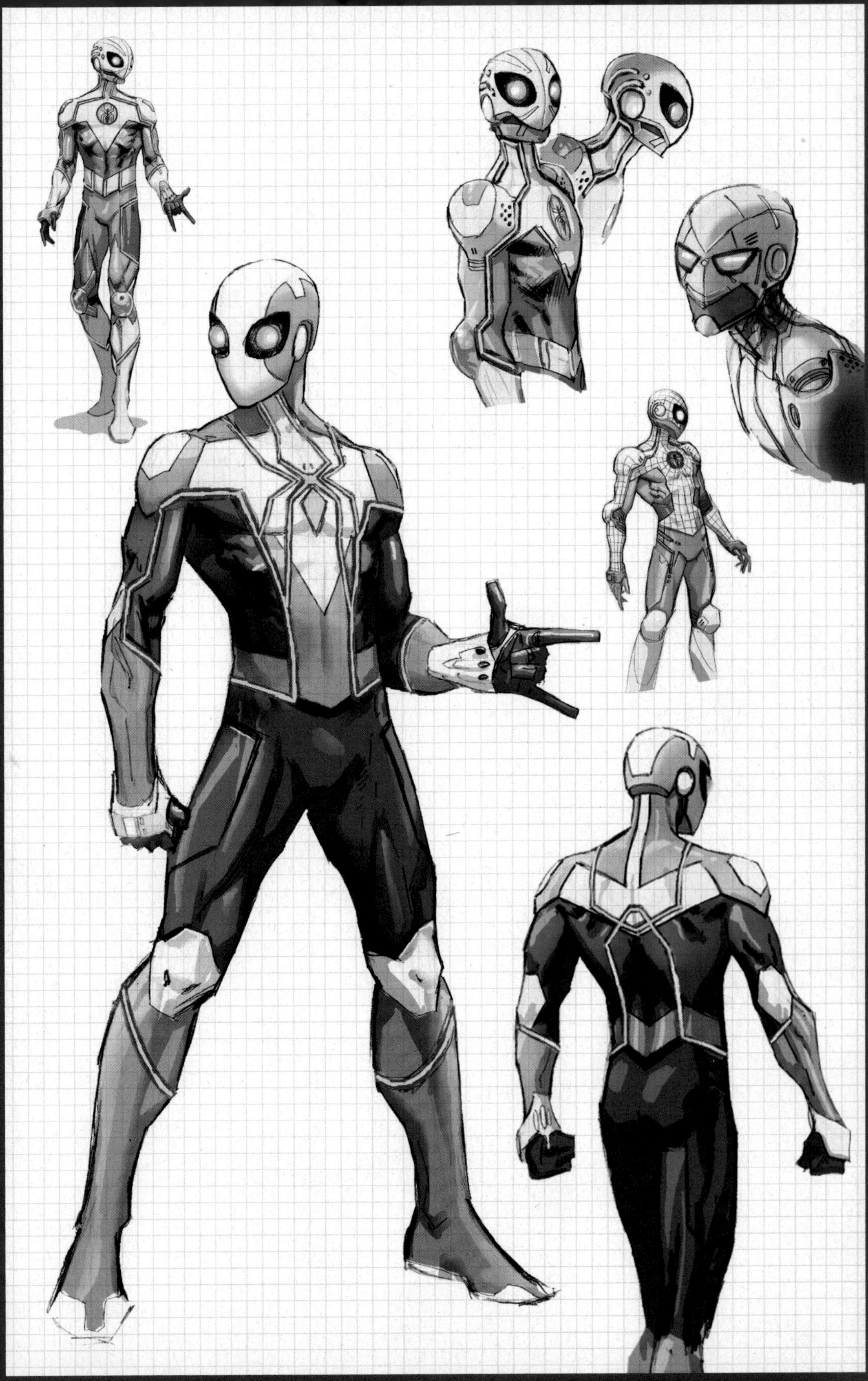

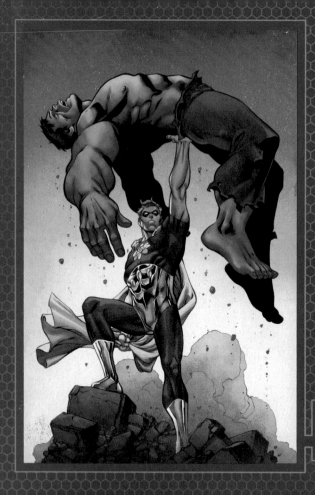

#63 HEROES REBORN VARIANT BY
CARLOS PACHECO, MARIANO TAIBO
& MATT MILLA

#64 HEROES REBORN VARIANT BY
CARLOS PACHECO, RAFAEL FONTERIZ
& RACHELLE ROSENBERG